accounting

7e

Charles T. Horngren Series in Accounting

Auditing and Assurance Services: An Integrated Approach, 11th ed.
Arens/Elder/Beasley

Governmental and Nonprofit Accounting: Theory and Practice, 8th ed.
Freeman/Shoulders

Financial Accounting, 6th ed.
Harrison/Horngren

Cases in Financial Reporting, 5th ed.
Hirst/McAnally

Cost Accounting: A Managerial Emphasis, 12th ed.
Horngren/Datar/Foster

Accounting, 7th ed.
Horngren/Harrison

Introduction to Financial Accounting, 9th ed.
Horngren/Sundem/Elliott

Introduction to Management Accounting, 13th ed.
Horngren/Sundem/Stratton

study guide for accounting

7e

Helen Brubeck
San Jose State University

Florence McGovern
Bergen Community College

PEARSON

Prentice Hall

Upper Saddle River, New Jersey 07458

Library of Congress Cataloging-in-Publication Data
Horngren, Charles T.
    Accounting / Charles T. Horngren, Walter T. Harrison, Jr. — 7th ed.
    p. cm.
    Includes bibliographical references and index.
    ISBN 0-13-243960-3 (hardback : alk. paper)
    1. Accounting.   I. Harrison, Walter T.   II. Title
HF5635.H8   2007
657—dc22   2006029536

Executive Editor: Jodi McPherson
VP/Editorial Director: Jeff Shelstad
Developmental Editors: Claire Hunter, Ralph Moore
Executive Marketing Manager: Sharon Koch
Marketing Assistant: Patrick Barbera
Associate Director, Production Editorial: Judy Leale
Production Editor: Michael Reynolds
Permissions Supervisor: Charles Morris
Manufacturing Manager: Arnold Vila
Creative Director: Maria Lange
Cover Design: Solid State Graphics
Director, Image Resource Center: Melinda Patelli
Manager, Rights and Permissions: Zina Arabia
Manager, Visual Research: Beth Brenzel
Manager, Cover Visual Research & Permissions: Karen Sanatar
Image Permission Coordinator: Nancy Seise
Photo Researcher: Diane Austin
Manager, Print Production: Christy Mahon
Composition/Full-Service Project Management: BookMasters, Inc.
Printer/Binder: RR Donnelley–Willard
Typeface: 10/12 Sabon

Credits and acknowledgments borrowed from other sources and reproduced, with permission, in this textbook appear on the appropriate page within text.

Pearson Education LTD.   Pearson Education Australia PTY, Limited
Pearson Education Singapore, Pte. Ltd   Pearson Education North Asia Ltd
Pearson Education, Canada, Ltd   Pearson Educación de Mexico, S.A. de C.V.
Pearson Education–Japan   Pearson Education Malaysia, Pte. Ltd

10 9 8 7 6 5 4 3 2
ISBN 0-13-179211-3

Brief Contents

Contents

14 Corporations: Retained Earnings and the Income Statement   688

16 The Statement of Cash Flows   782

22 **The Master Budget and Responsibility Accounting 1100**

To Billie Harrison, who taught me excellence

The *Accounting, 7e*, Demo Doc System: For professors whose greatest joy is hearing students say "I get it!"

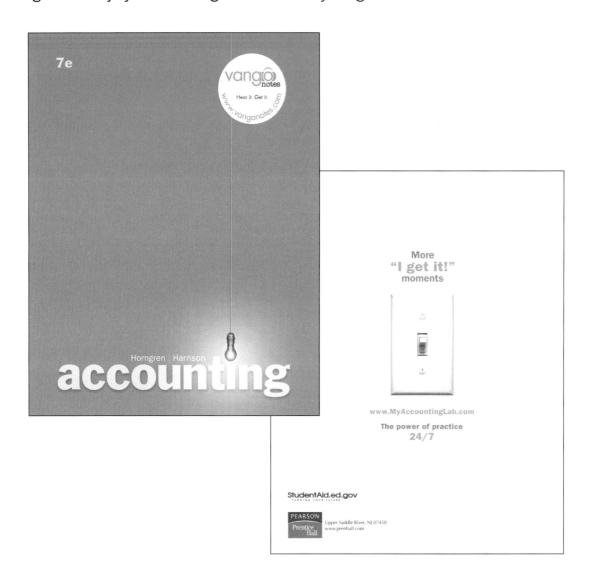

Help your students achieve "I get it!" moments when you're with them AND when you're NOT.

When you're there showing how to solve a problem in class, students "get it." When you're not there, they get stuck—it's only natural.

Our system is designed to help you deliver the best "I get it!" moments. (Instructor's Edition, Instructor Demo Docs)

But it's the really tricky situations that no one else has zeroed in on— the 2 A.M. outside-of-class moments, when you're not there—that present the greatest challenge.

That's where we come in, at these "they have the book, but they don't have you" moments. *Accounting 7e's* Demo Doc System will help in those critical times. That's what makes this package different from all other textbooks.

The *Accounting 7e,* Demo Doc System provides the vehicle for you and your students to have more "I get it!" moments inside and outside of class.

THE ACCOUNTING, 7e, DEMO DOC SYSTEM

Duplicate the classroom experience anytime, anywhere with Horngren & Harrison's *Accounting, Seventh Edition*

How The System Works

- The Demo Docs are entire problems worked through step-by-step, from start to finish, with the kind of comments around them that YOU would say in class. They exist in the first four chapters of this text to support the critical accounting cycle chapters, in the Study Guide both in print and in FLASH versions, and as a part of the instructor package for instructors to use in class.

- The authors have created a "no clutter" layout so that critical content is clear and easily referenced.

- Consistency is stressed across all mediums: text, student, and instructor supplements.

- MyAccountingLab is an online homework system that combines "I get it!" moments with the power of practice.

The System's Backbone

Demo Docs in the Text, the Study Guide, and MyAccountingLab.

▶ *NEW* **DEMO DOCS** – Introductory accounting students consistently tell us, "When doing homework, I get stuck trying to solve problems the way they were demonstrated in class." Instructors consistently tell us, "I have so much to cover in so little time; I can't afford to go backward and review homework in class." Those challenges inspired us to develop Demo Docs. Demo Docs are comprehensive worked-through problems, available for nearly every chapter of our introductory accounting text, to help students when they are trying to solve exercises and problems on their own. The idea is to help students duplicate the classroom experience outside of class. Entire problems that mirror end-of-chapter material are shown solved and annotated with explanations written in a conversational style, essentially imitating what an instructor might say if standing over a student's shoulder. All Demo Docs will be available online in Flash and in print so students can easily refer to them when and where they need them.

Chapter 2: Demo Doc

Debit/Credit Transaction Analysis

Demo Doc: To make sure you understand this material, work through the following demonstration 'demo doc' with detailed comments to help you see the concept within the framework of a worked-through problem.

Learning Objectives 1–4

On September 1, 2008, Michael Moe opened Moe's Mowing, a company that provides mowing and landscaping services. During the month of September, the business incurred the following transactions:

   a. To begin operations, Michael deposited $10,000 of personal funds in the business's bank account. The business received the cash and gave Michael capital (owner's equity).

   b. The business purchased equipment for $3,500 on account.

   c. The business purchased office supplies for $800 cash.

   d. The business provided $2,600 of services to a customer on account.

   e. The business paid $500 cash toward the equipment previously purchased on account in transaction b.

   f. The business received $2,000 in cash for services provided to a new customer.

   g. The business paid $200 cash to repair equipment.

   h. The business paid $900 cash in salary expense.

   i. The business received $2,100 cash from customers on account.

   j. Michael withdrew $1,500 cash from the business for personal use.

Requirements

1. Create blank T-accounts for the following accounts: Cash; Accounts Receivable; Supplies; Equipment; Accounts Payable; Michael Moe, Capital; Michael Moe, Withdrawals; Service Revenue; Salary Expense; Repair Expense.

2. Journalize the transactions and show how they are recorded in T-accounts. Use the table in Exhibit 2-17 to help with the journal entries.

EXHIBIT 2-17   The Rules of Debit and Credit

	Increase	Decrease
Assets	debit	credit

MyAccountingLab – This online homework and assessment tool supports the same theme as the text and resources by providing "I get it!" moments inside and outside of class. It is in MyAccountingLab where "I get it!" moments meet the power of practice. MyAccountingLab is about helping students at their teachable moment, whether that is 1 P.M. or 1 A.M. MyAccountingLab is packed with algorithmic problems because practice makes perfect. It is also packed with the exact same end-of-chapter material in the text that you are used to assigning for homework. MyAccountingLab features the same look and feel for exercises and problems in journal entries and financial statements so that students are familiar and comfortable working in it. Because it includes a Demo Doc for each of the end-of-chapter exercises and problems that students can refer to as they work through the question, it extends The System just one step further by providing students with the help they need to succeed when you are not with them.

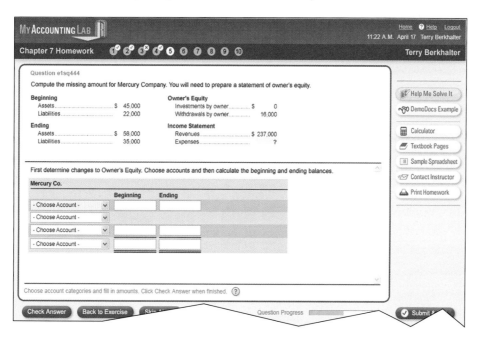

The System's Details

CHAPTERS 1–4 We know it's critical that students have a solid understanding of the fundamentals and language surrounding the accounting cycle before they can move to practice. To that end, we're spending extra time developing the accounting cycle chapters (Chs 1–4) to make sure they will help students succeed. We're adding extra visuals, additional comprehensive problems, and a Demo Doc per chapter to give students additional support to move on through the material successfully. You'll be able to stay on schedule in the syllabus because students understand the accounting cycle.

CONSISTENCY – The entire package matters. Consistency in terminology and problem set-ups from one medium to another—test bank to study guide to MyAccountingLab—is critical to your success in the classroom. So when students ask "Where do the numbers come from?," they can go to our text **or** go online and see what to do. If it's worded one way in the text, you can count on it being worded the same way in the supplements.

CLUTTER-FREE – This edition is built on the premise of "Less is More." Extraneous boxes and features, non-essential bells and whistles—they are all gone. The authors know that excess crowds out what really matters—the concepts, the problems, and the learning objectives. Instructors asked for fewer "features" in favor of less clutter and better cross-referencing, and Horngren/Harrison, *Accounting, 7e,* is delivering on that wish. And we've redone all of the end-of-chapter exercises and problems with a renewed focus on the critical core concepts.

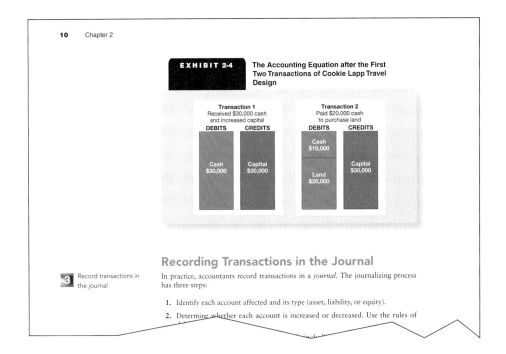

EXHIBIT 2-4 The Accounting Equation after the First Two Transactions of Cookie Lapp Travel Design

Transaction 1
Received $30,000 cash
and increased capital

DEBITS	CREDITS
Cash $30,000	Capital $30,000

Transaction 2
Paid $20,000 cash
to purchase land

DEBITS	CREDITS
Cash $10,000 Land $20,000	Capital $30,000

Recording Transactions in the Journal

3 Record transactions in the journal

In practice, accountants record transactions in a *journal*. The journalizing process has three steps:

1. Identify each account affected and its type (asset, liability, or equity).
2. Determine whether each account is increased or decreased. Use the rules of

INSTRUCTOR SUPPLEMENTS

Instructor's Edition Featuring *Instructor Demo Docs*

▶ **The New Look of the Instructor's Edition**

We've asked a lot of instructors how we can help them successfully implement new course-delivery methods (e.g. online) while maintaining their regular campus schedule of classes and academic responsibilities. In response, we developed a system of instruction for those of you who are long on commitment and expertise—but short on time and assistance.

The primary goal of the Instructor's Edition is **ease of implementation, using any delivery method**—traditional, self-paced, or online. That is, the Instructor's Edition quickly answers for you, the professor, the question "What must the student do?" Likewise, the Instructor's Edition quickly answers for the student "What must I do?," offers time-saving tips with "best of" categories for in class discussion, and strong examples to illustrate difficult concepts to a wide variety of students. The Instructor's Edition also offers a quick one-shot cross-reference at the exact point of importance with key additional teaching resources, so everything is in one place. The Instructor's Edition includes summaries and teaching tips, pitfalls for new students, and "best of" practices from instructors from across the world.

▶ **The Instructor's Edition also includes *Instructor Demo Docs***

In ***Instructor Demo Docs***, we walk the students through how to solve a problem as if it were the first time they've seen it. There are no lengthy passages of text. Instead, bits of expository text are woven into the steps needed to solve the problem, in the exact sequence—for you to provide at the teachable ***"I get it!"*** moment. This is the point at which the student has a context within which he or she can understand the concept. We provide conversational text around each of the steps so the student stays engaged in solving the problem. We provide notes to the instructor for key teaching points around the Demo Docs, and "best of" practice tid-bits before each ***Instructor Demo Doc***.

The ***Instructor Demo Docs*** are written with all of your everyday classroom realities in mind—and trying to save your time in prepping new examples each time your book changes. Additionally, algorithmic versions of these Demo Docs are provided to students in their student guide. We keep the terminology consistent with the text, so there are no surprises for students as they try and work through a problem the first time.

Solutions Transparencies

These transparency masters are the **Solutions Manual** in an easy-to-use format for class lectures.

Instructor's Resource Center CD or www.prenhall.com/horngren

The password-protected site and resource CD includes the following:
- **The Instructor's Edition with *Instructor Demo Docs***
- **Problem Set C**

- **Solutions Manual with Interactive Excel Solutions**

  The Solutions Manual contains solutions to all end-of-chapter questions, multiple-choice questions, short exercises, exercise sets, problems sets, and Internet exercises. The Solutions Manual is available in Microsoft Excel, Microsoft Word, and in print. You can access the solutions in MS Excel and MS Word formats by visiting the Instructor's Resource Center on the Prentice Hall catalog site at www.prenhall.com/horngren or on the Instructor's CD. You will need a Pearson Educator username and password to retrieve materials from the Web site.

  Solutions to select end-of-chapter exercises and problems are available in **interactive MS Excel format** so that instructors can present material in dynamic, step-by-step sequences in class. The interactive solutions were prepared by Kathleen O'Donnell of the State University of New York, Onondaga Community College.

- **Test Bank**

The test item file includes more than 2,000 questions:
  - Multiple Choice
  - Matching
  - True/False
  - Computational Problems
  - Essay

- **Test Bank** is formatted for use with WebCT, Blackboard, and Course Compass.

- **PowerPoints (instructor and student)** summarize and reinforce key text materials. They capture classroom attention with original problems and solved step-by-step exercises. These walk-throughs are designed to help facilitate classroom discussion and demonstrate where the numbers come from and what they mean to the concept at hand. There are approximately 35 slides per chapter. PowerPoints are available on the Instructor's CD and can be downloaded from www.prenhall.com/horngren.

New *MyAccountingLab* Online Homework and Assessment Manager

The **"I get it!"** moment meets **the power of practice**. The power of repetition when you "get it" means learning happens. **MyAccountingLab** is about helping students at their teachable moments, whether it's 1 P.M. or 1 A.M.

MyAccountingLab is an online homework and assessment tool, packed with algorithmic versions of every text problem, because practice makes perfect. It's also packed with the exact same end-of-chapter material that you're used to assigning for homework. Additionally, **MyAccountingLab** includes:

1. A **Demo Doc** for each of the end-of-chapter exercises and problems that students can refer to as they work through the questions.

2. A **Guided Solution** to the exact problem they are working on. It helps students when they're trying to solve a problem the way it was demonstrated in class.

3. A full **e-book** so the students can reference the book at the point of practice.

4. New **topic specific videos** that walk students through difficult concepts.

Companion Web Site–www.prenhall.com/Horngren

The book's Web site at www.prenhall.com/horngren—contains the following:

- Self-study quizzes—interactive study guide for each chapter
- MS Excel templates that students can use to complete homework assignments for each chapter (e-working papers)
- Samples of the Flash Demo Docs for students to work through the accounting cycle

Online Courses with WebCT/BlackBoard/Course Compass

Prentice Hall offers a link to MyAccountingLab through the Bb and WebCT Course Management Systems.

Classroom Response Systems (CRS)

CRS is an exciting new wireless polling technology that makes large and small classrooms even more interactive, because it enables instructors to pose questions to their students, record results, and display those results instantly. Students can easily answer questions using compact remote-control–type transmitters. Prentice Hall has partnerships with leading classroom response-systems providers and can show you everything you need to know about setting up and using a CRS system. Prentice Hall will provide the classroom hardware, text-specific PowerPoint slides, software, and support.

Visit **www.prenhall.com/crs** to learn more.

STUDENT SUPPLEMENTS

Runners Corporation PT Lab Manual

Containing numerous simulated real-world examples, the **Runners Corporation** practice set is available complete with data files for Peachtree, QuickBooks, and PH General Ledger. Each practice set also includes business stationery for manual entry work.

A-1 Photography-Manual PT Lab Manual

Containing numerous simulated real-world examples, the **A-1 Photography** practice set is available complete with data files for Peachtree, QuickBooks, and PH General Ledger. Each set includes business stationery for manual entry work.

Study Guide including Demo Docs and e-Working Papers

Introductory accounting students consistently tell us, "When doing homework, I get stuck trying to solve problems the way they were demonstrated in class." Instructors consistently tell us, "I have so much to cover in so little time; I can't afford to go backwards and review homework in class." Those challenges inspired us to develop Demo Docs. Demo Docs are comprehensive worked-through problems available for nearly every chapter of our introductory accounting text to help students when they are trying to solve exercises and problems on their own. The idea is to help students duplicate the classroom experience outside of class. Entire problems that mirror end-of-chapter material are shown solved and annotated with explanations written in a conversational style, essentially imitating what an instructor might say if standing over a student's shoulder. All Demo Docs will be available in the Study Guide—in print and on CD in Flash, so students can easily refer to them when they need them. The Study Guide also includes a summary overview of key topics and multiple-choice and short-answer questions for students to test their knowledge. Free electronic working papers are included on the accompanying CD.

MyAccountingLab Online Homework and Assessment Manager

The **"I get it!"** moment meets *power of practice*. The power of repetition when you "get it" means that learning happens. **MyAccountingLab** is about helping students at their teachable moment, whether that is 1 P.M. or 1 A.M.

MyAccountingLab is an online homework and assessment tool, packed with algorithmic versions of every text problem because practice makes perfect. It's also packed with the exact same end-of-chapter that you're used to assigning for homework. Additionally, **MyAccountingLab** includes:

1. A **Demo Doc** for each of the end-of-chapter exercises and problems that students can refer to as they work through the question.

2. A **Guided Solution** to the exact problem they are working on. It helps students when they're trying to solve a problem the way it was demonstrated in class.

3. A full **e-book** so the students can reference the book at the point of practice.

4. New **topic specific videos** that walk students through difficult concepts.

PowerPoints

For student use as a study aide or note-taking guide, these PowerPoint slides may be downloaded at the companion Web site at www.prenhall.com/horngren.

Companion Web Site–www.prenhall.com/Horngren

The book's Web site at www.prenhall.com/horngren—contains the following:

- Self-study quizzes—interactive study guide for each chapter
- MS Excel templates that students can use to complete homework assignments for each chapter (e-working papers)
- Samples of the Flash Demo Docs for students to work through the accounting cycle.

Classroom Response Systems (CRS)

CRS is an exciting new wireless polling technology that makes large and small classrooms even more interactive because it enables instructors to pose questions to their students, record results, and display those results instantly. Students can easily answer questions using compact remote-control-type transmitters. Prentice Hall has partnerships with leading classroom response-systems providers and can show you everything you need to know about setting up and using a CRS system. Prentice Hall will provide the classroom hardware, text-specific PowerPoint slides, software, and support.

Visit **www.prenhall.com/crs** to learn more.

- **VangoNotes in MP3 Format**

   Students can study on the go with VangoNotes, chapter reviews in downloadable MP3 format that offer brief audio segments for each chapter:

   - Big Ideas: the vital ideas in each chapter
   - Practice Test: lets students know if they need to keep studying
   - Key Terms: audio "flashcards" that review key concepts and terms
   - Rapid Review: a quick drill session—helpful right before tests

   Students can learn more at **www.vangonotes.com**

Hear it. Get It.

partnership with Audible®Education

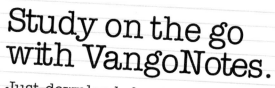

Study on the go with VangoNotes.

Just download chapter reviews from your text and listen to them on any mp3 player. Now wherever you are-- whatever you're doing--you can study by listening to the following for each chapter of your textbook:

Big Ideas: Your "need to know" for each chapter

Practice Test: A gut check for the Big Ideas--tells you if you need to keep studying

Key Terms: Audio "flashcards" to help you review key concepts and terms

Rapid Review: A quick drill session--use it right before your test

VangoNotes.com

Acknowledgments

We'd like to thank the following contributors:

Florence McGovern *Bergen Community College*
Sherry Mills *New Mexico State University*

Suzanne Oliver *Okaloosa Walton Junior College*
Helen Brubeck *San Jose State University*

We'd like to extend a special thank you to the following members of our advisory panel:

Jim Ellis *Bay State College, Boston*
Mary Ann Swindlehurst *Carroll Community College*
Andy Williams *Edmonds Community College*
Donnie Kristof-Nelson *Edmonds Community College*
Joan Cezair *Fayetteville State University*
David Baglia *Grove City College*

Anita Ellzey *Harford Community College*
Cheryl McKay *Monroe County Community College*
Todd Jackson *Northeastern State University*
Margaret Costello Lambert *Oakland Community College*
Al Fagan *University of Richmond*

We'd also like to thank the following reviewers:

Shi-Mu (Simon) Yang *Adelphi University*
Thomas Stolberg *Alfred State University*
Thomas Branton *Alvin Community College*
Maria Lehoczky *American Intercontinental University*
Suzanne Bradford *Angelina College*
Judy Lewis *Angelo State University*
Roy Carson Anne *Arundel Community College*
Paulette Ratliff-Miller *Arkansas State University*
Joseph Foley *Assumption College*
Jennifer Niece *Assumption College*
Bill Whitley *Athens State University*
Shelly Gardner *Augustana College*

Becky Jones *Baylor University*
Betsy Willis *Baylor University*
Michael Robinson *Baylor University*
Kay Walker-Hauser *Beaufort County Community College, Washington*
Joe Aubert *Bemidji State University*
Calvin Fink *Bethune Cookman College*
Michael Blue *Bloomsburg University*
Scott Wallace *Blue Mountain College*
Lloyd Carroll *Borough Manhattan Community College*
Ken Duffe *Brookdale Community College*
Chuck Heuser *Brookdale Community College*
Shafi Ullah *Broward Community College South*
Lois Slutsky *Broward Community College South*
Ken Koerber *Bucks County Community College*

Julie Browning *California Baptist University*
Richard Savich *California State University—San Bernardino*
David Bland *Cape Fear Community College*
Robert Porter *Cape Fear Community College*
Vickie Campbell *Cape Fear Community College*
Cynthia Thompson *Carl Sandburg College—Carthage*

Liz Ott *Casper College*
Joseph Adamo *Cazenovia College*
Julie Dailey *Central Virginia Community College*
Jeannie Folk *College of DuPage*
Lawrence Steiner *College of Marin*
Dennis Kovach *Community College Allegheny County—Allegheny*
Norma Montague *Central Carolina Community College*
Debbie Schmidt *Cerritos College*
Janet Grange *Chicago State University*
Bruce Leung *City College of San Francisco*
Pamela Legner *College of DuPage*
Bruce McMurrey *Community College of Denver*
Martin Sabo *Community College of Denver*
Jeffrey Jones *Community College of Southern Nevada*
Tom Nohl *Community College of Southern Nevada*
Christopher Kelly *Community College of Southern Nevada*
Patrick Rogan *Cosumnes River College*
Kimberly Smith *County College of Morris*

Jerold Braun *Daytona Beach Community College*
Greg Carlton *Davidson County Community College*
Irene Bembenista *Davenport University*
Thomas Szczurek *Delaware County Community College*
Charles Betts *Delaware Technical and Community College*
Patty Holmes *Des Moines Area Community College—Ankeny*
Tim Murphy *Diablo Valley College*

Phillipe Sammour *Eastern Michigan University*
Saturnino (Nino) Gonzales *El Paso Community College*
Lee Cannell *El Paso Community College*
John Eagan *Erie Community College*

Ron O'Brien *Fayetteville Technical Community College*
Patrick McNabb *Ferris State University*
John Stancil *Florida Southern College*
Lynn Clements *Florida Southern College*
Alice Sineath *Forsyth Technical Community College*
James Makofske *Fresno City College*
Marc Haskell *Fresno City College*
James Kelly *Ft. Lauderdale City College*

Christine Jonick *Gainesville State College*
Bruce Lindsey *Genesee Community College*
Constance Hylton *George Mason University*
Cody King *Georgia Southwestern State University*
Lolita Keck *Globe College*
Kay Carnes *Gonzaga University, Spokane*
Carol Pace *Grayson County College*
Rebecca Floor *Greenville Technical College*
Geoffrey Heriot *Greenville Technical College*
Jeffrey Patterson *Grove City College*
Lanny Nelms *Gwinnet Technical College*
Chris Cusatis *Gwynedd Mercy College*

Tim Griffin *Hillsborough Community College*
Clair Helms *Hinds Community College*
Michelle Powell *Holmes Community College*
Greg Bischoff *Houston Community College*
Donald Bond *Houston Community College*
Marina Grau *Houston Community College*
Carolyn Fitzmorris *Hutchinson Community College*

Susan Koepke *Illinois Valley Community College*
William Alexander *Indian Hills Community College—Ottumwa*
Dale Bolduc *Intercoast College*
Thomas Carr *International College of Naples*
Lecia Berven *Iowa Lakes Community College*
Nancy Schendel *Iowa Lakes Community College*
Michelle Cannon *Ivy Tech*
Vicki White *Ivy Tech*
Chuck Smith *Iowa Western Community College*

Stephen Christian *Jackson Community College*
DeeDee Daughtry *Johnston Community College*
Richard Bedwell *Jones County Junior College*

Ken Mark *Kansas City Kansas Community College*
Ken Snow *Kaplan Education Centers*
Charles Evans *Keiser College*
Bunney Schmidt *Keiser College*
Amy Haas *Kingsborough Community College*

Jim Racic *Lakeland Community College*
Doug Clouse *Lakeland Community College*

Patrick Haggerty *Lansing Community College*
Patricia Walczak *Lansing Community College*
Humberto M. Herrera *Laredo Community College*
Christie Comunale *Long Island University*
Ariel Markelevich *Long Island University*
Randy Kidd *Longview Community College*
Kathy Heltzel *Luzerne County Community College*
Lori Major *Luzerne County Community College*

Fred Jex *Macomb Community College*
Glenn Owen *Marymount College*
Behnaz Quigley *Marymount College*
Penny Hanes *Mercyhurst College, Erie*
John Miller *Metropolitan Community College*
Denise Leggett *Middle Tennessee State University*
William Huffman *Missouri Southern State College*
Ted Crosby *Montgomery County Community College*
Beth Engle *Montgomery County Community College*
David Candelaria *Mount San Jacinto College*
Linda Bolduc *Mount Wachusett Community College*

Barbara Gregorio *Nassau Community College*
James Hurat *National College of Business and Technology*
Denver Riffe *National College of Business and Technology*
Asokan Anandarajan *New Jersey Institute of Technology*
Robert Schoener *New Mexico State University*
Stanley Carroll *New York City Technical College of CUNY*
Audrey Agnello *Niagara County Community College*
Catherine Chiang *North Carolina Central University*
Karen Russom *North Harris College*
Dan Bayak *Northampton Community College*
Elizabeth Lynn Locke *Northern Virginia Community College*
Debra Prendergast *Northwestern Business College*
Nat Briscoe *Northwestern State University*
Tony Scott *Norwalk Community College*

Deborah Niemer *Oakland Community College*
John Boyd *Oklahoma City Community College*
Kathleen O'Donnell *Onondaga Community College*
J.T. Ryan *Onondaga Community College*

Toni Clegg *Palm Beach Atlantic College*
David Forsyth *Palomar College*
John Graves *PCDI*
Carla Rich *Pensacola Junior College*
Judy Grotrian *Peru State College*
Judy Daulton *Piedmont Technical College*
John Stone *Potomac State College*
Betty Habershon *Prince George's Community College*

Kathi Villani *Queensborough Community College*

William Black *Raritan Valley Community College*
Verne Ingram *Red Rocks Community College*
Paul Juriga *Richland Community College*
Patty Worsham *Riverside Community College*
Margaret Berezewski *Robert Morris College*
Phil Harder *Robert Morris College*
Shifei Chung *Rowan University of New Jersey*

Charles Fazzi *Saint Vincent College*
Lynnette Yerbuy *Salt Lake Community College*
Susan Blizzard *San Antonio College*
Hector Martinez *San Antonio College*
Audrey Voyles *San Diego Miramar College*
Margaret Black *San Jacinto College*
Merrily Hoffman *San Jacinto College*
Randall Whitmore *San Jacinto College*
Carroll Buck *San Jose State University*
Cynthia Coleman *Sandhills Community College*
Barbara Crouteau *Santa Rosa Junior College*
Pat Novak *Southeast Community College*
Susan Pallas *Southeast Community College*
Al Case *Southern Oregon University*
Gloria Worthy *Southwest Tennessee Community College*
Melody Ashenfelter *Southwestern Oklahoma State University*
Douglas Ward *Southwestern Community College*
Brandi Shay *Southwestern Community College*
John May *Southwestern Oklahoma State University*
Jeffrey Waybright *Spokane Community College*
Renee Goffinet *Spokane Community College*
Susan Anders *ST Bonaventure University*
John Olsavsky *SUNY at Fredonia*
Peter Van Brunt *SUNY College of Technology at Delhi*

David L. Davis *Tallahassee Community College*
Kathy Crusto-Way *Tarrant County Community College*
Sally Cook *Texas Lutheran University*
Bea Chiang *The College of New Jersey*
Matt Hightower *Three Rivers Community College*

Susan Pope *University of Akron*
Joe Woods *University of Arkansas*
Allen Blay *University of California, Riverside*

Barry Mishra *University of California, Riverside*
Laura Young *University of Central Arkansas*
Jane Calvert *University of Central Oklahoma*
Bambi Hora *University of Central Oklahoma*
Joan Stone *University of Central Oklahoma*
Kathy Terrell *University of Central Oklahoma*
Harlan Etheridge *University of Louisiana*
Pam Meyer *University of Louisiana*
Sandra Scheuermann *University of Louisiana*
Tom Wilson *University of Louisiana*
Lawrence Leaman *University of Michigan*
Larry Huus *University of Minnesota*
Brian Carpenter *University of Scranton*
Ashraf Khallaf *University of Southern Indiana*
Tony Zordan *University of St. Francis*
Gene Elrod *University of Texas, Arlington*
Cheryl Prachyl *University of Texas, El Paso*
Karl Putnam *University of Texas, El Paso*
Stephen Rockwell *University of Tulsa*
Chula King *University of West Florida*
Charles Baird *University of Wisconsin – Stout*

Mary Hollars *Vincennes University*
Lisa Nash *Vincennes University*
Elaine Dessouki *Virginia Wesleyan College*

Sueann Hely *West Kentucky Community and Technical College*
Darlene Pulliam *West Texas A&M University, Canyon*
Judy Beebe *Western Oregon University*
Michelle Maggio *Westfield State College*
Kathy Pellegrino *Westfield State College*
Nora McCarthy *Wharton County Junior College*
Sally Stokes *Wilmington College*
Maggie Houston *Wright State University*

Gerald Caton *Yavapai College*
Chris Crosby *York Technical College*
Harold Gellis *York College of CUNY*

About the Authors

Charles T. Horngren is the Edmund W. Littlefield Professor of Accounting, Emeritus, at Stanford University. A graduate of Marquette University, he received his M.B.A. from Harvard University and his Ph.D. from the University of Chicago. He is also the recipient of honorary doctorates from Marquette University and DePaul University.

A Certified Public Accountant, Horngren served on the Accounting Principles Board for six years, the Financial Accounting Standards Board Advisory Council for five years, and the Council of the American Institute of Certified Public Accountants for three years. For six years, he served as a trustee of the Financial Accounting Foundation, which oversees the Financial Accounting Standards Board and the Government Accounting Standards Board.

Horngren is a member of the Accounting Hall of Fame.

A member of the American Accounting Association, Horngren has been its President and its Director of Research. He received its first annual Outstanding Accounting Educator Award.

The California Certified Public Accountants Foundation gave Horngren its Faculty Excellence Award and its Distinguished Professor Award. He is the first person to have received both awards.

The American Institute of Certified Public Accountants presented its first Outstanding Educator Award to Horngren.

Horngren was named Accountant of the Year, Education, by the national professional accounting fraternity, Beta Alpha Psi.

Professor Horngren is also a member of the Institute of Management Accountants, from whom he has received its Distinguished Service Award. He was a member of the Institute's Board of Regents, which administers the Certified Management Accountant examinations.

Horngren is the author of other accounting books published by Prentice-Hall: *Cost Accounting: A Managerial Emphasis*, Twelfth Edition, 2006 (with Srikant Datar and George Foster*); Introduction to Financial Accounting*, Ninth Edition, 2006 (with Gary L. Sundem and John A. Elliott*); Introduction to Management Accounting*, Thirteenth Edition, 2005 (with Gary L. Sundem and William Stratton); *Financial Accounting*, Sixth Edition, 2006 (with Walter T. Harrison, Jr.).

Horngren is the Consulting Editor for Prentice-Hall's Charles T. Horngren Series in Accounting.

Walter T. Harrison, Jr. is Professor Emeritus of Accounting at the Hankamer School of Business, Baylor University. He received his B.B.A. degree from Baylor University, his M.S. from Oklahoma State University, and his Ph.D. from Michigan State University.

Professor Harrison, recipient of numerous teaching awards from student groups as well as from university administrators, has also taught at Cleveland State Community College, Michigan State University, the University of Texas, and Stanford University.

A member of the American Accounting Association and the American Institute of Certified Public Accountants, Professor Harrison has served as Chairman of the Financial Accounting Standards Committee of the American Accounting Association, on the Teaching/Curriculum Development Award Committee, on the Program Advisory

Committee for Accounting Education and Teaching, and on the Notable Contributions to Accounting Literature Committee.

Professor Harrison has lectured in several foreign countries and published articles in numerous journals, including *Journal of Accounting Research*, *Journal of Accountancy*, *Journal of Accounting and Public Policy*, *Economic Consequences of Financial Accounting Standards*, *Accounting Horizons*, *Issues in Accounting Education*, and *Journal of Law and Commerce*.

He is co-author of *Financial Accounting*, Sixth Edition, 2006 (with Charles T. Horngren), published by Prentice Hall. Professor Harrison has received scholarships, fellowships, and research grants or awards from PriceWaterhouse Coopers, Deloitte & Touche, the Ernst & Young Foundation, and the KPMG Foundation.

accounting

7e

12 Partnerships

WHAT YOU PROBABLY ALREADY KNOW

You probably already know that some couples sign a prenuptial agreement before getting married. A prenuptial agreement usually provides guidance as to the distribution of assets held before marriage and those acquired during marriage. The disposition of individual debt acquired before marriage may be addressed, as well as nonfinancial or lifestyle topics. The purpose of this agreement is to confirm in writing what the future marriage partners believe is fair and appropriate. Preparing written documentation avoids misunderstandings and poor communication.

This is exactly the reason why it is strongly recommended that a written partnership agreement be prepared. Important issues should be included in the partnership agreement, such as the share of profits (or losses) each partner will take, the responsibilities of each partner, voluntary withdrawal or death of a partner, provisions for the termination of the partnership, and other important guidelines.

Learning Objectives

 Identify the characteristics of a partnership.

Some of the characteristics of a partnership include limited life, mutual agency, unlimited liability, co-ownership of property, and no partnership tax. It is advisable to create a written partnership agreement containing important components of the partnership business in case the partnership dissolves. *Review these characteristics in the "Characteristics of a Partnership" section of your textbook. Be sure to also review the advantages and disadvantages of a partnership in Exhibit 12-2 (p. 598) and the different types of partnerships in Exhibit 12-3 (p. 599).*

 Account for partner investments.

When the partners invest personal assets in the partnership, they are recorded at market value. If liabilities are assumed by the partnership, they are also recorded and the partners' Capital accounts are credited for the net assets. *Review the "Start-up of a Partnership" in the main text.*

 Allocate profits and losses to the partners.

Profits and losses are shared by the partners in accordance with the terms of the partnership agreement. Typical arrangements may indicate that profits and losses are split based on each partner's investment, service, or some other percentage of fractional bases. If there is no provision for allocating profits and losses in the agreement, they are split evenly. The net income or loss that is closed out into Income Summary is then closed out to the partners' Capital accounts in accordance with the indicated allocation. *Review the examples included under the "Sharing Profits and Losses, and Partner Drawings" in the main text.*

 Account for the admission of a new partner.

When a new partner is admitted, the old partnership is dissolved and a new partnership agreement should be created. This may occur in one of the following ways:

• One partner selling directly to an outside individual who is agreeable to the partners. The outgoing partner's Capital is debited and the new partner's Capital is credited for the same amount.

• A partner can join a partnership by contributing assets into the business. The new partner's Capital account may be given credit for the market value of the assets at (a) an amount exactly equal to the market value of the assets recorded on the books, (b) an amount less than the market value of the assets recorded on the books, which provides a bonus to the existing partners, or (c) an amount more than the market value of the assets recorded on the books, which provides a bonus to the new partner.

Review "Admission by Investing in the Partnership" in the main text for specific examples of partners contributing assets to the business.

 Account for a partner's withdrawal from the firm.

A partner may die or decide to withdraw from the partnership. The withdrawal of a partner results in the dissolution of the partnership agreement. A withdrawal may occur in one of the following ways:

• A partner's interest may be satisfied upon death by paying the appropriate Capital amount as indicated in the partnership agreement.

• A remaining partner may purchase the deceased partner's interest. The continuing partner's Capital is increased for the same amount as the Capital account eliminated for the withdrawing partner.

• A partner can withdraw by receiving cash equal to (a) the book value of the Capital account, (b) an amount less than the book value of the Capital account, providing a bonus to the remaining partners, or (c) an amount more than the book value of the Capital account, providing a bonus to the withdrawing partner.

Review "Withdrawal of a Partner" in the main text for specific examples of the withdrawal of net assets from the business.

 Account for the liquidation of a partnership.

A liquidation means that the business is going to cease operations. When this happens, the business will (a) sell the assets and allocate the gain or loss to the partners' Capital accounts based on the partnership agreement, (b) pay all of the partnership liabilities, and (c) distribute the remaining cash to the partners based on their Capital balances.

Review Exhibit 12-5 (p. 613) to see the impact of a liquidation on the related account balances.

 Prepare partnership financial statements.

Partnership financial statements are similar to those of a sole proprietorship, except there is more than one owner. *Review Exhibit 12-6, Financial Statements of a Partnership (p. 614).*

Demo Doc 1

Partnerships

Learning Objectives 1–7

The Goode Partnership wants to admit Hanna Storm as a new partner on January 1, 2008. On this date, Goode had the following information:

Cash	$25,000	Liabilities	$35,000
Other assets	60,000	Ned Frist, capital	35,000
		Janice Wright, capital	15,000
Total assets	$85,000	Total liabilities and capital	$85,000

Janice has a 30% share of the profits, whereas Ned has a 70% share.

Requirements

1. Suppose Janice Wright sold her entire interest to Hanna for $40,000. Journalize the transfer of ownership. What are the Capital balances for each partner after the transfer is made?

2. (Ignoring Requirement 1) Suppose instead that the Goode Partnership were to admit Hanna as a third partner by selling her a 40% interest for $40,000 cash. Compute Hanna's Capital balance and journalize her investment. What are the Capital balances for each partner after the investment is made?

3. (Ignoring Requirement 1) Prepare the balance sheet of the Goode Partnership after Hanna is admitted to the partnership.

4. Assume that Hanna was not admitted to the partnership. During 2008, Goode earned $20,000 of net income (in cash). How much profit is allocated to each partner (Janice and Ned)? Does the partnership pay income taxes on this profit?

5. (Continuing on from Requirement 4) On January 1, 2009, the Goode Partnership was liquidated. All noncash assets were sold for $90,000, after which all liabilities were paid. How much does each partner receive upon liquidation?

Demo Doc 1 Solutions

Requirement 1

 2 Account for partner investments

4 Account for the admission of a new partner

5 Account for a partner's withdrawal from the firm

Suppose Janice Wright sold her entire interest to Hanna for $40,000. Journalize the transfer of ownership. What are the Capital balances for each partner after the transfer is made?

Part 1	Part 2	Part 3	Part 4	Part 5	Demo Doc Complete

If Hanna purchases Janice's interest in the partnership, it is an outside transaction of ownership. The only portion recorded in the accounting records is the name change on the Capital account. Janice's Capital account decreases (a debit) and Hanna's Capital account increases (a credit) by $15,000.

Janice Wright, Capital	15,000	
Hanna Storm, Capital		15,000

The Capital balances are as they were before the transaction, with the exception of the name change:

Before Transaction		After Transaction	
Janice Wright, capital	$15,000	Hanna Storm, capital	$15,000
Ned Frist, capital	35,000	Ned Frist, capital	35,000
Total capital	$50,000	Total capital	$50,000

Once Janice withdraws from the business, the old partnership (between Janice and Ned) is dissolved. A new partnership is formed between Hanna and Ned. The new partnership can even bear the same name as the old one (and will in this example).

Requirement 2

2 Account for partner investments

4 Account for the admission of a new partner

(Ignoring Requirement 1) Suppose instead that the Goode Partnership were to admit Hanna as a third partner by selling her a 40% interest for $40,000 cash. Compute Hanna's Capital balance and journalize her investment. What are the Capital balances for each partner after the investment is made?

Part 1	**Part 2**	Part 3	Part 4	Part 5	Demo Doc Complete

Hanna has purchased a 40% interest in the total partnership's capital. *Regardless* of how much she pays for her share, her capital will be 40% of the *total capital after the purchase.*

Capital before purchase ($15,000 + $35,000)	$50,000
Hanna's investment in capital	40,000
Total capital after purchase	$90,000

So Hanna's share of the capital after her investment is:

$$40\% \times \$90,000 = \$36,000$$

Because Hanna has purchased an interest, the Capital balances of Janice and Ned are adjusted.

Janice and Ned now have $90,000 − $36,000 = $54,000 capital between them. This new capital amount will be split between them using their *original* partnership percentages.

Janice's Capital account is now:

$$\$54,000 \times 30\% = \$16,200$$

This is an increase of:

$$\$16,200 - \$15,000 = \$1,200$$

Ned's Capital account is now:

$$\$54,000 \times 70\% = \$37,800$$

This is an increase of:

$$\$37,800 - \$35,000 = \$2,800$$

Before Transaction		After Transaction	
Janice Wright, capital	$15,000	Janice Wright, capital	$16,200
Ned Frist, capital	35,000	Ned Frist, capital	37,800
		Hanna Storm, capital	36,000
Total capital	$50,000	Total capital	$90,000

Because Hanna paid $4,000 more for her share than the Capital amount that is being recorded ($36,000), the difference is split *proportionately* by the preexisting partners by the preexisting percentages.

For the partnership as a whole, assets increase (a debit) by Hanna's cash investment of $40,000.

Hanna's Capital account increases (a credit) by $36,000, Janice's Capital increases (a credit) by its adjustment of $4,000 × 30% = $1,200, and Ned's Capital increases (a credit) by its adjustment of $4,000 × 70% = $2,800.

Cash	40,000	
Janice Wright, Capital		1,200
Ned Frist, Capital		2,800
Hanna Storm, Capital		36,000

Requirement 3

7 Prepare partnership
financial statements

(Ignoring Requirement 1) Prepare the balance sheet of the Goode Partnership after Hanna is admitted to the partnership.

Part 1	Part 2	**Part 3**	Part 4	Part 5	Demo Doc Complete

The Cash balance increases to:

$$\$25,000 + \$40,000 = \$65,000$$

Hanna Storm, Capital has a balance of $36,000.
   Ned Frist, Capital increases to:

$$\$35,000 + \$2,800 = \$37,800$$

Janice Wright, Capital increases to:

$$\$15,000 + \$1,200 = \$16,200$$

Liabilities and other assets have not changed.

<table>
<tr><td colspan="4" align="center">THE GOODE PARTNERSHIP
Balance Sheet
January 1, 2008</td></tr>
<tr><td>Cash</td><td align="right">$ 65,000</td><td>Liabilities</td><td align="right">$ 35,000</td></tr>
<tr><td>Other assets</td><td align="right">60,000</td><td>Ned Frist, capital</td><td align="right">37,800</td></tr>
<tr><td></td><td></td><td>Hanna Storm, capital</td><td align="right">36,000</td></tr>
<tr><td></td><td></td><td>Janice Wright, capital</td><td align="right">16,200</td></tr>
<tr><td>Total assets</td><td align="right">$125,000</td><td>Total liabilities and capital</td><td align="right">$125,000</td></tr>
</table>

Requirement 4

1 Identify the characteristics of a partnership

3 Allocate profits and losses to the partners

Assume that Hanna was not admitted to the partnership. During 2008, Goode earned $20,000 of net income (in cash). How much profit is allocated to each partner (Janice and Ned)? Does the partnership pay income taxes on this profit?

Part 1	Part 2	Part 3	**Part 4**	Part 5	Demo Doc Complete

Profits are allocated in this partnership based on stated percentages.

Janice receives 30% of the profits, so she is allocated 30% × $20,000 = $6,000 of profit.

Ned receives 70% of the profits, so he is allocated 70% × $20,000 = $14,000 of profit.

After this allocation, Goode has the following balance sheet:

Cash	$ 45,000	Liabilities	$ 35,000
Other assets	60,000	Ned Frist, capital	49,000
		Janice Wright, capital	21,000
Total assets	$105,000	Total liabilities and capital	$105,000

Cash has increased from earning net income of $20,000 and the Capital balances for Janice and Ned have been increased for their profit allocation.

Adjusted Cash balance:

$$\$25,000 + \$20,000 = \$45,000$$

Adjusted Janice Wright, Capital balance:

$$\$15,000 + \$6,000 = \$21,000$$

Adjusted Ned Frist, Capital balance:

$$\$35,000 + \$14,000 = \$49,000$$

Note that *allocation* of profit *does not necessarily mean distribution* of profit. Just as shareholders do not receive all profits a company earns as dividends, partners do not receive all income allocations as a cash distribution.

The partnership does *not* pay taxes on this profit. Instead, Janice and Ned are taxed on their individual tax returns for their allocation of profits.

Requirement 5

6 Account for the liquidation of a partnership

(Continuing on from Requirement 4) On January 1, 2009, the Goode Partnership was liquidated. All noncash assets were sold for $90,000, after which all liabilities were paid. How much does each partner receive upon liquidation?

Part 1	Part 2	Part 3	Part 4	**Part 5**	Demo Doc Complete

The sale of the other assets increases Cash (a debit) by $90,000 and decreases Other Assets (a credit) by $60,000, their book value.

The remaining "gain" of $90,000 − $60,000 = $30,000 is split among Janice and Ned according to their profit-sharing proportions. This "gain" is shown as an increase to Janice's and Ned's Capital accounts.

Janice receives 30% × $30,000 = $9,000 of the "gain."

Ned receives 70% × $30,000 = $21,000 of the "gain."

Jan. 1	Cash	90,000	
	Other Assets		60,000
	Janice Wright, Capital (30% × $30,000)		9,000
	Ned Frist, Capital (70% × $30,000)		21,000

The liabilities were paid after the noncash assets were sold. This is a decrease (a debit) to Liabilities of $35,000 and a decrease to Cash (a credit) of $35,000.

Jan. 1	Liabilities	35,000	
	Cash		35,000

After these transactions, Janice has a Capital balance of $21,000 + $9,000 = $30,000 and Ned has a Capital balance of $49,000 + $21,000 = $70,000.

The cash payment received on liquidation is *the amount of the Capital balances*. So Janice receives $30,000 cash and Ned receives $70,000 cash on liquidation.

Part 1	Part 2	Part 3	Part 4	Part 5	**Demo Doc Complete**

Quick Practice Questions

True/False

_____ 1. A single partner can commit the entire firm to a legal liability.

_____ 2. A partnership has an unlimited life.

_____ 3. If the partnership agreement specifies a method for allocating profits but not losses, then losses are shared in a different proportion from profits.

_____ 4. Partnership profits and losses may be allocated based on capital contributions but not on service.

_____ 5. The journal entry to close a partner's Drawing account involves a debit to the partner's Drawing account.

_____ 6. A new partner may be admitted to a partnership by purchasing some of an existing partner's interest.

_____ 7. A bonus paid to the existing partners by a new partner decreases the old partners' Capital accounts.

_____ 8. The resignation of a partner dissolves the partnership.

_____ 9. When a partner withdraws from the partnership, the withdrawing partner's Capital account is always debited for its balance.

_____ 10. Cash is distributed to partners in accordance with the net income agreement in the partnership liquidation process.

Multiple Choice

1. **Which of the following is _not_ an advantage of a partnership?**
    a. Limited liability
    b. Ease of formation
    c. Combined resources
    d. Combined experience and talent

2. **Which of the following is true for a limited partnership?**
    a. Must have at least two general partners
    b. Is illegal in most states
    c. Must have at least one general partner
    d. None of the above

3. Which of the following applies to the partnership characteristic of co-ownership of property?
   a. Any asset a partner invests in the partnership becomes the joint property of all the partners.
   b. General partners co-own all assets, but limited partners do not.
   c. General partners own a larger percentage of the assets of a partnership than do limited partners.
   d. All partnership assets are co-owned by any banks making loans to the partnership.

4. Equipment with a cost of $100,000 and accumulated depreciation of $30,000 is contributed to a new partnership by Jay Bergen. The current market value of the equipment is $105,000. The replacement value of the equipment is $135,000. At what amount is the equipment recorded on the partnership books?
   a. $70,000
   b. $100,000
   c. $105,000
   d. $135,000

5. Mac and Molly formed a partnership with capital contributions of $80,000 and $120,000, respectively. Their partnership agreement called for (1) Mac to receive a $20,000 salary, (2) each partner to receive 10% based on initial capital contributions, and (3) the remaining income or loss to be divided equally. If net income for the current year is $80,000, what amount is credited to Mac's Capital account?
   a. $27,000
   b. $35,000
   c. $43,000
   d. $48,000

6. Which of the following would be recorded in the closing entry if partner A's share of net income is $35,000 and partner B's share of net income is $45,000?
   a. Credit to A's Capital account for $40,000
   b. Credit to B's Capital account for $40,000
   c. Debit to A's Capital account for $35,000
   d. Debit to Income Summary for $80,000

7. Elliott, Barry, Ben, and Jerry formed a partnership agreeing to divide profits and losses in a 2:3:4:1 relationship, respectively. Assuming that the business earned a profit of $165,000, what are Elliott and Jerry's shares, respectively?
   a. $33,000; $49,500
   b. $49,500; $16,500
   c. $60,000; $33,000
   d. $33,000; $16,500

8. Which of the following is included on a partnership balance sheet?
   a. A category for assets contributed by each partner
   b. A category for liabilities incurred by each partner
   c. An ending Drawing account balance for each partner
   d. An ending Capital account balance for each partner

9. Black and Blue formed a partnership, agreeing to share profits equally. After closing entries, the balances in their Capital accounts are $36,000 and $45,000, respectively. Blue sells her interest in the partnership to White for $52,000. Which of the following would be recorded on the books of the partnership?
   a. Credit White, Capital for $45,000
   b. Debit Cash for $52,000
   c. Credit White, Capital for $52,000
   d. Debit Blue, Capital for $52,000

10. The net income agreement for Forsyth and Guilford states net income and net loss shall be divided in a ratio of beginning Capital balances. The net loss for the current year is $50,000. On January 1 of the current year, the Capital balances were as follows: Forsyth, $55,000; Guilford, $65,000. During the current year, Forsyth withdrew $40,000 and Guilford withdrew $25,000. What are the Capital balances for Forsyth and Guilford, respectively, as of December 31 of the current year?
    a. Debit $7,917; Credit $12,917
    b. Credit $7,917; Credit $12,917
    c. Debit $7,917; Debit $12,917
    d. Debit $12,917; Credit $7,917

Quick Exercises

12-1. Wallingford, Albright, and Rowe have recently formed a partnership by investing $45,000, $60,000, and $35,000, respectively. They are considering several methods of allocating income and losses.

Requirement

1. Compute the partners' shares of profits and losses under each of the following plans:

   a. Net income is $31,800 and the partners could not agree on a plan for net income/loss division.
   b. The net loss is $18,000 and the partners agreed to share in the profits based on a 2:2:1 ratio. The agreement did not address losses.
   c. Net income is $31,800 and the partners agreed to share profits based on the relationship of their initial Capital balances.
   d. The net loss is $38,000 and the partners agreed to share profits and losses based on 15% to Wallingford, 50% to Albright, and 35% to Rowe.

Round all answers to the nearest whole dollar.

Item	Wallingford	Albright	Rowe	Total
a.				
b.				
c.				
d.				

12-2. Browning and Douglas are partners who agree to admit Taylor to their partnership. Browning has a Capital balance of $51,000 and Douglas has a Capital balance of $70,000. Browning and Douglas share net income in the ratio of 2:8. Prepare journal entries to admit Taylor to the partnership based on the following independent agreements. Round all amounts to the nearest dollar.

  a. Taylor invests $66,000 cash into the partnership for a 20% interest.
  b. Taylor invests $66,000 cash into the partnership for a 30% interest.
  c. Taylor purchases one-third of Browning's Capital for $25,000.
  d. Taylor purchases one-half of Douglas's Capital for $32,000.

General Journal				
Date	Accounts		Debit	Credit

General Journal				
Date	Accounts		Debit	Credit

General Journal				
Date	Accounts		Debit	Credit

General Journal				
Date	Accounts		Debit	Credit

12-3. Peter, Paul, and Mary are partners in the Sing Song Company and share profits and losses in a ratio of 4:4:2, respectively. Mary has been contemplating retirement. The partners' current Capital account balances, after closing entries, are $49,000, $98,000, and $147,000, respectively. The new net income agreement for Peter and Paul will be 4:2.

Requirement

1. Journalize the following transactions involving the retirement of Mary. Round to the nearest dollar if necessary:

a. The partners agree to revalue the assets. Land with a cost of $90,000 has a current market value of $127,000.

b. Inventory with a cost of $50,000 has a current market value of $35,000.

c. After the assets are revalued, the partnership agrees to give Mary $75,000 cash and a note payable for $65,000.

General Journal				
Date	Accounts		Debit	Credit

General Journal				
Date	Accounts		Debit	Credit

General Journal				
Date	Accounts		Debit	Credit

12-4. Chandler, Cherry, and Cline are partners in the CCC Company. They share profits and losses in a 3:5:2 ratio and have just closed their books for the period. The current balances in their Capital accounts are $63,000, $49,000, and $94,000, respectively. Chandler has decided to withdraw from the partnership. Prior to the withdrawal of Chandler, the partners agreed that the assets needed to be revalued. Land with a cost of $55,000 has a current market value of $88,000. Inventory with a cost of $75,000 has a current market value of $60,000. Cherry and Cline have agreed to share net income in a 2:3 ratio.

Requirements

1. Prepare the journal entries required to revalue the assets.

General Journal				
Date	Accounts		Debit	Credit

General Journal				
Date	Accounts		Debit	Credit

2. Journalize the withdrawal of Chandler under each of the following independent assumptions:

    a. The partnership gives cash to Chandler equal to his Capital balance.
    b. The paFrtnership gives $76,000 cash to Chandler.
    c. The partnership gives $56,000 cash to Chandler.

General Journal				
Date	Accounts		Debit	Credit

General Journal				
Date	Accounts		Debit	Credit

General Journal				
Date	Accounts		Debit	Credit

12-5. On August 1, 2008, Wheat, Bran, and Oats agree to liquidate their partnership. Wheat has a Capital balance of $90,000, Bran has a Capital balance of $37,500, and Oats has a Capital balance of $30,000. The partners share net income/net loss in a ratio of 4:3:3. Accounts payable amount to $60,000. Assets are shown on the balance sheet at $40,000 of cash and $177,500 of noncash assets. All the noncash assets are sold for $188,000.

Requirement

1. Journalize the following:

    a. Sell the noncash assets.
    b. Pay the liabilities.
    c. Distribute the remaining cash to the partners.

	General Journal		
Date	Accounts	Debit	Credit

	General Journal		
Date	Accounts	Debit	Credit

	General Journal		
Date	Accounts	Debit	Credit

Do It Yourself! Question 1

Waters Partners wants to admit River Kline as a new partner on January 1, 2008. On this date, Waters had the following information:

Cash	$100,000	Liabilities	$ 80,000
Other assets	100,000	Brooke Daniels, capital	30,000
		Rainer Linfoot, capital	90,000
Total assets	$200,000	Total liabilities and capital	$200,000

Brooke Daniels has a 25% share of the profits, whereas Rainer Linfoot has a 75% share.

Requirements

2 Account for partner investments

4 Account for the admission of a new partner

1. Suppose Waters were to admit River as a partner by selling him a 30% interest for $70,000 cash. Compute River's Capital balance and journalize his investment. What are the Capital balances for each partner after the investment is made?

General Journal				
Date	Accounts		Debit	Credit

Before Transaction		After Transaction	

2 Account for partner investments

4 Account for the admission of a new partner

5 Account for a partner's withdrawal from the firm

2. (Ignoring Requirement 1) Suppose instead Brooke Daniels sold her entire interest to River for $50,000. Journalize the transfer of ownership. What are the Capital balances for each partner after the transfer is made?

	General Journal		
Date	Accounts	Debit	Credit

Before Transaction		After Transaction	

1 Identify the characteristics of a partnership

3 Allocate profits and losses to the partners

3. Assume that River was not admitted to the partnership. During 2008, Waters earned $80,000 of net income (in cash). How much profit is allocated to each partner (Brooke and Rainer)?

Account for the
liquidation of a
partnership

4. (Continuing on from Requirement 3) On January 1, 2009, Waters Partners was liquidated. All noncash assets were sold for $150,000, after which all liabilities were paid. How much does each partner receive upon liquidation?

General Journal				
Date	Accounts		Debit	Credit

General Journal				
Date	Accounts		Debit	Credit

Quick Practice Solutions

True/False

<u> T </u>   1. A single partner can commit the entire firm to a legal liability. (p. 597)

<u> F </u>   2. A partnership has an unlimited life.

        False—A partnership has a *limited* life. (p. 597)

<u> F </u>   3. If the partnership agreement specifies a method for allocating profits but not losses, then losses are shared in a different proportion from profits.

        False—If only a method of sharing profits is stated in the partnership agreement, then losses are shared the same way. (p. 601)

<u> F </u>   4. Partnership profits and losses may be allocated based on capital contributions but not on service.

        False—Partnership profits and losses may be allocated based on service. (p. 601)

<u> F </u>   5. The journal entry to close a partner's Drawing account involves a debit to the partner's Drawing account.

        False—The journal entry to close a partner's Drawing account involves a *credit* to the partner's Drawing account. (p. 603)

<u> T </u>   6. A new partner may be admitted to a partnership by purchasing some of an existing partner's interest. (p. 604)

<u> F </u>   7. A bonus paid to the existing partners by a new partner decreases the old partners' Capital accounts.

        False—A bonus paid to the existing partners by a new partner *increases* the old partners' Capital accounts. (p. 606)

<u> T </u>   8. The resignation of a partner dissolves the partnership. (p. 608)

<u> T </u>   9. When a partner withdraws from the partnership, the withdrawing partner's Capital account is always debited for its balance. (p. 609)

<u> F </u> 10. Cash is distributed to partners in accordance with the net income agreement in the partnership liquidation process.

        False—Cash is distributed to partners based on their Capital balances. (pp. 611–613)

Multiple Choice

1. **Which of the following is *not* an advantage of a partnership?** (p. 597)
   a. Limited liability
   b. Ease of formation
   c. Combined resources
   d. Combined experience and talent

2. **Which of the following is true for a limited partnership?** (p. 598)
   a. Must have at least two general partners
   b. Is illegal in most states
   c. Must have at least one general partner
   d. None of the above

3. Which of the following applies to the partnership characteristic of co-ownership of property? (p. 597)
   a. Any asset a partner invests in the partnership becomes the joint property of all the partners.
   b. General partners co-own all assets, but limited partners do not.
   c. General partners own a larger percentage of the assets of a partnership than do limited partners.
   d. All partnership assets are co-owned by any banks making loans to the partnership.

4. Equipment with a cost of $100,000 and accumulated depreciation of $30,000 is contributed to a new partnership by Jay Bergen. The current market value of the equipment is $105,000. The replacement value of the equipment is $135,000. At what amount is the equipment recorded on the partnership books? (pp. 600–601)
   a. $70,000
   b. $100,000
   c. $105,000
   d. $135,000

5. Mac and Molly formed a partnership with capital contributions of $80,000 and $120,000, respectively. Their partnership agreement called for (1) Mac to receive a $20,000 salary, (2) each partner to receive 10% based on initial capital contributions, and (3) the remaining income or loss to be divided equally. If net income for the current year is $80,000, what amount is credited to Mac's Capital account? (pp. 601–603)
   a. $27,000
   b. $35,000
   c. $43,000
   d. $48,000

6. Which of the following would be recorded in the closing entry if partner A's share of net income is $35,000 and partner B's share of net income is $45,000? (pp. 601–603)
   a. Credit to A's Capital account for $40,000
   b. Credit to B's Capital account for $40,000
   c. Debit to A's Capital account for $35,000
   d. Debit to Income Summary for $80,000

7. Elliott, Barry, Ben, and Jerry formed a partnership agreeing to divide profits and losses in a 2:3:4:1 relationship, respectively. Assuming that the business earned a profit of $165,000, what are Elliott and Jerry's shares, respectively? (pp. 601–603)
   a. $33,000; $49,500
   b. $49,500; $16,500
   c. $60,000; $33,000
   d. $33,000; $16,500

8. Which of the following is included on a partnership balance sheet? (p. 601)
   a. A category for assets contributed by each partner
   b. A category for liabilities incurred by each partner
   c. An ending Drawing account balance for each partner
   d. An ending Capital account balance for each partner

9. Black and Blue formed a partnership, agreeing to share profits equally. After closing entries, the balances in their Capital accounts are $36,000 and $45,000, respectively. Blue sells her interest in the partnership to White for $52,000. Which of the following would be recorded on the books of the partnership? (pp. 604–605)

    a. Credit White, Capital for $45,000
    b. Debit Cash for $52,000
    c. Credit White, Capital for $52,000
    d. Debit Blue, Capital for $52,000

10. The net income agreement for Forsyth and Guilford states net income and net loss shall be divided in a ratio of beginning Capital balances. The net loss for the current year is $50,000. On January 1 of the current year, the Capital balances were as follows: Forsyth, $55,000; Guilford, $65,000. During the current year, Forsyth withdrew $40,000 and Guilford withdrew $25,000. What are the Capital balances for Forsyth and Guilford, respectively, as of December 31 of the current year? (pp. 601–603)

    a. Debit $7,917; Credit $12,917
    b. Credit $7,917; Credit $12,917
    c. Debit $7,917; Debit $12,917
    d. Debit $12,917; Credit $7,917

Quick Exercises

12-1.   Wallingford, Albright, and Rowe have recently formed a partnership by investing $45,000, $60,000, and $35,000, respectively. They are considering several methods of allocating income and losses. (p. 601)

Requirement

1. Compute the partners' shares of profits and losses under each of the following plans:

   a. Net income is $31,800 and the partners could not agree on a plan for net income/loss division.
   b. The net loss is $18,000 and the partners agreed to share in the profits based on a 2:2:1 ratio. The agreement did not address losses.
   c. Net income is $31,800 and the partners agreed to share profits based on the relationship of their initial Capital balances.
   d. The net loss is $38,000 and the partners agreed to share profits and losses based on 15% to Wallingford, 50% to Albright, and 35% to Rowe.

Round all answers to the nearest whole dollar.

Item	Wallingford	Albright	Rowe	Total
a.	$ 10,600	$ 10,600	$ 10,600	$ 31,800
b.	$ (7,200)	$ (7,200)	$ (3,600)	$ (18,000)
c.	$ 10,221	$ 13,629	$ 7,950	$ 31,800
d.	$ (5,700)	$ (19,000)	$ (13,300)	$ (38,000)

12-2.   Browning and Douglas are partners who agree to admit Taylor to their partnership. Browning has a Capital balance of $51,000 and Douglas has a Capital balance of $70,000. Browning and Douglas share net income in the ratio of 2:8. Prepare journal entries to admit Taylor to the partnership based on the following independent agreements. Round all amounts to the nearest dollar. (p. 604)

   a. Taylor invests $66,000 cash into the partnership for a 20% interest.
   b. Taylor invests $66,000 cash into the partnership for a 30% interest.
   c. Taylor purchases one-third of Browning's Capital for $25,000.
   d. Taylor purchases one-half of Douglas's Capital for $32,000.

General Journal

	Date	Accounts	Debit	Credit
a.		Cash	66,000	
		Browning, Capital		5,720
		Douglas, Capital		22,880
		Taylor, Capital		37,400

General Journal

	Date	Accounts	Debit	Credit
b.		Cash	66,000	
		Browning, Capital		1,980
		Douglas, Capital		7,920
		Taylor, Capital		56,100

General Journal

	Date	Accounts	Debit	Credit
c.		Browning, Capital	17,000	
		Taylor, Capital		17,000

General Journal

	Date	Accounts	Debit	Credit
d.		Douglas, Capital	35,000	
		Taylor, Capital		35,000

Calculations:

a. $66,000 + $51,000 + $70,000 = $187,000 Total Capital
$187,000 × 0.20 = $37,400 Taylor, Capital
$66,000 − $37,400 = $28,600 bonus to existing partners
$28,600 × 0.20 = $5,720, Browning, Capital
$28,600 × 0.80 = $22,880, Douglas, Capital

b. $187,000 (Total Capital) × 0.30 = $56,100, Taylor, Capital
$66,000 − $56,100 = $9,900, bonus to existing partners
$9,900 × 0.20 = $1,980, Browning, Capital
$9,900 × 0.80 = $7,920, Douglas, Capital

12-3. Peter, Paul, and Mary are partners in the Sing Song Company and share profits and losses in a ratio of 4:4:2, respectively. Mary has been contemplating retirement. The partners' current Capital account balances, after closing entries, are $49,000, $98,000, and $147,000, respectively. The new net income agreement for Peter and Paul will be 4:2. (p. 609)

Requirement

1. Journalize the following transactions involving the retirement of Mary. Round to the nearest dollar if necessary.

a. **The partners agree to revalue the assets. Land with a cost of $90,000 has a current market value of $127,000.**

b. Inventory with a cost of $50,000 has a current market value of $35,000.

c. After the assets are revalued, the partnership agrees to give Mary $75,000 cash and a note payable for $65,000.

		General Journal		
	Date	Accounts	Debit	Credit
a.		Land	37,000	
		Peter, Capital		14,800
		Paul, Capital		14,800
		Mary, Capital		7,400

		General Journal		
	Date	Accounts	Debit	Credit
b.		Peter, Capital	6,000	
		Paul, Capital	6,000	
		Mary, Capital	3,000	
		Inventory		15,000

		General Journal		
	Date	Accounts	Debit	Credit
c.		Mary, Capital	151,400	
		Peter, Capital		7,600
		Paul, Capital		3,800
		Cash		75,000
		Note Payable		65,000

Calculations:

a. $127,000 − $90,000 = $37,000
$37,000 × 0.40 = $14,800 allocated to Peter and Paul, Capital
$37,000 × 0.20 = $7,400 allocated to Mary, Capital

b. $50,000 − $35,000 = $15,000
$15,000 × 0.40 = $6,000 allocated to Peter and Paul, Capital
$15,000 × 0.20 = $3,000 allocated to Mary, Capital

c. $147,000 + $7,400 − $3,000 = $151,400 Mary, Capital
$151,400 − $75,000 − $65,000 = $11,400 bonus to Peter and Paul
$11,400 × (4/6) = $7,600 allocated to Peter, Capital
$11,400 × (2/6) = $3,800 allocated to Paul, Capital

12-4.   Chandler, Cherry, and Cline are partners in the CCC Company. They share profits and losses in a 3:5:2 ratio and have just closed their books for the period. The current balances in their Capital accounts are $63,000, $49,000, and $94,000, respectively. Chandler has decided to withdraw from the partnership. Prior to the withdrawal of Chandler, the partners agreed that the assets need to be revalued. Land with a cost of $55,000 has a current market value of $88,000. Inventory with a cost of $75,000 has a current market value of $60,000. Cherry and Cline have agreed to share net income in a 2:3 ratio. (pp. 608–611)

Requirements

1. Prepare the journal entries required to revalue the assets.

	Date	Accounts	Debit	Credit
		General Journal		
1a.		Land	33,000	
		Chandler, Capital		9,900
		Cherry, Capital		16,500
		Cline, Capital		6,600

	Date	Accounts	Debit	Credit
		General Journal		
1b.		Chandler, Capital	4,500	
		Cherry, Capital	7,500	
		Cline, Capital	3,000	
		Inventory		15,000

2. Journalize the withdrawal of Chandler under each of the following independent assumptions:

  a. The partnership gives cash to Chandler equal to his Capital balance.
  b. The partnership gives $76,000 cash to Chandler.
  c. The partnership gives $56,000 cash to Chandler.

	Date	Accounts	Debit	Credit
		General Journal		
2a.		Chandler, Capital	68,400	
		Cash		68,400

	Date	Accounts	Debit	Credit
		General Journal		
2b.		Chandler, Capital	68,400	
		Cherry, Capital	3,040	
		Cline, Capital	4,560	
		Cash		76,000

	Date	Accounts	Debit	Credit
		General Journal		
2c.		Chandler, Capital	68,400	
		Cherry, Capital		4,960
		Cline, Capital		7,440
		Cash		56,000

Calculations:

  1a. $88,000 - $55,000 = $33,000
      $33,000 \times 3/10 = $9,900
      $33,000 \times 5/10 = $16,500
      $33,000 \times 2/10 = $6,600

1b. $75,000 - $60,000 = $15,000$
$15,000 \times 3/10 = $4,500$
$15,000 \times 5/10 = $7,500$
$15,000 \times 2/10 = $3,000$

2a. $($63,000 + $9,900 - $4,500) = $68,400$

2b. $($76,000 - $68,400) \times 2/5 = $3,040$
$($76,000 - $68,400) \times 3/5 = $4,560$

2c. $68,400 - $56,000 = $12,400$
$12,400 \times 2/5 = $4,960$
$12,400 \times 3/5 = $7,440$

12-5. On August 1, 2008, Wheat, Bran, and Oats agree to liquidate their partnership. Wheat has a Capital balance of $90,000, Bran has a Capital balance of $37,500, and Oats has a Capital balance of $30,000. The partners share net income/net loss in a ratio of 4:3:3. Accounts payable amount to $60,000. Assets are shown on the balance sheet at $40,000 of cash and $177,500 of noncash assets. All the noncash assets are sold for $188,000. (pp. 611–613)

Requirement

1. Journalize the following:

    a. Sell the noncash assets.
    b. Pay the liabilities.
    c. Distribute the remaining cash to the partners.

	Date	Accounts	Debit	Credit
		General Journal		
a.		Cash	188,000	
		Wheat, Capital		4,200
		Bran, Capital		3,150
		Oats, Capital		3,150
		Noncash Assets		177,500

	Date	Accounts	Debit	Credit
		General Journal		
b.		Liabilities	60,000	
		Cash		60,000

	Date	Accounts	Debit	Credit
		General Journal		
c.		Wheat, Capital	94,200	
		Bran, Capital	40,650	
		Oats, Capital	33,150	
		Cash		168,000

Calculations:

    a. $188,000 - $177,500 = $10,500$
       $10,500 \times 4/10 = $4,200$
       $10,500 \times 3/10 = $3,150$

    c. $90,000 + $4,200 = $94,200$
       $37,500 + $3,150 = $40,650$
       $30,000 + $3,150 = $33,150$

Do It Yourself! Question 1 Solutions

Requirement

1. Suppose Waters were to admit River as a partner by selling him a 30% interest for $70,000 cash. Compute River's Capital balance and journalize his investment. What are the Capital balances for each partner after the investment is made?

Capital before purchase ($30,000 + $90,000)	$120,000
River's investment in capital	70,000
Total capital after purchase	$190,000

River Kline, Capital after investment:

$$30\% \times \$190,000 = \$57,000$$

Capital shared by original partners Brooke and Rainer:

$$\$190,000 - \$57,000 = \$133,000$$

Brooke Daniels, Capital balance:

$$\$133,000 \times 25\% = \$33,250$$

Rainer Linfoot, Capital balance:

$$\$133,000 \times 75\% = \$99,750$$

Cash		70,000	
	River Kline, Capital		57,000
	Brooke Daniels, Capital ($33,250 – $30,000)		3,250
	Ranier Linfoot, Capital ($99,750 – $90,000)		9,750

Before Transaction		After Transaction	
Brooke Daniels, capital	$ 30,000	Brooke Daniels, capital	$ 33,250
Rainer Linfoot, capital	90,000	Rainer Linfoot, capital	99,750
		River Kline, capital	57,000
Total capital	$120,000	Total capital	$190,000

2. (Ignoring Requirement 1) Suppose instead Brooke Daniels sold her entire interest to River for $50,000. Journalize the transfer of ownership. What are the Capital balances for each partner after the transfer is made?

River Kline, Capital	30,000	
Brooke Daniels, Capital		30,000

Before Transaction		After Transaction	
Brooke Daniels, capital	$ 30,000	River Kline, capital	$ 30,000
Rainer Linfoot, capital	90,000	Rainer Linfoot, capital	90,000
Total capital	$120,000	Total capital	$120,000

3. Assume that River was not admitted to the partnership. During 2008, Waters earned $80,000 of net income (in cash). How much profit is allocated to each partner (Brooke and Rainer)?

Brooke is allocated 25% × $80,000 = $20,000 of profit.

Rainer is allocated 75% × $80,000 = $60,000 of profit.

After this allocation, Waters has the following balance sheet:

Cash	$180,000	Liabilities	$ 80,000
Other assets	100,000	Brooke Daniels, capital	50,000
		Rainer Linfoot, capital	150,000
Total assets	$280,000	Total liabilities and capital	$280,000

Adjusted Cash balance:

$100,000 + $80,000 = $180,000

Adjusted Brooke Daniels, Capital balance:

$30,000 + $20,000 = $50,000

Adjusted Ranier Linfoot, Capital balance:

$90,000 + $60,000 = $150,000

4. (Continuing on from Requirement 3) On January 1, 2009, Waters Partners was liquidated. All noncash assets were sold for $150,000, after which all liabilities were paid. How much does each partner receive upon liquidation?

$$\text{"Gain"} = \$150,000 - \$100,000 = \$50,000$$

Jan. 1	Cash	150,000	
	Other Assets		100,000
	Brooke Daniels, Capital (25% × $50,000)		12,500
	Ranier Linfoot, Capital (75% × $50,000)		37,500

Jan. 1	Liabilities	80,000	
	Cash		80,000

After these transactions, Brooke has a Capital balance of:

$$\$50,000 + \$12,500 = \$62,500$$

Rainer has a Capital balance of:

$$\$150,000 + \$37,500 = \$187,500$$

Brooke receives $62,500 cash and Rainer receives $187,500 cash on liquidation.

The Power of Practice

For more practice using the skills learned in this chapter, visit MyAccountingLab. There you will find algorithmically generated questions that are based on these Demo Docs and your main textbook's Review and Assess Your Progress sections.

Go to MyAccountingLab and follow these steps:

1. Direct your URL to www.myaccountinglab.com.
2. Log in using your name and password.
3. Click the MyAccountingLab link.
4. Click Study Plan in the left navigation bar.
5. From the table of contents, select Chapter 12, Partnerships.
6. Click a link to work tutorial exercises.

13 Corporations: Paid-In Capital and the Balance Sheet

What You Probably Already Know

You probably already know that you can purchase shares of a company's stock as an investment. CNBC shows the trading price of various stocks as they take place and the daily prices are reported in your financial newspapers. Much of the trading taking place is between investors rather than from the issuing corporation.

One way that a corporation issues its shares of stock is in an initial public offering (IPO). A recent popular IPO is Google. Google was doing business for six years before its founders took the company public in August 2004. The IPO provided investors an opportunity to purchase Google stock at a stated offer price of $85 a share. The market price of the stock rose quickly in trading and a year and a half after the IPO, the stock traded at over $300 per share. The cash received from the sale of the Google stock and the shareholders' equity interest were recorded on the books of Google Corporation. In this chapter, we will see how to account for the equity transactions of a corporation.

Learning Objectives

1 Identify the characteristics of a corporation.

As a **separate legal entity,** a corporation can enter into contracts, own assets in its own name, and be sued. The owners of the corporation are the stockholders. Shares of stock can be transferred to others without affecting the operation of the business. *No mutual agency* means that the owners of a corporation (stockholders) cannot commit or obligate the corporation. Stockholders are not personally liable for the obligations of the corporation. The most that a stockholder can lose is the amount invested. This is known as *limited liability.* These are some of the characteristics of a corporation. *Review these and other characteristics in your textbook, and take note of Exhibit 13-1 (p. 639) for a list of advantages and disadvantages of the corporate form of business.*

2 Record the issuance of stock.

When a company incorporates, the **par** or **stated value,** if any, will be indicated in the articles of incorporation. It is usually a nominal amount assigned to a share of stock that represents the minimum legal stated capital and does not indicate the value or worth of the stock. When the stock is sold by the corporation, the Common Stock account is credited for the par or stated value. Usually, the stock is sold above par, which is considered a premium. The excess of the stock sales price over the par or stated value is the amount credited to the **Paid-In Capital in Excess of Par** account. *Review the accounting for stock issuances under "Issuing Common Stock" in the main text.*

3 Prepare the stockholders' equity section of a corporation's balance sheet.

The equity accounts are shown in the Stockholders' Equity section in the following order:

- Preferred Stock

- Common Stock

- Paid-In Capital in Excess of Par

- Retained Earnings

Review the Stockholders' Equity section of the balance sheet in Exhibit 13-7 (p. 650).

4 Account for cash dividends.

If the board of directors declares dividends, Retained Earnings is debited and Dividends Payable is credited. On the date of payment, the Liability is debited (reduced); Cash is also credited (reduced). *Read "Account for Cash Dividends" in the main text to review the dividend dates and learn the difference between cumulative and noncumulative preferred stock.*

5 Use different stock values in decision making.

Market value is the current price at which the stock is being offered for sale in the market. This value is of prime importance to investors. **Book value** indicates the amount of net assets that each common shareholder would receive if the assets were sold for the amount reported on the balance sheet. *Review the calculations of book value under "Different Values of Stock" in the main text.*

6 Evaluate return on assets and return on stockholders' equity.

Ratios to assess profitability include the rate of return on total assets and return on stockholders' equity. The rate of return on total assets indicates the amount of profitability per dollar of assets invested (net income + interest expense/average total assets). The rate of return on common stockholders' equity indicates the amount of profitability per dollar of common equity (net income − preferred dividends/average common stockholders' equity). Higher returns for both ratios are more favorable.

7 Account for the income tax of a corporation.

There may be differences between pretax income on the income statement and taxable income on the income tax return for a corporation. The income tax expense on the income statement is based on the pretax income on the income statement. However, the income tax payable liability on the balance sheet is based on the taxable income on the tax return. The difference between these two amounts results in a *deferred tax asset* or *deferred tax liability.*

Demo Doc 1

Common Stock

Learning Objectives 2, 3, 5, 6

Jack Inc. had the following information at December 31, 2008:

Stockholder's Equity	
Common Stock, 1,600,000 authorized, 350,000 issued and outstanding shares	$ 437,500
Additional Paid-In Capital	787,500
Retained Earnings	4,200,000
Total Stockholder's Equity	$5,425,000

Requirements

1. What are Jack's two main sources of corporate capital?

2. What is the par value per share of the common stock?

3. On average, what was the original issue price per share of common stock?

4. On February 12, 2009, Jack issued another 20,000 common shares for $5 cash per share. Journalize this transaction.

5. Jack earned net income of $150,000 and paid no dividends in 2009. There were no other equity transactions in 2009. Prepare the stockholder's equity section of Jack's balance sheet on December 31, 2009.

6. Calculate Jack's return on equity and book value per share for 2009.

Demo Doc 1 Solutions

Requirement 1

1 Identify the characteristics of a corporation

What are Jack's two main sources of corporate capital?

Part 1	Part 2	Part 3	Part 4	Part 5	Part 6	Demo Doc Complete

Corporate capital is another term for shareholder's equity.

Jack has paid-in capital. This is money that has been received from the stockholders. Jack also has retained earnings. This represents profits earned on the stockholders' behalf (that have not yet been distributed as dividends).

Every corporation has these two sources of capital.

Requirement 2

5 Use different stock values in decision making

What is the par value per share of the common stock?

Part 1	Part 2	Part 3	Part 4	Part 5	Part 6	Demo Doc Complete

Common Stock and Preferred Stock accounts hold *only* the par value of the *issued* shares. So the $437,500 in the Common Stock account represents the par value of *all* the issued shares.

$$\frac{\text{Par value}}{\text{per share}} = \frac{\text{Common stock balance}}{\text{Number of issued common shares}}$$

$$\frac{\text{Par value}}{\text{per share}} = \frac{\$437,500}{350,000 \text{ shares}}$$

$$= \textbf{\$1.25} \text{ per share}$$

Requirement 3

5 Use different stock values in decision making

On average, what was the original issue price per share of common stock?

Part 1	Part 2	Part 3	Part 4	Part 5	Part 6	Demo Doc Complete

When stock is issued for cash, the Cash account increases (a debit) for cash received. The Common Stock account increases (a credit) for the par value and the excess is Additional Paid-In Capital. Because the selling price per share is almost always more than the par value, this excess balancing amount to Additional Paid-In Capital is usually an increase (a credit).

We know that total debits must equal total credits for any transaction. In this case, the debit is the cash received and the credits are the increases to Common Stock and Additional Paid-In Capital. This means that:

$$\text{Cash received from share issuance} = \text{Common Stock} + \text{Additional Paid-In Capital}$$

So the total cash received from issuance of the common shares is:

$$\$1.25 \text{ par} \times 350{,}000 \text{ shares} = \$437{,}500$$
$$\$437{,}500 + \$787{,}500 = \$1{,}225{,}000$$

This amount represents all 350,000 issued shares.

$$\$1{,}225{,}000/350{,}000 \text{ shares} = \mathbf{\$3.50} \text{ cash received per share}$$

The balancing credit to Additional Paid-In Capital is ($3.50 received − $1.25 par) $2.25 × 350,000 shares = $787,500 additional cash paid.

Requirement 4

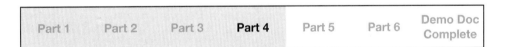

Record the issuance of stock

On February 12, 2009, Jack issued another 20,000 common shares for $5 cash per share. Journalize this transaction.

Part 1	Part 2	Part 3	**Part 4**	Part 5	Part 6	Demo Doc Complete

Cash increases (a debit) by $5 × 20,000 = $100,000.

Common Stock increases (a credit) by the par value of the new shares:

$$\$1.25 \times 20{,}000 = \$25{,}000$$

Additional Paid-In Capital is the excess cash paid:

$$(\$5 - \$1.25) \times \$3.75$$
$$\$3.75 \times 20{,}000 \text{ shares} = \$75{,}000$$

This is the balancing amount in the journal entry.

Cash ($5 × 20,000)		100,000	
Common Stock ($1.25 × 20,000)			25,000
Additional Paid-In Capital (to balance)			75,000

Requirement 5

Prepare the stockholders' equity section of a corporation balance sheet

Jack earned net income of $150,000 and paid no dividends in 2009. There were no other equity transactions in 2009. Prepare the stockholder's equity section of Jack's balance sheet on December 31, 2009.

Part 1	Part 2	Part 3	Part 4	**Part 5**	Part 6	Demo Doc Complete

Because of the stock issuance in Requirement 4, the number of outstanding common shares has increased to:

$$350,000 \text{ shares} + 20,000 \text{ shares} = 370,000 \text{ shares}$$

This must be shown for Common Stock as part of its descriptive line on the balance sheet.

The dollar amount in the Common Stock account has increased to:

$$\$437,500 + \$25,000 = \$462,500$$

The other impact of this transaction on stockholder's equity was to increase Additional Paid-In Capital to:

$$\$787,500 + \$75,000 = \$862,500$$

The net income earned by Jack will increase Retained Earnings to:

$$\$4,200,000 + \$150,000 = \$4,350,000$$

These new amounts create a new total stockholder's equity of $5,675,000.

Stockholder's Equity	
Common Stock, 1,600,000 authorized, 370,000 issued and outstanding shares	$ 462,500
Additional Paid-In Capital	862,500
Retained Earnings	4,350,000
Total Stockholder's Equity	$5,675,000

Requirement 6

6 Evaluate return on assets and return on stockholders' equity

Calculate Jack's return on equity and book value per share for 2009.

Part 1	Part 2	Part 3	Part 4	Part 5	**Part 6**	Demo Doc Complete

$$\text{Return on stockholder's equity} = \frac{\text{Net income} - \text{Preferred dividends}}{\text{Average common stockholder's equity}}$$

Common stockholder's equity means the total stockholder's equity less the preferred equity (that is, less any preferred stock or any additional paid-in capital relating to preferred stock).

Average common stockholder's equity is the *mathematical average* of the beginning and ending balances in Common Stockholder's Equity (that is, [beginning balance + ending balance]/2).

So using the data from this question:

$$\text{Return on stockholder's equity} = \frac{\$150,000 - \$0}{(\$5,425,000 + \$5,675,000)/2}$$

Return on stockholders' equity = 0.027 = 2.7%

$$\text{Book value per share} = \frac{\text{Common stockholders' equity}}{\text{Number of common shares outstanding}}$$

Using the data from this question:

$$\text{Book value per share} = \frac{\$5,675,000}{370,000 \text{ shares}}$$

$$= \mathbf{\$15.34} \text{ per share}$$

Part 1	Part 2	Part 3	Part 4	Part 5	Part 6	**Demo Doc Complete**

Demo Doc 2

Preferred Stock

Learning Objectives 2, 4

Jill Co. issued 25,000, 6%, $100 par cumulative preferred shares on January 1, 2008, for $120 cash per share. Jill had never issued preferred shares before this date. Jill paid the following cash dividends (in total, to *all* shares):

2008	$120,000
2009	$160,000
2010	$200,000

Requirements

1. Journalize the issuance of the preferred shares on January 1, 2008, and the payment of the preferred share dividends in 2008 (assuming the dividends were declared and paid on the same day).

2. How much in dividends is Jill supposed to pay to the preferred shareholders each year?

3. Did Jill pay all of the required dividends in each year? If not, what happens to the amount not paid? How much in dividends did the preferred and common shareholders receive each year?

Demo Doc 2 Solutions

Requirement 1

2 Record the issuance of stock

4 Account for cash dividends

Journalize the issuance of the preferred shares on January 1, 2008, and the payment of the preferred share dividends in 2008 (assuming the dividends were declared and paid on the same day).

Part 1	Part 2	Part 3	Demo Doc Complete

The issuance of preferred shares is the same as the issuance of common shares, except for the account title.

Cash is increased (a debit) by:

$$\$120 \times 25{,}000 = \$3{,}000{,}000$$

Preferred Stock is increased (a credit) by the par value of the new shares:

$$\$100 \times 25{,}000 = \$2{,}500{,}000$$

Additional Paid-In Capital is the excess cash paid:

$$(\$120 - \$100 \text{ par}) = \$20 \times 25{,}000 \text{ shares} = \$500{,}000$$

This is the balancing amount in the journal entry.

Cash ($120 × 25,000)		3,000,000	
Additional Paid-In Capital (to balance)			500,000
Preferred Stock ($100 × 25,000)			2,500,000

When dividends are paid, Retained Earnings is decreased because the shareholders are removing some of their capital from the company. So Retained Earnings is decreased (a debit) by $120,000.

Cash is also decreased (a credit) by $120,000.

Retained Earnings		120,000	
Cash			120,000

Requirement 2

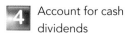

4 Account for cash dividends

How much in dividends is Jill supposed to pay to the preferred shareholders each year?

Part 1	**Part 2**	Part 3	Demo Doc Complete

Each year, every preferred share is *supposed* to receive:

$$\text{"Required" preferred share dividends} = \text{Par value per share} \times \text{Dividend percentage}$$

First, we should calculate the "required" annual dividends per share. In this case, it is:

$$\$100 \times 6\% = \$6 \text{ per share}$$

Because there are 25,000 outstanding preferred shares, this works out to $6 × 25,000 = **$150,000** in dividends per year for all preferred shares.

Requirement 3

4 Account for cash dividends

Did Jill pay all of the required dividends in each year? If not, what happens to the amount not paid? How much in dividends did the preferred and common shareholders receive each year?

Part 1	Part 2	**Part 3**	Demo Doc Complete

2008

Because $120,000 is less than the "required" $150,000, we know that Jill did *not* pay all of the required dividends in 2008.

The preferred shares only received:

$$\$120,000/25,000 \text{ shares} = \$4.80 \text{ per share}$$

The difference of $150,000 − $120,000 = $30,000 is <u>dividends in arrears</u>. This amount is *not* recorded in a transaction because it has not yet been declared and, therefore, is not a liability. Dividends in arrears do *not* appear on the balance sheet. However, they are disclosed in a *note* to the financial statements.

Because the full $150,000 was not paid, the entire $120,000 goes to the preferred shareholders as dividends. The common shareholders get no dividends in 2008.

2009

For 2009, Jill must not only pay the $150,000 annual "requirement" but first must also "catch up" on the dividends in arrears of $30,000 from 2008.

So in order to completely fulfill her obligation to the preferred shareholders, Jill must pay $30,000 + $150,000 = $180,000 in dividends to the preferred shareholders.

Because $160,000 is less than $180,000, we know that Jill did *not* pay all of the required dividends in 2009.

The difference of $180,000 − $160,000 = $20,000 is <u>dividends in arrears</u>.

Because the full $180,000 was not paid, the entire $160,000 goes to the preferred shareholders as dividends. The common shareholders get no dividends in 2009.

2010

In 2010, Jill is *supposed* to pay the annual $150,000 of dividends *plus* the $20,000 dividends in arrears from 2009 for a total of $170,000.

Because $200,000 is greater than $170,000, we know that Jill did pay all of the required dividends in 2010.

The $170,000 shown above goes to the preferred shareholders, while the rest ($200,000 − $170,000 = $30,000) goes to the common shareholders.

| Part 1 | Part 2 | Part 3 | **Demo Doc Complete** |

Demo Doc 3

Learning Objectives 1, 7

Joe Danson owns all outstanding common shares of Joseph Corp. The corporation earned net income before tax of $80,000 in 2008 and has an income tax rate of 40%.

Requirements

1. Is Joe Danson personally liable for the income taxes owed by Joseph Corp.?

2. Calculate the amount of income tax expense that will appear on Joseph Corp.'s 2008 income statement.

Demo Doc 3 Solutions

Requirement 1

1 Identify the characteristics of a corporation

Is Joe Danson personally liable for the income taxes owed by Joseph Corp.?

Part 1	Part 2	Demo Doc Complete

Corporations are liable for *their own* taxes. Even as the sole owner, Joe is not liable for the taxes of the corporation.

Requirement 2

7 Account for the income tax of a corporation

Calculate the amount of income tax expense that will appear on Joseph Corp.'s 2008 income statement.

Part 1	Part 2	Demo Doc Complete

Income tax expense
= Net income before tax × Tax rate
= $80,000 × 40% = $32,000

Part 1	Part 2	Demo Doc Complete

Quick Practice Questions

True/False

_____ 1. Stockholders in a corporation are personally liable for the debts of the corporation.

_____ 2. Most corporations have continuous lives regardless of changes in the ownership of their stock.

_____ 3. Par value is an arbitrary amount assigned by a company to a share of its stock.

_____ 4. A credit balance in Retained Earnings is referred to as a deficit.

_____ 5. When a corporation sells par value stock at an amount greater than par value, other income is reported on the income statement.

_____ 6. Dividends become a liability of the corporation on the payment date.

_____ 7. The owners of cumulative preferred stock must receive all dividends in arrears plus the current year's dividends before the common stockholders get a dividend.

_____ 8. A stock's market price is the price for which a person could buy or sell a share of the stock.

_____ 9. The book value of a stock is the amount of owners' equity on the company's books for each share of its stock.

_____ 10. The rate of return on total assets measures a company's success in using assets to earn income for those financing the business.

Multiple Choice

1. What is the document called that is used by a state to grant permission to form a corporation?
    a. Charter
    b. Proxy
    c. Stock certificate
    d. Bylaw agreement

2. Which of the following statements describing a corporation is true?
    a. Stockholders are the creditors of a corporation.
    b. A corporation is subject to greater governmental regulation than a proprietorship or a partnership.
    c. When ownership of a corporation changes, the corporation terminates.
    d. Stockholders own the business and manage its day-to-day operations.

3. Which of the following best describes paid-in capital?
    a. Investments by the stockholders of a corporation
    b. Investments by the creditors of a corporation
    c. Capital that the corporation has earned through profitable operations
    d. All of the above

4. Which of the following best describes retained earnings?
    a. It is classified as a liability on the corporate balance sheet.
    b. It does not appear on any financial statement.

c. It represents capital that the corporation has earned through profitable operations.

d. It represents investments by the stockholders of a corporation.

5. What individual(s) has the authority to obligate the corporation to pay dividends?
   a. Total stockholders
   b. The board of directors
   c. The president of the company
   d. The chief executive officer

6. A corporation issues 1,800 shares of $10 par value common stock in exchange for land with a current market value of $23,000. How would this be recorded in the Land account?
   a. Debited for $23,000
   b. Credited for $18,000
   c. Credited for $20,000
   d. Debited for $18,000

7. Which of the following would be recorded for the issuance of 55,000 shares of no-par common stock at $13.50 per share?
   a. Credit to Paid-In Capital in Excess of No-Par Value—Common for $742,500
   b. Credit to Common Stock for $742,500
   c. Credit to Cash for $742,500
   d. Debit to Paid-In Capital in Excess of No-Par Value—Common for $742,500

8. Which of the following is true for dividends?
   a. Dividends are a distribution of cash to the stockholders.
   b. Dividends decrease both the assets and the total stockholders' equity of the corporation.
   c. Dividends increase retained earnings.
   d. Both (a) and (b) are correct.

9. Dividends on cumulative preferred stock of $2,500 are in arrears for 2008. During 2009, the total dividends declared amount to $10,000. There are 6,000 shares of $10 par, 10% cumulative preferred stock outstanding and 10,000 shares of $5 par common stock outstanding. What is the total amount of dividends payable to each class of stock in 2009?
   a. $5,000 to preferred, $5,000 to common
   b. $6,000 to preferred, $4,000 to common
   c. $8,500 to preferred, $1,500 to common
   d. $10,000 to preferred, $0 to common

10. Which of the following is true about dividends in arrears?
    a. They are a liability on the balance sheet.
    b. They are dividends passed on cumulative preferred stock.
    c. They are dividends passed on noncumulative preferred stock.
    d. They are dividends passed on common stock.

Quick Exercises

13-1. Journalize the following transactions:

a. **Firm Body Corporation sells 12,000 shares of $10 par common stock for $13.00 per share.**

b. **Firm Body Corporation sells 5,000 shares of $50 par, 10% cumulative preferred stock for $59 per share.**

c. Received a building with a market value of $115,000 and issued 6,400 shares of $10 par common stock in exchange.

d. Firm Body Corporation reports net income of $66,000 at the end of its first year of operations.

General Journal				
Date	Accounts		Debit	Credit

General Journal				
Date	Accounts		Debit	Credit

General Journal				
Date	Accounts		Debit	Credit

General Journal				
Date	Accounts		Debit	Credit

13-2.   The following is a list of stockholders' equity accounts appearing on the balance sheet for O'Neil Corporation on December 31, 2008:

Common stock, $10 par value	$300,000
Paid-in capital in excess of par—common	200,000
Retained earnings	225,000
Preferred stock, $50 par value	125,000
Paid-in capital in excess of par—preferred	30,000

Determine the following:

a.   How many shares of preferred stock have been issued?

b. What was the average issuance price of the preferred stock per share?

c. How many shares of common stock have been issued?

d. What is total paid-in capital?

e. What is total stockholders' equity?

13-3. Bowen Corporation organized on January 1, 2008. Bowen Corporation has authorization for 90,000 shares of $10 par value common stock. As of December 31, 2008, Bowen has issued 50,000 shares of its common stock at an average issuance price of $15. Bowen also has authorization for 50,000 shares of 5%, $50 par value, noncumulative preferred stock. As of December 31, 2008, Bowen has issued 12,000 shares of preferred stock at an average issuance price of $68 per share. Bowen reports net income of $47,000 for its first year of operations ended December 31, 2008.

Requirement

1. Prepare the stockholders' equity section of the balance sheet for Bowen Corporation dated December 31, 2008.

13-4. Following is the stockholders' equity section of the balance sheet for Watson Corporation as of December 1, 2009:

Preferred stock, $100 par, 6% cumulative, 10,000 shares authorized, 7,500 shares issued	$ 750,000
Common stock, $10 par, 200,000 shares authorized, 130,000 shares issued	1,300,000
Paid-in capital in excess of par—common	520,000
Total paid-in capital	$2,570,000
Retained earnings	450,000
Total stockholders' equity	$3,020,000

Watson Corporation reports the following transactions for December 2009:

Dec. 5   Declared the required cash dividend on the preferred stock and a $0.40 dividend on the common stock.

20   Paid the dividends declared on December 5.

Requirements

1. Journalize the transactions.

	General Journal		
Date	Accounts	Debit	Credit

	General Journal		
Date	Accounts	Debit	Credit

2. What is the total stockholders' equity after posting the entries?

13-5.   Sparks Corporation has gathered the following data for the current year:

Net Income	$40,000
Interest Expense	6,000
Income Tax Expense	12,500
Preferred Dividends	3,600

Balance Sheet Data	Beginning of Year	End of Year
Current assets	$ 68,000	$ 81,000
Current liabilities	41,000	39,000
Plant assets	340,000	365,000
Long-term liabilities	100,000	90,000
Common stockholders' equity	217,000	267,000
Preferred stockholders' equity	50,000	50,000

Requirements

1. Calculate return on assets.

2. Calculate return on equity.

3. Comment on how these measures are used.

Do It Yourself! Question 1

Common Stock

Dinner Co. had the following information at December 31, 2008:

Stockholder's Equity	
Common Stock, 500,000 authorized, 50,000 issued and outstanding shares	$100,000
Additional Paid-In Capital	50,000
Retained Earnings	400,000
Total Stockholder's Equity	$550,000

Requirements

5 Use different stock values in decision making

1. What is the par value per share of the common stock?

5 Use different stock values in decision making

2. On average, what was the original issue price per share of the common stock?

2 Record the issuance of stock

3. On January 9, 2009, Dinner issued another 10,000 common shares for $4 cash per share. Journalize this transaction.

General Journal			
Date	Accounts	Debit	Credit

Do It Yourself! Question 1 | Chapter 13   **419**

Do It Yourself! Question 2

Preferred Stock

Lunch Corp. issued 5,000, 8%, $20 par cumulative preferred shares on January 1, 2008, for $25 cash per share. Lunch had never had preferred shares before this date. On December 31, 2008, Lunch paid $5,000 in cash dividends to its shareholders. On December 31, 2009, Lunch paid $15,000 in cash dividends to its shareholders.

Requirements

2 Record the issuance of stock

1. Journalize the issuance of the preferred shares on January 1, 2008.

	General Journal			
Date	Accounts		Debit	Credit

4 Account for cash dividends

2. How much in dividends is Lunch supposed to pay to the preferred shareholders each year?

4 Account for cash dividends

3. How much of the $5,000 paid as dividends in 2008 went to the preferred and common shareholders?

4 Account for cash dividends

4. How much of the $15,000 paid as dividends in 2009 went to the preferred and common shareholders?

Quick Practice Solutions

True/False

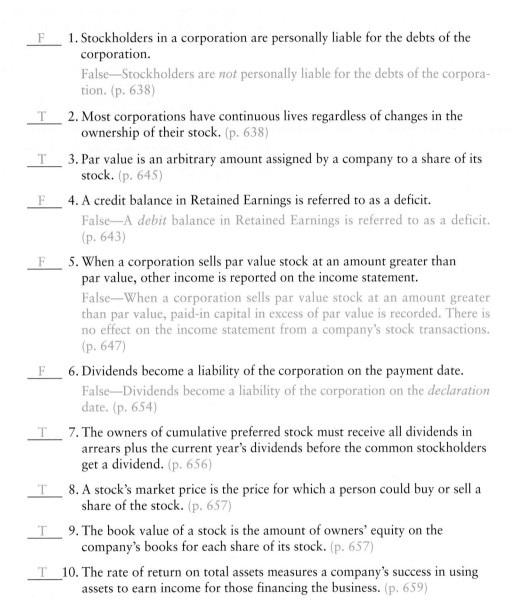

_F___ 1. Stockholders in a corporation are personally liable for the debts of the corporation.

False—Stockholders are *not* personally liable for the debts of the corporation. (p. 638)

_T___ 2. Most corporations have continuous lives regardless of changes in the ownership of their stock. (p. 638)

_T___ 3. Par value is an arbitrary amount assigned by a company to a share of its stock. (p. 645)

_F___ 4. A credit balance in Retained Earnings is referred to as a deficit.

False—A *debit* balance in Retained Earnings is referred to as a deficit. (p. 643)

_F___ 5. When a corporation sells par value stock at an amount greater than par value, other income is reported on the income statement.

False—When a corporation sells par value stock at an amount greater than par value, paid-in capital in excess of par value is recorded. There is no effect on the income statement from a company's stock transactions. (p. 647)

_F___ 6. Dividends become a liability of the corporation on the payment date.

False—Dividends become a liability of the corporation on the *declaration* date. (p. 654)

_T___ 7. The owners of cumulative preferred stock must receive all dividends in arrears plus the current year's dividends before the common stockholders get a dividend. (p. 656)

_T___ 8. A stock's market price is the price for which a person could buy or sell a share of the stock. (p. 657)

_T___ 9. The book value of a stock is the amount of owners' equity on the company's books for each share of its stock. (p. 657)

_T__10. The rate of return on total assets measures a company's success in using assets to earn income for those financing the business. (p. 659)

Multiple Choice

1. **What is the document called that is used by a state to grant permission to form a corporation?** (p. 638)
   a. Charter
   b. Proxy
   c. Stock certificate
   d. Bylaw agreement

2. **Which of the following statements describing a corporation is true?** (p. 639)
   a. Stockholders are the creditors of a corporation.
   b. A corporation is subject to greater governmental regulation than a proprietorship or a partnership.

c. When ownership of a corporation changes, the corporation terminates.

d. Stockholders own the business and manage its day-to-day operations.

3. **Which of the following best describes paid-in capital?** (p. 641)

   a. Investments by the stockholders of a corporation

   b. Investments by the creditors of a corporation

   c. Capital that the corporation has earned through profitable operations

   d. All of the above

4. **Which of the following best describes retained earnings?** (p. 641)

   a. It is classified as a liability on the corporate balance sheet.

   b. It does not appear on any financial statement.

   c. It represents capital that the corporation has earned through profitable operations.

   d. It represents investments by the stockholders of a corporation.

5. **What individual(s) has the authority to obligate the corporation to pay dividends?** (p. 654)

   a. Total stockholders

   b. The board of directors

   c. The president of the company

   d. The chief executive officer

6. **A corporation issues 1,800 shares of $10 par value common stock in exchange for land with a current market value of $23,000. How would this be recorded in the Land account?** (p. 648)

   a. Debited for $23,000

   b. Credited for $18,000

   c. Credited for $20,000

   d. Debited for $18,000

7. **Which of the following would be recorded for the issuance of 55,000 shares of no-par common stock at $13.50 per share?** (p. 648)

   a. Credit to Paid-In Capital in Excess of No-Par Value—Common for $742,500

   b. Credit to Common Stock for $742,500

   c. Credit to Cash for $742,500

   d. Debit Paid-In Capital in Excess of No-Par Value—Common for $742,500

8. **Which of the following is true for dividends?** (p. 654)

   a. Dividends are a distribution of cash to the stockholders.

   b. Dividends decrease both the assets and the total stockholders' equity of the corporation.

   c. Dividends increase retained earnings.

   d. Both (a) and (b) are correct.

9. **Dividends on cumulative preferred stock of $2,500 are in arrears for 2008. During 2009, the total dividends declared amount to $10,000. There are 6,000 shares of $10 par, 10% cumulative preferred stock outstanding and 10,000 shares of $5 par common stock outstanding. What is the total amount of dividends payable to each class of stock in 2009?** (pp. 654–657)

   a. $5,000 to preferred, $5,000 to common

   b. $6,000 to preferred, $4,000 to common

   c. $8,500 to preferred, $1,500 to common

   d. $10,000 to preferred, $0 to common

10. **Which of the following is true about dividends in arrears?** (p. 656)

    a. They are a liability on the balance sheet.

    b. They are dividends passed on cumulative preferred stock.

    c. They are dividends passed on noncumulative preferred stock.

    d. They are dividends passed on common stock.

Quick Exercise Solutions

13-1. Journalize the following transactions. (pp. 645–650)

a. **Firm Body Corporation sells 12,000 shares of $10 par common stock for $13.00 per share.**

b. **Firm Body Corporation sells 5,000 shares of $50 par, 10% cumulative preferred stock for $59 per share.**

c. **Received a building with a market value of $115,000 and issued 6,400 shares of $10 par common stock in exchange.**

d. **Firm Body Corporation reports net income of $66,000 at the end of its first year of operations.**

General Journal

	Date	Accounts	Debit	Credit
a.		Cash	156,000	
		Common Stock		120,000
		Paid-In Capital in Excess of Par—Common		36,000

General Journal

	Date	Accounts	Debit	Credit
b.		Cash	295,000	
		Preferred Stock		250,000
		Paid-In Capital in Excess of Par—Preferred		45,000

General Journal

	Date	Accounts	Debit	Credit
c.		Building	115,000	
		Common Stock		64,000
		Paid-In Capital in Excess of Par—Common		51,000

General Journal

	Date	Accounts	Debit	Credit
d.		Income Summary	66,000	
		Retained Earnings		66,000

13-2. The following is a list of stockholders' equity accounts appearing on the balance sheet for O'Neil Corporation on December 31, 2008:

Common stock, $10 par value	$300,000
Paid-in capital in excess of par—common	200,000
Retained earnings	225,000
Preferred stock, $50 par value	125,000
Paid-in capital in excess of par—preferred	30,000

Determine the following: (pp. 645–650)

a. How many shares of preferred stock have been issued?

$$\$125,000/\$50 = 2,500$$

b. What was the average issuance price of the preferred stock per share?

$$(\$125,000 + \$30,000)/2,500 = \$62$$

c. How many shares of common stock have been issued?

$$\$300,000/\$10 = 30,000$$

d. What is total paid-in capital?

$$\$300,000 + \$200,000 + \$125,000 + \$30,000 = \$655,000$$

e. What is total stockholders' equity?

$$\$655,000 + \$225,000 = \$880,000$$

13-3. Bowen Corporation organized on January 1, 2008. Bowen Corporation has authorization for 90,000 shares of $10 par value common stock. As of December 31, 2008, Bowen has issued 50,000 shares of its common stock at an average issuance price of $15. Bowen also has authorization for 50,000 shares of 5%, $50 par value, noncumulative preferred stock. As of December 31, 2008, Bowen has issued 12,000 shares of preferred stock at an average issuance price of $68 per share. Bowen reports net income of $47,000 for its first year of operations ended December 31, 2008.

Prepare the stockholders' equity section of the balance sheet for Bowen Corporation dated December 31, 2008. (pp. 645–650)

Bowen Corporation
Stockholders' Equity
December 31, 2008

Paid-in capital:	
Preferred stock, 5%, $50 par, 512,000 shares issued	$ 600,000
Paid-in capital in excess of par—preferred	216,000
Common stock, $10 par, 90,000 shares authorized, 50,000 shares issued	500,000
Paid-in capital in excess of par—common	250,000
Total paid-in capital	$1,566,000
Retained earnings	47,000
Total stockholders' equity	$1,613,000

13-4.   Following is the stockholders' equity section of the balance sheet for Watson Corporation as of December 1, 2009:

Preferred stock, $100 par, 6% cumulative, 10,000 shares authorized, 7,500 shares issued	$ 750,000
Common stock, $10 par, 200,000 shares authorized, 130,000 shares issued	1,300,000
Paid-in capital in excess of par—common	520,000
Total paid-in capital	$2,570,000
Retained earnings	450,000
Total stockholders' equity	$3,020,000

Watson Corporation reports the following transactions for December 2009: (pp. 654–657)

Dec. 5   Declared the required cash dividend on the preferred stock and a $0.40 dividend on the common stock.

20   Paid the dividends declared on December 5.

Requirements

1. Journalize the transactions.

General Journal			
Date	Accounts	Debit	Credit
12/5/09	Retained Earnings	97,000	
	Dividends Payable		97,000

General Journal			
Date	Accounts	Debit	Credit
12/20/09	Dividends Payable	97,000	
	Cash		97,000

2. What is the total stockholders' equity after posting the entries?

$2,923,000 ($3,020,000 − $97,000)

13-5.   Sparks Corporation has gathered the following data for the current year: (p. 659)

Net Income	$40,000
Interest Expense	6,000
Income Tax Expense	12,500
Preferred Dividends	3,600

Balance Sheet Data	Beginning of Year	End of Year
Current assets	$ 68,000	$ 81,000
Current liabilities	41,000	39,000
Plant assets	340,000	365,000
Long-term liabilities	100,000	90,000
Common stockholders' equity	217,000	267,000
Preferred stockholders' equity	50,000	50,000

Requirements

1. Calculate return on assets.

$40,000 + $6,000 = $46,000
$46,000/$427,000* = 10.8%

*$68,000 + $3,40,000 = $408,000
$81,000 + $365,000 = $446,000
$408,000 + $446,000 = $854,000
$854,000/2 = $427,000

2. Calculate return on equity.

$40,000 − $3,600 = $36,400
$36,400/$242,000* = 15.0%

*$217,000 + $267,000 = $484,000
$484,000/2 = $427,000

3. Comment on how these measures are used.

The return on assets is used as a standard profitability measure that shows the company's success in using its assets to generate income. It helps investors compare one company to another, especially within the same industry.

The return on equity is used as a standard profitability measure that shows the relationship between net income and average common stockholders' equity. The higher the rate of return, the more successful the company.

Do It Yourself! Question 1 Solutions

Requirements

1. What is the par value per share of the common stock?

$$\begin{aligned}\text{Par value per share} &= \frac{\$100,000}{50,000 \text{ shares}} \\ &= \$2 \text{ per share}\end{aligned}$$

2. On average, what was the original issue price per share of the common stock?

Total cash received from issuance of the common shares (par + additional paid-in capital):

$$\$100,000 + \$50,000 = \$150,000$$

$$\frac{\$150,000}{50,000 \text{ shares}} = \$3 \text{ cash received per share}$$

3. On January 9, 2009, Dinner issued another 10,000 common shares for $4 cash per share. Journalize this transaction.

Cash ($4 × 10,000)		40,000	
Additional Paid-In Capital (to balance)			20,000
Common Stock ($2 × 10,000)			20,000

$$\$4 \text{ paid} - \$2 \text{ par} = \$2 \text{ excess cash}$$

$$\$2 \text{ excess cash} \times 10,000 \text{ shares} = \text{Additional Paid-In Capital } \$20,000 \text{ balancing amount}$$

Do It Yourself! Question 2 Solutions

Requirements

1. Journalize the issuance of the preferred shares on January 1, 2008.

Cash ($25 × 5,000)	125,000	
Additional Paid-In Capital (to balance)		25,000
Common Stock ($20 × 5,000)		100,000

2. How much in dividends is Lunch supposed to pay to the preferred shareholders each year?

Preferred shareholders are *supposed* to receive:

$$\$20 \text{ par} \times 8\% = \$1.60 \text{ per share annually}$$

$\$1.60 \times 5,000 = \mathbf{\$8,000}$ dividends per year for all outstanding preferred shares

3. How much of the $5,000 paid as dividends in 2008 went to the preferred and common shareholders?

The full $8,000 was not paid; therefore, the entire $5,000 goes to the preferred shareholders. Common shareholders get nothing.

$$\$8,000 - \$5,000 = \$3,000 \text{ of dividends in arrears}$$

4. How much of the $15,000 paid as dividends in 2009 went to the preferred and common shareholders?

Preferred shareholders received:

$$\$8,000 + \$3,000 = \$11,000$$

Common shareholders received:

$$\$15,000 - \$11,000 = \$4,000$$

The Power of Practice

For more practice using the skills learned in this chapter, visit MyAccountingLab. There you will find algorithmically generated questions that are based on these Demo Docs and your main textbook's Review and Assess Your Progress sections.

Go to MyAccountingLab and follow these steps:

1. Direct your URL to www.myaccountinglab.com.
2. Log in using your name and password.
3. Click the MyAccountingLab link.
4. Click Study Plan in the left navigation bar.
5. From the table of contents, select Chapter 13, Corporations: Paid-In Capital and the Balance Sheet.
6. Click a link to work tutorial exercises.

14 Corporations: Retained Earnings and the Income Statement

WHAT YOU PROBABLY ALREADY KNOW

You probably already know that it can be helpful to look back at past history to predict the future. Let's assume that you want to join a gym that will cost you $50 a month. You have decided that although you have savings, you don't want to join if you can't afford to pay for it from your normal monthly earnings. Before you sign the contract, you may calculate your monthly finances. Assume you looked at the previous month's financial activity and found the following:

Revenues:		Expenses:	
Wages earned and received from employer	$ 850	Rent and utilities	$625
Birthday gifts	200	Insurance and gas	75
		College application fee	100
		Food and entertainment	150
Total revenues:	$1,050	Total expenses:	$950

Although there is an excess of revenues over expenses of $100, it cannot be assumed that this is what will occur in the future. The birthday gifts and the college application fee are unusual nonrecurring types of financial events. If those two items are eliminated, the recurring wage revenue of $850 equals the recurring monthly expenses of $850 and your conclusion would be that the gym membership is not affordable. The same concept holds for businesses. Those financial transactions that are nonrecurring and should not be considered when making future projections are identified and segregated from the routine operating results on the income statement.

Learning Objectives

 Account for stock dividends.

The board of directors may declare a stock dividend instead of a cash dividend. A **stock dividend** gives each shareholder more shares of stock based on the number of shares currently owned. Similar to a cash dividend, Retained Earnings is reduced (debited). However, unlike a cash dividend, a liability is not credited because there is no claim on assets; common stock is credited. *Review Exhibit 14-2 (p. 692) for the accounting of a stock dividend.*

2 Distinguish stock splits from stock dividends.

A **stock split** increases the number of shares issued and outstanding and reduces the par or stated value proportionately. A 3-for-1 split means that each shareholder receives 2 more shares for each 1 currently held and the par or stated value is 1/3 of the amount before the split. There is **no journal entry required** for a stock split because there is no impact on the financial position of the company.

A stock dividend increases (credits) the Common Stock and Paid-In Capital in Excess of Par accounts for the additional shares issued. The dividend, a return of equity to the shareholders, also decreases (debits) Retained Earnings. *Review Exhibit 14-5 (p. 694) for a comparison of stock dividends and splits.*

3 Account for treasury stock.

Treasury stock is when the company buys back its own shares from existing shareholders. The cost of the shares is debited to a contra equity account, Treasury Stock. If the treasury stock is subsequently sold, Cash is debited, Treasury Stock is credited for the cost of the shares, and Paid-In Capital from Treasury Stock Transactions is debited or credited for the difference, if any. *Review the impact of treasury stock on stockholders' equity in Exhibit 14-6 (p. 697).*

4 Report restrictions on retained earnings.

A **restriction on retained earnings** means that some of the Retained Earnings balance is not available for dividend declaration. The purpose of a restriction is to provide for a minimum amount of equity to remain in Retained Earnings. A restriction may be self-imposed or required by creditors or others. *See the required note to the financial statements under "Restrictions on Retained Earnings" in the main text.*

5 Analyze a corporate income statement.

The income statement reports **income from continuing operations,** which represents the results of operations that can be expected to proceed in the future. Below continuing operations, there may be special items that do not recur. These items, listed below, are shown individually net of tax on the income statement after continuing operations but before net income.

- **Discontinued operations**—The financial results of a discontinued segment of the business. The segment must be able to be separately identified operationally and for reporting purposes from the remainder of the entity.

- **Extraordinary gains and losses**—The financial effect of events that are **both** unusual (not expected to occur) and infrequent (not expected to recur).

Earnings per share, the net income earned per outstanding share of common stock, must be shown at the bottom of the income statement. This is probably the most important indicator used by analysts and investors for profitability analysis. *Review the multistep income statement containing special items in Exhibit 14-8 (p. 704). Observe the combined income statement and retained earnings statement in Exhibit 14-10 (p. 707) and the presentation of comprehensive income in Exhibit 14-11 (p. 709).*

Demo Doc 1

Stock Splits and Dividends

Learning Objectives 1, 2

On December 31, 2008, Tinker Corp. had 25,000, $1.20 par common shares outstanding with a market price of $9 per share.

Retained Earnings had a balance of $60,000, but there was no balance in Additional Paid-In Capital.

Requirements

1. On January 1, 2009, Tinker split its common stock 3 for 1. Give the journal entry for the split. What are the par and market values per share after the split? How does this split impact stockholder's equity?

2. On February 1, 2009, Tinker issued a 20% stock dividend. Give the journal entry for this dividend. What is the par value per share after the dividend? How does this dividend impact stockholder's equity?

3. On March 1, 2009, Tinker declared and paid a cash dividend of $0.60 per common share. Give the journal entry for this dividend. How does this dividend impact stockholder's equity?

Demo Doc 1 Solutions

Requirement 1

2 Distinguish stock splits from stock dividends

On January 1, 2009, Tinker split its common stock 3 for 1. Give the journal entry for the split. What are the par and market values per share after the split? How does this split impact stockholder's equity?

Part 1	Part 2	Part 3	Demo Doc Complete

Before the split, Tinker has 25,000 common shares.
With a 3-for-1 split, there will be **3** new shares **for** every **1** old share.

$$\begin{array}{ccccc}\text{Number of shares after} & = & \text{Number of shares before} & \times & \text{Split ratio} \\ \text{stock split} & & \text{stock split} & & \end{array}$$

$$\begin{array}{ccccc}\text{Number of shares after} & = & 25{,}000 & \times & \dfrac{3}{1} \\ \text{stock split} & & & & \end{array}$$

$$= 75{,}000 \text{ shares}$$

Another result of the split is that the par value and the market price are also split.

$$\begin{array}{ccccc}\text{Par value per} & = & \text{Par value per} & \times & \dfrac{1}{\text{Split ratio}} \\ \text{share after split} & & \text{share before split} & & \end{array}$$

$$\begin{array}{ccccc}\text{Par value per} & = & \$1.20 & \times & \dfrac{1}{3} \\ \text{share after split} & & & & \end{array}$$

$$= \mathbf{\$0.40} \text{ per share}$$

$$\begin{array}{ccccc}\text{Market price per} & = & \text{Market price per share} & \times & \dfrac{1}{\text{Split ratio}} \\ \text{share after split} & & \text{before split} & & \end{array}$$

$$\begin{array}{ccccc}\text{Market price per} & = & \$9 & \times & \dfrac{1}{3} \\ \text{share after split} & & & & \end{array}$$

$$= \mathbf{\$3} \text{ per share}$$

There has been *no change* to the account balance of Common Stock. It remains the same, only it is now spread across more shares (resulting in a lower par value per share, as shown above).

The net impact on common stock is *zero*. Essentially, this means that *there is no journal entry for a stock split*. However, a stock split is described in the notes to the financial statements.

Because there is no journal entry, total equity is *not* impacted by the stock split.

Requirement 2

On February 1, 2009, Tinker issued a 20% stock dividend. Give the journal entry for this dividend. What is the par value per share after the dividend? How does this dividend impact stockholder's equity?

Part 1	**Part 2**	Part 3	Demo Doc Complete

This is a small stock dividend because the dividend percentage (20%) is less than 25%.

Remember that after the stock split of January 1, Tinker has 75,000 common shares outstanding with a market price of $3 per share and a par value of $0.40 per share.

With a stock dividend, new shares are issued to existing shareholders.

$$\begin{array}{c} \text{Number of new shares} \\ \text{issued for stock} \\ \text{dividend} \end{array} = \begin{array}{c} \text{Shares outstanding} \\ \text{before dividend} \end{array} \times \begin{array}{c} \text{Stock} \\ \text{dividend \%} \end{array}$$

$$\begin{array}{c} \text{Number of new shares} \\ \text{issued for stock} \\ \text{dividend} \end{array} = \quad 75,000 \quad \times \quad 20\%$$

$$= \textbf{15,000 new shares}$$

Each of these new shares is *identical* to the shares that existed before the stock dividend. They have the same characteristics as the common shares that existed before the stock dividend. The par value of the new shares issued is $0.40 per share, as it is for the other common shares.

So Common Stock increases (a credit) by:

$$15,000 \text{ new shares} \times \$0.40 \text{ par} = \$6,000$$

With *any* dividend, there is a decrease (a debit) to Retained Earnings because the shareholders are receiving some of their value/equity back from the company.

In the case of a small stock dividend, this value is the *market value* of the new shares issued.

So in this case, Retained Earnings decreases (a debit) by:

$$15,000 \text{ new shares} \times \$3 \text{ market price per share} = \$45,000$$

The difference between these two amounts is balanced to Additional Paid-In Capital—in this case, an increase (a credit) of:

$$\$45,000 - \$6,000 = \$39,000$$

Feb. 1	Retained Earnings (15,000 × $3)	45,000	
	Additional Paid-In Capital (to balance)		39,000
	Common Stock (15,000 × $0.40)		6,000

All of these accounts are part of the equity section. This means that there is an equal debit (decrease) and credit (increase) impact to the equity section. We are simply shifting value from Retained Earnings to Paid-In Capital.

This means that *total* equity *does not change* as a result of this transaction.

	Before Stock Dividend		After Stock Dividend
Common Stock	$30,000		$36,000
Additional Paid-In Capital	0		39,000
Retained Earnings	60,000		15,000
Total Equity	$90,000	(same)	$90,000

Requirement 3

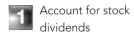 Account for stock dividends

On March 1, 2009, Tinker declared and paid a cash dividend of $0.60 per common share. Give the journal entry for this dividend. How does this dividend impact stockholder's equity?

Part 1	Part 2	**Part 3**	Demo Doc Complete

Cash will decrease (a credit) by the amount of dividends paid. After the stock dividend of February 1, there are 75,000 + 15,000 = 90,000 shares outstanding. Therefore, the cash paid is:

$$90,000 \text{ shares} \times \$0.60 \text{ per share} = \$54,000$$

With *any* dividend, there is a decrease to Retained Earnings (a debit). In this case, it is a decrease of the cash paid of $54,000.

March 1	Retained Earnings	54,000	
	Cash (90,000 × $0.60)		54,000

Part 1	Part 2	Part 3	**Demo Doc Complete**

Demo Doc 2

Treasury Stock

Learning Objectives 3, 4

On January 1, 2008, Unter Inc. purchased 4,000 shares of treasury stock for $10 each. At this time, Paid-In Capital, Treasury Stock had a balance of $0.

Quentin sold the treasury stock as follows:

April 1, 2008	Sold 1,000 shares for $12 cash each.
July 1, 2008	Sold 2,500 shares for $9.50 cash each.
October 1, 2008	Sold 500 shares for $8.25 cash each.

Requirements

1. Journalize all of Unter's treasury stock transactions.

2. Suppose instead of holding onto the common stock purchased as treasury stock, Unter retired the stock on January 2, 2008. Would it be possible for Unter to later reissue the stock?

Demo Doc 2 Solutions

Requirement 1

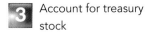 Account for treasury stock

Journalize all of Unter's treasury stock transactions.

Part 1	Part 2	Demo Doc Complete

On January 1, 2008, Unter Inc. purchased 4,000 shares of treasury stock for $10 cash each. At this time, Paid-In Capital, Treasury Stock had a balance of $0.

The Common Stock account represents all *issued* common shares. When the company purchases treasury stock, these shares are still issued but are *no longer outstanding*. To represent this decrease in the number of outstanding shares, the Treasury Stock account has a debit balance. It is a *contra equity* account.

When treasury stock is purchased, the Treasury Stock account increases (a debit) by the cost of the treasury shares:

$$4,000 \times \$10 \text{ share} = \$40,000$$

Cash decreases (a credit) by $40,000.

Jan. 1	Treasury Stock	40,000	
	Cash (4,000 × $10)		40,000

April 1, 2008: Sold 1,000 shares for $12 cash each.

Cash increases (a debit) by:

$$1,000 \text{ shares} \times \$12 = \$12,000$$

Treasury Stock decreases (a credit) by the *original cost* of the treasury shares:

$$1,000 \text{ shares} \times \$10 = \$10,000$$

The difference between these two amounts is a balancing amount to Paid-In Capital, Treasury Stock of ($12,000 − $10,000) = $2,000 credit (increase).

April 1	Cash (1,000 × $12)	12,000	
	Paid-In Capital, Treasury Stock (to balance)		2,000
	Treasury Stock (1,000 × $10)		10,000

July 1, 2008: Sold 2,500 shares for $9.50 cash each.

Cash increases (a debit) by:

$$2,500 \text{ shares} \times \$9.50 = \$23,750$$

Treasury Stock decreases (a credit) by the *original cost* of the treasury shares:

$$2,500 \text{ shares} \times \$10 = \$25,000$$

The difference between these two amounts is a balancing amount to Paid-In Capital, Treasury Stock. This is a debit (decrease) of:

$$\$25,000 - \$23,750 = \$1,250$$

Note that we *cannot* have a *debit/negative balance* in Paid-In Capital, Treasury Stock. However, from the entry on April 1, we know that there is a balance of $2,000. This is more than enough to cover a $1,250 debit.

July 1	Cash (2,500 × $9.50)	23,750	
	Paid-In Capital, Treasury Stock (to balance)	1,250	
	Treasury Stock (2,500 × $10)		25,000

After this transaction, Paid-In Capital, Treasury Stock has a balance of $750 credit:

Paid-In Capital, Treasury Stock

		Bal.	0
		Apr. 1	2,000
July 1	1,250		
		Bal.	750

Treasury Stock

Jan. 1	40,000		
		Apr. 1	10,000
		Mar. 1	25,000
Bal.	5,000		

October 1, 2008: Sold 500 shares for $8.25 cash each.

Cash increases (a debit) by:

$$500 \text{ shares} \times \$8.25 = \$4,125$$

Treasury Stock decreases (a credit) by the *original cost* of the treasury shares:

$$500 \text{ shares} \times \$10 = \$5,000$$

The difference between these two amounts would normally be a balancing amount to Paid-In Capital, Treasury Stock, but in this case, the difference is a debit (a decrease) of:

$$\$5,000 - \$4,125 = \$875$$

There is only $750 in the Paid-In Capital, Treasury Stock account. This is not enough to cover the debit that would normally be required.

Instead, we take *as much as possible* from the Paid-In Capital, Treasury Stock account. This means that we debit for the $750 left in the account. The remaining ($875 − $750) = $125 is balanced to Retained Earnings (debit/decrease).

Oct. 1	Cash (500 × $8.25)	4,125	
	Paid-In Capital, Treasury Stock	750	
	Retained Earnings (to balance)	125	
	Treasury Stock (500 × $10)		5,000

Requirement 2

4 Report restrictions on retained earnings

Suppose instead of holding onto the common stock purchased as treasury stock, Unter retired the stock on January 2, 2008. Would it be possible for Unter to later reissue the stock?

Part 1	Part 2	Demo Doc Complete

When stock is retired, the stock certificates are *canceled*. This means that the stock ceases to exist.

Retired/canceled stock can no longer be reissued.

Part 1	Part 2	**Demo Doc Complete**

Demo Doc 3

Income Statement Presentation and Earnings per Share _____

Learning Objective 5

Vater Industries had the following information for the year ended December 31, 2008:

Common stock, $0.50 par	$ 7,000
Preferred stock, $20 par, 10%	20,000
Treasury Stock (2,000 shares at cost)	8,000
Extraordinary items (before tax)	30,000
Tax impact of extraordinary items	(9,000)
Tax impact of income from continuing operations	(65,000)
Income from continuing operations (before tax)	200,000
Tax impact of discontinued operations	11,000
Discontinued operations (before tax)	(40,000)

During 2008, Vater paid all required dividends for the preferred stock and also paid dividends of $1 per share on the common stock.

Requirements

1. Prepare the lower portion of Vater's income statement for the year ended December 31, 2008, beginning with income from continuing operations, including earnings per share calculations.

2. Why are discontinued operations and extraordinary items not included as part of income from continuing operations?

Demo Doc 3 Solutions

Requirement 1

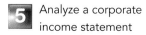

Analyze a corporate income statement

Prepare the lower portion of Vater's income statement for the year ended December 31, 2008, beginning with income from continuing operations, including earnings per share calculations.

Part 1	Part 2	Part 3	Part 4	Demo Doc Complete

First, we must get the final numbers to be reported on the income statement for these items. Each of these items is reported *after tax*, so we must combine the pretax numbers with their tax impacts to get the after-tax numbers.

Income from continuing operations (after tax):

$$\$200,000 - \$65,000 = \$135,000$$

Discontinued operations (net of tax):

$$-\$40,000 + \$11,000 = -\$29,000$$

Extraordinary items (net of tax):

$$\$30,000 - \$9,000 = \$21,000$$

Remember that discontinued operations and extraordinary items can be positive *or* negative. In this question, discontinued operations are negative and the extraordinary item is a gain, but either item could also be in the opposite direction. To help recall the order of presentation on this part of the income statement, remember that it is alphabetical: CDE.

C   Income from Continuing Operations

D   Income from Discontinued Operations

E   Extraordinary Items

So the first part of the income statement is:

Income from continuing operations	$135,000
− Discontinued operations (net of tax)	(29,000)
+ Extraordinary items (net of tax)	21,000
Net Income	$127,000

Part 1	Part 2	Part 3	Part 4	Demo Doc Complete

Next, we must calculate the earnings per share ratios for each of these items.

$$\text{Basic earnings per share} = \frac{\text{Net income} - \text{Preferred share dividends}}{\text{Average number of common shares outstanding}}$$

Notice that there is *no mention* of *common* share dividends because it is *irrelevant* whether or not common share dividends are paid. Net income (after the preferred dividends) goes to the common shareholders. Whether they "receive" this income as an increase to retained earnings or as a cash dividend, it still belongs to the common shareholders.

Therefore, payment of common stock dividends is ignored in the EPS calculation.

It is *only* the preferred dividends (money that does *not* go to the common shareholders) that is subtracted.

So we ignore the common stock dividends in our earnings per share calculation.

We still need the number of common shares outstanding for the earnings per share calculation. The common stock account represents the par value of all issued shares.

So the number of issued common shares is:

$$\$7{,}000/\$0.50 \text{ par per share} = 14{,}000 \text{ shares}$$

To get the number of outstanding common shares, we must take out the treasury stock:

$$\begin{array}{c} \text{Number of outstanding} \\ \text{shares} \end{array} = \begin{array}{c} \text{Number of issued} \\ \text{shares} \end{array} - \begin{array}{c} \text{Number of treasury} \\ \text{shares} \end{array}$$

$$\begin{array}{c} \text{Number of outstanding} \\ \text{shares} \end{array} = \quad 14{,}000 \quad - \quad 2{,}000$$

$$= 12{,}000 \text{ shares of common stock outstanding}$$

The \$20,000 in the Preferred Stock account represents the par value of *all* preferred stock. Therefore, we can calculate that the preferred share dividends paid in 2008:

$$10\% \times \$20{,}000 = \$2{,}000$$

For income from continuing operations, basic earnings per share is:

$$\begin{array}{c} \text{Basic earnings} \\ \text{per share} \end{array} = \frac{\text{Income} - \text{Preferred share dividends}}{\text{Average number of common shares outstanding}}$$

$$= \frac{\$135{,}000 - \$2{,}000}{12{,}000 \text{ common shares}}$$

$$= \mathbf{\$11.08} \text{ per share}$$

The portion of earnings per share relating to discontinued operations is:

$$\begin{array}{c} \text{Basic earnings} \\ \text{per share} \end{array} = \frac{\text{Income}}{\text{Average number of common shares outstanding}}$$

$$= \frac{-\$29{,}000}{12{,}000 \text{ common shares}}$$

$$= \mathbf{-\$2.42} \text{ per share}$$

The portion of earnings per share relating to extraordinary items is:

$$\begin{array}{c} \text{Basic earnings} \\ \text{per share} \end{array} = \frac{\text{Income}}{\text{Average number of common shares outstanding}}$$

$$= \frac{\$21{,}000}{12{,}000 \text{ common shares}}$$

$$= \mathbf{\$1.75} \text{ per share}$$

For net income, basic earnings per share is:

$$\text{Basic earnings per share} = \frac{\text{Income} - \text{Preferred share dividends}}{\text{Average number of common shares outstanding}}$$

$$= \frac{\$127,000 - \$2,000}{12,000 \text{ common shares}}$$

$$= \mathbf{\$10.41} \text{ per share (rounded down)}$$

As a check, we can add up the portions of earnings per share from the other items:

$$\$11.08 - \$2.42 + \$1.75 = \$10.41$$

Part 1	Part 2	**Part 3**	Part 4	Demo Doc Complete

The full income statement is:

Income from continuing operations	$135,000
+ Discontinued operations (net of tax)	(29,000)
− Extraordinary items (net of tax)	21,000
Net income	$127,000

Earnings per share:

Income from continuing operations	$11.08
Discontinued operations	(2.42)
Extraordinary items	1.75
Net income	$10.41

Requirement 2

Analyze a corporate income statement

Why are discontinued operations and extraordinary items not included as part of income from continuing operations?

Part 1	Part 2	Part 3	**Part 4**	Demo Doc Complete

Accountants must make financial statements helpful to investors (and other people) making decisions. One of the things the users of financial statements want to know is how much profit/income they can expect the business to make in the future. Income from *continuing* operations helps with estimating future profits because it involves income from business activities that will go on (that is, continue) into the future.

Discontinued operations are business activities that are ceasing (such as a subsidiary of the company that is in the process of being sold).

Extraordinary items are supposed to be one-time occurrences (by definition—unusual and infrequent) such as an earthquake.

These numbers are not helpful if you are trying to predict *future* profit levels. The discontinued operations will be gone in the future and the extraordinary events will not happen again. They will have *no* future impact.

These items are legitimately part of net income (and so are included there) but they are separated from income from continuing operations to make it easier for users of financial statements to understand what they can expect to see on future income statements. An analyst who is trying to predict *future* income would *only* use income from continuing operations because this is the only part of net income that will have a future impact (in other words, is *continuing* on into the future).

| Part 1 | Part 2 | Part 3 | Part 4 | **Demo Doc Complete** |

Quick Practice Questions

True/False

_____ 1. A stock dividend is a distribution by a corporation of its own stock to its stockholders.

_____ 2. Stock dividends increase total stockholders' equity.

_____ 3. A stock split reduces the number of outstanding shares of stock and the par value of the stock.

_____ 4. When treasury stock is purchased, the balance in the Common Stock account remains unchanged.

_____ 5. A corporation purchases 200 shares of its $10 par common stock for $12 per share. Subsequently, all 200 shares are resold for $13 per share. The amount of revenue from these transactions is $200.

_____ 6. Only outstanding shares of stock receive cash and stock dividends.

_____ 7. Earnings per share is computed by dividing net income less preferred dividends by the average number of common shares outstanding.

_____ 8. Stock dividends may cause the price of the stock to increase.

_____ 9. Prior-period adjustments adjust retained earnings for discontinued operations.

_____ 10. Comprehensive income is the company's change in total stockholders' equity from all sources other than from its owners.

Multiple Choice

1. What is the effect of a stock dividend distribution on a stockholder's ownership percentage?
   a. It increases.
   b. It decreases.
   c. It can increase or decrease depending on the type of stock dividend.
   d. It will stay the same.

2. What is the ownership percentage used as a cutoff point for distinguishing between a small and a large stock dividend?
   a. 15%
   b. 10%
   c. 25%
   d. 50%

3. What entry is made to record a 2-for-1 stock split?
   a. Credit to Common Stock
   b. Credit to Retained Earnings
   c. Debit to Retained Earnings
   d. There is no journal entry for a stock split.

4. **What effect does the purchase of treasury stock have on the number of a corporation's shares?**
   a. It causes issued shares to exceed authorized shares.
   b. It causes outstanding shares to exceed issued shares.
   c. It causes outstanding shares to exceed authorized shares.
   d. It causes outstanding shares to be less than issued shares.

5. **What type of account is Treasury Stock?**
   a. Contra asset
   b. Liability
   c. Contra liability
   d. Contra Stockholders' Equity account

6. **What is the effect of a common stock retirement?**
   a. It decreases the number of shares of common stock outstanding.
   b. It increases the balance in the Common Stock account.
   c. It decreases the number of shares of common stock issued.
   d. Both (a) and (c) are correct.

7. **Which of the following is true for restrictions on retained earnings?**
   a. They are usually reported in the notes to the financial statements.
   b. They happen frequently.
   c. They are disclosed on the income statement.
   d. They reduce total assets on the balance sheet.

8. **The Gain on Sale of Machinery account would appear on the income statement as which of the following?**
   a. Extraordinary gain
   b. Component of income from discontinued operations
   c. Component of net sales
   d. Component of income from continuing operations

9. **To be considered an extraordinary item on the income statement, the event must be which of the following?**
   a. Unusual but not infrequent
   b. Both infrequent and unusual
   c. Neither infrequent nor unusual
   d. Infrequent but not unusual

10. **Net income for a corporation for the current year amounts to $200,000. The corporation currently has outstanding 5,000 shares of 5%, cumulative $100 par preferred stock and 20,000 shares of $20 par common stock. What is the numerator to be used in the earnings-per-share calculation?**
    a. $175,000
    b. $195,000
    c. $200,000
    d. $225,000

Quick Exercises

14-1.   Jonathan Corporation reports the following transactions for 2009:

Jan. 10   Sold 6,000 shares of 9%, noncumulative $50 par, preferred stock for $85 per share.

Feb. 19   Sold 3,000 shares of $10 par common stock for $15 per share.

Oct. 12 The board announced a 15% stock dividend on the common stock. The current market price of the common stock is $22 per share. Jonathan Corporation has 120,000 shares of common stock outstanding on October 12.

Requirement

1. Journalize the above transactions.

General Journal			
Date	Accounts	Debit	Credit

General Journal			
Date	Accounts	Debit	Credit

General Journal			
Date	Accounts	Debit	Credit

14-2. Following is the stockholders' equity section of the balance sheet of Fairfield Corporation as of November 1, 2009:

FAIRFIELD CORPORATION
Stockholders' Equity
November 1, 2009

Paid-in capital:	
Preferred stock, 6%, noncumulative $50 par, 10,000 authorized,	
6,500 shares issued	$ 325,000
Common stock, $10 par, 300,000 shares authorized,	
120,000 shares issued	1,200,000
Paid-in capital in excess of par—common	420,000
Total paid-in capital	$1,945,000
Retained earnings	467,200
Total stockholders' equity	$2,412,200

Fairfield Corporation reported the following transactions during November 2009:

Nov. 1 Declared the required annual cash dividend on the preferred stock and a $0.70 dividend on the common stock.

15 Paid the dividends declared on November 1.

16 Distributed a 10% common stock dividend. The market value of the common stock is $20 per share.

30 The board of directors announced a 2-for-1 stock split.

Requirement

1. Show the dollar amount of the effect of each transaction on both total paid-in capital and total stockholders' equity.

Date	Total paid-in capital	Total stockholders' equity

14-3.   Victory Corporation reported the following stockholders' equity items on December 31, 2008:

Preferred stock, 5%, cumulative $100 par, 7,000 shares authorized, 1,000 shares issued	$100,000
Paid-in-capital in excess of par—preferred	55,000
Common stock, $50 par, 10,000 shares authorized, 5,000 shares issued	250,000
Paid-in capital in excess of par—common	235,000
Retained earnings	455,300
Treasury common stock, at cost, 700 shares	96,000

Requirements

1. Compute the:

    a.   Number of shares of common stock outstanding

    b.   Number of shares of preferred stock outstanding

    c.   Average issue price of common stock

d. Average issue price of preferred stock

2. Assume that Victory Corporation declares a 4-for-1 stock split. Compute the:

    a. Number of shares of common outstanding

    b. Par value

14-4. Clean Wash Corporation reported the following stockholders' equity on January 1, 2008:

<table>
<tr><td colspan="2" align="center">CLEAN WASH CORPORATION
Stockholders' Equity
January 1, 2008</td></tr>
<tr><td>Paid-in capital:</td><td></td></tr>
<tr><td> Preferred stock, 5%, cumulative $50 par, 30,000 authorized,</td><td></td></tr>
<tr><td>   7,500 shares issued</td><td>$ 375,000</td></tr>
<tr><td> Paid-in capital in excess of par—preferred</td><td>18,750</td></tr>
<tr><td> Common stock, $1 par, 200,000 shares authorized,</td><td></td></tr>
<tr><td>   135,000 shares issued</td><td>135,000</td></tr>
<tr><td> Paid-in capital in excess of par—common</td><td>472,500</td></tr>
<tr><td>Total paid-in capital</td><td>$1,001,250</td></tr>
<tr><td>Retained earnings</td><td>218,500</td></tr>
<tr><td>Total stockholders' equity</td><td>$1,219,750</td></tr>
</table>

Requirements

1. On June 15, 2008, the board of directors announced a 10% common stock dividend when the market price of the stock was $6 per share. Journalize the stock dividend.

<table>
<tr><td colspan="5" align="center">General Journal</td></tr>
<tr><td>Date</td><td>Accounts</td><td></td><td>Debit</td><td>Credit</td></tr>
<tr><td></td><td></td><td></td><td></td><td></td></tr>
<tr><td></td><td></td><td></td><td></td><td></td></tr>
<tr><td></td><td></td><td></td><td></td><td></td></tr>
<tr><td></td><td></td><td></td><td></td><td></td></tr>
</table>

2. What effect did the distribution of the common stock dividend have on the following?

    a. Total assets

    b. Total liabilities

    c. Total paid-in capital

    d. Total stockholders' equity

14-5.   On June 1, 2008, Hauser Corporation purchased 2,600 shares of its $10 par value common stock for $12.50 per share. The 2,600 shares had originally been issued for $11.25 per share. Hauser Corporation sold 1,700 of its treasury shares on August 4, 2008, for $14.75 per share.

Journalize the transactions on June 1 and August 4, 2008.

General Journal				
Date	Accounts		Debit	Credit

General Journal				
Date	Accounts		Debit	Credit

Do It Yourself! Question 1

Stock Splits and Dividends

On December 31, 2008, Garbage Inc. had 12,000 common shares outstanding with a market price of $8 per share and a par value of $2 per share.

Requirements

1. On January 1, 2009, Garbage issued a 15% stock dividend. Journalize this dividend.

	General Journal			
Date	Accounts		Debit	Credit

2. On January 2, 2009, Garbage split its common stock 2 for 1. Journalize the split. What are the par and market values per share after the split?

	General Journal			
Date	Accounts		Debit	Credit

3. On January 3, 2009, Garbage declared and paid a cash dividend of $0.30 per common share. Journalize this dividend.

	General Journal			
Date	Accounts		Debit	Credit

Do It Yourself! Question 2

Treasury Stock

On January 1, 2008, Hartnick Co. purchased 1,000 shares of treasury stock for $7 cash each. At this time, Paid-In Capital, Treasury Stock had a balance of $0.

Hartnick sold the treasury stock as follows:

February 1, 2008	Sold 200 shares for $10 cash each
March 1, 2008	Sold 500 shares for $6 cash each
April 1, 2008	Sold 300 shares for $6.50 cash each

Requirement

1. Journalize all of Hartnick's treasury stock transactions.

	General Journal		
Date	Accounts	Debit	Credit

	General Journal		
Date	Accounts	Debit	Credit

	General Journal		
Date	Accounts	Debit	Credit

	General Journal		
Date	Accounts	Debit	Credit

Do It Yourself! Question 3

Income Statement Presentation and Earnings per Share

Gate Corp. had the following information for the year ended December 31, 2008:

Common stock, $0.50 par	$ 200,000
Preferred stock, $50 par, 8%	500,000
Tax impact of discontinued operations	(80,000)
Discontinued operations (before tax)	400,000
Extraordinary items (before tax)	(100,000)
Tax impact of extraordinary items	30,000
Tax impact of income from continuing operations	(750,000)
Income from continuing operations (before tax)	2,500,000

During the year, Gate paid all required dividends for the preferred stock and also paid dividends of $1 per share on the common stock. Gate has no treasury stock.

Requirement

1. Prepare the lower portion of Gate's income statement for the year ended December 31, 2008, beginning with income from continuing operations, including earnings-per-share calculations.

Quick Practice Solutions

True/False

_T_   1. A stock dividend is a distribution by a corporation of its own stock to its stockholders. (p. 691)

_F_   2. Stock dividends increase total stockholders' equity.

     False—Stock dividends have *no effect* on total stockholders' equity. (p. 691)

_F_   3. A stock split reduces the number of outstanding shares of stock and the par value of the stock.

     False—A stock split *increases* the number of outstanding shares of stock and reduces the par value of the stock. (p. 693)

_T_   4. When treasury stock is purchased, the balance in the Common Stock account remains unchanged. (p. 694)

_F_   5. A corporation purchases 200 shares of its $10 par common stock for $12 per share. Subsequently, all 200 shares are resold for $13 per share. The amount of revenue from these transactions is $200.

     False—Revenue is not recorded from a company's stock transactions. Paid-In Capital from the sale of treasury stock is credited for $200. (pp. 691–692)

_T_   6. Only outstanding shares of stock receive cash and stock dividends. (p. 691)

_T_   7. Earnings per share is computed by dividing net income less preferred dividends by the average number of common shares outstanding. (p. 706)

_F_   8. Stock dividends may cause the price of the stock to increase.

     False—Stock dividends may cause the price of the stock to *decrease* because of the increased supply of the stock. (p. 691)

_F_   9. Prior-period adjustments correct retained earnings for discontinued operations.

     False—Prior-period adjustments correct retained earnings for *errors made in prior periods.* (p. 708)

_T_ 10. Comprehensive income is the company's change in total stockholders' equity from all sources other than from its owners. (p. 708)

Multiple Choice

1. What is the effect of a stock dividend distribution on a stockholder's ownership percentage? (p. 691)
   a. It increases.
   b. It decreases.
   c. It can increase or decrease depending on the type of stock dividend.
   d. It will stay the same.

2. What is the ownership percentage used as a cutoff point for distinguishing between a small and a large stock dividend? (p. 692)
   a. 15%
   b. 10%
   c. 25%
   d. 50%

3. **What entry is made to record a 2-for-1 stock split?** (p. 693)
   a. Credit to Common Stock
   b. Credit to Retained Earnings
   c. Debit to Retained Earnings
   d. There is no journal entry for a stock split.

4. **What effect does the purchase of treasury stock have on the number of a corporation's shares?** (p. 695)
   a. It causes issued shares to exceed authorized shares.
   b. It causes outstanding shares to exceed issued shares.
   c. It causes outstanding shares to exceed authorized shares.
   d. It causes outstanding shares to be less than issued shares.

5. **What type of account is Treasury Stock?** (p. 695)
   a. Contra asset
   b. Liability
   c. Contra liability
   d. Contra Stockholders' Equity account

6. **What is the effect of a common stock retirement?** (p. 697)
   a. It decreases the number of shares of common stock outstanding.
   b. It increases the balance in the Common Stock account.
   c. It decreases the number of shares of common stock issued.
   d. Both (a) and (c) are correct.

7. **Which of the following is true for restrictions on retained earnings?** (p. 697)
   a. They are usually reported in the notes to the financial statements.
   b. They happen frequently.
   c. They are disclosed on the income statement.
   d. They reduce total assets on the balance sheet.

8. **The Gain on Sale of Machinery account would appear on the income statement as which of the following?** (p. 704)
   a. Extraordinary gain
   b. Component of income from discontinued operations
   c. Component of net sales
   d. Component of income from continuing operations

9. **To be considered an extraordinary item on the income statement, the event must be which of the following?** (pp. 704–705)
   a. Unusual but not infrequent
   b. Both infrequent and unusual
   c. Neither infrequent nor unusual
   d. Infrequent but not unusual

10. **Net income for a corporation for the current year amounts to $200,000. The corporation currently has outstanding 5,000 shares of 5%, cumulative $100 par preferred stock and 20,000 shares of $20 par common stock. What is the numerator to be used in the earnings-per-share calculation?** (p. 706)
    a. $175,000
    b. $195,000
    c. $200,000
    d. $225,000

Quick Exercises

14-1. Jonathan Corporation reports the following transactions for 2009: (p. 691)

Jan. 10 Sold 6,000 shares of 9%, noncumulative $50 par, preferred stock for $85 per share.

Feb. 19 Sold 3,000 shares of $10 par common stock for $15 per share.

Oct. 12 The board announced a 15% stock dividend on the common stock. The current market price of the common stock is $22 per share. Jonathan Corporation has 120,000 shares of common stock outstanding on October 12.

Requirement

1. Journalize the above transactions.

General Journal

Date	Accounts	Debit	Credit
Jan. 10	Cash	510,000	
	Preferred Stock		300,000
	Paid-In Capital in Excess of Par—Preferred		210,000

General Journal

Date	Accounts	Debit	Credit
Feb. 19	Cash	45,000	
	Common Stock		30,000
	Paid-In Capital in Excess of Par—Common		15,000

General Journal

Date	Accounts	Debit	Credit
Oct. 12	Retained Earnings	396,000	
	Common Stock		180,000
	Paid-In Capital in Excess of Par—Common		216,000

14-2. Following is the stockholders' equity section of the balance sheet of Fairfield Corporation as of November 1, 2009: (pp. 691–692)

FAIRFIELD CORPORATION
Stockholders' Equity
November 1, 2009

Paid-in capital:	
Preferred stock, 6%, noncumulative $50 par, 10,000 authorized,	
6,500 shares issued	$ 325,000
Common stock, $10 par, 300,000 shares authorized,	
120,000 shares issued	1,200,000
Paid-in capital in excess of par—common	420,000
Total paid-in capital	$1,945,000
Retained earnings	467,200
Total stockholders' equity	$2,412,200

Fairfield Corporation reported the following transactions during November 2009:

Nov. 1 Declared the required annual cash dividend on the preferred stock and a $0.70 dividend on the common stock.

15 Paid the dividends declared on November 1.

16 Distributed a 10% common stock dividend. The market value of the common stock is $20 per share.

30 The board of directors announced a 2-for-1 stock split.

Requirements

1. Show the dollar amount of the effect of each transaction on both total paid-in capital and total stockholders' equity.

Date	Total paid-in capital	Total stockholders' equity
Nov. 1	No effect	Decrease of $103,500
Nov. 15	No effect	No effect
Nov. 16	Increase of $240,000	No effect
Nov. 30	No effect	No effect

14-3. Victory Corporation reported the following stockholders' equity items on December 31, 2008: (pp. 691–694)

Preferred stock, 5%, cumulative $100 par, 7,000 shares authorized, 1,000 shares issued	$100,000
Paid-in-capital in excess of par—preferred	55,000
Common stock, $50 par, 10,000 shares authorized, 5,000 shares issued	250,000
Paid-in capital in excess of par—common	235,000
Retained earnings	455,300
Treasury common stock, at cost, 700 shares	96,000

Requirements

1. Compute the:

    a. Number of shares of common stock outstanding

        $250,00/$50 per share = 5,000 shares
        5,000 shares − 700 shares = 4,300 shares

    b. Number of shares of preferred stock outstanding

        $100,000/$100 per share = 1,000 shares

    c. Average issue price of common stock

        $250,000 + $235,000 = $485,000
        $485,000/5,000 shares = $97 per share

    d. Average issue price of preferred stock

        $100,000 + $55,000 = $155,000
        $155,000/1,000 shares = $155 per share

2. Assume that Victory Corporation declares a 4-for-1 stock split. Compute the:

    a. Number of shares of common outstanding

$$4,300 \text{ shares} \times 4 = 17,200$$

    b. Par value

$$\$50/4 = \$12.50$$

14-4.   Clean Wash Corporation reported the following stockholders' equity on January 1, 2008: (pp. 691–696)

<table>
<tr><td colspan="2" align="center">CLEAN WASH CORPORATION
Stockholders' Equity
January 1, 2008</td></tr>
<tr><td>Paid-in capital:</td><td></td></tr>
<tr><td>Preferred stock, 5%, cumulative $50 par, 30,000 authorized,</td><td></td></tr>
<tr><td>   7,500 shares issued</td><td>$ 375,000</td></tr>
<tr><td>Paid-in capital in excess of par—preferred</td><td>18,750</td></tr>
<tr><td>Common stock, $1 par, 200,000 shares authorized,</td><td></td></tr>
<tr><td>   135,000 shares issued</td><td>135,000</td></tr>
<tr><td>Paid-in capital in excess of par—common</td><td>472,500</td></tr>
<tr><td>Total paid-in capital</td><td>$1,001,250</td></tr>
<tr><td>Retained earnings</td><td>218,500</td></tr>
<tr><td>Total stockholders' equity</td><td>$1,219,750</td></tr>
</table>

Requirements

1. On June 15, 2008, the board of directors announced a 10% common stock dividend when the market price of the stock was $6 per share. Prepare the necessary journal entry to record the stock dividend.

General Journal				
Date	Accounts		Debit	Credit
June 15	Retained Earnings		81,000	
	Common Stock			13,500
	Paid-In Capital in Excess of Par—Common			67,500

2. What effect did the distribution of the common stock dividend have on the following?

    a. Total assets

        No effect

    b. Total liabilities

        No effect

    c. Total paid-in capital

        Increase of $81,000

    d. Total stockholders' equity

        No effect

14-5. On June 1, 2008, Hauser Corporation purchased 2,600 shares of its $10 par value common stock for $12.50 per share. The 2,600 shares had originally been issued for $11.25 per share. Hauser Corporation sold 1,700 of its treasury shares on August 4, 2008, for $14.75 per share. (p. 696)

Journalize the transactions on June 1 and August 4, 2008.

General Journal			
Date	Accounts	Debit	Credit
June 1	Treasury Stock	32,500	
	Cash		32,500

General Journal			
Date	Accounts	Debit	Credit
Aug. 4	Cash	25,075	
	Treasury Stock		21,250
	Paid-In Capital from Treasury Stock Transactions		3,825

Do It Yourself! Question 1 Solutions

Stock Splits and Dividends

Requirements

1. On January 1, 2009, Garbage issued a 15% stock dividend. Journalize this dividend.

Number of new shares issued for stock dividend = 12,000 × 15% = 1,800 new shares

Jan. 1	Retained Earnings (1,800 × $8)	14,400	
	Additional Paid-In Capital (to balance)		10,800
	Common Stock (1,800 × $2)		3,600

2. On January 2, 2009, Garbage split its common stock 2 for 1. Journalize the split. What are the par and market values per share after the split?

Common shares before split = 12,000 + 1,800 = 13,800

Number of shares after stock split = 13,800 × 2/1 = 27,600 shares

Par value per share after split = $2 × 1/2 = **$1**

Market price per share after split = $8 × 1/2 = **$4**

There is no journal entry for a stock split.

3. On January 3, 2009, Garbage declared and paid a cash dividend of $0.30 per common share. Journalize this dividend.

Jan. 3	Retained Earnings	8,280	
	Cash (27,600 × $0.30)		8,280

Do It Yourself! Question 2 Solutions

Treasury Stock

Requirement

1. Journalize all of Hartnick's treasury stock transactions.

On January 1, 2008, Hartnick Co. purchased 1,000 shares of treasury stock for $7 cash each. At this time, Paid-In Capital, Treasury Stock had a balance of $0.

| Jan. 1 | Treasury Stock | 7,000 | |
| | Cash (1,000 × $7) | | 7,000 |

February 1, 2008: Sold 200 shares for $10 cash each.

Feb. 1	Cash (200 × $10)	2,000	
	Paid-In Capital, Treasury Stock (to balance)		600
	Treasury Stock (200 × $7)		1,400

March 1, 2008: Sold 500 shares for $6 cash each.

March 1	Cash (500 × $6)	3,000	
	Paid-In Capital, Treasury Stock (to balance)	500	
	Treasury Stock (500 × $7)		3,500

After this transaction:

Paid-In Capital, Treasury Stock				Treasury Stock			
		Bal.	0	Jan. 1	7,000		
		Feb. 1	600			Feb 1	1,400
Mar. 1	500					Mar. 1	3,500
		Bal.	100	Bal.	2,100		

April 1, 2008: Sold 300 shares for $6.50 cash each.

April 1	Cash (300 × $6.50)	1,950	
	Paid-In Capital, Treasury Stock	100	
	Retained Earnings (to balance)	50	
	Treasury Stock (300 × $7)		2,100

Do It Yourself! Question 3 Solutions

Income Statement Presentation and Earnings per Share

Requirement

1. Prepare the lower portion of Gate's income statement for the year ended December 31, 2008, beginning with income from continuing operations, including earnings-per-share calculations.

Income from Continuing Operations (after tax):

$$\$2,500,000 - \$750,000 = \$1,750,000$$

Discontinued Operations (net of tax):

$$\$400,000 - \$80,000 = \$320,000$$

Extraordinary Items (net of tax):

$$-\$100,000 + \$30,000 = -\$70,000$$

Net Income:

$$\$1,750,000 + \$320,000 - \$70,000 = \$2,000,000$$

Number of Common Shares Outstanding:

$$\$200,000/\$0.50 \text{ par per share} = 400,000 \text{ shares}$$

Preferred Share Dividends Paid:

$$8\% \times \$500,000 = \$40,000$$

For income from continuing operations, basic earnings per share is:

$$\frac{\$1,750,000 - \$40,000}{400,000 \text{ shares}} = \$4.275 \text{ per share}$$

The portion of earnings per share relating to discontinued operations is:

$$\frac{\$320,000}{400,000 \text{ shares}} = \$0.80 \text{ per share}$$

The portion of earnings per share relating to extraordinary items is:

$$\frac{-\$70{,}000}{400{,}000 \text{ shares}} = -\$0.175 \text{ per share}$$

For net income, basic earnings per share is:

$$\frac{\$2{,}000{,}000 - \$40{,}000}{400{,}000 \text{ shares}} = \$4.90 \text{ per share}$$

Income from continuing operations	$1,750,000
+ Discontinued operations (net of tax)	320,000
− Extraordinary items (net of tax)	(70,000)
Net income	$2,000,000

Earnings per share:

Income from continuing operations	$ 4.275
Discontinued operations	0.800
Extraordinary items	(0.175)
Net income	$ 4.900

The Power of Practice

For more practice using the skills learned in this chapter, visit MyAccountingLab. There you will find algorithmically generated questions that are based on these Demo Docs and your main textbook's Review and Assess Your Progress sections.

Go to MyAccountingLab and follow these steps:

1. Direct your URL to www.myaccountinglab.com.
2. Log in using your name and password.
3. Click the MyAccountingLab link.
4. Click Study Plan in the left navigation bar.
5. From the table of contents, select Chapter 14, Corporations: Retained Earnings and the Income Statement.
6. Click a link to work tutorial exercises.

15 Long-Term Liabilities

WHAT YOU PROBABLY ALREADY KNOW

You probably already know that when you purchase a home, you will likely need to obtain a mortgage. There are various types of mortgages to choose from, but a popular form is the fixed-rate mortgage. If you obtain a 30-year fixed mortgage, you know that you are locked into the interest rate specified in the mortgage contract for 30 years. Mortgage interest rates may increase or decrease in subsequent years, but it won't affect your fixed monthly payment. If the interest rate decrease is material enough, you may choose to refinance the mortgage to save future interest costs. Refinancing means that the old mortgage is paid off with a new mortgage loan. The characteristics of a bond are similar to a mortgage. The issuer of a bond has incurred a long-term liability and is committed to pay interest at the fixed interest rate included in the bond agreement. Sometimes issuers will refinance their debt if the interest rate decreases by issuing new bonds at the lower interest rate and paying off the higher-rate bonds. In this chapter, we will learn about bonds and how to account for them.

Learning Objectives

 Account for bonds payable.

A **bond** is a long-term liability that may be issued by corporations; local, state, or federal governments; and agencies. The **principal amount**, the amount on the bond certificate, is the amount that is to be paid to the investor on the maturity date. It is also the amount that is recorded in the Bond Payable account. Over the life of the bond, interest will be paid at the **stated rate**, the fixed interest rate for the bond. *Review "Issuing Bonds Payable to Borrow Money" in the main text for examples of accounting for bonds payable.*

 Measure interest expense by the straight-line amortization method.

A discount occurs when the bond is sold for less than the principal amount. When the stated rate of interest is less than the market rate of interest, a bond is sold at a discount. A premium occurs when the bond is sold for more than the principal amount. When the stated rate of interest is higher than the market rate of interest, a bond is sold at a premium. A Discount on Bonds Payable and a Premium on Bonds Payable need to be amortized into Interest Expense over the life of the bond. Amortization reduces the account balance and Interest Expense is the other account affected. A **discount** is a **debit**

balance; a premium is a credit balance. To reduce a debit balance, a credit entry must be made and then Interest Expense is debited. To reduce a credit balance, a debit entry must be made and then Interest Expense is credited. *Review "Straight-Line Amortization of Bond Discount" and "Straight-Line Amortization of Bond Premium" in the main text for illustrations on the calculation and accounting for amortization.*

 Account for retirement and conversion of bonds payable.

Some bonds are **callable,** which means that the issuer has the right to call, or pay them off at a stipulated redemption price, before the maturity date. When a company calls in the bonds, it is relieved of the net bond liability. This net amount, called the carrying amount, is equal to the Bonds Payable less Discount on Bonds Payable or plus Premium on Bonds Payable amounts. The company must pay the call price, a percentage of the face value of the bonds, to be relieved of that obligation. Similar to the disposal of a plant asset in Chapter 10, there may be a gain or loss that results and needs to be recorded. If the amount received (elimination of bond-carrying amount) is greater than the amount given up (call price), then a Gain on Retirement of Bonds Payable must be credited for the difference. If the amount received is less than the amount given up, then a Loss on Retirement of Bonds Payable must be debited for the difference. *Review "Retirement of Bonds Payable" in the main text.*

A **convertible bond** gives the bondholders the option to convert their investment from a bond into stock at a fixed conversion rate. The price to convert from a bond into equity shares is stipulated when the bonds are issued. The price is usually somewhat higher than the market price of the stock at that time. To record the conversion from a bond into equity:

- The book value of the bonds is eliminated. Bonds Payable is debited and any Discount on Bonds Payable is credited *or* Premium on Bonds Payable is debited.
- The book value of the bonds is assumed to be the purchase price of the stock issuance. As per Chapter 14, the Stock account is credited for the number of shares issued times the par or stated value, as applicable. The excess amount is credited to the Paid-In Capital in Excess of Par account.

Review "Convertible Bonds Payable" in the main text.

 Report liabilities on the balance sheet.

Similar to the handling of Notes Payable, the portion of the Bond Payable that is due within a year is classified as a current liability. Amounts due beyond one year are listed as long-term liabilities. *Review the illustration under "Reporting Liabilities on the Balance Sheet" in the main text.*

 Show the advantages and disadvantages of borrowing.

Borrowing may result in earning more money than the cost of the interest expense incurred. This concept of **leverage** is favorable because it serves to increase earnings per share. Borrowing has the disadvantage of creating a liability for the repayment of debt. Future interest payments will also be required. This increases the company's risk. *Review Exhibit 15-4 (p. 748) for an illustration of the earnings-per-share advantage of borrowing versus issuing stock.*

Demo Doc 1

Bonds Payable (straight-line amortization) _____

Learning Objectives 1, 3, 5

Blue Co. issued $50,000 maturity value of bonds payable for $51,788 cash on January 1, 2008. The bonds had a stated rate of 12%, but the market rate was 10%. Interest is paid semiannually and the bonds are due in two years.

Blue uses the straight-line method of amortization.

Requirements

1. Are these bonds issued at a discount or premium? How do you know?

2. Journalize Blue's issuance of the bonds on January 1, 2008.

3. Journalize Blue's first two interest payments on June 30, 2008, and December 31, 2008.

4. Show how the bonds would appear on Blue's December 31, 2008, balance sheet.

5. On January 2, 2009, 30% of the bonds were converted to 10,000 common shares with $1 par per share. Journalize this transaction.

6. On January 3, 2009, Blue purchased the remaining bonds from the marketplace for $36,000 cash. The bonds were immediately retired. Journalize this transaction.

Demo Doc 1 Solutions

Requirement 1

Are these bonds issued at a discount or premium? How do you know?

Part 1	Part 2	Part 3	Part 4	Part 5	Part 6	Demo Doc Complete

These bonds were issued at a **premium**. We know this because the cash received for the bonds is *more* than the maturity value and because the stated rate is *greater* than the market rate.

12% stated rate > 10% market rate

Requirement 2

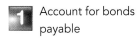 Account for bonds payable

Journalize Blue's issuance of the bonds on January 1, 2008.

Part 1	Part 2	Part 3	Part 4	Part 5	Part 6	Demo Doc Complete

Cash is increased (a debit) by $51,788.
Bonds Payable is increased (a credit) by the bonds' *maturity* value of $50,000.
The difference between these two amounts is balanced to Premium on Bonds Payable. The balancing amount is a credit of:

$51,788 − $50,000 = $1,788

Cash		51,788	
Premium on Bonds Payable (to balance)			1,788
Bonds Payable			50,000

Requirement 3

Account for bonds payable

Journalize Blue's first two interest payments on June 30, 2008, and December 31, 2008.

Part 1	Part 2	Part 3	Part 4	Part 5	Part 6	Demo Doc Complete

Under straight-line amortization, the premium will be amortized the *same amount* every interest period.

$$\frac{\text{Premium amortization}}{\text{each interest period}} = \frac{\text{Discount or Premium}}{\text{Number of interest periods}}$$

The bonds are due in two years and have two interest payments per year. This results in $2 \times 2 = 4$ interest payment periods.

$$\frac{\text{Premium amortization}}{\text{each interest period}} = \frac{\$1,788}{4}$$
$$= \$447$$

This means that *every* time interest expense is recorded, the premium will be amortized (that is, *decreased/debited*) by $447.
Cash will be decreased by the cash interest paid.

$$\frac{\text{Cash interest}}{\text{paid}} = \frac{\text{Maturity value} \times \text{Stated rate}}{\text{Number of interest payments per year}}$$

The question states that the bonds are semiannual; that is, they pay interest twice per year.

$$\frac{\text{Cash interest}}{\text{paid}} = \frac{\$50,000 \times 12\%}{2}$$
$$= \$3,000$$

Interest Expense is increased (a debit) by the balancing amount of:

$$\$3,000 - \$447 = \$2,553$$

Because the cash interest paid and the premium amortization *do not change* from period to period, the entry to record the interest expense and payment is *always* the same. So the entry for June 30, 2008, *and* December 31, 2008, is:

Interest Expense (to balance)	2,553	
Premium on Bonds Payable ($1,788/4)	447	
Cash (50,000 × 12%/2)		3,000

Requirement 4

Show how the bonds would appear on Blue's December 31, 2008, balance sheet.

Part 1	Part 2	Part 3	**Part 4**	Part 5	Part 6	Demo Doc Complete

The bonds are reported in the liabilities section of the balance sheet.
The premium is added to the bonds payable to create a net value.

Bonds payable	$50,000
plus Premium	894*
Bonds payable (net)	$50,894

*$1,788 − $1,447 (June amortization) − $1,447 (December amortization)

Requirement 5

1 Account for bonds payable

3 Account for retirement and conversion of bonds payable

On January 2, 2009, 30% of the bonds were converted to 10,000 common shares with $1 par per share. Journalize this transaction.

Part 1	Part 2	Part 3	Part 4	**Part 5**	Part 6	Demo Doc Complete

Immediately before this transaction, the premium had a balance of $894:

Bond Premium

		Bal.	0
		Jan. 1	1,788
June 30	447		
Dec. 31	447		
		Bal.	894

If 30% of the bonds are converted, then 30% of the maturity value is converted:

$$30\% \times \$50,000 = \$15,000$$

Also 30% of the premium is converted:

$$30\% \times \$894 = \$268 \text{ (rounded)}$$

Note the the values are rounded to the nearest dollar.

The bonds *will not exist* after the conversion, so the Bonds Payable account is decreased (a debit) by $15,000. The Premium is also decreased (a debit) by $268.

New common stock is issued for the conversion, so Common Stock is increased (a credit) by the par value of the new shares:

$$10,000 \times \$1 = \$10,000$$

The remainder is balanced to Additional Paid-In Capital. This balancing amount is:

$$\$15,000 + \$268 - \$10,000 = \$5,268$$

Bonds Payable ($50,000 × 30%)	15,000	
Premium on Bonds Payable ($894 × 30%)	268	
Additional Paid-In Capital (to balance)		5,268
Common Stock ($10,000 × $1)		10,000

Bond Premium

		Bal.	0
		Jan. 1	1,788
June 30	447		
Dec. 31	447		
Jan. 2	268		
		Bal.	626

Bonds Payable

		Bal.	0
		Jan. 1	50,000
Jan. 2	15,000		
		Bal.	35,000

Requirement 6

1 Account for bonds payable

3 Account for retirement and conversion of bonds payable

On January 3, 2009, Blue purchased the remaining bonds from the marketplace for $36,000 cash. The bonds were immediately retired. Journalize this transaction.

Part 1	Part 2	Part 3	Part 4	Part 5	**Part 6**	Demo Doc Complete

Because 30% of the bonds were converted to common stock, 100% − 30% = 70% remained. These bonds will be retired.

If 70% of the bonds are retired, then 70% of the maturity value is retired:

$$70\% \times \$50,000 = \$35,000$$

Also 70% of the premium is retired:

$$70\% \times \$894 = \$626$$

The bonds *will not exist* after retirement, so the Bonds Payable account is decreased (a debit) by $35,000. The Premium is also decreased (a debit) by $626.

Cash is decreased (a credit) by $36,000.

The remainder is balanced to a gain or loss. In this case, the balancing amount is a debit, so there is a *loss* of:

$$\$36,000 - \$626 - \$35,000 = \$374$$

Bonds Payable ($50,000 × 70%)	35,000	
Premium on Bonds Payable (70% × $894)	626	
Loss on Retirement (to balance)	374	
Cash		36,000

Part 1	Part 2	Part 3	Part 4	Part 5	Part 6	**Demo Doc Complete**

Demo Doc 2

Bonds Payable (effective-interest amortization) _____

Learning Objectives 1, 3, 5

Red Co. issued $2,000 maturity (face) value of bonds payable for $1,930 cash on January 1, 2008. The bonds had a stated rate of 8%, but the market rate was 10%. Interest is paid semiannually and the bonds are due in two years.

Red uses the effective interest method of amortization.

Requirements

1. Are these bonds issued at a discount or premium? How do you know?

2. Journalize Red's issuance of the bonds on January 1, 2008.

3. Prepare Red's effective-interest amortization table for the entire life of the bonds payable.

4. Journalize Red's first two interest payments on June 30, 2008, and December 31, 2008.

5. On January 2, 2009, 20% of the bonds were converted to 120 common shares with a $2 par value per share. Journalize this transaction.

6. On January 3, 2009, Red purchased the remaining bonds from the marketplace for $1,800 cash. The bonds were immediately retired. Journalize this transaction.

7. How do interest payments on bonds differ from dividend payments on preferred stock?

Demo Doc 2 Solutions

Requirement 1

Are these bonds issued at a discount or premium? How do you know?

Part 1	Part 2	Part 3	Part 4	Part 5	Part 6	Part 7	Part 8	Part 9	Part 10	Part 11	Demo Doc Complete

These bonds were issued at a **discount**. We know this because the cash received for the bonds is *less* than the maturity value and because the stated rate is *less* than the market rate.

8% stated rate < 10% market rate

Requirement 2

![1](account for bonds payable) Account for bonds payable

Journalize Red's issuance of the bonds on January 1, 2008.

Part 1	**Part 2**	Part 3	Part 4	Part 5	Part 6	Part 7	Part 8	Part 9	Part 10	Part 11	Demo Doc Complete

Cash is increased (a debit) by $1,930.

Bonds Payable is increased (a credit) by the bonds' *maturity* or face value of $2,000.

The difference between these two amounts is balanced to the Discount on Bonds Payable. The balancing amount is a debit of:

$2,000 − $1,930 = $70

	Cash	1,930	
	Discount on Bonds Payable (to balance)	70	
	Bonds Payable		2,000

Requirement 3

![1](account for bonds payable) Account for bonds payable

![2](measure interest expense) Measure interest expense by the straight-line amortization

Prepare Red's effective-interest amortization table for the entire life of the bonds payable.

Part 1	Part 2	**Part 3**	Part 4	Part 5	Part 6	Part 7	Part 8	Part 9	Part 10	Part 11	Demo Doc Complete

Interest Payment

The *cash interest payment is the same every interest period* and is calculated the same as under the straight-line method of amortization:

$$\text{Cash interest paid} = \frac{\text{Maturity value} \times \textbf{Stated rate}}{\text{Number of interest payments per year}}$$

The question states that the bonds are semiannual; that is, they pay interest twice per year.

$$\frac{\text{Cash interest}}{\text{paid}} = \frac{\$2,000 \times 8\%}{2}$$

$$= \$80$$

So every line in the Interest Payment column will show $80.

Part 1	Part 2	Part 3	**Part 4**	Part 5	Part 6	Part 7	Part 8	Part 9	Part 10	Part 11	Demo Doc Complete

Interest Expense

Under the effective-interest method, the interest expense is calculated as:

$$\frac{\text{Interest}}{\text{expense}} = \frac{\text{Carrying value} \times \textbf{Market rate}}{\text{Number of interest payments per year}}$$

The carrying value changes every time interest expense is recorded and the discount is amortized. This means that the *interest expense changes* as well.

The interest expense is calculated as:

06/30/08	$1,930 × 10%/2 = $96
12/31/08	$1,946 × 10%/2 = $97
06/30/09	$1,963 × 10%/2 = $98
12/31/09	$1,981 × 10%/2 = $99

Part 1	Part 2	Part 3	Part 4	**Part 5**	Part 6	Part 7	Part 8	Part 9	Part 10	Part 11	Demo Doc Complete

Discount Amortization

Under the effective-interest method, the *discount (or premium) is the balancing amount*. It is the difference between the cash interest payment and the interest expense.

The discount amortization is calculated as:

06/30/08	$96 − $80 = $16
12/31/08	$97 − $80 = $17
06/30/09	$98 − $80 = $18
12/31/09	$99 − $80 = $19

Discount Balance

The discount balance is the balance from the Discount T-account. By putting the discount amortization into the account, we can calculate the balance after each interest transaction.

Bond Discount

1/1/08	70		
		6/30/08	16
Bal.	54		
		12/31/08	17
Bal.	37		
		6/30/09	18
Bal.	19		
		12/31/09	19
Bal.	0		

Bond Carrying Value

The carrying value is the maturity value of the bonds combined with the discount (or premium).

The bonds' carrying value is calculated as the maturity value less the discount. After each interest period, this is:

01/01/08	$2,000 − $70 = $1,930
06/30/08	$2,000 − $54 = $1,946
12/31/08	$2,000 − $37 = $1,963
06/30/09	$2,000 − $19 = $1,981
12/31/09	$2,000 − $ 0 = $2,000

Combining all of this information into the amortization table, we get:

Date	Interest Payment	Interest Expense	Discount Amortization	Discount Balance	Bonds' Carrying Value
01/01/08				70	1,930
06/30/08	80	96	16	54	1,946
12/31/08	80	97	17	37	1,963
06/30/09	80	98	18	19	1,981
12/31/09	80	99	19	0	2,000

Requirement 4

Journalize Red's first two interest payments on June 30, 2008, and December 31, 2008.

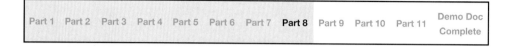

| Part 1 | Part 2 | Part 3 | Part 4 | Part 5 | Part 6 | Part 7 | **Part 8** | Part 9 | Part 10 | Part 11 | Demo Doc Complete |

June 30, 2008

Interest Expense is increased (a debit) by $96, as calculated in the table in Requirement 3.

Cash is decreased (a credit) by the cash interest paid of $80 (as calculated in Requirement 3).

The difference between these two amounts is balanced to Discount on Bonds Payable. The balancing amount is a credit of:

$$\$96 - \$80 = \$16$$

This is the discount amortization shown in Requirement 3.

Interest Expense (1,930 × 10%/2)	96	
Discount on Bonds Payable (to balance)		16
Cash (2,000 × 8%/2)		80

December 31, 2008

Interest Expense is increased (a debit) by $97, as calculated in the table in Requirement 3.

Cash is decreased (a credit) by the cash interest paid of $80 (as calculated in Requirement 3).

The difference between these two amounts is balanced to Discount on Bonds Payable. The balancing amount is a credit of:

$$\$97 - \$80 = \$17$$

This is the discount amortization shown in Requirement 3.

Interest Expense (1,946 × 10%/2)	97	
Discount on Bonds Payable (to balance)		17
Cash (2,000 × 8%/2)		80

Requirement 5

1 Account for bonds payable

3 Account for retirement and conversion of bonds payable

On January 2, 2009, 20% of the bonds were converted to 120 common shares with a $2 par value per share. Journalize this transaction.

Part 1	Part 2	Part 3	Part 4	Part 5	Part 6	Part 7	Part 8	**Part 9**	Part 10	Part 11	Demo Doc Complete

If 20% of the bonds are converted, then 20% of the maturity value is converted:

$$20\% \times \$2,000 = \$400$$

Also 20% of the discount is converted:

$$20\% \times \$37 = \$7$$

The bonds *will not exist* after the conversion, so the Bonds Payable account is decreased (a debit) by $400. The Discount on Bonds Payable is also decreased (a credit) by $7.

New common stock is issued for the conversion, so Common Stock is increased (a credit) by the par value of the new shares:

$$120 \times \$2 = \$240$$

The remainder is balanced to Additional Paid-In Capital. The balancing amount is:

$$\$400 - \$7 - \$240 = \$153$$

Bonds Payable ($2,000 × 20%)	400	
Discount on Bonds Payable ($37 × 20%)		7
Additional Paid-In Capital (to balance)		153
Common Stock (120 × $2)		240

Bond Discount					Bonds Payable		
Bal.	0					Bal.	0
Jan. 1	70					Jan. 1	2,000
		June 30	16	Jan. 2	400		
		Dec. 31	17			Bal.	1,600
		Jan. 2	7				
Bal.	30						

Requirement 6

1 Account for bonds payable

3 Account for retirement and conversion of bonds payable

On January 3, 2009, Red purchased the remaining bonds from the marketplace for $1,800 cash. The bonds were immediately retired. Journalize this transaction.

Part 1	Part 2	Part 3	Part 4	Part 5	Part 6	Part 7	Part 8	Part 9	**Part 10**	Part 11	Demo Doc Complete

Because 20% of the bonds were converted to common stock, $100\% - 20\% = 80\%$ remained. These bonds will be retired.

If 80% of the bonds are retired, then 80% of the maturity value is retired:

$$80\% \times \$2,000 = \$1,600$$

Also 80% of the discount is retired:

$$80\% \times \$37 = \$30$$

The bonds *will not exist* after retirement, so the Bonds Payable account is decreased (a debit) by $1,600. The Discount is also decreased (a credit) by $30.

Cash is decreased (a credit) by $1,800.

The remainder is balanced to a gain or loss. In this case, the balancing amount is a debit, so there is a *loss* of:

$$\$1,800 + \$30 - \$1,600 = \$230$$

Bonds Payable ($2,000 × 80%)	1,600	
Loss on Retirement (to balance)	230	
Discount on Bonds Payable (80% × $37)		30
Cash		1,800

Requirement 7

5 Show the advantages and disadvantages of borrowing

How do interest payments on bonds differ from dividend payments on preferred stock?

Part 1	Part 2	Part 3	Part 4	Part 5	Part 6	Part 7	Part 8	Part 9	Part 10	**Part 11**	Demo Doc Complete

If a company chooses to issue bonds instead of preferred stock, it will have a higher earnings-per-share ratio as a result.

However, large interest payments (and principal payments when the bonds mature) can lead to bankruptcy if the company is unable to pay off the debt.

Part 1	Part 2	Part 3	Part 4	Part 5	Part 6	Part 7	Part 8	Part 9	Part 10	Part 11	**Demo Doc Complete**

Quick Practice Questions

True/False

_____ 1. The journal entry to record selling $200,000 face value bonds at 98 will involve a credit to Bonds Payable for $196,000.

_____ 2. When a bond is issued at a discount, the discount has the effect of raising the interest expense on the bonds to the market rate of interest.

_____ 3. The carrying value of bonds will decrease each interest period if the bonds were sold at a discount.

_____ 4. The amount of discount amortized under the effective-interest method is the same amount each period.

_____ 5. Callable bonds give the issuer the benefit of being able to take advantage of low interest rates by paying off bonds whenever it is favorable to do so.

_____ 6. If convertible bonds were issued at a discount, the Discount on Bonds Payable must be credited when converting the bonds into common stock.

_____ 7. When reporting serial bonds on the balance sheet, the portion maturing within one year is shown as a current liability.

_____ 8. Earning more income on borrowed money than the related interest expense increases the earnings for common stockholders and is called using leverage.

_____ 9. Issuing bonds instead of stock generally is less risky to a corporation.

_____ 10. Bondholders are creditors of a corporation.

Multiple Choice

1. On January 2, 2008, Lot Corporation issues $200,000 face value, 6% bonds for $196,000. What can be concluded about the effective (market) rate of interest?
   a. It is less than 6%.
   b. It is more than 6%.
   c. It is equal to 6%.
   d. It is impossible to determine from the given data.

2. Dalton Corporation issues 50, $1,000 face value, 10% bonds at 102.5. The journal entry includes which of the following?
   a. A debit to Cash for $50,000
   b. A credit to Premium on Bonds Payable for $1,250
   c. A debit to Discount on Bonds Payable for $1,250
   d. A credit to Bonds Payable for $51,250

3. Jones Corporation issues $400,000, 10%, 5-year bonds at 103. What is the total *interest expense* over the life of the bonds?
   a. $40,000
   b. $188,000
   c. $200,000
   d. $212,000

4. What are bonds issued on the general credit of the issuing corporation called?
   a. Serial bonds
   b. Term bonds
   c. Debenture bonds
   d. Convertible bonds

5. What are bonds called when the maturities are spread over several dates?
   a. Term bonds
   b. Debenture bonds
   c. Serial bonds
   d. Callable bonds

6. What is the interest rate specified in the bond indenture called?
   a. Stated rate
   b. Discount rate
   c. Yield rate
   d. Effective rate

7. Which of the following statements about the discount on bonds payable is correct?
   a. It is added to bonds payable on the balance sheet.
   b. It is a contra asset.
   c. It is amortized over the life of the bonds.
   d. Both (b) and (c) are correct.

8. How is interest expense calculated under the effective-interest method of amortization?
   a. The market rate times the carrying value of the bonds
   b. The market rate times the face value of the bonds
   c. The stated rate times the carrying value of the bonds
   d. The stated rate times the face value of the bonds

9. A bond issued with a face value of $200,000 and a carrying amount of $195,500 is paid off at 98 1/2 and retired. What is the gain or loss on this transaction?
   a. $1,500 loss
   b. $1,500 gain
   c. $3,000 loss
   d. $3,000 gain

10. All *except* which of the following is an advantage of issuing stock?
    a. It is less risky to the issuing corporation.
    b. It creates no liabilities.
    c. It generally results in higher earnings per share.
    d. It creates no interest expense that must be paid.

Quick Exercises

15-1. For each of the following independent situations, state whether the bonds were issued at a premium, at a discount, or at par.

  a. Bonds with a face value of $50,000 were issued for $53,000.
  b. Bonds with a contract rate of 8% were issued to yield 7.5%.
  c. Bonds with a face value of $75,000 were issued for $75,000.
  d. Bonds with a contract rate of 8.25% were issued to yield 8.75%.
  e. Bonds with a face value of $110,000 were issued for $106,000.

15-2. Fox Corporation issued 10-year, 10%, $1,000,000 bonds on January 1, 2008. The bonds pay interest every June 30 and December 31. The bonds were issued for $1,065,000. Fox Corporation uses straight-line amortization for any discount or premium amortization.

Requirements

1. Journalize the following:

  a. Issue the bonds on January 1, 2008.
  b. Record the interest payment and amortize the premium or discount on June 30, 2008.

General Journal				
Date	Accounts		Debit	Credit

General Journal				
Date	Accounts		Debit	Credit

2. What is the carrying value of the bonds on June 30, 2008?

15-3. On April 1, 2008, Needy Corporation issued $3,000,000 of 8%, 10-year bonds dated April 1, 2008, with interest payments made each October 1 and April 1. The bonds are issued at 95. Needy Corporation amortizes any premium or discount using the straight-line method.

Requirement

1. Journalize the following transactions:

a. April 1, 2008, issue the bonds.

b. October 1, 2008, record the payment of interest and the amortization of any discount or premium.

c. December 31, 2008, record accrued interest and the amortization of any premium or discount.

General Journal			
Date	Accounts	Debit	Credit

General Journal			
Date	Accounts	Debit	Credit

General Journal			
Date	Accounts	Debit	Credit

15-4. Cary Corporation issued $800,000 of 9.5%, 8-year bonds on June 1, 2008. Interest is paid semiannually on December 1 and June 1 of each year. On the issuance date, the market rate of interest was 8.5%, resulting in a price of 103 1/2 for these bonds. The effective-interest method of amortizing the premium or discount is used.

Requirements

1. Journalize the following transactions:

a. June 1, 2008, issue the bonds.

b. December 1, 2008, record the first interest payment and the amortization of the premium.

c. Prepare the adjusting entry on December 31, 2008.

General Journal			
Date	Accounts	Debit	Credit

General Journal			
Date	Accounts	Debit	Credit

General Journal			
Date	Accounts	Debit	Credit

15-5.   Apex Corporation issued $500,000, callable, 10%, 10-year bonds at 93 on January 2, 2008. The bonds are callable at 102 anytime after January 2, 2010. On December 31, 2011, Apex Corporation calls the entire issuance.

Requirements

1. Compute the balance in the Premium or Discount account on December 31, 2011. Apex Corporation uses the straight-line method of amortization.

2. Prepare the entry to call the bonds on December 31, 2011.

General Journal			
Date	Accounts	Debit	Credit

Do It Yourself! Question 1

Bonds Payable (straight-line amortization)

Circle Inc. issued $20,000 maturity value of bonds payable for $19,337 cash on January 1, 2008. The bonds had a stated rate of 14%, but the market rate was 16%. Interest is paid semiannually and the bonds are due in two years.

Circle uses the straight-line method of amortization.

Requirements

1. Are these bonds issued at a discount or premium?

Account for bonds payable

2. Journalize Circle's issuance of the bonds on January 1, 2008.

General Journal				
Date	Accounts		Debit	Credit

Account for bonds payable

3. Journalize Circle's first two interest payments on June 30, 2008, and December 31, 2008.

General Journal				
Date	Accounts		Debit	Credit

General Journal				
Date	Accounts		Debit	Credit

Report liabilities on the balance sheet

4. Show how the bonds would appear on Circle's December 31, 2008, balance sheet.

1 Account for bonds payable

5. On January 2, 2009, 25% of the bonds were converted to 9,000 common shares with a $0.50 par value per share. Journalize this transaction.

3 Account for retirement and conversion of bonds payable

General Journal				
Date	Accounts		Debit	Credit

1 Account for bonds payable

6. On January 3, 2009, Circle purchased the remaining bonds from the marketplace for $14,000 cash. The bonds were immediately retired. Journalize this transaction.

3 Account for retirement and conversion of bonds payable

General Journal				
Date	Accounts		Debit	Credit

Do It Yourself! Question 2

Bonds Payable (effective-interest amortization)

Square Corp. issued $10,000 maturity value of bonds payable for $10,346 cash on January 1, 2008. The bonds had a stated rate of 14% but the market rate was 12%. Interest is paid semiannually and the bonds are due in two years.

Square Corp. uses the effective-interest method of amortization.

Requirements

1. Are these bonds issued at a discount or premium?

1 Account for bonds payable

2 Measure interest expense by the straight-line amortization.

2. Journalize Square's issuance of the bonds on January 1, 2008.

General Journal				
Date	Accounts		Debit	Credit

1 Account for bonds payable

2 Measure interest expense by the straight-line amortization

3. Prepare Square's effective-interest amortization table for the entire life of the bonds payable.

<table>
<tr><td>1</td><td>Account for bonds payable</td></tr>
</table>

4. Journalize Square's first two interest payments on June 30, 2008, and December 31, 2008.

<table>
<tr><td>2</td><td>Measure interest expense by the straight-line amortization</td></tr>
</table>

General Journal				
Date	Accounts		Debit	Credit

General Journal				
Date	Accounts		Debit	Credit

<table>
<tr><td>1</td><td>Account for bonds payable</td></tr>
</table>

5. On January 2, 2009, 50% of the bonds were converted to 3,000 common shares with a $1.50 par value per share. Journalize this transaction.

<table>
<tr><td>3</td><td>Account for retirement and conversion of bonds payable</td></tr>
</table>

General Journal				
Date	Accounts		Debit	Credit

<table>
<tr><td>1</td><td>Account for bonds payable</td></tr>
</table>

6. On January 3, 2009, Square purchased the remaining bonds from the marketplace for $6,000 cash. The bonds were immediately retired. Journalize this transaction.

<table>
<tr><td>3</td><td>Account for retirement and conversion of bonds payable</td></tr>
</table>

General Journal				
Date	Accounts		Debit	Credit

Quick Practice Solutions

True/False

F   1. The journal entry to record selling $200,000 face value bonds at 98 will involve a credit to Bonds Payable for $196,000.

     False—The journal entry to record selling $200,000 face value bonds at 98 will involve a credit to Bonds Payable for *$200,000.* (p. 738)

T   2. When a bond is issued at a discount, the discount has the effect of raising the interest expense on the bonds to the market rate of interest. (p. 738)

F   3. The carrying value of bonds will decrease each interest period if the bonds were sold at a discount.

     False—The carrying value of bonds will *increase* each interest period if the bonds were sold at a discount. (p. 739)

F   4. The amount of discount amortized each period under the effective-interest method is the same amount each period.

     False—The amount of discount amortized each period under the effective-interest method is a *different amount* each period. The *rate* of interest to calculate the amount of discount amortized each period is the same. (p. 771)

T   5. Callable bonds give the issuer the benefit of being able to take advantage of low interest rates by paying off bonds whenever it is favorable to do so. (p. 747)

T   6. If convertible bonds were issued at a discount, the Discount on Bonds Payable must be credited when converting the bonds into common stock. (p. 747)

T   7. When reporting serial bonds on the balance sheet, the portion maturing within one year is shown as a current liability. (p. 748)

T   8. Earning more income on borrowed money than the related interest expense increases the earnings for common stockholders and is called using leverage. (p. 749)

F   9. Issuing bonds instead of stock generally is less risky to a corporation.

     False—Issuing bonds instead of stock generally is *more* risky to a corporation. (p. 748)

T 10. Bondholders are creditors of a corporation. (p. 734)

Multiple Choice

1. On January 2, 2008, Lot Corporation issues $200,000 face value, 6% bonds for $196,000. What can be concluded about the effective (market) rate of interest? (p. 743)
   a. It is less than 6%.
   b. It is more than 6%.
   c. It is equal to 6%.
   d. It is impossible to determine from the given data.

2. Dalton Corporation issues 50, $1,000 face value, 10% bonds at 102.5. The journal entry includes which of the following? (p. 743)
   a. A debit to Cash for $50,000
   b. A credit to Premium on Bonds Payable for $1,250
   c. A debit to Discount on Bonds Payable for $1,250
   d. A credit to Bonds Payable for $51,250

3. Jones Corporation issues $400,000, 10%, 5-year bonds at 103. What is the total *interest expense* over the life of the bonds? (p. 743)
   a. $40,000
   b. $188,000
   c. $200,000
   d. $212,000

4. What are bonds issued on the general credit of the issuing corporation called? (p. 735)
   a. Serial bonds
   b. Term bonds
   c. Debenture bonds
   d. Convertible bonds

5. What are bonds called when the maturities are spread over several dates? (p. 734)
   a. Term bonds
   b. Debenture bonds
   c. Serial bonds
   d. Callable bonds

6. What is the interest rate specified in the bond indenture called? (p. 734)
   a. Stated rate
   b. Discount rate
   c. Yield rate
   d. Effective rate

7. Which of the following statements about the discount on bonds payable is correct? (p. 739)
   a. It is added to bonds payable on the balance sheet.
   b. It is a contra asset.
   c. It is amortized over the life of the bonds.
   d. Both (b) and (c) are correct.

8. How is interest expense calculated under the effective-interest method of amortization? (p. 771)
   a. The market rate times the carrying value of the bonds
   b. The market rate times the face value of the bonds
   c. The stated rate times the carrying value of the bonds
   d. The stated rate times the face value of the bonds

9. A bond issued with a face value of $200,000 and a carrying amount of $195,500 is paid off at 98 1/2 and retired. What is the gain or loss on this transaction? (p. 746)
   a. $1,500 loss
   b. $1,500 gain
   c. $3,000 loss
   d. $3,000 gain

10. All *except* which of the following is an advantage of issuing stock? (p. 748)
    a. It is less risky to the issuing corporation.
    b. It creates no liabilities.
    c. It generally results in higher earnings per share.
    d. It creates no interest expense that must be paid.

Quick Exercises

15-1. For each of the following independent situations, state whether the bonds were issued at a premium, at a discount, or at par. (p. 735)

   a. Bonds with a face value of $50,000 were issued for $53,000. Premium
   b. Bonds with a contract rate of 8% were issued to yield 7.5%. Premium
   c. Bonds with a face value of $75,000 were issued for $75,000. Par
   d. Bonds with a contract rate of 8.25% were issued to yield 8.75%. Discount
   e. Bonds with a face value of $110,000 were issued for $106,000. Discount

15-2. Fox Corporation issued 10-year, 10%, $1,000,000 bonds on January 1, 2008. The bonds pay interest every June 30 and December 31. The bonds were issued for $1,065,000. Fox Corporation uses straight-line amortization for any discount or premium amortization. (p. 743)

Requirements

1. Journalize the following:

   a. Issue the bonds on January 1, 2008.
   b. Record the interest payment and amortize the premium or discount on June 30, 2008.

General Journal			
Date	Accounts	Debit	Credit
Jan. 1	Cash	1,065,000	
	Bonds Payable		1,000,000
	Premium on Bonds Payable		65,000

General Journal			
Date	Accounts	Debit	Credit
June 30	Interest Expense	46,750	
	Premium on Bonds Payable	3,250	
	Cash		50,000

2. What is the carrying value of the bonds on June 30, 2008?

Carrying value = $1,000,000 + ($65,000 − $3,250) = $1,061,750.

15-3. On April 1, 2008, Needy Corporation issued $3,000,000 of 8%, 10-year bonds dated April 1, 2008, with interest payments made each October 1 and April 1. The bonds are issued at 95. Needy Corporation amortizes any premium or discount using the straight-line method. (p. 738)

Requirement

1. Journalize the following transactions:

a. April 1, 2008, issue the bonds.

b. October 1, 2008, record the payment of interest and the amortization of any discount or premium.

c. December 31, 2008, record accrued interest and the amortization of any premium or discount.

General Journal			
Date	Accounts	Debit	Credit
Apr. 1	Cash	2,850,000	
	Discount on Bonds Payable	150,000	
	Bonds Payable		3,000,000

General Journal			
Date	Accounts	Debit	Credit
Oct. 1	Interest Expense	127,500	
	Discount on Bonds Payable		7,500
	Cash		120,000

General Journal			
Date	Accounts	Debit	Credit
Dec. 31	Interest Expense	63,750	
	Discount on Bonds Payable		3,750
	Interest Payable		60,000

Calculations:

a. $3,000,000 × 0.95 = $2,850,000
   $3,000,000 − $2,850,000 = $150,000
b. $3,000,000 × 0.08 × 6/12 = $120,000
   $150,000 × 6/120 months = $7,500
c. $3,000,000 × 0.08 × 3/12 = $60,000
   $150,000 × 3/120 months = $3,750

15-4. Cary Corporation issued $800,000 of 9.5%, 8-year bonds on June 1, 2008. Interest is paid semiannually on December 1 and June 1 of each year. On the issuance date, the market rate of interest was 8.5%, resulting in a price of 103 1/2 for these bonds. The effective-interest method of amortizing the premium or discount is used. (p. 743)

Requirement

1. Journalize the following transactions:

a. June 1, 2008, issue the bonds.

b. December 1, 2008, record the first interest payment and the amortization of the premium.

c. Prepare the adjusting entry on December 31, 2008.

General Journal			
Date	Accounts	Debit	Credit
June 1	Cash	828,000	
	Bonds Payable		800,000
	Premium on Bonds Payable		28,000

General Journal			
Date	Accounts	Debit	Credit
Dec. 1	Interest Expense	35,190	
	Premium on Bonds Payable	2,810	38,000
	Cash		

General Journal			
Date	Accounts	Debit	Credit
Dec. 31	Interest Expense	5,845	
	Premium on Bonds Payable	488	
	Interest Payable		6,333

Calculations:

    a. $800,000 × 0.1035 = $828,000
    b. $800,000 × 0.095 × 6/12 = $38,000
       $800,000 + $28,000 = $828,000
       $828,000 × 0.085 × 6/12 = $35,190
    c. $800,000 × 0.095 × 1/12 = 6,333
       $800,000 + $28,000 − $2,810 = $825,190
       $825,190 × 0.085 × 1/2 = $5,845

15-5. Apex Corporation issued $500,000, 10%, 10-year bonds at 93 on January 2, 2008. The bonds are callable at 102 anytime after January 2, 2010. On December 31, 2011, Apex Corporation calls the entire issuance. (p. 746)

Requirement 1

Compute the balance in the Premium or Discount account on December 31, 2011. Apex Corporation uses the straight-line method of amortization.

1. $500,000 × 0.93 = $465,000

$500,000 − $465,000 = $35,000 discount

$35,000/10 years = $3,500 annual amortization of discount

$3,500 × 4 years = $14,000 amortized discount as of December 31, 2011

$35,000 − $14,000 = $21,000 unamortized discount as of December 31, 2011

Requirement 2

2. Prepare the entry to call the bonds on December 31, 2011.

	General Journal			
Date	Accounts		Debit	Credit
2011				
Dec. 31	Bonds Payable		500,000	
	Loss on Retirement of Bonds Payable		31,000	
	($500,000 + $21,000 − $510,000)			
	Discount on Bonds Payable			21,000
	Cash ($500,000 × 102%)			510,000

Do It Yourself! Question 1 Solutions

Bonds Payable (straight-line amortization)

Requirements

1. Are these bonds issued at a discount or premium?

These bonds were issued at a **discount.**

2. Journalize Circle's issuance of the bonds on January 1, 2008.

Cash	19,337	
Discount on Bonds Payable (to balance)	663	
Bonds Payable		20,000

3. Journalize Circle's first two interest payments on June 30, 2008, and December 31, 2008.

The entry for both June 30, 2008 and December 31, 2008 would be the same:

Interest Expense	1,566	
Discount on Bonds Payable ($663/4)		166
Cash $(20,000 \times 14\%/2)$		1,400

4. Show how the bonds would appear on Circle's December 31, 2008, balance sheet.

Bonds payable	$20,000
less Discount	(331)
Bonds payable (net)	$19,669

5. On January 2, 2009, 25% of the bonds were converted to 9,000 common shares with a $0.50 par value per share. Journalize this transaction.

Immediately before this transaction, the discount had a balance of $331.50:

Bond Discount

Bal.	0		
Jan. 1	663		
		June 30	166
		Dec. 31	166
Bal.	331.50		

Bonds Payable ($20,000 × 25%)	5,000	
Discount on Bonds Payable ($331 × 25%)		83
Additional Paid-In Capital (to balance)		417
Common Stock (9,000 × $0.50)		4,500

6. On January 3, 2009, Circle purchased the remaining bonds from the marketplace for $14,000 cash. The bonds were immediately retired. Journalize this transaction.

Bonds Payable ($20,000 × 75%)	15,000	
Gain on Retirement (to balance)		752
Discount on Bonds Payable (75% × 331)		248
Cash		14,000

Do It Yourself! Question 2 Solutions

Bonds Payable (effective-interest amortization)

Requirements

1. Are these bonds issued at a discount or premium?

These bonds were issued at a **premium**.

2. Journalize Square's issuance of the bonds on January 1, 2008.

Cash		10,346	
Premium on Bonds Payable (to balance)			346
Bonds Payable			10,000

3. Prepare Square's effective-interest amortization table for the entire life of the bonds payable.

Date	Interest Payment	Interest Expense	Premium Amortization	Premium Balance	Bonds' Carrying Value
01/01/08				346	10,346
06/30/80	700	621	79	267	10,267
12/31/08	700	617	83	184	10,184
06/30/09	700	611	89	95	10,095
12/31/09	700	605	95	0	10,000

4. Journalize Square's first two interest payments on June 30, 2008, and December 31, 2008.

June 30, 2008

Interest Expense (10,346 × 12%/2)	621	
Premium on Bonds Payable (to balance)	79	
Cash (10,000 × 14%/2)		700

December 31, 2008

Interest Expense (10,267 × 12%/2)	617	
Premium on Bonds Payable (to balance)	83	
Cash (10,000 × 14%/2)		700

5. On January 2, 2009, 50% of the bonds were converted to 3,000 common shares with a $1.50 par value per share. Journalize this transaction.

Bonds Payable ($10,000 × 50%)	5,000	
Premium on Bonds Payable ($184 × 50%)	92	
Additional Paid-In Capital (to balance)		592
Common Stock (3,000 × $1.50)		4,500

6. On January 3, 2009, the remaining bonds were purchased by Square from the marketplace for $6,000 cash. The bonds were immediately retired. Journalize this transaction.

Bonds Payable ($10,000 × 50%)	5,000	
Premium on Bonds Payable (50% × $184)	92	
Loss on Retirement (to balance)	908	
Cash		6,000

The Power of Practice

For more practice using the skills learned in this chapter, visit MyAccountingLab. There you will find algorithmically generated questions that are based on these Demo Docs and your main textbook's Review and Assess Your Progress sections.

Go to MyAccountingLab and follow these steps:

1. Direct your URL to www.myaccountinglab.com.
2. Log in using your name and password.
3. Click the MyAccountingLab link.
4. Click Study Plan in the left navigation bar.
5. From the table of contents, select Chapter 15, Long-Term Liabilities.
6. Click a link to work tutorial exercises.

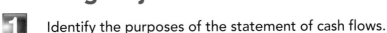

16 Statement of Cash Flows

WHAT YOU PROBABLY ALREADY KNOW

If you find yourself short of cash occasionally, it is not uncommon to wonder where all of the money has gone. You probably already know that you need to keep track of all cash received and spent for a period of time to find out the answer. Not only does that show you the *amount* of money coming in and going out, but you would also identify the *source* of the cash received and the *use* of the cash spent. Identifying the cash activities in your life helps you to predict your future cash flows based on past history, review the decisions you have made in your financial life that result in the creation and disbursement of cash, and assess your ability to meet future financial obligations. The same issues are important to a business. In this chapter, we will see how the statement of cash flows provides this information for an entity.

Learning Objectives

1 Identify the purposes of the statement of cash flows.

The statement of cash flows helps to:

- Predict future cash flows. Recall from Chapter 15 the concept of income from continuing operations and special items. Those results are used to make predictions about the future.
- Evaluate management decisions. The cash-flow result of management's decisions is reflected in the statement of cash flows.
- Predict ability to pay debts and dividends. Investors and creditors will review past cash flows to assess the risk of nonpayment of debt and dividends.

2 Distinguish among operating, investing, and financing cash flows.

The statement of cash flows includes all transactions that increase or decrease Cash. These items are included in one of the following three categories:

- **Operating**—Activities that affect the income statement and current assets and current liabilities on the balance sheet. These transactions include inflows such as cash receipts from customers, interest, and dividends. Outflows include cash paid to employees and suppliers. *It is most important to have a positive net cash inflow for this activity.*

- **Investing**—Activities that affect long-term assets. These transactions include cash inflows from the sale of plant, property, and equipment; investments; and the collection from long-term loans. Outflows include the cash payment to purchase plant, property, and equipment; make investments; and make loans.
- **Financing**—Activities that affect long-term liabilities and owners' equity. These transactions include cash inflows from the sale of stock and issuance of long-term debt. Cash outflows include the payment of dividends and the repayment of debt.

Refer to Exhibit 16-2 (p. 786) for the relationship between the activity categories and the balance sheet classifications.

 Prepare the statement of cash flows by the indirect method.

The **indirect method** reconciles from net income on the income statement to cash from operating activities. The schedule begins with accrual-basis net income and identifies the adjustments or items of difference to convert from the accrual basis of accounting to a cash basis for operating activities. Some of the adjustments include:

- Eliminating such noncash expenses as depreciation, depletion, and amortization—these expenses need to be added to net income to eliminate the expense from net income.
- Eliminating the gains or losses included in net income—gains need to be deducted from net income and losses need to be added to net income to eliminate these from net income. The full proceeds of sale are included as an investing activity.
- Changes in the current assets and current liabilities—review the "Changes in the Current Assets and the Current Liabilities" section in the main text for the rules. Review the rationale for the rules.

This can be a challenging concept. Review carefully the "Cash Flows from Operating Activities" section of the main text and Exhibit 16-7 (p. 791).

 Prepare the statement of cash flows by the direct method (Appendix A).

The **direct method** lists the amount of cash receipts and cash payments from operating activities by major category. The FASB recommends the direct method, but most corporations use the indirect method, which requires less work. *Review the direct method of presenting operating activities in Exhibit 16A-1 (p. 828).*

Demo Doc 1

Statement of Cash Flows (Indirect Method)

Learning Objectives 2, 3

Indirect Method

Tanker Inc. had the following information at December 31, 2008:

TANKER INC.
Balance Sheet
December 31, 2008

Assets	2008	2007	Change	Liabilities	2008	2007	Change
Current:				Current:			
Cash	$ 700	$1,160	$(460)	Accounts payable	$ 680	$ 530	$150
Accounts receivable	300	420	(120)				
Inventory	800	750	50	Long-term notes payable	660	815	
Prepaid insurance	120	90	30				
				Total liabilities	$1,340	$1,345	
Furniture	1,500	1,400					
Less acc. depn.	(400)	(475)		Owners' Equity			
Net	1,100	925		Common stock (no par)	$1,800	$1,800	
				Retained earnings	880	200	
Total assets	$3,020	$3,345		Less treasury stock	(1,000)	0	
				Total equity	$1,680	$2,000	
				Total liabilities and equity	$3,020	$3,345	

TANKER INC.
Income Statement
Year Ended December 31, 2008

Sales revenue	$3,400
Less cost of goods sold	(1,750)
Gross margin	$1,650
Depreciation expense	$ (110)
Insurance expense	(230)
Other operating expenses	(390)
Gain on sale of furniture	80
Net income	$1,000

Other Information

- Every year, Tanker declares and pays cash dividends.
- During 2008, Tanker sold old furniture for $90 cash. Tanker also bought new furniture by making a cash down payment and signing a $200 note payable.
- During 2008, Tanker repaid $500 of notes payable in cash and borrowed new long-term notes payable for cash.
- During 2008, Tanker purchased treasury stock for cash. No treasury stock was sold.

Requirement

1. Prepare Tanker's statement of cash flows for the year ended December 31, 2008, using the indirect method.

Demo Doc 1 Solution

Requirement 1

2 Distinguish among operating, investing, and financing cash flows

3 Prepare the statement of cash flows by the indirect method

Prepare Tanker's statement of cash flows for the year ended December 31, 2008.

Part 1	Part 2	Part 3	Demo Doc Complete

Operating Activities

We first set up the statement of cash flows with the proper title and then start with operating activities.

Net Income

The first item is net income. Because net income is positive, it is added to the Cash balance. Therefore, we add (that is, positive number) $1,000 on our cash-flow statement.

Depreciation Expense

Net income includes depreciation expense, which must be removed because it is a 100% noncash item. Remember, no cash was "spent" for depreciation, yet it was still deducted to arrive at the net income number. Because depreciation expense was *subtracted* to calculate net income, we *add* it back to remove it.

Gain on Sale of Furniture

After depreciation, we must look for gains and losses on disposal of long-term assets. These are treated in a manner similar to the depreciation. No cash was "earned" for the gain, yet it was still added to arrive at the net income number. The gain on sale of furniture was *added* to calculate net income, so we *subtract* it to remove it.

Accounts Receivable

After looking at net income and the depreciation and gain adjustments, we need to incorporate the changes in current assets and current liabilities.

The increases and decreases in these accounts do not tell us whether to add or subtract these items on the cash-flow statement.

The first current asset (other than cash) is Accounts Receivable. On the balance sheet we see:

Assets	2008	2007	Change
Current:			
Cash	$700	$1,160	$(460)
Accounts receivable	300	420	(120)

We must add the $120 decrease in Accounts Receivable. There are two ways to reason this out:

1. Accounts Receivable went down. Why? Tanker is collecting more of the cash that its customers owe. How does this affect Cash? It increases Cash; therefore, we should add the number on the cash-flow statement.

2. Accounts Receivable went down. This is a decrease in an asset, which is a credit. If this credit is balanced out by the Cash account, that would be a debit to Cash, which is an increase. If Cash is increased, we should add the number on the cash-flow statement.

Notice that in both of these cases, we are adding or subtracting on the cash-flow statement because of the item's effect on *cash flow*. *It doesn't matter if Accounts Receivable went up or down; what matters is how that affects cash flow.*

Inventory

Let's try the two ways with the next current asset: Inventory. On the balance sheet, we see:

Assets	2008	2007	Change
Current:			
Cash	$700	$1,160	$(460)
Accounts receivable	300	420	(120)
Inventory	800	750	50

During the year, Inventory increased by $50.

1. Why did Inventory increase? Tanker is purchasing inventory with cash. Therefore, this has a negative effect on cash flow.

2. If Inventory increased, this is an increase in an asset, which is a debit. If this is balanced out by Cash, then Cash is credited, which is a negative effect on cash flow.

Prepaid Insurance

The last current asset is Prepaid Insurance. On the balance sheet, we see:

Assets	2008	2007	Change
Current:			
Cash	$700	$1,160	$(460)
Accounts receivable	300	420	(120)
Inventory	800	750	50
Prepaid insurance	120	90	30

During the year, Prepaid Insurance increased by $30.

1. Why did Prepaid Insurance increase? Tanker paid more insurance costs in advance. This has a negative effect on cash flow.

2. If Prepaid Insurance is increased, this is an increase in an asset, which is a debit. If this is balanced out by Cash, then Cash is credited, which is a negative effect on cash flow.

Accounts Payable

The last part of operating activities is to look at the changes in current liabilities. The only current liability in this question is Accounts Payable. On the balance sheet, we see:

Liabilities	2008	2007	Change
Current:			
Accounts payable	$680	$530	$150

During the year, Accounts Payable increased by $150.

1. Why did Accounts Payable increase? Tanker is not paying all of its bills. This means that it is holding onto its cash, which is a positive effect on cash flow.

2. If Accounts Payable increased, this is an increase in a liability, which is a credit. If this is balanced out by Cash, then Cash is debited, which is a positive effect on cash flow.

We total these numbers, and we are finished with operating activities. The completed operating activities section would appear as:

Operating Activities	
Net income	$1,000
Depreciation expense	110
Gain on sale of furniture	(80)
Decrease in accounts receivable	120
Increase in inventory	(50)
Increase in prepaid insurance	(30)
Increase in accounts payable	150
Total cash flow provided by operating activities	$1,220

Investing Activities

2 Distinguish among operating, investing, and financing cash flows

3 Prepare the statement of cash flows by the indirect method

Part 1	**Part 2**	Part 3	Demo Doc Complete

Investing activities looks at cash purchases and cash disposals of long-term assets. This means that we need to know how much cash was paid to purchase new furniture and how much cash was received when Tanker sold some of the old furniture. Do we have any of these numbers right away? Yes, we are told in the question that Tanker signed a $200 note payable to purchase new furniture. We also know that the old furniture was sold for $90 cash.

Before we do anything else, we should point out that the $200 note payable is a <u>noncash transaction</u>. Although we will *need* to use it in our analysis, it will *not* appear on the main body of the cash-flow statement. Instead, it will appear in a note for noncash investing and financing activities:

Noncash Investing and Financing Activities	
Purchase of furniture with note payable	$200

We need to calculate the *cash* Tanker paid to purchase new furniture. To do this, we need to analyze the Furniture (Net) T-account:

Furniture (Net)

Bal. 12/31/07	925		
	increases	decreases	
Bal. 12/31/08	1,100		

We know that the Furniture (Net) account increased and decreased. What caused that account to increase? Well, it would increase if Tanker bought new furniture. So obviously the cash paid *and* the note signed for new furniture went into this account.

What would cause the Furniture (Net) account to decrease?

If Tanker sold furniture, we would decrease the account, *but* it would be decreased by the *book* value (that is, the *net* amount) of the furniture sold. Remember, the book value is another term for *net* value. We are looking at net value in the T-account, so the Furniture (Net) account decreases by its *net/book* value.

We know that some furniture was sold, so obviously this decrease occurred.

We know that this furniture was sold for $90 cash, but this is *not* the net book value (NBV) of the furniture sold. This amount is still unknown.

However, we can calculate this amount using the gain/loss formula:

Gain or loss on sale of fixed assets

= Cash received on sale of fixed assets
− NBV of fixed assets sold

For this example, this becomes:

Gain on sale of furniture

= Cash received on sale of furniture
− NBV of furniture sold

So: $80 = $90 2 NBV of furniture sold.
Therefore, the NBV of furniture sold is $10.

What else would decrease Furniture (Net)? Well, when Tanker takes depreciation expense, don't we decrease the net value of its assets? We know from the income statement that depreciation expense is $110. Let's now put all of the numbers in and see what comes out:

Furniture (Net)

Bal. 12/31/07	925		
Cash Purchases	X		
Noncash Purchases	200		
		NBV Furniture Sold	10
		Depreciation Expense	110
Bal. 12/31/08	1,100		

So X = Cash paid to purchase furniture = $95.

To summarize, this is how we find missing information for long-term assets:

1. Set up a T-account for the net value of the asset.

2. Fill in as much information as you can in the T-account (such as beginning and ending balances, depreciation expense, and purchases or net book value of disposals).

3. Solve for any missing information.

4. If there is more than one number missing, or if the missing information is not the number you need, use the gain/loss formula to calculate any remaining information.

Now we can put our two numbers, $90 and $95, into the statement of cash flows. *Cash* purchases of equipment were $95. Did this cause Cash to increase or decrease? Obviously, it is a decrease because Tanker *paid* cash, so we will subtract it. Cash received on sale of equipment is $90, which is an increase to Cash, so we will add it.

Remember that for investing activities, we *cannot* combine these two items. They *must* be listed separately because they are two separate transactions.

Totaling these numbers completes investing activities.

The completed investing activities section would appear as:

Investing Activities	
Cash paid to purchase new furniture	$(95)
Cash proceeds from sale of furniture	90
Total cash flow provided by investing activities	$ (5)

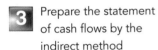

Financing Activities

Part 1	Part 2	**Part 3**	Demo Doc Complete

Financing activities deals with long-term liabilities (debt) and equity accounts. First, we will look at long-term liabilities.

There are new notes payable (for which Tanker received cash) and Tanker repaid some other notes.

Notes Payable

We need the cash numbers involved so that we can put them into the cash-flow statement. Do we have any of them immediately available to us?

Yes, we are told that Tanker repaid $500 of notes payable.

We also know that Tanker took out a noncash note (to purchase furniture) of $200. This noncash transaction has already been recorded in the note to the cash-flow statement (discussed under investing activities).

Knowing this, let us analyze the Notes Payable T-account:

Notes Payable		
	Bal. 12/31/07	815
decreases	increases	
	Bal. 12/31/08	660

What would cause this account to increase? Well, it would increase if Tanker took out new notes payable. What would cause it to decrease? It would decrease if Tanker paid off some of the notes. Let's put in that information:

Notes Payable			
Note Repayments	500	Bal. 12/31/07	815
		New Cash Notes	X
		New Noncash Notes	200
		Bal. 12/31/08	660

So we can calculate that new cash notes = X = $145.

Now we can put these numbers into the cash-flow statement. *Cash* received from new notes was $145. This increased Cash, so it has a positive effect on cash flow. Cash paid to repay old notes was $500. This decreased Cash, so it has a negative effect on cash flow.

Treasury Stock

Now we must analyze the changes in Tanker's equity. Tanker had some activity with treasury stock during the year. We know that Tanker purchased treasury stock.

Treasury Stock			
Bal. 12/31/07	0		
	increases	decreases	
Bal. 12/31/08	1,000		

What could cause this account to go up? It would go up if Tanker purchased treasury stock. What could cause it to go down? It would go down if treasury stock were sold. We know that there was no treasury stock sold, so looking at this again:

Treasury Stock			
Bal. 12/31/07	0		
Treasury Stock Purchased	X		
		Treasury Stock Sold	0
Bal. 12/31/08	1,000		

So we can calculate that treasury stock purchased = X = $1,000. This means that cash was paid by Tanker, which is a negative effect on cash flow.

Dividends

The other account in equity is Retained Earnings. The two major transactions impacting Retained Earnings are net income and dividends.

Net income was already listed in the operating activities section, so all that remains to be included in the financing activities section is dividend activity.

The Retained Earnings account looks like this:

Retained Earnings

	Bal. 12/31/07	200
decreases	increases	
	Bal. 12/31/08	880

What makes Retained Earnings go up? It goes up when Tanker earns net income. What makes it go down? It goes down when Tanker pays dividends. Putting this information in:

Retained Earnings

		Bal. 12/31/07	200
Cash Dividends Paid	X		
		Net Income	1,000
		Bal. 12/31/08	880

So cash dividends paid = X = $320. These were paid in cash so this has a negative effect on Cash.

Totaling these numbers completes financing activities. The completed financing activities section would appear as:

Financing Activities	
Cash proceeds from new notes	$ 145
Cash repayment of old notes	(500)
Cash purchase of treasury stock	(1,000)
Cash dividends paid	(320)
Total cash flow provided by financing activities	$(1,675)

Now we must combine operating activities, investing activities, and financing activities to get the total cash flow (the change in cash during the year).

Next, we show the Cash balance from the prior year (December 31, 2007) and add it to total cash flow to get this year's Cash balance (December 31, 2008).

TANKER INC.
Statement of Cash Flows
Year Ended December 31, 2008

Operating Activities	
Net income	$ 1,000
+ Depreciation expense	110
− Gain on sale of furniture	(80)
+ Decrease in accounts receivable	120
− Increase in inventory	(50)
− Increase in prepaid insurance	(30)
+ Increase in accounts payable	150
Total cash flow provided by operating activities	$ 1,220
Investing Activities	
Cash paid to purchase new furniture	$ (95)
Cash proceeds from sale of furniture	90
Total cash flow provided by investing activities	$ (5)
Financing Activities	
Cash proceeds from new notes	$ 145
Cash repayment of old notes	(500)
Cash purchase of treasury stock	(1,000)
Cash dividends paid	(320)
Total cash flow provided by financing activities	$(1,675)
Total cash flow (change in Cash balance)	$ 460
Cash, December 31, 2007	$ 1,160
Cash, December 31, 2008	$ 700
Noncash Investing and Financing Activities	
Purchase of furniture with note payable	$ 200

Part 1	Part 2	Part 3	**Demo Doc Complete**

Demo Doc 2

Statement of Cash Flows (Direct Method) _____

Learning Objectives 1, 2, 4

Pages in Text

Direct Method

Use the information for Tanker Inc. in the previous question:

TANKER INC.
Balance Sheet
December 31, 2008

Assets	2008	2007	Change	Liabilities	2008	2007	Change
Current:				Current:			
Cash	$ 700	$1,160	$(460)	Accounts payable	$ 680	$ 530	$150
Accounts receivable	300	420	(120)				
Inventory	800	750	50	Long-term notes payable	660	815	
Prepaid insurance	120	90	30				
				Total liabilities	$1,340	$1,345	
Furniture	1,500	1,400					
Less acc. depn.	(400)	(475)		**Owners' Equity**			
Net	1,100	925		Common stock (no par)	$1,800	$1,800	
				Retained earnings	880	200	
Total assets	$3,020	$3,345		Less treasury stock	(1,000)	0	
				Total equity	$1,680	$2,000	
				Total liabilities and equity	$3,020	$3,345	

TANKER INC.
Income Statement
Year Ended December 31, 2008

Sales revenue	$3,400
Less cost of goods sold	(1,750)
Gross margin	$1,650
Depreciation expense	$ (110)
Insurance expense	(230)
Other operating expenses	(390)
Gain on sale of furniture	80
Net income	$1,000

Requirements

1. Prepare the operating activities section of Tanker's statement of cash flow using the direct method.

2. How is the information a cash-flow statement provides different from the information an income statement provides?

Demo Doc 2 Solution

Distinguish among
operating, investing,
and financing cash
flows

Prepare the statement
of cash flows by the
direct method
(Appendix A)

Requirement 1

Prepare the operating activities section of Tanker's statement of cash flows using the direct method.

Part 1	Part 2	Demo Doc Complete

We need to list all of the cash transactions involved in Tanker's day-to-day business operations. To do this, we should look at the income statement to get an idea of what these transactions are.

Cash Received from Customers

What is the first item on the income statement? Revenues. How does this translate into a cash transaction? Revenues should result in customers giving Tanker cash, so the appropriate line on the direct method cash-flow statement is "cash received from customers."

For each income statement account that is not 100% cash, there is always a balance sheet account to record the related accrual. In this case, Accounts Receivable (on the balance sheet) takes care of revenues when cash has not yet been collected.

Accounts Receivable		
Bal. 12/31/07	420	
	increases	decreases
Bal. 12/31/08	300	

What could cause this account to increase? It would increase if Tanker had more sales. What could cause it to decrease? It would decrease if Tanker collected the cash. We know from the income statement that sales were $3,400, so:

Accounts Receivable		
Bal. 12/31/07	420	
Sales Revenue	3,400	
		Cash Collected X
Bal. 12/31/08	300	

X = cash collected from customers = $3,520. This is the amount for the direct method cash-flow statement.

Cash Paid to Suppliers

The next line on the income statement is cost of goods sold. How does this relate to a cash transaction? In order to get the goods Tanker sold, it must buy the items from a supplier and pay for them. So the appropriate line on the cash-flow statement is "cash paid to suppliers." Accounts Payable is the balance sheet account that takes care of bills to suppliers that have not yet been paid.

Accounts Payable		
		Bal. 12/31/07 530
	decreases	increases
		Bal. 12/31/08 680

What could cause this account to increase? It would increase if Tanker had more bills (that is, if Tanker were to purchase inventory from its suppliers). What could cause it to decrease? It would decrease if Tanker paid the cash it owed to the suppliers. However, we don't know how much inventory was purchased.

We can figure this out using the inventory formula from Chapter 6:

$$\text{COGS} = \text{Beginning inventory} + \text{Purchases} - \text{Ending inventory}$$

$$\$1,750 = \$750 + \text{Purchases} - \$800$$

$$\text{Purchases} = \$1,800$$

Putting this into the Accounts Payable T-account:

Accounts Payable

Cash Payments	X	Bal. 12/31/07	530
		Inventory Purchases	1,800
		Bal. 12/31/08	680

X = Cash payments to suppliers = $1,650. This is the amount for the direct method cash-flow statement.

The next item on the income statement is depreciation expense. Because we know that this is 100% noncash, we can ignore it for the direct method.

Cash Paid as Insurance

Next is insurance expense. This would result in "cash paid as insurance." To calculate this number, we need to analyze the Prepaid Insurance account.

Prepaid Insurance

Bal. 12/31/07	90		
increases		decreases	
Bal. 12/31/08	120		

What could cause this account to increase? It would increase if Tanker paid more insurance in advance. What could cause it to decrease? It would decrease if Tanker incurred that insurance expense. We know from the income statement that insurance expense was $230.

Prepaid Insurance

Bal. 12/31/07	90		
Cash Payments	X		
		Insurance Expense	230
Bal. 12/31/08	120		

X = Cash paid as insurance = $260. This is the amount for the direct method statement of cash flows.

Following insurance expense are other expenses. Let's leave this until the end.

After this is the gain on sale of furniture. This is noncash and, therefore, does not impact a direct method cash-flow statement.

Other Cash Expenses

Now we come back to other expenses. Are there any other current asset or current liability accounts with which we have not yet dealt? No, we have analyzed all of them. This means that there is no accrual portion (that is, no *noncash* portion) of these expenses. So we can just assume that they were *all paid in cash*. Therefore, the last line in the operating activities section is "other cash expenses" of $390.

Operating Activities	
Cash collected from customers	$3,520
Cash paid to suppliers	(1,650)
Cash paid for insurance	(260)
Other cash expenses	(390)
Cash flow provided by operating activities	$1,220

Notice that the "cash flow provided by operating activities" of $1,220 is the *same* total we calculated under the indirect method. It is *always* the case that cash flow from operating activities is the same under the direct and indirect methods. This is a good check to confirm that our calculations were correct.

Remember that the investing and financing activities are the same under both methods. So the rest of Tanker's cash-flow statement (investing activities to the end) would be identical to what is shown in Demo Doc 1.

Requirement 2

How is the information a cash-flow statement provides different from the information an income statement provides?

Part 1	**Part 2**	Demo Doc Complete

The income statement shows the determination of net income. Net income is calculated on an accrual basis.

This means that net income not only includes cash transactions *but also* includes noncash transactions. We record revenue earned and expenses incurred *regardless* of whether or not cash has been received or paid.

The cash-flow statement shows the determination of cash flow (that is, the change in the Cash balance during the year). Because the cash-flow statement distills all transactions down to their cash components only, it is missing certain noncash transactions that are included in net income. Cash flow is actually net income *under the cash basis of accounting.*

So the primary difference is that the income statement is prepared under the accrual basis of accounting whereas the cash-flow statement is prepared under the cash basis of accounting.

Part 1	Part 2	**Demo Doc Complete**

Quick Practice Questions

True/False

_____ 1. The statement of cash flows helps to inform the reader about all of the differences between net income and cash flows from operations.

_____ 2. A company may have net income but still have a net cash outflow.

_____ 3. Cash payments for interest expense would be classified as a financing activity.

_____ 4. Free cash flow is a measure of cash adequacy that focuses on the amount of cash available from operations after paying for planned investments in long-term assets.

_____ 5. Purchases of plant assets for cash would be classified as a financing activity.

_____ 6. Under the indirect method, depreciation expense would be subtracted from net income in the operating activities.

_____ 7. The majority of U.S. corporations use the direct method in preparing the statement of cash flows.

_____ 8. Under the indirect method, the acquisition of land through the issuance of common stock would be an investing activity on the statement of cash flows.

_____ 9. When using the indirect method, a loss on sale of equipment is added to net income under the operating activities.

_____10. Interest received on a bond investment would be shown as an investing cash inflow.

Multiple Choice

1. Which of the following statements is *incorrect*?
   a. A statement of cash flows is a basic financial statement required by GAAP.
   b. A statement of cash flows is dated for a period of time as opposed to a point in time.
   c. One purpose of a statement of cash flows is to predict future cash flows.
   d. The statement of cash flows may be combined with the stockholders' equity section of the balance sheet.

2. The operating activities section has a relationship with which part of the balance sheet?
   a. Current assets and current liabilities
   b. Long-term assets
   c. Owners' equity and all liabilities
   d. Owners' equity and long-term liabilities

3. Dividend payments would be included in which section of the statement of cash flows?
   a. Operating activities
   b. Financing activities
   c. Investing activities
   d. Dividend payments are not included on the statement of cash flows.

4. Cash dividends received would be included in which section of the statement of cash flows?
   a. Operating activities
   b. Financing activities
   c. Investing activities
   d. Cash dividends received are not included on the statement of cash flows.

5. The purchase of treasury stock would be included in which section of the statement of cash flows?
   a. Operating activities
   b. Financing activities
   c. Investing activities
   d. The purchase of treasury stock is not included on the statement of cash flows.

6. Activities that create revenues and expenses are included in which section of the statement of cash flows?
   a. Investing activities
   b. Operating activities
   c. Financing activities
   d. Noncash investing and financing activities

7. Where are noncash investing and financing activities reported?
   a. The financing activities section of the statement of cash flows
   b. The investing activities section of the statement of cash flows
   c. Both (a) and (b) are correct
   d. An accompanying schedule to the statement of cash flows

8. Where is the gain resulting from the sale of equipment shown under the indirect method?
   a. In the operating activities section as a deduction
   b. In the operating activities section as an addition
   c. In the investing activities section as an addition
   d. In the financing activities section as a deduction

9. Wilson Companys 2008 income statement reports depreciation expense of $25,000. How would depreciation be shown on the statement of cash flows using the direct method for 2008?
   a. As an addition under financing activities
   b. As a deduction under operating activities
   c. As an addition under operating activities
   d. It would not be reported.

10. Which of the following would be shown as a deduction to net income under the operating activities section using the indirect method?
   a. Depletion expense
   b. Increase in Accounts Payable account balance for the period
   c. Increase in Inventory balance for the period
   d. Decrease in Accounts Receivable account balance for the period

Quick Exercises

16-1. Your best friend just lost his job because the company he was working for went bankrupt. He was complaining to you that even though the company had been profitable for three years in a row, it still went out of business. He asks you how this can happen.

Requirements

1. Explain the most likely reason for the company's declaring bankruptcy. Could your friend have seen it coming? How?

2. Discuss the four purposes of the statement of cash flows.

16-2. State whether each of the following events should be classified as an operating activity (O), investing activity (I), financing activity (F), shown in a separate schedule of noncash investing and financing activities (N), or not disclosed on the statement of cash flows (NA).

    _____ a. Received cash dividends
    _____ b. Retired bonds payable by issuing common stock
    _____ c. Paid for merchandise purchased on account
    _____ d. Paid interest on a short-term note payable
    _____ e. Received stock dividends
    _____ f. Paid for a three-year insurance policy on property
    _____ g. Issued preferred stock in exchange for land
    _____ h. Issued common stock for cash
    _____ i. Received cash from sale of land
    _____ j. Purchased equipment for cash

16-3. Using the following data, prepare the operating activities section of a statement of cash flows for Washington Corporation for the year ended December 31, 2008. Assume the indirect method is used.

Increase in salary payable	$ 1,500
Decrease in accounts payable	2,000
Increase in accounts receivable	3,500
Net income	98,000
Decrease in inventory	5,800
Increase in prepaid expenses	1,200
Depreciation expense—equipment	5,000
Depreciation expense—buildings	7,500
Gain on sale of equipment	1,300
Loss on sale of patent	2,500

WASHINGTON CORPORATION
Statement of Cash Flows
Year Ended December 31, 2008

16-4. For each of the following events, determine if it should be classified as an operating activity (O), investing activity (I), or financing activity (F). Then determine the increase or decrease to the Cash account using the indirect method.

Transaction Description	Type of Activity	Cash Inflow (Outflow)
a. Declared cash dividends of $21,000 during the current period. Dividends payable on January 1 were $1,500; the December 31 balance was $2,300.	_____	_____
b. Interest income on the income statement for the current period is $22,000. Interest receivable on January 1 was $2,700; the December 31 balance was $2,250.	_____	_____
c. Issued $1,000,000, 10-year, 10% bonds at 102.	_____	_____
d. Sales on account for the current period amount to $160,000. The January 1 balance in Accounts Receivable was $95,000; the December 31 balance was $106,000.	_____	_____
e. Purchased equipment for $215,000 cash.	_____	_____
f. Sold 1,000 shares of $20 par common stock for cash at $29.	_____	_____
g. Salary expense on the income statement for the current year is $151,500. The Salary Payable balance on January 1 was $20,300; the December 31 balance was $17,800.	_____	_____

16-5.   Aycoth Inc. gathered the following data from its accounting records for the year ended December 31, 2008:

Depreciation expense	$ 15,900
Payment of income taxes	24,500
Collections of accounts receivable	166,700
Purchase of treasury stock	40,000
Declaration of stock dividend	65,000
Loss on sale of plant assets	8,400
Collection of dividend revenue	13,800
Payments of salaries and wages	83,600
Cash sales	102,900
Net income	61,200
Acquisition of land	73,500
Payment of interest	19,400
Interest received on investments	3,100
Issuance of bonds payable	500,000
Increase in accounts payable	20,300
Payments to suppliers	170,300
Acquisition of equipment by issuing long-term note payable	50,000

Prepare the operating activities section of the statement of cash flows using the direct method.

AYCOTH INC.
Partial Statement of Cash Flows
Year Ended December 31, 2008

Do It Yourself! Question 1

Indirect Method

Clean Co. had the following information at December 31, 2008:

CLEAN CO.
Balance Sheet
December 31, 2008

Assets	2008	2007	Change	Liabilities	2008	2007	Change
Current:				Current:			
Cash	$ 460	$ 320	$140	Accounts payable	$ 800	$ 540	$260
Accounts receivable	510	420	90				
Inventory	710	750	(40)	Long-term notes payable	600	900	
Prepaid rent	170	250	(80)	Total liabilities	$1,400	$1,440	
Equipment	1,350	1,500		**Owner's Equity**			
Less acc. depn.	(400)	(650)		Common stock (no par)	$ 200	$ 150	
Net	950	850		Retained earnings	1,200	1,000	
Total assets	$2,800	$2,590		Total equity	$1,400	$1,150	
				Total liabilities and equity	$2,800	$2,590	

CLEAN CO.
Income Statement
Year Ended December 31, 2008

Sales revenue		$1,800
Less cost of goods sold		(960)
Gross margin		$ 840
Depreciation expense		$ (90)
Rent expense		(140)
Other operating expenses		(195)
Loss on sale of equipment		(55)
Net income		$ 360

Other Information

- Every year, Clean declares and pays cash dividends.

- During 2008, Clean sold old equipment for cash. Clean also bought new equipment for $120 cash and a $140 note payable.

- During 2008, Clean repaid $600 of notes payable in cash and borrowed new long-term notes payable for cash.

- During 2008, new common stock was issued. No stock was retired.

Requirement

1) Prepare Clean's statement of cash flows for the year ended December 31, 2008, using the indirect method.

Do It Yourself! Question 2

Direct Method

Use the information for Clean Inc. in the previous question.

Requirement

1. Prepare the operating activities section of Clean's statement of cash flows using the direct method.

Quick Practice Solutions

True/False

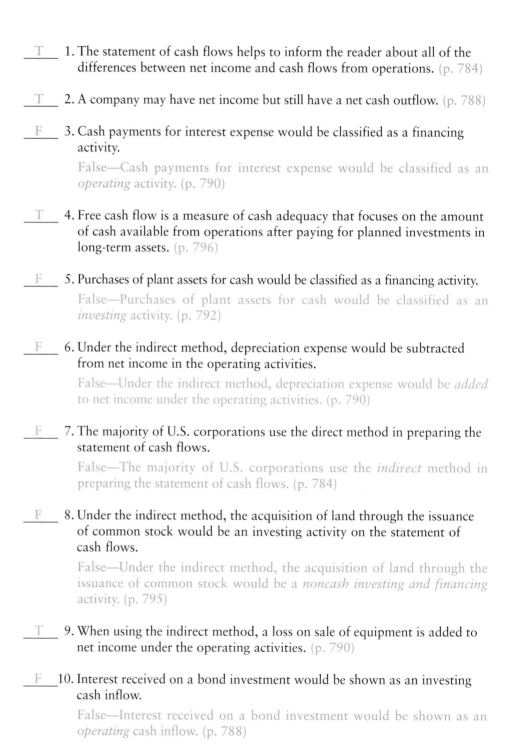

___T___ 1. The statement of cash flows helps to inform the reader about all of the differences between net income and cash flows from operations. (p. 784)

___T___ 2. A company may have net income but still have a net cash outflow. (p. 788)

___F___ 3. Cash payments for interest expense would be classified as a financing activity.

   False—Cash payments for interest expense would be classified as an *operating* activity. (p. 790)

___T___ 4. Free cash flow is a measure of cash adequacy that focuses on the amount of cash available from operations after paying for planned investments in long-term assets. (p. 796)

___F___ 5. Purchases of plant assets for cash would be classified as a financing activity.

   False—Purchases of plant assets for cash would be classified as an *investing* activity. (p. 792)

___F___ 6. Under the indirect method, depreciation expense would be subtracted from net income in the operating activities.

   False—Under the indirect method, depreciation expense would be *added* to net income under the operating activities. (p. 790)

___F___ 7. The majority of U.S. corporations use the direct method in preparing the statement of cash flows.

   False—The majority of U.S. corporations use the *indirect* method in preparing the statement of cash flows. (p. 784)

___F___ 8. Under the indirect method, the acquisition of land through the issuance of common stock would be an investing activity on the statement of cash flows.

   False—Under the indirect method, the acquisition of land through the issuance of common stock would be a *noncash investing and financing* activity. (p. 795)

___T___ 9. When using the indirect method, a loss on sale of equipment is added to net income under the operating activities. (p. 790)

___F___ 10. Interest received on a bond investment would be shown as an investing cash inflow.

   False—Interest received on a bond investment would be shown as an *operating* cash inflow. (p. 788)

Multiple Choice

1. Which of the following statements is incorrect? (p. 784)
   a. A statement of cash flows is a basic financial statement required by GAAP.
   b. A statement of cash flows is dated for a period of time as opposed to a point in time.
   c. One purpose of a statement of cash flows is to predict future cash flows.
   d. The statement of cash flows may be combined with the stockholders' equity section of the balance sheet.

2. The operating activities section has a relationship with which part of the balance sheet? (p. 788)
   a. Current assets and current liabilities
   b. Long-term assets
   c. Owners' equity and all liabilities
   d. Owners' equity and long-term liabilities

3. Dividend payments would be included in which section of the statement of cash flows? (p. 794)
   a. Operating activities
   b. Financing activities
   c. Investing activities
   d. Dividend payments are not included on the statement of cash flows.

4. Cash dividends received would be included in which section of the statement of cash flows? (p. 788)
   a. Operating activities
   b. Financing activities
   c. Investing activities
   d. Cash dividends received are not included on the statement of cash flows.

5. The purchase of treasury stock would be included in which section of the statement of cash flows? (p. 794)
   a. Operating activities
   b. Financing activities
   c. Investing activities
   d. The purchase of treasury stock is not included on the statement of cash flows.

6. Activities that create revenues and expenses are included in which section of the statement of cash flows? (p. 788)
   a. Investing activities
   b. Operating activities
   c. Financing activities
   d. Noncash investing and financing activities

7. Where are noncash investing and financing activities reported? (p. 795)
   a. The financing activities section of the statement of cash flows
   b. The investing activities section of the statement of cash flows
   c. Both (a) and (b) are correct
   d. An accompanying schedule to the statement of cash flows

8. Where is the gain resulting from the sale of equipment shown under the indirect method? (p. 790)
   a. In the operating activities section as a deduction
   b. In the operating activities section as an addition
   c. In the investing activities section as an addition
   d. In the financing activities section as a deduction

9. Wilson Company's 2008 income statement reports depreciation expense of $25,000. How would depreciation be shown on the statement of cash flows using the direct method for 2008? (p. 831)
   a. As an addition under financing activities
   b. As a deduction under operating activities
   c. As an addition under operating activities
   d. It would not be reported.

10. Which of the following would be shown as a deduction to net income under the operating activities section using the indirect method? (p. 790)
    a. Depletion expense
    b. Increase in Accounts Payable account balance for the period
    c. Increase in Inventory balance for the period
    d. Decrease in Accounts Receivable account balance for the period

Quick Exercises

16-1. Your best friend just lost his job because the company he was working for went bankrupt. He was complaining to you that even though the company had been profitable for three years in a row, it still went out of business. He asks you how this can happen. (p. 784)

Requirements

1. Explain the most likely reason for the company's declaring bankruptcy. Could your friend have seen it coming? How?

A profitable company is one in which revenues exceed expenses on an accrual basis. This does not necessarily mean that the company is generating enough cash to pay its bills. The most likely reason your friend's company went bankrupt is the lack of cash. If your friend had access to the statement of cash-flows, the cash flow problems would have likely been evident.

2. Discuss the four purposes of the statement of cash flows.

The four purposes of the statement of cash flows are as follows:

1. To help predict future cash flows
2. To evaluate management decisions
3. To determine the company's ability to pay dividends to stockholders and interest and principal to creditors
4. To show the relationship of net income to changes in the business's cash

16-2. State whether each of the following events should be classified as an operating activity (O), investing activity (I), financing activity (F), shown in a separate schedule of noncash investing and financing activities (N), or not disclosed on the statement of cash flows (NA). (pp. 788–796)

O	a.	Received cash dividends
N	b.	Retired bonds payable by issuing common stock
O	c.	Paid for merchandise purchased on account
O	d.	Paid interest on a short-term note payable
NA	e.	Received stock dividends
O	f.	Paid for a three-year insurance policy on property
N	g.	Issued preferred stock in exchange for land
F	h.	Issued common stock for cash
I	i.	Received cash from sale of land
I	j.	Purchased equipment for cash

16-3. Using the following data, prepare the operating activities section of a statement of cash flows for Washington Corporation for the year ended December 31, 2008. Assume the indirect method is used. (pp. 788–791)

Increase in salary payable	$ 1,500
Decrease in accounts payable	2,000
Increase in accounts receivable	3,500
Net income	98,000
Decrease in inventory	5,800
Increase in prepaid expenses	1,200
Depreciation expense—equipment	5,000
Depreciation expense—buildings	7,500
Gain on sale of equipment	1,300
Loss on sale of patent	2,500

WASHINGTON CORPORATION
Statement of Cash Flows
Year Ended December 31, 2008

Cash flows from operating activities:		
Net income		$ 98,000
Adjustments to reconcile net income to net cash provided by operating activities:		
Depreciation on equipment	$5,000	
Depreciation on buildings	7,500	
Loss on sale of patent	2,500	
Gain on sale of equipment	(1,300)	
Increase in accounts receivable	(3,500)	
Increase in prepaid expenses	(1,200)	
Decrease in inventory	5,800	
Increase in salary payable	1,500	
Decrease in accounts payable	(2,000)	14,300
Net cash inflow from operating activities		$112,300

16-4.   For each of the following events, determine if it should be classified as an operating activity (O), investing activity (I), or financing activity (F). Then determine the cash inflow or (outflow). (pp. 788–796)

Transaction Description	Type of Activity	Cash Inflow (Outflow)
a. Declared cash dividends of $21,000 during the current period. Dividends payable on January 1 were $1,500; the December 31 balance was $2,300.	F	$(20,200)
b. Interest income on the income statement for the current period is $22,000. Interest receivable on January 1 was $2,700; the December 31 balance was $2,250.	O	$22,450
c. Issued $1,000,000, 10-year, 10% bonds at 102.	F	$1,020,000
d. Sales on account for the current period amount to $160,000. The January 1 balance in accounts Receivable was $95,000; the December 31 balance was $106,000.	O	$149,000
e. Purchased equipment for $215,000 cash.	I	$(215,000)
f. Sold 1,000 shares of $20 par common stock for cash at $29.	F	$29,000
g. Salary expense on the income statement for the current year is $151,500. The Salary Payable balance on January 1 was $20,300; the December 31 balance was $17,800.	O	$(154,000)

16-5. Aycoth Inc. gathered the following data from its accounting records for the year ended December 31, 2008: (pp. 829–831)

Depreciation expense	$ 15,900
Payment of income taxes	24,500
Collections of accounts receivable	166,700
Purchase of treasury stock	40,000
Declaration of stock dividend	65,000
Loss on sale of plant assets	8,400
Collection of dividend revenue	13,800
Payments of salaries and wages	83,600
Cash sales	102,900
Net income	61,200
Acquisition of land	73,500
Payment of interest	19,400
Interest received on investments	3,100
Issuance of bonds payable	500,000
Increase in accounts payable	20,300
Payments to suppliers	170,300
Acquisition of equipment by issuing long-term note payable	50,000

Prepare the operating activities section of the statement of cash flows using the direct method.

AYCOTH INC.
Partial Statement of Cash Flows
Year Ended December 31, 2008

Cash flows from operating activities:		
Receipts:		
Collections from customers	$ 269,600*	
Interest received	3,100	
Dividends received	13,800	
Total cash receipts		$286,500
Payments:		
To suppliers	$(170,300)	
To employees	(83,600)	
For interest	(19,400)	
For income tax	(24,500)	
Total cash payments		(297,800)
Net cash outflow from operating activities		$ (11,300)

*($166,700 + $102,900 = $269,600)

Do It Yourself! Question 1 Solutions

Requirements

2 Distinguish among operating, investing, and financing cash flows

3 Prepare the statement of cash flows by the indirect method

1. Prepare Clean's statement of cash flows for the year ended December 31, 2008, using the indirect method.

Calculations: Investing Activities

The $140 note payable is a <u>noncash transaction</u>.

Equipment (Net)			
Bal. 12/31/07	850		
Cash Purchases	120		
Noncash Purchases	140		
		NBV Equipment Sold	X
		Depreciation Expense	90
Bal. 12/31/08	950		

$$X = \text{NBV of equipment sold} = \$70$$
$$\text{Loss} = -\$55 = \text{Cash received} - \$70$$
$$\text{Cash received on sale of equipment} = \$15$$

2 Distinguish among operating, investing, and financing cash flows

3 Prepare the statement of cash flows by the indirect method

Calculations: Financing Activities

Notes Payable			
		Bal. 12/31/07	900
Note Repayments	600		
		New Cash Notes	X
		New Noncash Notes	140
		Bal. 12/31/08	600

$$\text{New cash notes} = X = \$160$$

Common Stock			
		Bal. 12/31/07	150
Retirements	0		
		New Stock Issued	X
		Bal. 12/31/08	200

$$\text{New stock issued} = X = \$50$$

Retained Earnings

		Bal. 12/31/07	1,000
Cash Dividends Paid	X		
		Net Income	360
		Bal. 12/31/08	1,200

Cash dividends paid = X = $160

CLEAN CO.
Statement of Cash Flows
Year Ended December 31, 2008

Operating Activities	
Net income	$ 360
+ Depreciation expense	90
+ Loss on sale of equipment	55
– Increase in accounts receivable	(90)
+ Decrease in inventory	40
+ Decrease in prepaid rent	80
+ Increase in accounts payable	260
Total cash flow provided by operating activities	$ 795
Investing Activities	
Cash paid to purchase new equipment	$(120)
Cash proceeds from sale of equipment	15
Total cash flow provided by investing activities	$(105)
Financing Activities	
Cash proceeds from new notes	$ 160
Cash repayment of old notes	(600)
Cash proceeds from new stock issue	50
Cash dividends paid	(160)
Total cash flow provided by financing activities	$(550)
Total cash flow (change in Cash during year)	$ 140
Cash, December 31, 2007	$ 320
Cash, December 31, 2008	$ 460
Noncash Investing and Financing Activities	
Purchase of equipment with note payable	$ 140

Do It Yourself! Question 2 Solutions

Requirements

2 Distinguish among operating, investing, and financing cash flows

4 Prepare the statement of cash flows by the direct method (Appendix A)

1. Prepare the operating activities section of Clean's statement of cash flows using the direct method.

Accounts Receivable

Bal. 12/31/07	420		
Sales Revenue	1,800		
		Cash Collected	X
Bal. 12/31/08	510		

X = Cash collected from customers = $1,710

COGS = $960 = $750 + purchases − $710

Purchases = $920

Accounts Payable

		Bal. 12/31/07	540
Cash Payments	X		
		Inventory Purchases	920
		Bal. 12/31/08	800

X = Cash payments to suppliers = $660

Prepaid Rent

Bal. 12/31/07	250		
Cash Payments	X		
		Rent Expense	140
Bal. 12/31/08	170		

X = Cash paid as rent = $60

Operating Activities	
Cash collected from customers	$1,710
Cash paid to suppliers	(660)
Cash paid for rent	(60)
Other cash expenses	(195)
Cash flow from operating activities	$ 795

The Power of Practice

For more practice using the skills learned in this chapter, visit MyAccountingLab. There you will find algorithmically generated questions that are based on these Demo Docs and your main textbook's Review and Assess Your Progress sections.

Go to MyAccountingLab and follow these steps:

1. Direct your URL to www.myaccountinglab.com.
2. Log in using your name and password.
3. Click the MyAccountingLab link.
4. Click Study Plan in the left navigation bar.
5. From the table of contents, select Chapter 16, The Statement of Cash Flows.
6. Click a link to work tutorial exercises.

17 Financial Statement Analysis

What You Probably Already Know

For years now, you have been a student and have taken many exams. You probably already know that there may be typical responses you have upon receiving your grade. Your first reaction may be the level of satisfaction you have with your grade compared to your previous grades received in that class and the established grading norms for your institution. You may then ask your friends what grade they received so that you can compare your results to them. The instructor may announce the average exam results and you could then determine if you performed better or worse than the average. Students often like to assess their performance by comparing their grade to a standard, their peers, and the average. Businesses often do the same thing. In this chapter, you study various techniques and ratios that a business will use to assess its performance using comparisons to previous results, competitors, and the industry average.

Learning Objectives

 Perform a horizontal analysis.

Horizontal analysis provides comparisons of financial information over time. To analyze a line item in the financial statements, the difference between the current and earlier time period amounts is computed. The dollar amount change of the line item between the periods is useful, but it is more informative to determine the percentage change by dividing the dollar change (current period amount, or this year's balance minus earlier period amount, or last year's balance) by the earlier period amount. *Review the horizontal analysis of the income statement and the balance sheet in Exhibits 17-2 and 17-3 (pp. 850–851).*

 Perform a vertical analysis.

Vertical analysis provides comparisons of individual items on a financial statement to a relative base. The base, which serves as the denominator, is usually net sales for the income statement and total assets for the balance sheet. The vertical analysis percentage is calculated by dividing each financial statement item amount by the relevant base of net sales *or* total assets.

The vertical analysis percentage is shown next to the item amount on the financial statement. *Review the vertical analysis of the income statement and the balance sheet in Exhibits 17-4 and 17-5 (pp. 853–854).*

3 Prepare and use common-size financial statements.

A **common-size statement** is similar to the vertical analysis but shows only the vertical analysis percentages of each item in the financial statement. This presentation permits ready comparisons between companies of various sizes. *Review the common-size comparison of Google versus Yahoo! in Exhibit 17-6 (p. 855).*

4 Compute the standard financial ratios.

Financial ratios are helpful to assess a company's performance and financial position. Trends can be determined and comparisons to competing companies can be made. Various ratios are presented to measure the following:

- Ability to pay current liabilities
- Ability to sell inventory and collect receivables
- Ability to pay long-term debt
- Profitability
- Return on stock investment

Review "Using Ratios to Make Decisions" in the main text for descriptions and formulas for the financial ratios.

Demo Doc 1

Financial Statement Analysis

Learning Objectives 1–4

MeMe Co. had the following information at December 31, 2008:

MEME CO.
Balance Sheet
December 31, 2008 and 2007

(Dollar amounts in millions)	2008	2007
Assets		
Cash	$150	$130
Accounts receivable	80	145
Inventory	130	190
Total assets	$360	$465
Liabilities		
Accounts payable	90	140
Loans payable	140	220
Total liabilities	$230	$360
Stockholders' Equity		
Common stock	20	10
Retained earnings	110	95
Total stockholders' equity	$130	$105
Total liabilities and equity	$360	$465

MEME CO.
Income Statement
Years Ended December 31, 2008 and 2007

(Dollar amounts in millions)	2008	2007
Sales revenue	$650	$580
Less cost of goods sold	430	350
Gross profit	$220	$230
Salary expense	120	140
Rent expense	70	80
Net income	$ 30	$ 10

At December 31, 2006, MeMe's inventory was $160 and total equity was $95.

Requirements

1. Prepare horizontal and vertical analyses for MeMe's financial statements.

2. Calculate MeMe's inventory turnover and rate of return on stockholder's equity ratios for both years.

Demo Doc 1 Solutions

Requirement 1

1 Perform a horizontal analysis

Prepare horizontal and vertical analyses for MeMe's financial statements.

Part 1	Part 2	Part 3	Demo Doc Complete

Horizontal Analysis

As its name implies, horizontal analysis goes *across* the rows of the financial statements, looking at *one* account and how it has changed.

For *each* number on the balance sheet and income statement, we calculate the dollar change and the percent change.

$$\frac{\text{Dollar}}{\text{change}} = \frac{\text{This year's}}{\text{balance}} - \frac{\text{Last year's}}{\text{balance}}$$

So in the dollar change of Accounts Receivable and Sales Revenue:

$$\text{Accounts Receivable} = \$80 - \$145 = \$(65)\text{ change}$$
$$\text{Sales Revenue} = \$650 - \$580 = \$70\text{ change}$$

Notice that the negative value on the change in Accounts Receivable indicates that this account has decreased, whereas the positive value on the change in Sales Revenue indicates that this account has increased.

Extra care must be taken when using this calculation on expenses (because they are presented as subtracted/negative numbers on the income statement). The *absolute value* of the expense (that is, ignoring the fact that it is already a negative number) must be used to calculate dollar change. In the dollar change of COGS and Rent Expense:

$$\text{COGS} = \$430 - \$350 = \$80\text{ change}$$
$$\text{Rent Expense} = \$70 - \$80 = \$(10)\text{ change}$$

Again, the positive value indicates that COGS increased and the negative value indicates that Rent Expense decreased.

$$\frac{\text{Percent}}{\text{change}} = \frac{\text{Dollar change}}{\text{Last year's balance}}$$

So in the percent change of Accounts Receivable and Sales Revenue:

$$\frac{\text{Accounts}}{\text{Receivable}} = \frac{\$(65)}{\$145}\text{ change}$$
$$= (44.8)\%\text{ change}$$

$$\frac{\text{Sales}}{\text{Revenue}} = \frac{\$70}{\$580}$$
$$= 12.1\%\text{ change}$$

Again, the percent change numbers are negative for Accounts Receivable (which decreased in 2008) and positive for Sales Revenue (which increased in 2008).

The percent change is calculated the same way for expenses, again using the *absolute value* of the expenses. In the percent change of COGS and Rent Expense:

$$COGS = \frac{\$80}{\$350}$$
$$= \mathbf{22.9\%} \text{ change}$$

$$\text{Rent Expense} = \frac{-\$10}{\$80}$$
$$= \mathbf{(12.5)\%} \text{ chang}$$

MEME CO.
Horizontal Analysis of Balance Sheet
Years Ended December 31, 2008 and 2007

(Dollar amounts in millions)	2008	2007	Increase (Decrease) Amount	Percent
Assets				
Cash	$150	$130	$ 20	15.4%
Accounts receivable	80	145	(65)	(44.8)
Inventory	130	190	(60)	(31.6)
Total assets	$360	$465	$(105)	(22.6)
Liabilities				
Accounts payable	90	140	(50)	(35.7)%
Loans payable	140	220	(80)	(36.4)
Total liabilities	$230	$360	$(130)	(36.1)
Stockholders' Equity				
Common stock	20	10	10	100.0%
Retained earnings	110	95	15	15.8
Total stockholders' equity	$130	$105	$ 25	23.8%
Total liabilities and equity	$360	$465	$(105)	(22.6)%

MEME CO.
Horizontal Analysis of Comparative Income Statement
Years Ended December 31, 2008 and 2007

(Dollar amounts in millions)	2008	2007	Increase (Decrease) Amount	Percent
Sales revenue	$650	$580	$ 70	12.1%
Less cost of goods sold	430	350	80	22.9
Gross profit	$220	$230	(10)	(4.3)
Salary expense	120	140	(20)	(14.3)
Rent expense	70	80	(10)	(12.5)
Net income	$ 30	$ 10	$ 20	200.0%

2 Perform a vertical analysis

3 Prepare and use common-size financial statements

Vertical Analysis

Part 1	**Part 2**	Part 3	Demo Doc Complete

As its name implies, vertical analysis takes *each* number on the financial statements and compares it to others in the same year (that is, *down* the columns of the financial statements). Vertical analysis is sometimes called common-size analysis because it allows two companies of different sizes to be compared (through the use of percentages).

Balance Sheet Vertical Analysis

On the **balance sheet,** each number, whether it is before an asset, a liability, or an equity account is calculated as a percentage of *total assets.*

$$\text{Vertical analysis percent (balance sheet)} = \frac{\text{Account balance}}{\text{Total assets}}$$

So in the case of Accounts Receivable:

$$\text{Vertical analysis percent (2008 Accounts Receivable)} = \frac{\$80}{\$360}$$
$$= \mathbf{22.2\%}$$

In other words, about 22% of all the assets in 2008 are in Accounts Receivable.

Income Statement Vertical Analysis

On the **income statement,** each number is calculated as a percentage of **net** *sales revenues.*

$$\text{Vertical analysis percent (income statement)} = \frac{\text{Account balance}}{\text{Net sales revenues}}$$

So in the case of Gross Profit:

$$\begin{array}{r} \text{Vertical analysis percent} \\ \text{(2008 Gross Profit)} \end{array} = \frac{\$220}{\$650}$$
$$= \mathbf{33.8\%}$$

This means that for every dollar in sales revenues, $0.338 went to Gross Profit. For expenses, the calculation is the same. So in the cases of COGS and Rent Expense:

$$\begin{array}{r} \text{Vertical analysis percent} \\ \text{(2008 COGS)} \end{array} = \frac{\$430}{\$650}$$
$$= \mathbf{66.2\%}$$
$$\begin{array}{r} \text{Vertical analysis percent} \\ \text{(2008 Rent Expense)} \end{array} = \frac{\$70}{\$650}$$
$$= \mathbf{10.8\%}$$

MEME CO.
Vertical Analysis of Balance Sheet
December 31, 2008 and 2007

(Dollar amounts in millions)	2008	2008 %	2007	2007 %
Assets				
Cash	$150	41.7%	$130	28.0%
Accounts receivable	80	22.2	145	31.1 *
Inventory	130	36.1	190	40.9
Total assets	$360	100.0%	$465	100.0%
Liabilities				
Accounts payable	$ 90	25.0%	$140	30.1%
Loans payable	140	38.9	220	47.3
Total liabilities	$230	63.9%	$360	77.4%
Stockholders' Equity				
Common stock	$ 20	5.5 *%	$ 10	2.2%
Retained earnings	110	30.6	95	20.4
Total stockholders' equity	$130	36.1%	$105	22.6%
Total liabilities and equity	$360	100.0%	$465	100.0%

*Rounded down to balance.

MEME CO.
Vertical Analysis of Comparative Income Statement
Years Ended December 31, 2008 and 2007

	2008	2008 %	2007	2007 %
Net sales revenue	$650	100.0%	$580	100.0%
Less cost of goods sold	430	66.2	350	60.3
Gross profit	$220	33.8%	$230	39.7%
Salary expense	120	18.4 *	140	24.1
Rent expense	70	10.8	80	13.8
Net income	$ 30	4.6%	$ 10	1.7%

*Rounded to balance.

Requirement 2

4 Compute the standard financial ratios

Calculate MeMe's inventory turnover and rate of return on stockholder's equity ratios for both years.

Part 1	Part 2	**Part 3**	Demo Doc Complete

$$\frac{\text{Inventory}}{\text{turnover}} = \frac{\text{COGS}}{\text{Average inventory}}$$

Remember that "average" (when used in a financial ratio) generally means the beginning balance plus the ending balance divided by two.

$$\begin{array}{l} 2008 \\ \text{Inventory} \\ \text{turnover} \end{array} = \frac{\$430}{[\frac{1}{2}(190+130)]}$$

$$= \textbf{2.7 times}$$

$$\begin{array}{l} 2007 \\ \text{Inventory} \\ \text{turnover} \end{array} = \frac{\$350}{[\frac{1}{2}(160+190)]}$$

$$= \textbf{2 times}$$

$$\begin{array}{l} \text{Rate of return on} \\ \text{stockholders' equity} \end{array} = \frac{\text{Net income} - \text{Prefered dividends}}{\text{Average common stockholders' equity}}$$

$$\begin{array}{l} \text{2008 Rate of return on} \\ \text{stockholders' equity} \end{array} = \frac{[\$30-\$0]}{\frac{1}{2}(\$105+\$130)}$$

$$= \textbf{25.5\%}$$

$$\begin{array}{l} \text{2007 Rate of return on} \\ \text{stockholders' equity} \end{array} = \frac{[\$10-\$0]}{\frac{1}{2}(\$95+\$105)}$$

$$= \textbf{10\%}$$

Part 1	Part 2	Part 3	**Demo Doc Complete**

Quick Practice Questions

True/False

_____ 1. It is generally considered more useful to know the percentage change in financial statement amounts from year to year than to know the absolute dollar amount of their change.

_____ 2. Benchmarking may be done against an industry average or against a key competitor.

_____ 3. Vertical analysis of financial statements reveals changes in items on the financial statements over time.

_____ 4. Inventory turnover is the ratio of average inventory to cost of goods sold.

_____ 5. Book value per share of common stock has no relationship to market value.

_____ 6. A high current ratio means that a company's current assets represent a relatively large portion (or ratio) of total liabilities.

_____ 7. The debt ratio measures the ability to pay current liabilities.

_____ 8. The acid-test (quick) ratio includes the sum of Cash, Net Accounts Receivable, and Inventory in the numerator

_____ 9. Earnings per share indicates the net income earned for each share of common and preferred stock.

_____ 10. A signal of financial trouble may include cash flow from operations being lower than net income from period to period.

Multiple Choice

1. Horizontal analysis can be described as which of the following?
   a. Percentage changes in various financial statement amounts from year to year
   b. The changes in individual financial statement amounts as a percentage of some related total
   c. The change in key financial statement ratios over a certain time frame or horizon
   d. None of the above

2. Trend percentages can be considered a form of which of the following?
   a. Ratio analysis
   b. Vertical analysis
   c. Profitability analysis
   d. Horizontal analysis

3. In 2008, net sales were $1,600,000 and in 2009, net sales were $1,750,000. How is the percent change calculated?
   a. Divide $1,600,000 by $1,750,000
   b. Divide $1,750,000 by $1,600,000
   c. Divide $150,000 by $1,750,000
   d. Divide $150,000 by $1,600,000

4. Vertical analysis can be described as which of the following?
   a. Percentage changes in the balances shown in comparative financial statements
   b. The change in key financial statement ratios over a specified period of time
   c. The dollar amount of the change in various financial statement amounts from year to year
   d. Individual financial statement items expressed as a percentage of a base (which represents 100%)

5. What is the base that is used when performing vertical analysis on an income statement?
   a. Net sales
   b. Gross sales
   c. Gross profit
   d. Total expenses

6. What is the base that is used when performing vertical analysis on a balance sheet?
   a. Total assets
   b. Stockholders' equity
   c. Total liabilities
   d. Net assets

7. Which ratio measures the ability to pay long-term debt?
   a. Rate of return on net sales
   b. Earnings per share
   c. Times-interest-earned ratio
   d. Acid-test (quick) ratio

8. Which of the following would be most helpful in the comparison of different-sized companies?
   a. Performing horizontal analysis
   b. Looking at the amount of income earned by each company
   c. Comparing working capital balances
   d. Preparing common-size financial statements

9. Which ratio(s) help(s) in the analysis of working capital?
   a. Current ratio
   b. Acid-test ratio
   c. Debt ratio
   d. Both a and b are correct

10. Assume that collections from customers on account are being received faster. Which of the following would be true?
    a. The accounts receivable turnover would be higher.
    b. The days' sales in receivables would be higher.
    c. The current ratio would be higher.
    d. None of the above.

Quick Exercises

17-1. Selected items from the balance sheet and income statement follow for the Brothers Company for 2007 and 2008.

Requirement

1. Calculate the amount of the change and the percentage of change for each item.

	2007	2008	$ Change	% Change
Cash	$121,000	$100,000	_____	_____
Accounts receivable	117,000	125,000	_____	_____
Merchandise inventory	70,000	85,000	_____	_____
Accounts payable	63,500	50,000	_____	_____
Sales	144,000	135,000	_____	_____
Cost of goods sold	74,000	67,500	_____	_____

17-2. The income statement for Commerce Corporation for the year ended December 31, 2007, follows:

COMMERCE CORPORATION
Income Statement
Year Ended December 31, 2007

Net sales		$661,000
Expenses:		
Cost of goods sold	$268,500	
Selling expenses	45,000	
General expenses	49,300	
Interest expense	35,000	
Income tax expense	30,000	
Total expenses		427,800
Net income		$233,200

Requirements

1. Prepare a vertical analysis of the income statement showing appropriate percentages for each item listed.

COMMERCE CORPORATION
Vertical Analysis of Income Statement
Year Ended December 31, 2007

2. What additional information would you need to determine whether these percentages are good or bad?

17-3. Financial ratios and analytical functions follow.

Requirement

1. Match the function with the appropriate ratio.

Functions:

    a. Gives the amount of net income earned for each share of the company's common stock

    b. Measures the number of times operating income can cover interest expense

    c. Shows ability to pay all current liabilities if they come due immediately

    d. Shows the percentage of a stock's market value returned to stockholders as dividends each period

    e. Measures ability to collect cash from credit customers

    f. Measures ability to pay current liabilities with current assets

    g. Indicates the market price of $1 of earnings

    h. Measures the difference between current assets and current liabilities

    i. Indicates percentage of assets financed with debt

    j. Shows the percentage of each sales dollar earned as net income

Ratios:

    1. _____ Dividend yield

    2. _____ Rate of return on net sales

    3. _____ Accounts receivable turnover

    4. _____ Working capital

    5. _____ Debt ratio

    6. _____ Current ratio

    7. _____ Price/earnings ratio

    8. _____ Times-interest-earned ratio

    9. _____ Acid-test ratio

    10. _____ Earnings per share of common stock

17-4. Using the following data for Dream Corporation for 2008, calculate the ratios that follow:

Market price per share of common stock at 12/31/08	$ 9.00
Net income	50,000.00
Number of common shares outstanding	25,000.00
Dividend per share of common stock	$ 0.71

    a. earnings per share of common stock

    b. price/earnings ratio

    c. dividend yield

17-5. Following are selected data from the comparative income statement and balance sheet for Deerfield Corporation for the years ended December 31, 2008 and 2007:

	2008	2007
Net sales (all on credit)	$97,600	$93,000
Cost of goods sold	53,500	52,500
Gross profit	44,700	40,500
Income from operations	16,300	15,000
Interest expense	3,100	3,500
Net income	9,800	9,000
Cash	7,700	7,500
Accounts receivable, net	10,700	12,500
Inventory	20,000	26,000
Prepaid expenses	1,000	900
Total current assets	39,400	46,900
Total long-term assets	50,000	67,000
Total current liabilities	32,000	44,500
Total long-term liabilities	11,000	39,800
Common stock, no par*	10,000	10,000
Retained earnings	25,400	19,600

*NOTE: Two thousand shares of common stock have been issued and outstanding since the company started operations. During the entire fiscal year ended December 31, 2008, the stock was selling for $45 per share.

Requirement

1. Calculate the following ratios at December 31, 2008:

a. Acid-test ratio

b. Inventory turnover

c. Days' sales in receivables

d. Book value per share of common stock

e. Price/earnings ratio

f. Rate of return on total assets

g. Times-interest-earned ratio

h. Current ratio

i. Debt ratio

Do It Yourself! Question 1

Tykes Inc. had the following information at December 31, 2008:

TYKES INC.
Balance Sheet
December 31, 2008 and 2007

(Dollar amounts in millions)	2008	2007
Assets		
Cash	$400	$300
Accounts receivable	290	350
Inventory	150	220
Total assets	$840	$870
Liabilities		
Accounts payable	140	75
Loans payable	450	600
Total liabilities	590	675
Stockholders' Equity		
Common stock	40	40
Retained earnings	210	155
Total stockholders' equity	250	195
Total liabilities and equity	$840	$870

TYKES INC.
Income Statement
Years Ended December 31, 2008 and 2007

(Dollar amounts in millions)	2008	2007
Sales revenue	$1,200	$1,000
Less cost of goods sold	800	600
Gross profit	400	400
Insurance expense	200	190
Interest expense	60	80
Net income	$ 140	$ 130

At December 31, 2006, Tykes's inventory was $200 million and total equity was $165 million.

Requirements

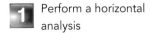

Perform a horizontal analysis

1. Prepare a horizontal analysis of Tykes's financial statements.

TYKES INC.
Horizontal Analysis of Balance Sheet
December 31, 2008 and 2007

(Dollar amounts in millions)	2008	2007	Increase (Decrease)	
			Amount	Percent
Assets				
Cash	$400	$300		
Accounts receivable	290	350		
Inventory	150	220		
Total assets	$840	$870		
Liabilities				
Accounts payable	140	75		
Loans payable	450	600		
Total liabilities	590	675		
Stockholders' Equity				
Common stock	40	40		
Retained earnings	210	155		
Total stockholders' equity	250	195		
Total liabilities and equity	$840	$870		

TYKES INC.
Horizontal Analysis of Comparative Income Statement
Years Ended December 31, 2008 and 2007

(Dollar amounts in millions)	2008	2007	Increase (Decrease)	
			Amount	Percent
Sales revenue	$1,200	$1,000		
Less cost of goods sold	800	600		
Gross profit	400	400		
Insurance expense	200	190		
Interest expense	60	80		
Net income	$ 140	$ 130		

2. Prepare a vertical analysis of Tykes's financial statements.

TYKES INC.
Vertical Analysis of Balance Sheet
December 31, 2008 and 2007

(Dollar amounts in millions)	2008	2008 %	2007	2007 %
Assets				
Cash	$400		$300	
Accounts receivable	290		350	
Inventory	150		220	
Total assets	$840		$870	
Liabilities				
Accounts payable	140		75	
Loans payable	450		600	
Total liabilities	590		675	
Stockholders' Equity				
Common stock	40		40	
Retained earnings	210		155	
Total stockholders' equity	250		195	
Total liabilities and equity	$840		$870	

TYKES INC.
Vertical Analysis of Comparative Income Statement
Years Ended December 31, 2008 and 2007

(Dollar amounts in millions)	2008	2008 %	2007	2007 %
Net sales revenue	$1,200		$1,000	
Less cost of goods sold	800		600	
Gross profit	400		400	
Insurance expense	200		190	
Interest expense	60		80	
Net income	$ 140		$ 130	

3. Calculate Tykes's inventory turnover and rate of return on stockholder's equity ratios for both years.

Quick Practice Solutions

True/False

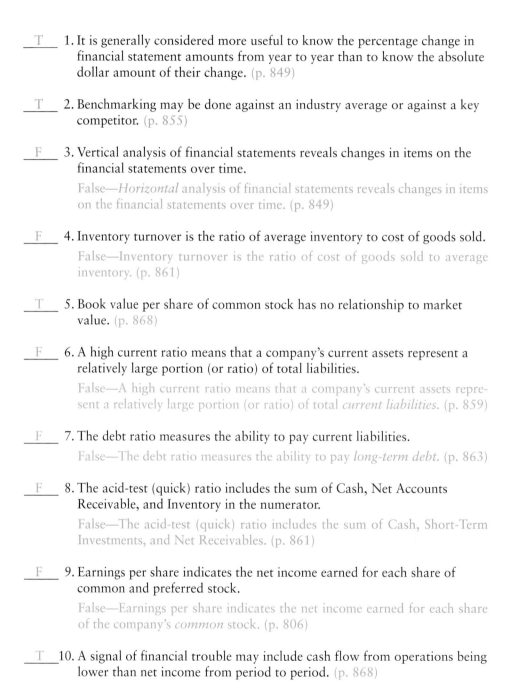

T___ 1. It is generally considered more useful to know the percentage change in financial statement amounts from year to year than to know the absolute dollar amount of their change. (p. 849)

T___ 2. Benchmarking may be done against an industry average or against a key competitor. (p. 855)

F___ 3. Vertical analysis of financial statements reveals changes in items on the financial statements over time.

   False—*Horizontal* analysis of financial statements reveals changes in items on the financial statements over time. (p. 849)

F___ 4. Inventory turnover is the ratio of average inventory to cost of goods sold.

   False—Inventory turnover is the ratio of cost of goods sold to average inventory. (p. 861)

T___ 5. Book value per share of common stock has no relationship to market value. (p. 868)

F___ 6. A high current ratio means that a company's current assets represent a relatively large portion (or ratio) of total liabilities.

   False—A high current ratio means that a company's current assets represent a relatively large portion (or ratio) of total *current liabilities*. (p. 859)

F___ 7. The debt ratio measures the ability to pay current liabilities.

   False—The debt ratio measures the ability to pay *long-term debt*. (p. 863)

F___ 8. The acid-test (quick) ratio includes the sum of Cash, Net Accounts Receivable, and Inventory in the numerator.

   False—The acid-test (quick) ratio includes the sum of Cash, Short-Term Investments, and Net Receivables. (p. 861)

F___ 9. Earnings per share indicates the net income earned for each share of common and preferred stock.

   False—Earnings per share indicates the net income earned for each share of the company's *common* stock. (p. 806)

T___10. A signal of financial trouble may include cash flow from operations being lower than net income from period to period. (p. 868)

Multiple Choice

1. Horizontal analysis can be described as which of the following? (p. 849)
   a. Percentage changes in various financial statement amounts from year to year
   b. The changes in individual financial statement amounts as a percentage of some related total
   c. The change in key financial statement ratios over a certain time frame or horizon
   d. None of the above

2. Trend percentages can be considered a form of which of the following? (p. 852)
   a. Ratio analysis
   b. Vertical analysis
   c. Profitability analysis
   d. Horizontal analysis

3. In 2008, net sales were $1,600,000 and in 2009, net sales were $1,750,000. How is the percent change calculated? (p. 850)
   a. Divide $1,600,000 by $1,750,000
   b. Divide $1,750,000 by $1,600,000
   c. Divide $150,000 by $1,750,000
   d. Divide $150,000 by $1,600,000

4. Vertical analysis can be described as which of the following? (p. 853)
   a. Percentage changes in the balances shown in comparative financial statements
   b. The change in key financial statement ratios over a specified period of time
   c. The dollar amount of the change in various financial statement amounts from year to year
   d. Individual financial statement items expressed as a percentage of a base (which represents 100%)

5. What is the base that is used when performing vertical analysis on an income statement? (p. 852)
   a. Net sales
   b. Gross sales
   c. Gross profit
   d. Total expenses

6. What is the base that is used when performing vertical analysis on a balance sheet? (p. 853)
   a. Total assets
   b. Stockholders' equity
   c. Total liabilities
   d. Net assets

7. Which ratio measures the ability to pay long-term debt? (p. 864)
   a. Rate of return on net sales
   b. Earnings per share
   c. Times-interest-earned ratio
   d. Acid-test (quick) ratio

8. **Which of the following would be most helpful in the comparison of different-sized companies?** (p. 853)
   a. Performing horizontal analysis
   b. Looking at the amount of income earned by each company
   c. Comparing working capital balances
   d. Preparing common-size financial statements

9. **Which ratio(s) help(s) in the analysis of working capital?** (p. 859)
   a. Current ratio
   b. Acid-test ratio
   c. Debt ratio
   d. Both a and b are correct

10. **Assume that collections from customers on account are being received faster. Which of the following would be true?** (p. 862)
    a. The accounts receivable turnover would be higher.
    b. The days' sales in receivables would be higher.
    c. The current ratio would be higher.
    d. None of the above.

Quick Exercises

17-1. Selected items from the balance sheet and income statement follow for the Brothers Company for 2007 and 2008. (p. 850)

Requirement

1. Calculate the amount of the change and the percentage of change for each item.

	2007	2008	$ Change	% Change
Cash	$121,000	$100,000	$21,000	21.0%
Accounts receivable	117,000	125,000	(8,000)	(6.4)
Merchandise inventory	70,000	85,000	(15,000)	(17.6)
Accounts payable	63,500	50,000	13,500	27.0
Sales	144,000	135,000	9,000	6.7
Cost of goods sold	74,000	67,500	6,500	9.6

17-2.   The income statement for Commerce Corporation for the year ended December 31, 2007, follows: (p. 853)

COMMERCE CORPORATION
Income Statement
Year Ended December 31, 2007

Net sales			$661,000
Expenses:			
	Cost of goods sold	$268,500	
	Selling expenses	45,000	
	General expenses	49,300	
	Interest expense	35,000	
	Income tax expense	30,000	
Total expenses			427,800
Net income			$233,200

Requirements

1. Prepare a vertical analysis of the income statement showing appropriate percentages for each item listed.

COMMERCE CORPORATION
Vertical Analysis of Income Statement
Year Ended December 31, 2007

		Amount	Percentage
Net sales		$661,000	100.0%
Expenses			
Cost of goods sold		268,500	40.6
Selling expenses		45,000	6.8
General expenses		49,300	7.5
Interest expense		35,000	5.3
Income tax expense		30,000	4.5
Total expenses		427,800	64.7
Net income		$233,200	35.3%

2. What additional information would you need to determine whether these percentages are good or bad?

Additional information to determine whether these percentages are good or bad might include:

- industry averages to compare to Commerce Corporation
- the change in each line item percentage over a relevant period of time

17-3. Financial ratios and analytical functions follow. (p. 859)

Requirement

1. Match the function with the appropriate ratio.

Functions:

    a. Gives the amount of net income earned for each share of the company's common stock
    b. Measures the number of times operating income can cover interest expense
    c. Shows ability to pay all current liabilities if they come due immediately
    d. Shows the percentage of a stock's market value returned to stockholders as dividends each period
    e. Measures ability to collect cash from credit customers
    f. Measures ability to pay current liabilities with current assets
    g. Indicates the market price of $1 of earnings
    h. Measures the difference between current assets and current liabilities
    i. Indicates percentage of assets financed with debt
    j. Shows the percentage of each sales dollar earned as net income

Ratios:

    1. _d_ Dividend yield
    2. _j_ Rate of return on net sales
    3. _e_ Accounts receivable turnover
    4. _h_ Working capital
    5. _i_ Debt ratio
    6. _f_ Current ratio
    7. _g_ Price/earnings ratio
    8. _b_ Times-interest-earned ratio
    9. _c_ Acid-test ratio
    10. _a_ Earnings per share of common stock

17-4. Using the following data for Dream Corporation for 2008, calculate the ratios that follow: (p. 866)

Market price per share of common stock at 12/31/08	$ 9.00
Net income	50,000
Number of common shares outstanding	25,000
Dividend per share of common stock	0.71

    a. earnings per share of common stock
        $50,000/25,000 = $2.00
    b. price/earnings ratio
        $9.00/$2.00 = 4.5
    c. dividend yield
        $0.71/$9.00 = 0.08

17-5. Following are selected data from the comparative income statement and balance sheet for Deerfield Corporation for the years ended December 31, 2008 and 2007: (p. 859)

	2008	2007
Net sales (all on credit)	$97,600	$93,000
Cost of goods sold	53,500	52,500
Gross profit	44,700	40,500
Income from operations	16,300	15,000
Interest expense	3,100	3,500
Net income	9,800	9,000
Cash	7,700	7,500
Accounts receivable, net	10,700	12,500
Inventory	20,000	26,000
Prepaid expenses	1,000	900
Total current assets	39,400	46,900
Total long-term assets	50,000	67,000
Total current liabilities	32,000	44,500
Total long-term liabilities	11,000	39,800
Common stock, no par*	10,000	10,000
Retained earnings	25,400	19,600

*NOTE: Two thousand shares of common stock have been issued and outstanding since the company started operations. During the entire fiscal year ended December 31, 2008, the stock was selling for $45 per share.

Requirement

1. Calculate the following ratios at December 31, 2008:

    a. Acid-test ratio

$$(\$7{,}700 + \$10{,}700)/\$32{,}000 = 0.58$$

    b. Inventory turnover

$$\frac{\$53{,}500}{(\$20{,}000+\$26{,}000)/2} = 2.33$$

    c. Days' sales in receivables

$$\frac{(\$10{,}700+\$12{,}500)/2}{\$97{,}600/365} = 43.4 \text{ days}$$

    d. Book value per share of common stock

$$\frac{\$10{,}000+\$25{,}400}{2{,}000} = \$17.70$$

    e. Price/earnings ratio

$$\frac{\$45}{\$9{,}800/2{,}000} = 9.18$$

    f. Rate of return on total assets

$$\frac{\$9{,}800+\$3{,}100}{(\$39{,}400+\$50{,}000+\$46{,}900+\$67{,}000)/2} = 0.13$$

    g. Times-interest-earned ratio

$$\frac{\$16{,}300}{\$3{,}100} = 5.26 \text{ times}$$

    h. Current ratio

$$\frac{\$39{,}400}{\$32{,}000} = 1.23$$

    i. Debt ratio

$$\frac{\$32{,}000+\$11{,}000}{\$39{,}400+\$50{,}000} = 0.48$$

Do It Yourself! Question 1 Solutions

Requirements

1. Prepare a horizontal analysis for Tykes's financial statements.

TYKES INC.
Horizontal Analysis of Balance Sheet
December 31, 2008 and 2007

(Dollar amounts in millions)	2008	2007	Increase	(Decrease)
			Amount	Percent
Assets				
Cash	$400	$300	$100	33.3%
Accounts receivable	290	350	(60)	(17.1)
Inventory	150	220	(70)	(31.8)
Total assets	$840	$870	$ (30)	(3.4)
Liabilities				
Accounts payable	140	75	65	86.7
Loans payable	450	600	(150)	(25.0)
Total liabilities	$590	$675	(85)	(12.6)
Stockholders' Equity				
Common stock	40	40	0	0.0
Retained earnings	210	155	55	35.5
Total stockholders' equity	$250	$195	55	28.2
Total liabilities and equity	$840	$870	$ (30)	(3.4)%

TYKES INC.
Horizontal Analysis of Comparative Income Statement
Years Ended December 31, 2008 and 2007

(Dollar amounts in millions)	2008	2007	Increase	(Decrease)
			Amount	Percent
Sales revenue	$1,200	$1,000	$200	20.0%
Less cost of goods sold	800	600	$200	33.3
Gross profit	400	400	0	0.0
Insurance expense	200	190	10)	5.3
Interest expense	60	80	(20)	(25.0)
Net income	$ 140	$ 130	$ 10	7.7%

2. Prepare a vertical analysis for Tykes's financial statements.

TYKES INC.
Vertical Analysis of Balance Sheet
December 31, 2008 and 2007

(Dollar amounts in millions)	2008	2008 %	2007	2007 %
Assets				
Cash	$400	47.6%	$300	34.5%
Accounts receivable	290	34.5	350	40.2
Inventory	150	17.9	220	25.3
Total assets	$840	100.0%	$870	100.0%
Liabilities				
Accounts payable	140	16.7%	75	8.6%
Loans payable	450	53.5	600	69.0
Total liabilities	590	70.2	675	77.6
Stockholders' Equity				
Common stock	40	4.8	40	4.6
Retained earnings	210	25.0	155	17.8
Total stockholders' equity	250	29.8	195	22.4
Total liabilities and equity	$840	100.0%	$870	100.0%

TYKES INC.
Vertical Analysis of Comparative Income Statement
Years Ended December 31, 2008 and 2007

(Dollar amounts in millions)	2008	2008 %	2007	2007 %
Net sales revenue	$1,200	100.0%	$1,000	100.0%
Less cost of goods sold	800	66.7	600	60.0
Gross profit	400	33.3	400	40.0
Insurance expense	200	16.6	190	19.0
Interest expense	60	5.0	80	8.0
Net income	$ 140	11.7%	$ 130	13.0%

3. Calculate Tykes's inventory turnover and rate of return on stockholder's equity ratios for both years.

$$\begin{array}{c} 2008 \\ \text{Inventory} \\ \text{turnover} \end{array} = \frac{\$800}{\frac{1}{2}(220+150)}$$

$$= \textbf{4.3 times}$$

$$\begin{array}{c} 2007 \\ \text{Inventory} \\ \text{turnover} \end{array} = \frac{\$600}{\frac{1}{2}(200+220)}$$

$$= \textbf{2.9 times}$$

$$\begin{array}{c} \text{2008 Rate of return on} \\ \text{stockholder's equity} \end{array} = \frac{\$140-\$0}{\frac{1}{2}(\$195+\$250)}$$

$$= \textbf{62.9\%}$$

$$\begin{array}{c} \text{2007 Rate of return on} \\ \text{stockholder's equity} \end{array} = \frac{\$130-\$0}{\frac{1}{2}(\$165+\$195)}$$

$$= \textbf{72.2\%}$$

The Power of Practice

For more practice using the skills learned in this chapter, visit MyAccountingLab. There you will find algorithmically generated questions that are based on these Demo Docs and your main textbook's Review and Assess Your Progress sections.

Go to MyAccountingLab and follow these steps:

1. Direct your URL to www.myaccountinglab.com.
2. Log in using your name and password.
3. Click the MyAccountingLab link.
4. Click Study Plan in the left navigation bar.
5. From the table of contents, select Chapter 17, Financial Statement Analysis.
6. Click a link to work tutorial exercises.

18 Introduction to Management Accounting

WHAT YOU PROBABLY ALREADY KNOW

If you have ever baked a cake, you probably already know that there are ingredients that are required to produce the desired result. You may use a mix that only requires eggs and water, or you may follow a recipe where you must add in all of the ingredients separately. Whichever it may be, you know that the more ingredients necessary to make the cake, the more costly it is. Assume you ask your sister to apply the icing because you're short on time and offer to pay her $5. The amount paid for her services (labor) adds to the cost of the cake. It is certain that without utilities to run the mixer and the oven, you could not make the cake. In business, this would be referred to as overhead. So, it seems that there is a cost of materials, labor, and overhead to make the cake. In this chapter, we will study these three components of cost for manufacturers.

Learning Objectives

 Identify trends in the business environment and the role of management accountability.

Some of the changes that have taken place over recent years include an increasing shift toward a service economy, global competition and increasing opportunities for worldwide expansion, time-based competition (including ERP, e-commerce, and JIT management), and an increased focus on promoting continuous improvement in the quality of goods and services produced (total quality management). *Review the section called "Today's Business Environment" in the main text, as well as management's accountability to stakeholders in Exhibit 18-2 (p. 901).*

2 Distinguish management accounting from financial accounting.

Management accounting provides financial and nonfinancial information to managers and other internal users of information. The data help management plan and control the operations of the business. **Financial accounting** provides financial information to users outside of the business such as creditors, investors, and governmental agencies. *Review management accounting versus financial accounting in Exhibit 18-3 (p. 902).*

Classify costs and prepare an income statement for a service company.

All of the costs of a service company are considered period costs. **Period costs** include selling, general, and administrative costs that are included as expenses on the income statement in the period incurred. There is no inventory for a service company and therefore none of the costs incurred are inventoriable. Similarly, there is no cost of goods sold on the income statement. *Review the income statement for a service company in Exhibit 18-4 (p. 904).*

 Classify costs and prepare an income statement for a merchandising company.

Some costs are **inventoriable product costs**, included in the cost of inventory on the balance sheet, until sold. These costs include the total cost of purchasing the inventory, plus the freight that may be required to obtain the goods. When the inventory is sold, it becomes cost of goods sold, one of the largest expenses on the income statement for a merchandising company. Recall from Chapter 5 the calculation of cost of goods sold for a periodic inventory system is to add beginning inventory, purchases, and freight in and subtract ending inventory. Review the income statement for a merchandising company in Exhibit 18-5 (p. 905).

 Classify costs and prepare an income statement for a manufacturing company.

Manufacturers have three stages and accounts for inventory: raw materials (including the components, ingredients, or parts used in manufacturing), work in process (including raw materials that have some degree of work done but not completed), and finished goods (completed and ready for sale). The inventoriable product costs in finished goods for a manufacturing company include the elements of cost required to make the goods, including direct materials, direct labor, and manufacturing overhead.

As described under Objective 4, merchandisers consider the cost of purchases and freight in to determine the cost of goods sold. Because manufacturers don't purchase their inventory, the cost of the goods manufactured must be considered to calculate the cost of goods sold for manufacturers. The approach, similar to that used to calculate the cost of goods sold for a merchandiser, is to start with beginning inventory, add direct materials, labor, and manufacturing overhead, and subtract ending inventory. *Review the inventoriable product and period costs analysis in Exhibit 18-8 (p. 911). Also, review the income statement for a manufacturing company in Exhibit 18-7 (p. 911) and carefully study the schedule of cost of goods manufactured, which can be particularly troublesome, in Exhibit 18-10 (p. 913).*

6 Use reasonable standards to make ethical judgments.

It is more important than ever to be mindful of making ethical judgments. Professional accounting associations have standards of ethical conduct, as do most other professions. In addition, employees are often provided with a code of ethics from their employer. Management accountants are required to maintain their professional competence, preserve the confidentiality of the information they handle, and act with integrity and objectivity. *Review the excerpt of the Institute of Management Accountants' Standards of ethical conduct in Exhibit 18-11 (p. 914).*

Demo Doc 1

Introduction to Management Accounting

Learning Objectives 1–4

Dark Spray Tanning has hired you as their new management accountant. Data for the month ended April 30, 2010 are as follows:

Wages expense	$ 8,000
Supply expense	3,000
Utility expense	2,000
Rent expense	1,000
Service revenue	17,000

Requirements

1. Your new boss has heard of the term *management accountability,* **but doesn't really understand what it means. Explain the concept of management accountability.**

2. Explain to your boss the scope of information you can produce as a management accountant.

3. Prepare an income statement for Dark Spray Tanning for the month ended April 30, 2010.

4. In the month of May, Dark Spray decided to sell tanning spray. Based on the following data, prepare Dark Spray's income statement for the month ended May 31, 2010.

Wages expense	$11,000
Supply expense	3,000
Utility expense	2,000
Rent expense	1,000
Sales revenue	30,000*
Purchases	15,000
Ending inventory	6,000

* Assume that 100% of sales revenue is from selling tanning spray.

5. Suppose Dark Spray sold 900 bottles of tanning spray in the month of May. What is its cost per bottle?

Demo Doc 1 Solutions

Requirement 1

Distinguish
management
accounting from
financial accounting

Your new boss has heard of the term management accountability, but
doesn't really understand what it means. Explain the concept of
management accountability.

Part 1	Part 2	Part 3	Part 4	Part 5	Demo Doc Complete

Management accountability is the idea that the manager is responsible to manage the resources of the organization. There are many groups and individuals, called stakeholders, who have an interest in an organization (that is, owners, creditors, customers, suppliers, and the various government organizations). To satisfy the needs of these stakeholders, managers are required to provide information that communicates the decisions made and the results obtained from these decisions.

Management accountability requires two forms of accounting:

- financial accounting for external reporting, and
- management accounting for internal planning, controlling, and decision making.

Remember, planning means choosing goals and deciding how to achieve them. Controlling means evaluating the results of business operations by comparing the actual results to the plan.

Requirement 2

Identify trends in the
business environment
and the role of
management
accountability

Explain to your boss the scope of information you can produce as a
management accountant.

Part 1	**Part 2**	Part 3	Part 4	Part 5	Demo Doc Complete

Management accounting provides more detailed and timely information than does financial accounting. Managers use this information to:

- identify ways to cut costs
- set prices that will be competitive and yet yield profits
- identify the most profitable products and customers so the sales force can focus on key profit makers
- evaluate employees' job performance

Chapter 18 | Demo Doc 1 Solutions

Requirement 3

3 Classify costs and prepare an income statement for a service company

Prepare an income statement for Dark Spray Tanning for the month ended April 30, 2010.

| Part 1 | Part 2 | **Part 3** | Part 4 | Part 5 | Demo Doc Complete |

As you recall from earlier chapters, an income statement reports the organization's revenues and expenses for a period of time.

Dark Spray is a service company, so all of its costs are period costs and it doesn't carry an inventory of product, so there is no cost of goods sold on its income statement. Period costs are costs incurred and expensed in the current accounting period.

Dark Spray's period costs include all expenses for the month of April (wages, supplies, utilities, and rent). Dark Spray's period costs are $8,000 + $3,000 + $2,000 + $1,000 = $14,000 for the month of April 2010.

Here is the income statement for Dark Spray for the month of April 2010.

DARK SPRAY TANNING
Income Statement
Month Ended April 30, 2010

Service revenue				$17,000	100%
Expenses:					
	Wages expense	$8,000			
	Supply expense	3,000			
	Utility expense	2,000			
	Rent expense	1,000			
Total expenses				14,000	82%
Operating income				$ 3,000	18%

Notice that Dark Spray has no cost of goods sold because it is a service company. Its largest expense on the income statement is for employee salaries. They also had an 18% profit margin for the month of April.

Requirement 4

In the month of May, Dark Spray decided to sell tanning spray. Based on the following data, prepare Dark Spray's income statement for the month ended May 31, 2010.

Wages expense	$11,000
Supply expense	3,000
Utility expense	2,000
Rent expense	1,000
Sales revenue	30,000*
Purchases	15,000
Ending inventory	6,000

* Assume that 100% of sales revenue is from selling tanning spray.

Part 1	Part 2	Part 3	**Part 4**	Part 5	Demo Doc Complete

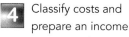 Classify costs and prepare an income statement for a merchandising company

Because Dark Spray has purchased products from a supplier that they now resell, Dark Spray is now a merchandiser (retailer). Dark Spray now maintains an inventory.

Dark Spray's income statement will now have cost of goods sold as a major expense. Any product that is not sold in one period will be shown as an asset called merchandise inventory. Merchandise inventory is NOT an expense until it is sold—then the expense becomes cost of goods sold.

The goods available for sale are computed by adding purchases during the period to beginning inventory. Ending inventory is subtracted from cost of goods available for sale to get cost of goods sold. Cost of goods sold is subtracted from sales revenue to get gross profit. Consider the following formula:

$$\begin{array}{l} \quad \text{Beginning Inventory} \\ + \ \underline{\text{Purchases}} \\ \quad \text{Goods Available for Sale} \\ - \ \underline{\text{Ending Inventory}} \\ \quad \text{Cost of Goods Sold} \end{array}$$

So in the case of Dark Spray:

	Beginning Inventory	$ 0
+	Purchases	15,000
	Goods Available for Sale	15,000
−	Ending Inventory	6,000
	Cost of Goods Sold	$ 9,000

Subtract $9,000 from sales revenue of $30,000 for a gross profit of $21,000.

Here is Dark Spray's income statement for the month ended May 31, 2010:

DARK SPRAY TANNING
Income Statement
Month Ended May 31, 2010

Sales revenue		$30,000	100%
Cost of goods sold:			
Beginning inventory	$ 0		
Purchases	15,000		
Cost of goods available for sale	15,000		
Ending inventory	(6,000)		
Cost of goods sold		9,000	30%
Gross profit		21,000	70%
Operating expenses:			
Wages expense	11,000		
Supply expense	3,000		
Utility expense	2,000		
Rent expense	1,000	17,000	57%
Operating income		$ 4,000	13%

Gross profit is what remains from sales after the cost of goods sold is subtracted from sales revenue. Gross profit is then used to cover operating expenses and yield a profit (or loss). Managers want to keep an eye on the gross profit percentage, which is a measure of profitability, to make sure that it doesn't fluctuate too much from period to period.

In this case, Dark Spray had a gross profit percentage of 70% and a 13% profit margin. These are calculated as follows:

$$\text{Gross Profit Percentage} = \frac{\text{Gross Profit}}{\text{Sales Revenue}}$$

$$\text{Dark Spray's Gross Profit Percentage} = \frac{\$21,000}{\$30,000}$$

$$= 70\%$$

$$\text{Profit Margin} = \frac{\text{Operating Income}}{\text{Sales Revenue}}$$

$$\text{Dark Spray's Profit Margin} = \frac{\$4,000}{\$30,000}$$

$$= 13\%$$

What this means is that Dark Spray generates $0.70 from each dollar of revenue for the period, which is used to cover its operating expenses and then generate operating income.

Profit margin represents the percentage of revenue that the company keeps as earnings. In this case, Dark Spray generates $0.13 from every revenue dollar as income. Managers watch this as well to make sure that it doesn't drop from period to period. Even if overall earnings increase, it's still possible for a company's profit margin to diminish if, for example, costs increase at a rate greater than sales. This would raise a flag to managers that they may need to exhibit greater control over costs.

Requirement 5

Suppose Dark Spray sold 900 bottles of tanning spray in the month of May. What is its cost per bottle?

Part 1	Part 2	Part 3	Part 4	**Part 5**	Demo Doc Complete

Cost per unit is determined by dividing total cost by the number of units. Knowing the costs the company incurs per unit it sells helps managers make pricing decisions. They obviously want to make sure they are charging their customers enough to cover their own costs and generate a profit. To calculate the cost per unit:

$$\text{Cost per unit} = \frac{\text{Total cost of goods sold}}{\text{Total number of units sold}}$$

Dark Spray wants to know its cost for each bottle of tanning spray it sells. In this case, the total cost of selling 900 bottles is $9,000. So:

$$\text{Cost per bottle} = \frac{\$9,000}{900 \text{ bottles}}$$

$$= \mathbf{\$10} \text{ per bottle}$$

Managers will use the per-unit cost information to help them make better decisions. Knowing that their per-unit cost is $10, Dark Spray managers may decide they need to adjust their price.

Part 1	Part 2	Part 3	Part 4	Part 5	**Demo Doc Complete**

Demo Doc 2

Manufacturing Companies

Learning Objectives 5, 6

Chase Toys produces toys for dogs. The following information was available for the month ended November 30, 2010 (assume no beginning or ending raw materials inventory):

Sales revenue	$106,500
Direct materials used	32,000
Direct labor	16,000
Manufacturing overhead*	17,000
Beginning work in process	8,000
Ending work in process	6,000
Operating expenses	32,000
Finished goods, Nov. 1, 2010	4,000
Finished goods, Nov. 30, 2010	7,200

* All indirect production costs are included in manufacturing overhead.

Requirements

1. Prepare a schedule of cost of goods manufactured for the month ended November 30, 2010.

2. Prepare an income statement for the month ended November 30, 2010.

3. At an internal Chase Toys meeting, you learned that Chase Toys has developed a new product that is expected to produce record profits. Before Chase Toys went public with this product, you advised your girlfriend to invest in Chase Toys. Which standard of ethical conduct for management accountants did you violate? Explain.

Demo Doc 2 Solutions

Requirement 1

5 Classify costs and prepare an income statement for a manufacturing company

Prepare a schedule of cost of goods manufactured for the month ended November 30, 2010.

Part 1	Part 2	Part 3	Demo Doc Complete

The cost of goods manufactured summarizes the manufacturing activities that took place for the month of November 2010.

The three manufacturing costs—direct materials, direct labor, and manufacturing overhead—are added together to get the total manufacturing costs incurred during November ($32,000 + $16,000 + $17,000 = $65,000). These are added to beginning inventory to yield the total accountable manufacturing costs. Ending inventory is then subtracted from total accountable manufacturing costs to get cost of goods manufactured. Consider the following formula:

Beginning Work In Process	
+ Direct Materials used	
+ Direct Labor used	
+ Factory / Manufacturing Overhead applied	
Current Manufacturing Costs	
− Ending Work In Process	
Cost of Goods Manufactured	

So for Chase Toys:

Beginning Work In Process	$ 8,000
+ Direct Materials used	32,000
+ Direct Labor used	16,000
+ Factory / Manufacturing Overhead applied	17,000
Current Manufacturing Costs	73,000
− Ending Work In Process	6,000
Cost of Goods Manufactured	$67,000

Here is Chase Toys' schedule of cost of goods manufactured for the month ended November 30, 2010:

CHASE TOYS
Schedule of Cost of Goods Manufactured
Month Ended November 30, 2010

Beginning work in process inventory		$ 8,000
Add: Direct materials used	$32,000	
Direct labor	16,000	
Manufacturing overhead	17,000	
Total manufacturing costs incurred during the period		65,000
Total accountable manufacturing costs		73,000
Less: Ending work in process		(6,000)
Cost of goods manufactured		$67,000

Notice the similarity between calculating cost of goods manufactured and calculating cost of goods sold for a merchandiser: Start with the beginning inventory balance, increase it for the additions during the period, and subtract the ending inventory balance.

The cost of goods manufactured becomes part of the finished goods inventory, which will be shown as an asset until the period in which it is sold, when it flows to cost of goods sold.

Note that the inventoriable product costs in Finished Goods for a manufacturing company include the elements of cost required to make the goods. These include:

- **Direct materials**—Physical components required to manufacture the product and that can be traced directly to the finished good.
- **Direct labor**—Labor of employees who work directly on the finished product.
- **Manufacturing overhead**—Includes all of the manufacturing costs other than direct materials and direct labor. These typically include factory costs such as insurance, depreciation, and utilities. Overhead also includes **indirect materials** (low value materials that cannot be traced directly to a finished product) and **indirect labor** (supportive factory labor of janitors, managers, and equipment operators that cannot be traced directly to a finished product).

Requirement 2

Prepare an income statement for the month ended November 30, 2010.

5 Classify costs and prepare an income statement for a manufacturing company

Part 1	**Part 2**	Part 3	Demo Doc Complete

The Cost of Goods Manufactured account summarizes the activities that take place in a manufacturing plant over a period of time. It represents the manufacturing cost of goods that Chase Toys finished during November.

Cost of goods sold is computed as follows:

	Beginning Inventory	$ 4,000
+	Cost of Goods Manufactured	67,000
	Cost of Goods Available for Sale	71,000
−	Ending Inventory	7,200
	Cost of Goods Sold	$63,800

Following is Chase Toys' income statement for the month of November:

CHASE TOYS
Income Statement
Month Ended November 30, 2010

Sales revenue		$106,500	100%
Cost of goods sold:			
Beginning finished goods inventory	$ 4,000		
Cost of goods manufactured	67,000		
Cost of goods available for sale	71,000		
Ending finished goods inventory	(7,200)		
Cost of goods sold		63,800	60%
Gross profit		42,700	40%
Operating expenses		32,000	30%
Operating income		$ 10,700	10%

Notice how the cost of goods manufactured amount computed on the schedule in requirement 1 is part of finished goods here—the only inventory that is ready to sell. It becomes part of cost of goods sold on the income statement.

Note that Finished Goods for a manufacturer is like the Inventory account for a merchandiser. In both cases, these accounts represent the inventory that is complete and available to be sold.

Requirement 3

6 Use reasonable standards to make ethical judgments

At an internal Chase Toys meeting, you learned that Chase Toys has developed a new product that is expected to produce record profits. Before Chase Toys went public with this product, you advised your girlfriend to invest in Chase Toys. Which standard of ethical conduct for management accountants did you violate? Explain.

Part 1	Part 2	**Part 3**	Demo Doc Complete

Providing confidential company information to your girlfriend is a clear violation of the **confidentiality standard**. Employees must refrain from disclosing confidential information acquired in the course of work except when authorized, unless legally obligated to do so.

Part 1	Part 2	Part 3	**Demo Doc Complete**

Quick Practice Questions

True/False

_____ 1. A system that integrates all of a company's worldwide functions, departments, and data is called supply-chain management.

_____ 2. A budget is a quantitative expression of a plan that helps managers coordinate and implement the plan.

_____ 3. Goods that are partway through the manufacturing process, but not yet complete, are referred to as materials inventory.

_____ 4. Manufacturers use labor, plant, and equipment to convert raw materials into new finished products.

_____ 5. Period costs are operating costs that are expensed in the period in which the goods are sold.

_____ 6. Indirect labor and indirect materials are part of manufacturing overhead.

_____ 7. Trends in the modern business environment include the shift to a service economy and the rise of the global marketplace.

_____ 8. Management has a responsibility to meet regulatory obligations to federal and local government agencies.

_____ 9. Total quality management applies only to manufacturers and promotes the creation of superior products.

_____ 10. The cost of goods manufactured is equal to the sum of direct materials used, direct labor, and manufacturing overhead.

Multiple Choice

1. The primary goal of financial accounting is to provide information to which of the following?
   a. Investors
   b. Creditors
   c. Company managers
   d. Both a and b

2. Which of the following is true about management accounting?
   a. Management accounting provides information to customers.
   b. Management accounting provides information that is required to be audited by certified public accountants.
   c. Management accounting primarily focuses on reporting on the company as a whole on a quarterly or annual basis.
   d. Management accounting is not restricted by GAAP.

3. **Manufacturers may have which accounts on their balance sheet?**
   a. Materials, Work in Process, and Finished Goods
   b. Merchandise, Materials, and Finished Goods
   c. Direct Materials, Direct Labor, and Manufacturing Overhead
   d. Work in Process, Materials, and Manufacturing Overhead

4. **In which category would glue or fasteners to manufacture a table be included?**
   a. Direct materials
   b. Manufacturing overhead
   c. Period costs
   d. Indirect labor

5. **Inventoriable product costs include which of the following?**
   a. Marketing costs
   b. Costs of direct materials, direct labor, and manufacturing overhead used to produce a product
   c. Costs of direct materials and direct labor used to produce a product
   d. Period costs, overhead, and direct labor

6. **When do inventoriable costs become expenses?**
   a. When the manufacturing process begins
   b. When the manufacturing process is completed
   c. When the direct materials are purchased
   d. When the units in inventory are sold

7. **In which category would selling and administrative costs be included?**
   a. Direct materials
   b. Manufacturing overhead
   c. Period costs
   d. Work in process

8. **All *except* which of the following are manufacturing overhead costs?**
   a. Materials used directly in the manufacturing process of the product
   b. Insurance on factory equipment
   c. Salaries of production supervisors
   d. Property tax on factory building

9. **Cost of goods sold for a manufacturer equals cost of goods manufactured plus which of the following?**
   a. Beginning work in process inventory less ending work in process inventory
   b. Ending work in process inventory less beginning work in process inventory
   c. Beginning finished goods inventory less ending finished goods inventory
   d. Ending finished goods inventory less beginning finished goods inventory

10. **At the beginning of 2008, the Taylor Company's Work in Process Inventory account had a balance of $30,000. During 2008, $68,000 of direct materials were used in production, and $66,000 of direct labor costs were incurred. Manufacturing overhead in 2008 amounted to $90,000. The cost of goods manufactured was $220,000 in 2008. What is the balance in the work in process inventory on December 31, 2008?**
    a. $34,000
    b. $24,000
    c. $66,000
    d. $6,000

Quick Exercises

18-1. Use the correct number to categorize each item that follows:

1. Direct materials
2. Selling and general expenses
3. Manufacturing overhead
4. Direct labor

a. _____ rent expense on factory building

b. _____ sales supplies used

c. _____ factory supplies used

d. _____ indirect materials used

e. _____ wages of assembly line personnel

f. _____ cost of primary material used to make product

g. _____ depreciation on office equipment

h. _____ rent on office facilities

i. _____ insurance expired on factory equipment

j. _____ utilities incurred in the office

k. _____ advertising expense

l. _____ taxes paid on factory building

18-2. The Carter Company reports the following information for 2007:

Sales	$70,600
Direct materials used	7,300
Depreciation on factory equipment	4,700
Indirect labor	5,900
Direct labor	11,300
Factory rent	4,200
Factory utilities	1,200
Sales salary expense	16,300
Office salary expense	8,900
Indirect materials	1,200

Compute the following:

a. Inventoriable product costs

b. Period costs

18-3. Indicate whether each of the following costs is a product cost or a period cost:

    a. _____ direct materials used

    b. _____ factory utilities

    c. _____ salespersons' commissions

    d. _____ plant manager's salary

    e. _____ indirect materials used

    f. _____ depreciation on store equipment

    g. _____ indirect labor incurred

    h. _____ advertising expense

    i. _____ direct labor incurred

    j. _____ factory machinery repairs and maintenance

    k. _____ depreciation on factory machinery

    l. _____ office supplies used

    m. _____ plant insurance expired

18-4. South State Company financial information for the year ended December 31, 2008 follows:

Direct materials used	$71,000
Direct labor incurred	37,000
Indirect labor	2,700
Indirect materials used	1,600
Other factory costs:	
Utilities	3,100
Maintenance	4,500
Supplies	1,800
Depreciation	7,900
Property taxes	2,600

There was no beginning or ending finished goods inventory, but work in process inventory began the year with a $5,500 balance and ended the year with a $7,500 balance.

Requirement

1. Prepare a schedule of cost of goods manufactured for South State Company for the year ending December 31, 2008.

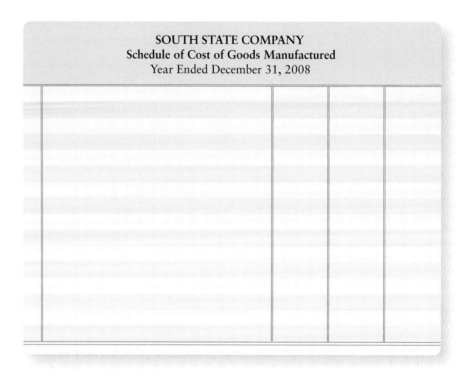

SOUTH STATE COMPANY
Schedule of Cost of Goods Manufactured
Year Ended December 31, 2008

18-5.   Briefly describe a just-in-time management philosophy.

Do It Yourself! Question 1

Introduction to Management Accounting

Stay Fit Exercise Company has hired you as their new management accountant. Data for the month ended February 28, 2010 is as follows:

Wages expense	$22,000
Supply expense	3,000
Utility expense	1,000
Rent expense	4,500
Service revenue	32,000

Requirements

1. Your new boss has heard of the term *total quality management,* **but doesn't really understand what it means. Explain the concept of total quality management.**

2. Prepare an income statement for Stay Fit for the month ended February 28, 2010.

3. In the month of March, Stay Fit decided to sell exercise balls. Based on the following data, prepare Stay Fit's income statement for the month ended March 31, 2010. Calculate Stay Fit's gross profit percentage and profit margin (round to the nearest percentage point).

Wages expense	$24,000
Supply expense	3,000
Utility expense	1,000
Rent expense	4,500
Sales revenue	42,000*
Purchases	8,000
Ending inventory	2,000

*Assume that 100% of sales revenue is from selling exercise balls.

4. Suppose Stay Fit sold 375 exercise balls in the month of March. What is its cost per ball?

Do It Yourself! Question 2

Manufacturing Companies

Theme Cans Company produces metal popcorn cans. The following information was available for the month ended August 31, 2010:

Sales	$104,250
Direct materials used	36,000
Direct labor	25,000
Manufacturing overhead	12,000
Beginning work in process	5,000
Ending work in process	3,000
Operating expenses	28,400
Finished goods, Aug. 1, 2010	2,500
Finished goods, Aug. 30, 2010	5,200

Requirements

1. Prepare a schedule of cost of goods manufactured for the month ended August 31, 2010.

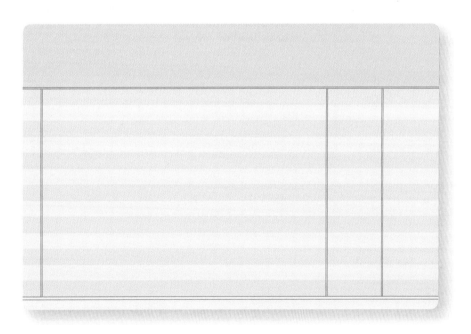

2. Prepare Theme Cans' income statement for the month ended August 31, 2010.

3. As the management accountant for Theme Cans, you are in the process of purchasing new software for the company. One of the suppliers of software gave you a brand new set of expensive golf clubs. Was the acceptance of the golf clubs a violation of any management accountant standard of ethical conduct? Explain.

Quick Practice Solutions

True/False

   F   1. A system that integrates all of a company's worldwide functions, departments, and data is called supply-chain management.

          False—A system that integrates all of a company's worldwide functions, departments, and data is called *enterprise resource planning.* (p.903)

   T   2. A budget is a quantitative expression of a plan that helps managers coordinate and implement the plan. (p. 901)

   F   3. Goods that are partway through the manufacturing process, but not yet complete, are referred to as materials inventory.

          False—Goods that are partway through the manufacturing process, but not yet complete, are referred to as *work in process.* (p. 909)

   T   4. Manufacturers use labor, plant, and equipment to convert raw materials into new finished products. (p. 909)

   F   5. Period costs are operating costs that are expensed in the period in which the goods are sold.

          False—Period costs are operating costs that are expensed in the *period incurred.* (p. 904)

   T   6. Indirect labor and indirect materials are part of manufacturing overhead. (p. 909)

   T   7. Trends in the modern business environment include the shift to a service economy and the rise of the global marketplace. (pp. 902–903)

   T   8. Management has a responsibility to meet regulatory obligations to federal and local government agencies. (p. 901)

   F   9. Total quality management applies only to manufacturers and promotes the creation of superior products.

          False—Total quality management promotes the creation of *superior products and services.* It applies to entities other than manufacturers. (p. 903)

   F 10. The cost of goods manufactured is equal to the sum of direct materials used, direct labor, and manufacturing overhead.

          False—The cost of goods manufactured is equal to the sum of direct materials used, direct labor, and manufacturing overhead *plus* beginning work in process inventory *minus* ending work in process inventory. (p. 912)

Multiple Choice

1. The primary goal of financial accounting is to provide information to which of the following? (p. 901)
   a. Investors
   b. Creditors
   c. Company managers
   d. Both a and b

2. Which of the following is true about management accounting? (pp. 901–902)
   a. Management accounting provides information to customers.
   b. Management accounting provides information that is required to be audited by certified public accountants.
   c. Management accounting primarily focuses on reporting on the company as a whole on a quarterly or annual basis.
   d. Management accounting is not restricted by GAAP.

3. Manufacturers may have which accounts on their balance sheet? (p. 909)
   a. Materials, Work in Process, and Finished Goods
   b. Merchandise, Materials, and Finished Goods
   c. Direct Materials, Direct Labor, and Manufacturing Overhead
   d. Work in Process, Materials, and Manufacturing Overhead

4. In which category would glue or fasteners to manufacture a table be included? (p. 909)
   a. Direct materials
   b. Manufacturing overhead
   c. Period costs
   d. Indirect labor

5. Inventoriable product costs include which of the following? (p. 909)
   a. Marketing costs
   b. Costs of direct materials, direct labor, and manufacturing overhead used to produce a product
   c. Costs of direct materials and direct labor used to produce a product
   d. Period costs, overhead, and direct labor

6. When do inventoriable costs become expenses? (pp. 909–911)
   a. When the manufacturing process begins
   b. When the manufacturing process is completed
   c. When the direct materials are purchased
   d. When the units in inventory are sold

7. In which category would selling and administrative costs be included? (p. 904)
   a. Direct materials
   b. Manufacturing overhead
   c. Period costs
   d. Work in process

8. All *except* which of the following are manufacturing overhead costs? (p. 910)
   a. Materials used directly in the manufacturing process of the product
   b. Insurance on factory equipment
   c. Salaries of production supervisors
   d. Property tax on factory building

9. Cost of goods sold for a manufacturer equals cost of goods manufactured plus which of the following? (p. 905)
   a. Beginning work in process inventory less ending work in process inventory
   b. Ending work in process inventory less beginning work in process inventory
   c. Beginning finished goods inventory less ending finished goods inventory
   d. Ending finished goods inventory less beginning finished goods inventory

10. At the beginning of 2008, the Taylor Company's Work in Process Inventory account had a balance of $30,000. During 2008, $68,000 of direct materials were used in production, and $66,000 of direct labor costs were incurred. Manufacturing overhead in 2008 amounted to $90,000. The cost of goods manufactured was $220,000 in 2008. What is the balance in the work in process inventory on December 31, 2008? (p. 912)
    a. $34,000
    b. $24,000
    c. $66,000
    d. $6,000

Quick Exercises

18-1. Use the correct number to categorize each item that follows: (p. 909)

1. Direct materials
2. Selling and general expenses
3. Manufacturing overhead
4. Direct labor

a. 3   rent expense on factory building

b. 2   sales supplies used

c. 3   factory supplies used

d. 3   indirect materials used

e. 4   wages of assembly line personnel

f. 1   cost of primary material used to make product

g. 2   depreciation on office equipment

h. 2   rent on office facilities

i. 3   insurance expired on factory equipment

j. 2   utilities incurred in the office

k. 2   advertising expense

l. 3   taxes paid on factory building

18-2.   The Carter Company reports the following information for 2007:

Sales	$70,600
Direct materials used	7,300
Depreciation on factory equipment	4,700
Indirect labor	5,900
Direct labor	11,300
Factory rent	4,200
Factory utilities	1,200
Sales salary expense	16,300
Office salary expense	8,900
Indirect materials	1,200

Compute the following: (p. 909)

a.   Inventoriable product costs
$7,300 + $4,700 + $5,900 + $11,300 + $4,200 + $1,200 + $1,200
= $35,800

b.   Period costs
$16,300 + $8,900 = $25,200

18-3.   Indicate whether each of the following costs is a product cost or a period cost: (p. 909)

a.   product   direct materials used

b.   product   factory utilities

c.   period   salespersons' commissions

d.   product   plant manager's salary

e.   product   indirect materials used

f.   period   depreciation on store equipment

g.   product   indirect labor incurred

h.   period   advertising expense

i.   product   direct labor incurred

j.   product   factory machinery repairs and maintenance

k.   product   depreciation on factory machinery

l.   period   office supplies used

m.   product   plant insurance expired

18-4. South State Company financial information for the year ended December 31, 2008, follows:

Direct materials used	$71,000
Direct labor incurred	37,000
Indirect labor	2,700
Indirect materials used	1,600
Other factory costs:	
Utilities	3,100
Maintenance	4,500
Supplies	1,800
Depreciation	7,900
Property taxes	2,600

There was no beginning or ending finished goods inventory, but work in process inventory began the year with a $5,500 balance and ended the year with a $7,500 balance. (p. 913)

Requirement

1. Prepare a schedule of cost of goods manufactured for South State Company for the year ending December 31, 2008.

SOUTH STATE COMPANY
Schedule of Cost of Goods Manufactured
Year Ended December 31, 2008

Beginning work in process inventory			$ 5,500
Add:			
Direct materials used		$71,000	
Direct labor		37,000	
Manufacturing overhead:			
Indirect labor	$2,700		
Indirect materials	1,600		
Utilities	3,100		
Maintenance	4,500		
Supplies	1,800		
Depreciation	7,900		
Property taxes	2,600	24,200	
Total manufacturing costs incurred			
during the year			132,200
Total manufacturing costs to account for			137,700
Less: Ending work in process inventory			(7,500)
Cost of goods manufactured			$130,200

18-5.   Briefly describe a just-in-time management philosophy. (p. 903)

In a just-in-time system, an organization purchases materials and produces products just when they are needed in the production process. Goods are not produced until it is time for them to be shipped to a customer. The goal is to have zero inventory because holding inventory does not add value to the product. Reducing inventory and speeding the production process reduces throughput time—the time between buying raw materials and selling the finished products.

Manufacturers adopting just-in-time depend on their suppliers to make on-time deliveries of perfect-quality raw materials. JIT requires close communication with suppliers.

Companies that adopt JIT must strive for perfect quality. Defects stop production lines. To avoid disrupting production, defects must be rare.

Do It Yourself! Question 1 Solutions

Requirements

1 Distinguish management accounting from financial accounting

1. Your new boss has heard of the term total quality management, but doesn't really understand what it means. Explain the concept of total quality management.

Total quality management is a management philosophy that promotes the goal of providing customers with superior products and services. Companies achieve this goal by continuously improving quality and reducing or eliminating defects and waste. Companies design and build quality into their products and services rather than depending on finding and fixing defects later.

3 Classify costs and prepare an income statement for a service company

2. Prepare an income statement for Stay Fit for the month ended February 28, 2010.

STAY FIT EXERCISE COMPANY
Income Statement
Month Ended February 28, 2010

Service revenue		$32,000	100%
Expenses:			
Wages expense	$22,000		
Rent expense	4,500		
Supply expense	3,000		
Utility expense	1,000		
Total expenses		30,500	95%
Operating income		$ 1,500	5%

3. In the month of March, Stay Fit decided to sell exercise balls. Based on the following data, prepare Stay Fit's income statement for the month ended March 31, 2010. Calculate Stay Fit's gross profit percentage and profit margin (round to the nearest percentage point).

Wages expense	$24,000
Supply expense	3,000
Utility expense	1,000
Rent expense	4,500
Sales revenue	42,000*
Purchases	8,000
Ending inventory	2,000

*Assume that 100% of sales revenue is from selling exercise balls.

Classify costs and prepare an income statement for a merchandising company

STAY FIT EXERCISE COMPANY
Income Statement
Month Ended February 28, 2010

Sales revenue			$42,000	100%
Cost of goods sold:				
Beginning inventory		$ 0		
Purchases		8,000		
Cost of goods available for sale		8,000		
Ending inventory		(2,000)		
Cost of goods sold			6,000	14%
Gross profit			36,000	86%
Operating expenses:				
Wages expense		24,000		
Rent expense		4,500		
Supply expense		3,000		
Utility expense		1,000	32,500	77%
Operating income			$ 3,500	8%

$$\text{Gross Profit Percentage} = \frac{\text{Gross Profit}}{\text{Sales Revenue}}$$

$$\text{Stay Fit's Gross Profit Percentage} = \frac{\$36,000}{42,000}$$

$$= 86\%$$

$$\text{Profit Margin} = \frac{\text{Operating Income}}{\text{Sales Revenue}}$$

$$\text{Stay Fit's Profit Margin} = \frac{\$3,500}{42,000}$$

$$= 8\%$$

4. Suppose Stay Fit sold 375 exercise balls in the month of March. What is its cost per ball?

$$\text{Cost per unit} \quad = \quad \frac{\text{Total cost of goods sold}}{\text{Total number of units sold}}$$

$$\text{Cost per ball} \quad = \quad \frac{\$6,000}{375 \text{ balls}}$$

$$= \mathbf{\$16} \text{ per ball}$$

Do It Yourself! Question 2 Solutions

Requirements

5 Classify costs and prepare an income statement for a manufacturing company

1. Prepare a schedule of cost of goods manufactured for the month ended August 31, 2010.

THEME CANS
Schedule of Cost of Goods Manufactured
Month Ended August 31, 2010

Beginning work in process inventory		$ 5,000
Add: Direct materials used	$36,000	
Direct labor	25,000	
Manufacturing overhead	12,000	
Total manufacturing costs incurred during the period		73,000
Total accountable manufacturing costs		78,000
Less: Ending work in process		(3,000)
Cost of goods manufactured		$75,000

5 Classify costs and prepare an income statement for a manufacturing company

2. Prepare Theme Cans' income statement for the month ended August 31, 2010.

THEME CANS
Income Statement
Month Ended August 31, 2010

Sales revenue		$104,250	100%
Cost of goods sold:			
Beginning finished goods inventory	$ 2,500		
Cost of goods manufactured	75,000		
Cost of goods available for sale	77,500		
Ending finished goods inventory	(5,200)		
Cost of goods sold		72,300	69%
Gross profit		31,950	31%
Operating expenses		28,400	27%
Operating income		$ 3,550	3%

 Use reasonable standards to make ethical judgments

3. As the management accountant for Theme Cans, you are in the process of purchasing new software for the company. One of the suppliers of software gave you a brand new set of expensive golf clubs. Was the acceptance of the golf clubs a violation of any management accountant standard of ethical conduct? Explain.

The **integrity standard** indicates that the accountant must refuse any gift, favor, or hospitality that would influence *or would appear to influence* actions. The acceptance of a new set of golf clubs is a gift that would appear to influence actions.

The Power of Practice

For more practice using the skills learned in this chapter, visit MyAccountingLab. There you will find algorithmically generated questions that are based on these Demo Docs and your main textbook's Review and Assess Your Progress sections.

Go to MyAccountingLab and follow these steps:

1. Direct your URL to www.myaccountinglab.com.
2. Log in using your name and password.
3. Click the MyAccountingLab link.
4. Click Study Plan in the left navigation bar.
5. From the table of contents, select Chapter 18, Introduction to Management Accounting.
6. Click a link to work tutorial exercises.

19 Job Order Costing

WHAT YOU PROBABLY ALREADY KNOW

If you own a car, you may have already had the unpleasant task of taking your car to a repair shop. Then you probably already know that before work is performed, a cost estimate is usually stated as a certain amount for parts and an hourly amount for labor. The hourly labor charge is much higher than the employees are paid. The charge must be sufficient to cover such overhead costs of running the shop as rent, utilities, maintenance, and supplies. An additional amount is added on top of the costs to create a profit. It is very important to be able to accurately identify all of the projected costs and estimated hours of work that will take place to calculate the cost per hour. In this chapter, we will study how an overhead rate is calculated and allocated to jobs performed.

Learning Objectives

1 Distinguish between job order costing and process costing.

Job order costing accumulates costs for each unique job, assignment, or batch. A construction company, photographer, and law firm may use job order costing because the required work may vary among customers and clients. Other companies operate by performing a similar set of production steps or processes. These companies would use a process costing system, which accumulates the costs for each process or department. A cereal manufacturer, bank, and automotive manufacturer might all use process costing.

2 Record materials and labor transactions in a manufacturer's job order costing system.

A job cost record is created when the job is started. All of the costs of production will be recorded on this record: direct materials used, direct labor used, and manufacturing overhead. In Demo Doc 1, you will see how materials and labor transactions are recorded in a manufacturer's job order costing system. *Review the "Decision Guidelines—Job Order Costing: Tracing Direct Materials and Direct Labor" section in the main text.*

3   Record manufacturing overhead transactions in a manufacturer's job order costing system.

Manufacturing overhead includes factory depreciation, repairs, insurance, utilities, and other factory costs. The accumulation of these costs is debited to Manufacturing Overhead and credited to the appropriate accounts, as you will see in Demo Doc 2.

4   Record transactions for completion and sales of finished goods and adjustment for under- or overallocated manufacturing overhead.

As goods continue to be worked on and completed, the costs will transfer from the Work in Process Inventory account to the Finished Goods inventory account. The inventory costs remain in the Finished Goods asset account until they are sold. When the goods are sold, two entries are required under the perpetual inventory system, as we learned in Chapter 5. One entry is made to record the sale on account or for cash. The other entry removes the cost of inventory and charges Cost of Goods Sold. Manufacturing Overhead is debited for the actual overhead costs and credited for the assigned overhead costs. At year-end, as you will see in Demo Doc 2, the balance in Manufacturing Overhead should be transferred into Cost of Goods Sold.

5   Calculate unit costs for service companies.

The costs for service companies include the labor component and the other indirect office costs. The hourly cost per employee can be calculated as follows:

$$\text{Hourly Labor Cost} = \frac{\text{Salary and Fringe Benefits}}{\text{Total Number of Hours Worked}}$$

Other indirect office costs may include rent, utilities, taxes, and support salaries. An hourly cost for indirect costs can be calculated as follows:

$$\text{Predetermined Indirect Cost Allocation Rate} = \frac{\text{Total Expected Indirect Costs}}{\text{Total Direct Labor Hours}}$$

To determine the cost of a job, the actual number of hours applied to the job should be multiplied by the hourly labor cost and the predetermined indirect cost allocation rate.

Demo Doc 1

Job Order Costing for Manufacturers _____

Learning Objectives 1, 2

Clarence Douglas manufactures specialized art for his customers. Suppose Douglas has the following transactions during March:

a. **Purchased raw materials on account, $67,000.**

b. **Materials costing $45,000 were requisitioned for production. Of this total, $5,000 were indirect materials.**

c. **Labor time records show that direct labor of $30,000 and indirect labor of $2,000 were incurred, but not yet paid.**

Requirements

1. Why would Douglas use the job order costing system?

2. What document would Douglas use to accumulate direct materials, direct labor, and manufacturing overhead costs assigned to each individual job? How do managers use this document to direct and control operations?

3. Prepare summary journal entries for each transaction.

Demo Doc 1 Solutions

Requirement 1

1 Distinguish between job order costing and process costing

Why would Douglas use the job order costing system?

Part 1	Part 2	Part 3	Demo Doc Complete

Companies that manufacture batches of unique or specialized products would use a job order costing system to accumulate costs for each job or batch. Because Douglas manufactures specialized art for his customers and the required work may vary from customer to customer, Douglas would use the job order costing system. You will learn about the process costing system, which accumulates costs for production processes as opposed to individual jobs, in Chapter 20.

Requirement 2

2 Record materials and labor in a job order costing system

What document would Douglas use to accumulate direct materials, direct labor, and manufacturing overhead costs assigned to each individual job? How do managers use this document to direct and control operations?

Part 1	**Part 2**	Part 3	Demo Doc Complete

Douglas would use a job cost record to accumulate direct materials, direct labor, and manufacturing overhead costs assigned to each individual job. Managers use job cost records to determine how much each job (and each unit in the job) costs to produce. Managers use cost information to help them set prices and control costs. Cost data help managers identify their most profitable products so that marketing can concentrate on selling these products. Managers also use cost data to make outsourcing decisions and to prepare the company's financial statements.

Managers also use the job cost record to see how they can use materials and labor more efficiently. For example, if a job's costs exceed its budget, managers must do a better job controlling costs on future jobs, or raise the sale price on similar jobs, to be sure that the company remains profitable.

Similarly, managers use labor time records to control labor costs. Together, labor time records and job cost records help managers determine whether employees are working efficiently. If they spend longer than expected on a job, it may not yield a profit.

Managers also use the materials inventory subsidiary ledger to control inventory levels.

Requirement 3

2 Record materials and labor in a job order costing system

Prepare summary journal entries for each transaction.

Part 1	Part 2	**Part 3**	Demo Doc Complete

a. Purchased raw materials on account, $67,000.

When materials are purchased on account, you want to record the increase in materials inventory, so you would debit Materials Inventory (an asset) by the cost of the materials, $67,000.

You also want to record the increase in liability, so you would credit Accounts Payable (a liability) by $67,000 because this amount is still payable.

Materials Inventory		67,000	
Accounts Payable			67,000
To record the purchase of materials on account.			

2 Record materials and labor in a job order costing system

b. Materials costing $45,000 were requisitioned for production. Of this total, $5,000 were indirect materials.

When materials are requisitioned, it means that they move from materials inventory into production to be used. You want to record this movement in the appropriate accounts.

If the materials can be directly traceable to a job, Work in Process will be debited (increased). If the materials do not represent a major component and cannot be traced directly to a job, they are considered indirect materials and are debited to Manufacturing Overhead (increased).

Because $40,000 ($45,000 total materials less $5,000 indirect materials) of the materials can be traced to specific jobs, this amount goes directly into Work in Process Inventory, increasing that asset by $40,000.

The $5,000 in indirect materials is debited (an increase) to Manufacturing Overhead.

Because we are taking all materials out of the Materials Inventory, we reduce this asset with a credit for the total ($45,000).

Work in Process Inventory (direct material)		40,000	
Manufacturing Overhead (indirect material)		5,000	
Materials Inventory			45,000
To record direct and indirect materials used.			

Record materials and labor in a job order costing system

c. Labor time records show that direct labor of $30,000 and indirect labor of $2,000 were incurred, but not yet paid.

First, we debit (increase) Manufacturing Wages for the full amount of labor, direct and indirect, to accumulate total labor costs. We then credit Wages Payable to show the increased liability to our employees.

Manufacturing Wages		32,000	
Wages Payable			32,000
To record the direct and indirect labor incurred.			

The manufacturing wages need to be assigned to the appropriate accounts. A *labor time record* is completed by each employee who works directly on a job. Each of the jobs and hours worked are identified on the record.

In this case, some of the labor, $30,000, can be traced to specific jobs. This amount, called direct labor, is assigned as a debit (increase) to the asset Work in Process Inventory. The rest of the labor, $2,000, is for indirect labor such as maintenance and janitorial services, and cannot be traced to specific jobs. Therefore, it is debited to Manufacturing Overhead (increased).

Manufacturing Wages is credited for the full amount (a decrease), bringing its balance to zero.

Work in Process Inventory (direct labor)		30,000	
Manufacturing Overhead (indirect labor)		2,000	
Manufacturing Wages			32,000
To record the direct and indirect labor used.			

Part 1	Part 2	Part 3	**Demo Doc Complete**

Demo Doc 2

Allocating Manufacturing Overhead _____

Learning Objectives 3, 4

Macho Mike Machine Shop manufactures specialized metal products per its customer's specifications. Macho Mike uses direct labor cost to allocate their manufacturing overhead. Macho Mike expects to incur $160,000 of manufacturing overhead costs and to use $400,000 of direct labor cost during 2010.

During November 2010, Macho Mike's Machine Shop had the following selected transactions:

a. **Actual indirect manufacturing labor incurred was $4,200.**

b. **Actual indirect materials used, $3,000.**

c. **Other manufacturing overhead incurred, $2,800 (credit accounts payable).**

d. **Allocated overhead for November (the machine shop incurred $36,000 of direct labor cost during the month).**

e. **Finished jobs that totaled $6,500 on their job cost records.**

f. **Sold inventory for $70,000 (on account) that cost $42,000 to produce.**

Requirements

1. Compute the predetermined manufacturing overhead rate for Macho Mike.

2. Journalize the transactions.

3. Prepare the journal entry to close the ending balance of manufacturing overhead.

Demo Doc 2 Solutions

Requirement 1

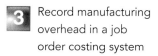

Record manufacturing
overhead in a job
order costing system

Compute the predetermined manufacturing overhead rate for Macho Mike.

Part 1	Part 2	Part 3	Demo Doc Complete

Because Macho Mike uses direct labor cost to allocate overhead to jobs, the predetermined manufacturing overhead rate is computed as follows:

$$\frac{\text{Total estimated manufacturing overhead costs}}{\text{Total estimated direct labor cost}}$$

In this case, the estimated manufacturing overhead cost equals $160,000 / estimated direct labor cost of $400,000 = 0.40, or a predetermined manufacturing overhead rate = 40% of *actual* direct labor cost. Another way to think of this is for every $1 spent on direct labor, we incur $0.40 of manufacturing overhead.

It's important to remember that this rate is determined at the beginning of the period, *before* any production has started. This is because actual overhead costs and the actual quantity of the allocation base are not known until the end of the period, so managers need this estimate to make decisions and allocate overhead to individual jobs throughout the period.

Because the allocation base used may be direct labor hours, direct labor cost, machine hours, and other bases, it's important to label this rate accordingly. The predetermined manufacturing overhead rate is multiplied by the allocation base activity to determine the amount of overhead applied to each of the jobs.

Requirement 2

Journalize the transactions.

Part 1	**Part 2**	Part 3	Demo Doc Complete

a. Actual indirect manufacturing labor incurred was $4,200.

b. Actual indirect materials used, $3,000.

Record manufacturing
overhead in a job
order costing system

c. Other manufacturing overhead incurred, $2,800 (credit accounts payable).

In this case, all actual manufacturing overhead costs incurred during the period are debited to Manufacturing Overhead because they cannot be traced to any specific job (that is, they are indirect costs). So Manufacturing Overhead is debited (increased) by:

$$\$4,200 + \$3,000 + \$2,800 = \$10,000$$

Indirect manufacturing labor results in a decrease of $4,200 to Manufacturing Wages (a credit).

Indirect materials used results in a decrease of $3,000 to Materials Inventory (a credit), because the materials have been used and are therefore removed from materials inventory.

Other manufacturing overhead is credited (an increase) to Accounts Payable, as indicated in the question, $2,800.

Manufacturing Overhead		10,000	
Manufacturing Wages			4,200
Materials Inventory			3,000
Accounts Payable			2,800

3 Record manufacturing overhead in a job order costing system

d. Allocate overhead for November (the machine shop incurred $36,000 of direct labor cost during the month).

To determine the total overhead allocated to jobs in November, multiply the actual direct labor cost ($36,000) by the predetermined allocation rate of 40% (from requirement 1):

$$\$36,000 \text{ (direct labor cost)} \times 0.40 \text{ (predetermined overhead rate)} = \$14,400 \text{ allocated overhead for November}$$

Allocate the overhead to work in process by debiting (increasing) Work in Process Inventory and crediting (decreasing) Manufacturing Overhead by $14,400.

Work in Process Inventory		14,400	
Manufacturing Overhead			14,400

4 Record completion and sales of finished goods and the adjustment for under- or overallocated overhead

e. Finished jobs that totaled $6,500 on their job cost records.

When the goods are completed, they are transferred from Work in Process to Finished Goods. This reflects work in process that leaves the plant floor and is moved into the finished goods storage area. This is accomplished by debiting (increasing) Finished Goods inventory by $6,500 and crediting (decreasing) Work in Process Inventory by $6,500.

Finished Goods Inventory		6,500	
Work in Process Inventory			6,500

4 Record completion and sales of finished goods and the adjustment for under- or overallocated overhead

f. Sold inventory for $70,000 (on account) that cost $42,000 to produce.

Debit the asset Accounts Receivable to record the increased amount of $70,000 that is owed to Macho Mike. Credit (increase) the revenue account, Sales Revenue, by the same amount.

Debit (increase) the expense Cost of Goods Sold to record the cost of the sale. Because the goods are no longer in the finished goods inventory, we must credit Finished Goods Inventory to reduce that asset account.

Accounts Receivable	70,000	
Sales Revenue		70,000
Cost of Goods Sold	42,000	
Finished Goods Inventory		42,000

Requirement 3

Prepare the journal entry to close the ending balance of manufacturing overhead.

Part 1	Part 2	**Part 3**	Demo Doc Complete

The balance of the Manufacturing Overhead account should be zero at the end of the accounting period. To achieve this, if Manufacturing Overhead has a debit balance, then you would credit Manufacturing Overhead and debit Cost of Goods Sold. If Manufacturing Overhead has a credit balance, then you would debit Manufacturing Overhead and credit Cost of Goods Sold.

In this case, manufacturing overhead was overallocated, because the overhead allocated to Work in Process Inventory ($14,400 from requirement 2, transaction **d**) is *more* than the amount actually incurred ($4,200 + $3,000 + $2,800 = $10,000—from transactions **a, b,** and **c**).

This results in a credit balance of $4,400 to Manufacturing Overhead. To close the ending balance, we then debit Manufacturing Overhead by $4,400 and credit Cost of Goods Sold by $4,400.

Manufacturing Overhead	4,400	
Cost of Goods Sold		4,400

Why? Because Macho Mike allocated too much manufacturing overhead to each job, resulting in cost of goods sold being too high (meaning the jobs were charged too much overhead during the period). To close the balance in Manufacturing Overhead, Macho Mike applies a decrease to Cost of Goods Sold.

Part 1	Part 2	Part 3	**Demo Doc Complete**

Quick Practice Questions

True/False

_____ 1. Process costing is used by companies that produce large numbers of identical units in a continuous fashion.

_____ 2. A food and beverage company would most likely use a job order costing system.

_____ 3. A job cost record is a document that accumulates direct materials, direct labor, and manufacturing overhead costs assigned to each individual job.

_____ 4. For jobs that the company has started but not yet finished, the job cost records form the subsidiary ledger for the general ledger account Work in Process Inventory.

_____ 5. When materials are requisitioned for a job, the Materials Inventory account is debited.

_____ 6. A labor time record identifies the employee, the amount of time spent on a particular job, and the labor cost charged to the job.

_____ 7. Manufacturing Overhead is credited for actual manufacturing overhead costs incurred throughout the year.

_____ 8. The allocation base is a common denominator that links indirect manufacturing overhead costs to the cost objects.

_____ 9. Work in Process Inventory is credited for the cost of direct labor in a job order costing system.

_____ 10. The required adjustment for an underallocation of manufacturing overhead results in a credit to Cost of Goods Sold.

Multiple Choice

1. What are the two basic types of costing systems?
   a. Job order costing and process costing
   b. Periodic costing and perpetual costing
   c. Product costing and materials inventory costing
   d. Periodic costing and process costing

2. Which type of business can use a job order costing system?
   a. Service and manufacturing businesses
   b. Manufacturing and merchandising businesses
   c. Service and merchandising businesses
   d. Service, merchandising, and manufacturing businesses

3. Which of the following industries is most likely to use a process costing system?
   a. Paint
   b. Aircraft
   c. Construction
   d. Unique furniture accessories

4. Which of the following companies is most likely to use job order costing?
   a. Kellogg's Cereal Company
   b. Elizabeth's Custom Furniture Company

    c. ExxonMobil Oil Refinery

    d. DuPont Chemical Company

5. Which of the following would be necessary to record the purchase of materials on account using a job order costing system?

    a. Credit to Work in Process Inventory

    b. Debit to Accounts Payable

    c. Debit to Materials Inventory

    d. Debit to Work in Process Inventory

6. Which of the following would be debited to record the direct materials used?

    a. Finished Goods Inventory

    b. Materials Inventory

    c. Work in Process Inventory

    d. Cost of Goods Manufactured

7. Which of the following would be debited to assign direct labor costs actually incurred?

    a. Finished Goods Inventory

    b. Manufacturing Overhead

    c. Wages Payable

    d. Work in Process Inventory

8. Which of the following would be debited to assign the costs of indirect labor?

    a. Manufacturing Overhead

    b. Work in Process Inventory

    c. Finished Goods Inventory

    d. Wages Payable

9. What is the document that is prepared by manufacturing personnel to request materials for the production process?

    a. Materials requisition

    b. Cost ticket

    c. Job order card

    d. Manufacturing ticket

10. Opaque Corporation uses a job order costing system. The Work in Process Inventory balance on December 31, 2007, consists of Job No. 120, which has a balance of $19,000. Job No. 120 has been charged with manufacturing overhead of $5,100. Opaque allocates manufacturing overhead at a predetermined rate of 85% of direct labor cost. What is the amount of direct materials charged to Job No. 120?

    a. $7,565

    b. $5,900

    c. $7,000

    d. $7,900

Quick Exercises

19-1.   State whether each the following companies would be more likely to use a job order costing system or a process costing system:

    a.   custom furniture manufacturer _____

    b.   paint manufacturer_____

    c.   carpet manufacturer _____

    d.   concrete manufacturer _____

    e.   home builder _____

    f.   soft drink bottler _____

    g.   custom jewelry manufacturer _____

19-2. Gadgets Company has two departments, X and Y. Manufacturing overhead is allocated based on direct labor cost in Department X and direct labor hours in Department Y. The following additional information is available:

Estimated Amounts		
	Department X	Department Y
Direct labor costs	$249,600	$427,500
Direct labor hours	24,960	45,000
Manufacturing overhead costs	259,000	262,000

Actual data for completed Job No. 140 is as follows:		
Direct materials requisitioned	$23,700	$48,600
Direct labor cost	34,400	38,800
Direct labor hours	4,300	3,800

Requirements

1. Compute the predetermined manufacturing overhead rate for Department X.

2. Compute the predetermined manufacturing overhead rate for Department Y.

3. What is the total manufacturing overhead cost for Job No. 140?

4. If Job No. 140 consists of 350 units of product, what is the average unit cost of this job?

19-3. Peterson Corporation uses a job order costing system.

Journalize the following transactions in Peterson's general journal for the current month:

a. Purchased materials on account, $74,000.

b. Requisitioned $47,700 of direct materials and $6,500 of indirect materials for use in production.

c. Factory payroll incurred and due to employees, $72,000.

d. Allocated factory payroll, 85% direct labor, 15% indirect labor.

e. Recorded depreciation on factory equipment of $10,500 and other manufacturing overhead of $45,900 (credit accounts payable).

f. Allocated manufacturing overhead based on 130% of direct labor cost.

g. Cost of completed production for the current month, $155,000.

h. Cost of finished goods sold, $131,000; selling price, $183,000 (all sales on account).

General Journal

Date	Accounts	Debit	Credit

General Journal

Date	Accounts	Debit	Credit

General Journal

Date	Accounts	Debit	Credit

General Journal

Date	Accounts	Debit	Credit

General Journal

Date	Accounts	Debit	Credit

General Journal

Date	Accounts	Debit	Credit

General Journal

Date	Accounts	Debit	Credit

General Journal

Date	Accounts	Debit	Credit

General Journal

Date	Accounts	Debit	Credit

19-4. The following activities took place in the Work in Process Inventory account during April:

Work in process balance, April 1	$ 15,000
Direct materials used	123,000

Total manufacturing labor incurred in April was $163,500 and 75% of manufacturing labor represents direct labor. The predetermined manufacturing overhead rate is 120% of direct labor cost. Actual manufacturing overhead costs for April amounted to $150,000.

Two jobs were completed with total costs of $118,000 and $85,000, respectively. They were sold on account for $258,000 and $150,000, respectively.

Requirements

1. Compute the balance in Work in Process Inventory on April 30.

2. Journalize the following:
   a. Direct materials used in April.
   b. The total manufacturing labor incurred in April.
   c. The entry to assign manufacturing labor to the appropriate accounts.
   d. The allocated manufacturing overhead for April.
   e. The entry to move the completed jobs into finished goods inventory.
   f. The entry to sell the two completed jobs on account.

General Journal				
Date	Accounts		Debit	Credit

General Journal				
Date	Accounts		Debit	Credit

General Journal				
Date	Accounts		Debit	Credit

General Journal				
Date	Accounts		Debit	Credit

General Journal				
Date	Accounts		Debit	Credit

General Journal				
Date	Accounts		Debit	Credit

19-5.   The following account balances as of January 1, 2008, were selected from the general ledger of Browning Manufacturing Company:

Work in process inventory	$ 0
Materials inventory	21,000
Finished goods inventory	44,000

Additional data:

a.   Actual manufacturing overhead for January amounted to $59,000.
b.   Total direct labor cost for January was $56,000.
c.   The predetermined manufacturing overhead rate is based on direct labor cost. The budget for 2008 called for $300,000 of direct labor cost and $369,000 of manufacturing overhead costs.
d.   The only job unfinished on January 31, 2008, was Job No. 410, for which total labor charges were $5,600 (700 direct labor hours) and total direct material charges were $10,000.
e.   Cost of direct materials placed in production during January totaled $100,000. There were no indirect material requisitions during January 2008.
f.   January 31 balance in Materials Inventory was $29,000.
g.   Finished Goods Inventory balance on January 31 was $30,000.

Requirements

1. Determine the predetermined manufacturing overhead rate.

2. Determine the amount of materials purchased during January.

3. Determine cost of goods manufactured for January.

4. Determine the Work in Process Inventory balance on January 31.

5. Determine cost of goods sold for January.

6. Determine whether manufacturing overhead is overallocated or underallocated. What is the account balance at January 31?

Do It Yourself! Question 1

Bell Boxers is a customized clothing manufacturer. Bell has the following transactions:

a. **Purchased raw materials on account, $20,000.**

b. **Materials costing $15,000 were requisitioned for production. Of this total, $1,500 worth were indirect materials.**

c. **Labor time records show that direct labor of $24,000 and indirect labor of $3,000 were incurred, but not yet paid.**

Requirements

1. Why would Bell Boxers use the job order costing system?

2. What document would Bell Boxers use to accumulate direct materials, direct labor, and manufacturing overhead costs assigned to each job?

3. Journalize each transaction.

		General Journal		
	Date	Accounts	Debit	Credit

		General Journal		
	Date	Accounts	Debit	Credit

		General Journal		
	Date	Accounts	Debit	Credit

		General Journal		
	Date	Accounts	Debit	Credit

Do It Yourself! Question 2

Quality Cabinet Maker manufactures specialized cabinets. Because of its unique specialization, Quality Cabinet is labor-intensive, so it uses direct labor cost to allocate its overhead. Quality Cabinet expects to incur $240,000 of manufacturing overhead costs and to use $300,000 of direct labor cost during 2010.

During May 2010, Quality Cabinet actually incurred $22,000 of direct labor cost and recorded the following transactions:

a. **Indirect actual manufacturing labor, $5,100.**

b. **Indirect actual materials used, $6,200.**

c. **Other manufacturing overhead incurred, $7,000 (credit accounts payable).**

d. **Allocated overhead for May.**

e. **Transferred 45,000 of product to finished goods.**

f. **Sold product on account, $60,000; cost of the product, $33,000.**

Requirements

1. Compute the predetermined manufacturing overhead for Quality.

2. Journalize the transactions in the general journal.

General Journal				
Date	Accounts		Debit	Credit

General Journal				
Date	Accounts		Debit	Credit

General Journal				
Date	Accounts		Debit	Credit

	Date	Accounts	Debit	Credit

General Journal

	Date	Accounts	Debit	Credit

General Journal

	Date	Accounts	Debit	Credit

General Journal

	Date	Accounts	Debit	Credit

General Journal

3. Prepare the journal entry to close the ending balance of Manufacturing Overhead.

	Date	Accounts	Debit	Credit

Quick Practice Solutions

True/False

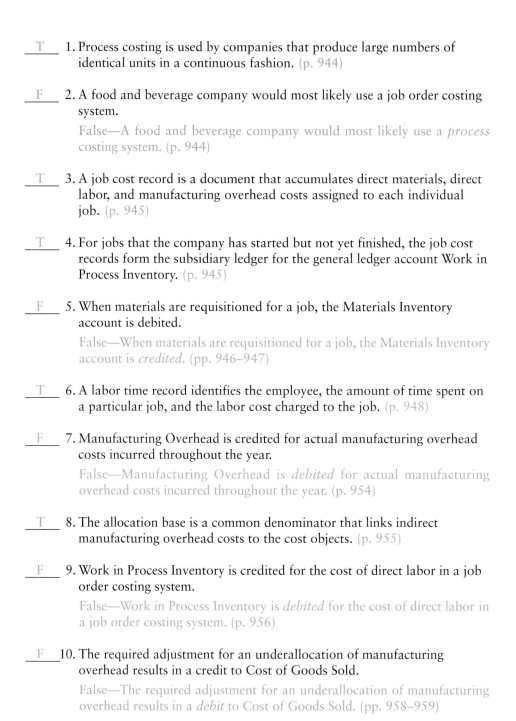

__T__ 1. Process costing is used by companies that produce large numbers of identical units in a continuous fashion. (p. 944)

__F__ 2. A food and beverage company would most likely use a job order costing system.

    False—A food and beverage company would most likely use a *process* costing system. (p. 944)

__T__ 3. A job cost record is a document that accumulates direct materials, direct labor, and manufacturing overhead costs assigned to each individual job. (p. 945)

__T__ 4. For jobs that the company has started but not yet finished, the job cost records form the subsidiary ledger for the general ledger account Work in Process Inventory. (p. 945)

__F__ 5. When materials are requisitioned for a job, the Materials Inventory account is debited.

    False—When materials are requisitioned for a job, the Materials Inventory account is *credited*. (pp. 946–947)

__T__ 6. A labor time record identifies the employee, the amount of time spent on a particular job, and the labor cost charged to the job. (p. 948)

__F__ 7. Manufacturing Overhead is credited for actual manufacturing overhead costs incurred throughout the year.

    False—Manufacturing Overhead is *debited* for actual manufacturing overhead costs incurred throughout the year. (p. 954)

__T__ 8. The allocation base is a common denominator that links indirect manufacturing overhead costs to the cost objects. (p. 955)

__F__ 9. Work in Process Inventory is credited for the cost of direct labor in a job order costing system.

    False—Work in Process Inventory is *debited* for the cost of direct labor in a job order costing system. (p. 956)

__F__ 10. The required adjustment for an underallocation of manufacturing overhead results in a credit to Cost of Goods Sold.

    False—The required adjustment for an underallocation of manufacturing overhead results in a *debit* to Cost of Goods Sold. (pp. 958–959)

Multiple Choice

1. What are the two basic types of costing systems? (p. 944)
   a. Job order costing and process costing
   b. Periodic costing and perpetual costing
   c. Product costing and materials inventory costing
   d. Periodic costing and process costing

2. Which type of business can use a job order costing system? (p. 944)
   a. Service and manufacturing businesses
   b. Manufacturing and merchandising businesses
   c. Service and merchandising businesses
   d. Service, merchandising, and manufacturing businesses

3. Which of the following industries is most likely to use a process costing system? (p. 944)
   a. Paint
   b. Aircraft
   c. Construction
   d. Unique furniture accessories

4. Which of the following companies is most likely to use job order costing? (p. 944)
   a. Kellogg's Cereal Company
   b. Elizabeth's Custom Furniture Company
   c. Exxon Mobil Oil Refinery
   d. DuPont Chemical Company

5. Which of the following would be necessary to record the purchase of materials on account using a job order costing system? (p. 946)
   a. Credit to Work in Process Inventory
   b. Debit to Accounts Payable
   c. Debit to Materials Inventory
   d. Debit to Work in Process Inventory

6. Which of the following would be debited to record the direct materials used? (p. 946)
   a. Finished Goods Inventory
   b. Materials Inventory
   c. Work in Process Inventory
   d. Cost of Goods Manufactured

7. Which of the following would be debited to assign direct labor costs actually incurred? (p. 949)
   a. Finished Goods Inventory
   b. Manufacturing Overhead
   c. Wages Payable
   d. Work in Process Inventory

8. Which of the following would be debited to assign the costs of indirect labor? (p. 949)
   a. Manufacturing Overhead
   b. Work in Process Inventory
   c. Finished Goods Inventory
   d. Wages Payable

9. What is the document that is prepared by manufacturing personnel to request materials for the production process? (p. 947)
   a. Materials requisition
   b. Cost ticket
   c. Job order card
   d. Manufacturing ticket

10. Opaque Corporation uses a job order costing system. The Work in Process Inventory balance on December 31, 2007, consists of Job No. 120, which has a balance of $19,000. Job No. 120 has been charged with manufacturing overhead of $5,100. Opaque allocates manufacturing overhead at a predetermined rate of 85% of direct labor cost. What is the amount of direct materials charged to Job No. 120? (p. 954)
    a. $7,565
    b. $5,900
    c. $7,000
    d. $7,900

Quick Exercises

19-1. State whether each of the following companies would be more likely to use a job order costing system or a process costing system: (p. 944)

    a. custom furniture manufacturer   job order costing
    b. paint manufacturer   process costing
    c. carpet manufacturer   process costing
    d. concrete manufacturer   process costing
    e. home builder   job order costing
    f. soft drink bottler   process costing
    g. custom jewelry manufacturer   job order costing

19-2. Gadgets Company has two departments, X and Y. Manufacturing overhead is allocated based on direct labor cost in Department X and direct labor hours in Department Y. The following additional information is available: (p. 954)

Estimated Amounts	Department X	Department Y
Direct labor costs	$249,600	$427,500
Direct labor hours	24,960	45,000
Manufacturing overhead costs	259,000	262,000

Actual data for completed Job No. 140 is as follows:

	Department X	Department Y
Direct materials requisitioned	$23,700	$48,600
Direct labor cost	34,400	38,800
Direct labor hours	4,300	3,800

Requirements

1. Compute the predetermined manufacturing overhead rate for Department X.

$259,000/$249,600 = 104% of direct labor cost

2. Compute the predetermined manufacturing overhead rate for Department Y.

$262,000/45,000 hours = $5.82 per direct labor hour

3. What is the total manufacturing overhead cost for Job No.140?

Dept. X ($34,400×104%)	$35,776
Dept. Y ($5.82×3,800)	22,116
	$57,892

4. If Job No. 140 consists of 350 units of product, what is the average unit cost of this job?

$23,700 + $34,400 + $35,776 + $48,600 + $38,800 + $22,116 = $203,392

$203,392/350 units = $581.12

19-3.   Peterson Corporation uses a job order costing system. (pp. 945–957)

Journalize the following transactions in Peterson's general journal for the current month:

a. **Purchased materials on account, $74,000.**

b. **Requisitioned $47,700 of direct materials and $6,500 of indirect materials for use in production.**

c. **Factory payroll incurred and due to employees, $72,000.**

d. **Allocated factory payroll, 85% direct labor, 15% indirect labor.**

e. **Recorded depreciation on factory equipment of $10,500 and other manufacturing overhead of $45,900 (credit accounts payable).**

f. **Allocated manufacturing overhead based on 130% of direct labor cost.**

g. **Cost of completed production for the current month, $155,000.**

h. **Cost of finished goods sold, $131,000; selling price, $183,000 (all sales on account).**

		General Journal			
	Date	Accounts		Debit	Credit
a.		Materials Inventory		74,000	
		Accounts Payable			74,000

General Journal

	Date	Accounts	Debit	Credit
b.		Work in Process Inventory	47,700	
		Manufacturing Overhead	6,500	
		Materials Inventory		54,200

General Journal

	Date	Accounts	Debit	Credit
c.		Manufacturing Wages	72,000	
		Wages Payable		72,000

General Journal

	Date	Accounts	Debit	Credit
d.		Work in Process Inventory	61,200	
		Manufacturing Overhead	10,800	
		Manufacturing Wages		72,000

General Journal

	Date	Accounts	Debit	Credit
e.		Manufacturing Overhead	56,400	
		Accumulated Dep.—Factory Equip.		10,500
		Accounts Payable		45,900

General Journal

	Date	Accounts	Debit	Credit
f.		Work in Process Inventory	79,560	
		Manufacturing Overhead		79,560

General Journal

	Date	Accounts	Debit	Credit
g.		Finished Goods Inventory	155,000	
		Work in Process Inventory		155,000

General Journal

	Date	Accounts	Debit	Credit
h.		Accounts Receivable	183,000	
		Sales Revenue		183,000
		Cost of Goods Sold	131,000	
		Finished Goods Inventory		131,000

19-4. The following activities took place in the Work in Process Inventory account during April: (pp. 945–957)

Work in process balance, April 1	$ 15,000
Direct materials used	123,000

Total manufacturing labor incurred in April was $163,500 and 75% of manufacturing labor represents direct labor. The predetermined manufacturing overhead rate is 120% of direct labor cost. Actual manufacturing overhead costs for April amounted to $150,000.

Two jobs were completed with total costs of $118,000 and $85,000, respectively. They were sold on account for $258,000 and $150,000, respectively.

Requirements

1. Compute the balance in Work in Process Inventory on April 30.

$15,000 + $123,000 + (75% $\times$ $163,500)
+ (120% $\times$ $122,625) $-$ $118,000 $-$ $85,000
= $204,775

2. Journalize the following:

    a. Direct materials used in April.
    b. The total manufacturing labor incurred in April.
    c. The entry to assign manufacturing labor to the appropriate accounts.
    d. The allocated manufacturing overhead for April.
    e. The entry to move the completed jobs into finished goods inventory.
    f. The entry to sell the two completed jobs on account.

General Journal				
	Date	Accounts	Debit	Credit
a.		Work in Process Inventory	123,000	
		Materials Inventory		123,000

General Journal				
	Date	Accounts	Debit	Credit
b.		Manufacturing Wages	163,500	
		Wages Payable		163,500

General Journal				
	Date	Accounts	Debit	Credit
c.		Work in Process Inventory	122,625	
		Manufacturing Overhead	40,875	
		Manufacturing Wages		163,500

General Journal				
	Date	Accounts	Debit	Credit
d.		Work in Process Inventory	147,150	
		Manufacturing Overhead		147,150

General Journal

	Date	Accounts	Debit	Credit
e.		Finished Goods Inventory	203,000	
		Work in Process Inventory		203,000

General Journal

	Date	Accounts	Debit	Credit
f.		Accounts Receivable	408,000	
		Sales Revenue		408,000
		Cost of Goods Sold	203,000	
		Finished Goods Inventory		203,000

19-5.   The following account balances as of January 1, 2008, were selected from the general ledger of Browning Manufacturing Company: (pp. 945–957)

Work in process inventory	$ 0
Materials inventory	21,000
Finished goods inventory	44,000

Additional data:

a.   Actual manufacturing overhead for January amounted to $59,000.

b.   Total direct labor cost for January was $56,000.

c.   The predetermined manufacturing overhead rate is based on direct labor cost. The budget for 2008 called for $300,000 of direct labor cost and $369,000 of manufacturing overhead costs.

d.   The only job unfinished on January 31, 2008, was Job No. 410, for which total labor charges were $5,600 (700 direct labor hours) and total direct material charges were $10,000.

e.   Cost of direct materials placed in production during January totaled $100,000. There were no indirect material requisitions during January 2008.

f.   January 31 balance in Materials Inventory was $29,000.

g.   Finished Goods Inventory balance on January 31 was $30,000.

Requirements

1. Determine the predetermined manufacturing overhead rate.

$$\$369,000/\$300,000 = 123\% \text{ of direct labor cost}$$

2. Determine the amount of materials purchased during January.

$$\$21,000 + X - \$100,000 = \$29,000$$
$$-\$79,000 + X = \$29,000$$
$$X = \$108,000$$

3. Determine cost of goods manufactured for January.

$$\$56{,}000 + (123\% \times \$56{,}000)$$
$$+ \ \$100{,}000 - \$5{,}600 - \$10{,}000 - (123\% \times \$5{,}600)$$
$$= \$202{,}392$$

4. Determine the Work in Process Inventory balance on January 31.

$$\$5{,}600 + (123\% \times \$5{,}600) + \$10{,}000 = \$22{,}488$$

5. Determine cost of goods sold for January.

$$\$44{,}000 + \$202{,}392 - \$30{,}000 = \$216{,}392$$

6. Determine whether manufacturing overhead is overallocated or underallocated. What is the account balance at January 31?

$$\text{Actual manufacturing overhead} = \$59{,}000;$$
$$\text{Allocated manufacturing overhead} = \$68{,}880$$
$$\$68{,}880 - \$59{,}000 = \$9{,}880 \text{ overallocated}$$

Do It Yourself! Question 1 Solutions

Requirements

1 Distinguish between job order costing and process costing

1. Why would Bell Boxers use the job order costing system?

Companies that manufacture batches of unique or specialized products would use a job order costing system to accumulate costs for each job or batch. Because Bell Boxers manufactures specialized clothing for customers and the required work may vary from customer to customer, Bell would use the job order costing system.

2 Record materials and labor in a job order costing system

2. What document would Bell use to accumulate direct materials, direct labor, and manufacturing overhead costs assigned to each individual job?

Bell would use a job cost record to accumulate direct materials, direct labor, and manufacturing overhead costs assigned to each individual job.

2 Record materials and labor in a job order costing system

3. Journalize each transaction.

	Date	Accounts	Debit	Credit
		General Journal		
a.		Materials Inventory	20,000	
		Accounts Payable		20,000

	Date	Accounts	Debit	Credit
		General Journal		
b.		Work in Process Inventory	13,500	
		Manufacturing Overhead	1,500	
		Materials Inventory		15,000

	Date	Accounts	Debit	Credit
		General Journal		
c.		Manufacturing Wages	27,000	
		Wages Payable		27,000
		Work in Process Inventory	24,000	
		Manufacturing Overhead	3,000	
		Manufacturing Wages		27,000

Do It Yourself! Question 2 Solutions

Requirements

1. Compute the predetermined manufacturing overhead for Quality.

$240,000/$300,000 = 0.80$ or 80% of direct labor cost

3 Record manufacturing overhead in a job order costing system

2. Journalize the transactions in the general journal.

		General Journal		
	Date	Accounts	Debit	Credit
a.		Manufacturing Overhead	5,100	
		Manufacturing Wages		5,100

		General Journal		
	Date	Accounts	Debit	Credit
b.		Manufacturing Overhead	6,200	
		Materials Inventory		6,200

		General Journal		
	Date	Accounts	Debit	Credit
c.		Manufacturing Overhead	7,000	
		Accounts Payable		7,000

		General Journal		
	Date	Accounts	Debit	Credit
d.		Work in Process Inventory	17,600	
		Manufacturing Overhead		17,600

		General Journal		
	Date	Accounts	Debit	Credit
e.		Finished Goods Inventory	45,000	
		Work in Process Inventory		45,000

		General Journal		
	Date	Accounts	Debit	Credit
f.		Accounts Receivable	60,000	
		Sales Revenue		60,000
		Cost of Goods Sold	33,000	
		Finished Goods Inventory		33,000

4 Record completion and sales of finished goods and the adjustment for under- or overallocated overhead

3. Record the journal entry to close the ending balance of manufacturing overhead.

		Cost of Goods Sold	700	
		Manufacturing Overhead		700

The Power of Practice

For more practice using the skills learned in this chapter, visit MyAccountingLab. There you will find algorithmically generated questions that are based on these Demo Docs and your main textbook's Review and Assess Your Progress sections.

Go to MyAccountingLab and follow these steps:

1. Direct your URL to www.myaccountinglab.com.
2. Log in using your name and password.
3. Click the MyAccountingLab link.
4. Click Study Plan in the left navigation bar.
5. From the table of contents, select Chapter 19, Job Order Costing.
6. Click a link to work tutorial exercises.

20 Process Costing

WHAT YOU PROBABLY ALREADY KNOW

WHAT YOU PROBABLY ALREADY KNOW

Sometimes when you have the opportunity, like on vacation, you may want to catch up on reading several books of interest. Assume that you started reading three books and were approximately 2/3 done reading each of them at the end of the week. If you were asked how many books you finished reading, you would have to say none. But that would not indicate the amount of time spent during the week reading. You read 2/3 of each of the 3 books. This is *equivalent* to reading 2 complete books (2/3 × 3 = 2) over the course of the week. Using an equivalent number of books accurately quantifies the amount of work completed during the week. In this chapter, we will study the computation of inventory costs. To determine the cost of work in process, we will use this concept of equivalent units for those inventory items that are partially complete.

Learning Objectives

 Distinguish between the flow of costs in process costing and job order costing.

In Chapter 19, we learned that **job order costing** is an appropriate system for companies that produce unique jobs, batches, or assignments. **Process costing** is an appropriate system for companies that mass-produce many similar products in a continuous fashion such as food and beverage, paint, or chemical manufacturers. The flow of costs through both of these systems is similar. The three components of cost—direct materials, direct labor, and manufacturing overhead—are included in the product cost. After the goods are produced, they are transferred from Work in Process to Finished Goods. When the goods are sold, the costs are transferred from Finished Goods to Cost of Goods Sold. The difference between the two systems occurs during the processing stage. When direct materials, direct labor, and overhead are applied, the Work in Process account is debited under both systems. The job order costing system includes a subsidiary ledger of job cost records. The sum of the job cost records, which include the direct materials, direct labor, and manufacturing overhead for each job, should always equal the *one* Work in Process account balance. Under process costing, there may be a Work in Process account for *each* of the processing departments. The Work in Process costs will flow from department to department while in production until the product is complete and the costs are transferred into Finished Goods. *Review Exhibit 20-1 (p. 996) for a comparison between the cost flows of job order and process costing systems.*

Compute equivalent units.

Equivalent units express the amount of work done during a period in terms of fully complete units of output. This is necessary to calculate the cost incurred for each unit. At the end of the period, some of those costs will be transferred either to the next Work in Process account or to Finished Goods. To calculate equivalent units, the department's physical flow of inventory is first determined. Inputs must equal outputs. Beginning units in process plus those started in the department are the inputs or accountable units. The ending units in process and those completed and transferred out are the outputs, or units accounted for. Equivalent units are determined for direct materials and conversion costs separately for the outputs. Those units completed and transferred out are 100% complete for direct materials and conversion costs; the physical units and equivalent units are the same. For ending Work in Process units, a determination of the percentage complete for direct materials and conversion costs must be made. The physical units multiplied by the percentage complete equals the equivalent units. *Review Exhibits 20-2 to 20-6 (pp. 997–1003) and Summary Problem 1 for an illustration and calculation of equivalent units.*

 Use process costing to assign costs to units completed and to units in ending work in process inventory.

The direct materials and conversion costs are determined by adding the costs from beginning inventory, if any, to the costs added to the department for the period. The total costs are divided by the respective equivalent units to determine the cost per equivalent units, as shown in Demo Doc 1. The units completed will be assigned the full unit cost—direct materials plus conversion cost. The equivalent units of ending work in process are allocated the respective cost per equivalent unit to determine the cost of ending work in process inventory. *Review Exhibits 20-8 and 20-9 (pp. 1004–1005) and Summary Problem 1 for the calculation of costs to units completed and in ending work in process inventory.*

4 Use the weighted-average method to assign costs to units completed and to units in ending work in process inventory in a second department.

The procedure to calculate the cost to units completed and to units in ending work in process in a second department is similar to that described in objective 3. The difference is that there is a third column for the transferred in equivalent units and costs. All of the units completed and in ending work in process will be allocated the transferred in cost per unit. *Review Exhibits 20-12 to 20-16 (pp. 1012–1016) and Summary Problem 2 for illustrations of calculating and assigning costs to units completed and to units in ending work in process inventory in a second department.*

Demo Doc 1

Illustrating Process Costing _____

Learning Objectives 2, 3

Clear Bottled Water produces packaged water. Clear has two production departments: blending and packaging. In the blending department, materials are added at the beginning of the process. Conversion costs are added throughout the process for blending. Data for the month of April for the blending department are as follows:

Blending Department Data for April:	
Units:	
Beginning work in process	0 units
Started in production during April	116,000 units
Completed and transferred out to Packaging in April	98,000 units
Ending work in process inventory (70% completed)	18,000 units
Costs:	
Beginning work in process	$ 0
Costs added during April:	
Direct materials	54,520
Conversion costs	32,074
Total costs added during April	$86,594

Requirement

1. Use the four-step process to calculate (1) the cost of the units completed and transferred out to the packaging department, and (2) the total cost of the units in the blending department ending work in process inventory.

Demo Doc 1 Solution

Requirement 1

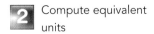 Compute equivalent
units

Use the four-step process to calculate (1) the cost of the units completed
and transferred out to the packaging department, and (2) the total cost of
the units in the blending department ending work in process inventory.

Steps 1 and 2: **Summarize the flow of physical units and compute output in
terms of equivalent units.**

Part 1	Part 2	Part 3	Demo Doc Complete

Total units to account for is the equivalent of units completed and transferred
out of packaging in April (98,000) plus the ending work in process inventory of
April 30 (18,000):

CLEAR BOTTLED WATER
Blending Department
Month Ended April 30, 2010

Flow of Production	Step 1 Flow of Physical Units	Step 2: Equivalent Units Direct Materials	Conversion Costs
Units to account for:			
Beginning work in process, March 31	0		
Started in production during April	116,000		
Total physical units to account for	116,000		

Materials are added at the beginning of the blending production process, so
equivalent units for materials is the same as the total units.

Completed units have 100% of their conversion costs (98,000).

Conversion costs are added evenly throughout the blending process, so the conversion equivalent units for ending work in process inventory are the total units in
ending work in process, 18,000, times the percent complete, 70% = 12,600.

Remember, conversion costs include both direct labor and manufacturing
overhead.

CLEAR BOTTLED WATER
Blending Department
Month Ended April 30, 2010

Flow of Production	Step 1 Flow of Physical Units	Step 2: Equivalent Units Direct Materials	Conversion Costs
Units to account for:			
Beginning work in process, March 31	0		
Started in production during April	116,000		
Total physical units to account for	116,000		
Units accounted for:			
Completed and transferred out during April	98,000	98,000	98,000
Ending work in process, April 30	18,000	18,000	12,600
Total physical units accounted for	116,000		
Equivalent units		116,000	110,600

From this, we can see that the total units accounted for is 116,000 units, with 98,000 completed units + 18,000 work in process units = 116,000 equivalent units for direct materials, and 98,000 completed units + 12,600 work in process units = 110,600 equivalent units for conversion costs.

3 Use process costing to assign costs to units completed and to units in ending work in process inventory

Step 3: Compute the cost per equivalent unit.

Part 1	Part 2	Part 3	Demo Doc Complete

The cost per equivalent unit is computed by dividing the costs added during the period by the equivalent units:

$$\text{Cost per equivalent unit for direct materials} = \frac{\text{Total direct material cost}}{\text{Equivalent units for direct material cost}}$$

$$\text{Cost per equivalent unit for conversion cost} = \frac{\text{Total conversion cost}}{\text{Equivalent units for conversion cost}}$$

We know from Step 1 that Clear has 116,000 accountable units. From the question, we know that Clear has $54,520 of total accountable direct materials costs in April.

Using the formula for cost per equivalent unit for direct materials, we divide the total direct materials costs of $54,520 by the equivalent units of materials, determined in Step 2 as 116,000 units = $0.47 per equivalent units for direct materials.

By using equivalent units, we are indicating that $32,074 of conversion costs will blend 110,600 units from the start of the blending process to the end of the blending process. To calculate costs per equivalent unit for conversion costs, we must divide the total conversion costs of $32,074 by the number of equivalent units for conversion, determined in Step 2 to be 110,600 = $0.29 per equivalent units for conversion costs.

CLEAR BOTTLED WATER
Blending Department
Month Ended April 30, 2010

| | Step 3: Cost per Equivalent Unit | |
	Direct Materials	Conversion Costs
Beginning work in process, March 31	$ 0	$ 0
Costs added during April	54,520	32,074
Total costs for April	$ 54,520	$ 32,074
Divide by equivalent units	÷ 116,000	÷ 110,600
Cost per equivalent unit	$ 0.47	$ 0.29

3 Use process costing to assign costs to units completed and to units in ending work in process inventory

Step 4: Assign costs to units completed and to units in ending work in process inventory.

| Part 1 | Part 2 | **Part 3** | Demo Doc Complete |

Because the units completed and transferred out were started and finished in the month of April, their cost is the full unit cost of $0.76. Shown another way:

$$98,000 \times \$0.47 = \$46,060 \text{ (direct materials) (100\%)}$$
$$98,000 \times \underline{\$0.29} = \$28,420 \text{ (conversion costs) (100\%)}$$
$$98,000 \times \$0.76 = \underline{\underline{\$74,480}}$$

The ending work in process is complete regarding materials because they are added in their entirety at the beginning of the mixing process.

The conversion costs in ending work in process are only 70% complete because conversion costs occur evenly throughout the mixing process. Multiplying each by their respective per-unit cost:

$$18,000 \times \$0.47 = \$\ 8,460 \text{ (direct materials) (100\%)}$$
$$12,600 \times \$0.29 = \$\ \underline{3,654}\ \text{ (conversion costs) (70\%)}$$
$$\underline{\underline{\$12,114}}$$

The solution to the problem is (1) the $74,480 cost of the goods completed and transferred out of the blending department to the packaging department during April added to (2) the $12,114 cost of the ending work in process in the blending department as of April 30 = total costs accounted for of $86,594.

CLEAR BOTTLED WATER
Blending Department
Month Ended April 30, 2010

		Step 4: Assign Costs		
		Direct Materials	Conversion Costs	Total
Units completed and transferred out to Packaging in April	[98,000 ×	($0.47 +	$0.29)]	= $74,480
Ending work in process, April 30:				
Direct materials	18,000 ×	0.47		= 8,460
Conversion costs	12,600 ×		0.29	= 3,654
Total ending work in process, March 31				$12,114
Total costs accounted for				$86,594

Part 1	Part 2	Part 3	**Demo Doc Complete**

Demo Doc 2

Weighted-Average Process Costing _____

Easy Flow produces tubes for toothpaste. Easy has two departments: molding and packaging. In the second department, packaging, conversion costs are incurred evenly throughout the process. Packaging materials are not added until the end of the packaging process. Costs in beginning work in process inventory include transferred in costs of $28,360, direct labor of $12,369, and manufacturing overhead of $10,000. October data from the packaging department are as follows:

EASY FLOW **Packaging Department** **Month Ended October 31, 2010**	Units	Dollars
Beginning inventory, Sept. 30 (60% complete)	5,700	$ 50,729
Production started:		
Transferred in	120,000	575,000
Direct materials		155,100
Conversion costs:		
Direct labor		240,000
Manufacturing overhead		185,000
Total conversion costs		$ 425,000
Total to account for	125,700	$1,205,829
Transferred out	110,000	$?
Ending inventory (30% complete)	15,700	$?

Easy Flow uses weighted-average process costing.

Requirements

1. Compute Easy Flow's equivalent units for the month of October.

2. Compute the cost per equivalent unit for October.

3. Assign the costs to units completed and transferred out and to ending inventory.

Demo Doc 2 Solutions

Requirement 1

2 Compute equivalent units

4 Use the weighted-average method to assign costs to units completed and to units in ending work in process inventory in a second department

Compute Easy Flow's equivalent units for the month of October.

Part 1	Part 2	Part 3	Part 4	Demo Doc Complete

The 110,000 units completed and transferred out are 100% completed regarding transferred in, direct materials, and conversion costs. That is why the equivalent units are 100%.

The ending work in process inventory is 100% complete regarding transferred in. In other words, Easy Flow doesn't need to transfer any additional costs from another department to complete the units in ending inventory.

Because direct materials are added at the end of the packaging process, they are zero completed in terms of work in process.

Units in ending inventory are only 30% finished in terms of conversion costs. Another way to think of this is that the conversion costs applied to the ending inventory so far will complete 15,700 units 30% of the way ($15,700 \times 0.30 = 4,710$), or those same conversion costs would complete 4,710 units 100% of the way.

EASY FLOW
Packaging Department
Month Ended October 31, 2010

	Equivalent Units		
	Transferred In	Direct Materials	Conversion Costs
Flow of Production			
Units accounted for:			
Completed and transferred out during October	110,000	110,000	110,000
Ending work in process inventory, October 31	15,700	0	4,710
Equivalent units	125,700	110,000	114,710

So the total equivalent units for the packaging department during October is 125,700 transferred-in units, 110,000 direct material units, and 114,710 conversion costs units.

Requirement 2

4 Use the weighted-average method to assign costs to units completed and to units in ending work in process inventory in a second department

Compute the cost per equivalent unit for October.

Part 1	**Part 2**	Part 3	Part 4	Demo Doc Complete

Determine total costs for each of the three categories. We know from the question that we have beginning inventory of $28,360 transferred-in costs and $22,369 in conversion costs ($12,369 for direct labor and $10,000 manufacturing over-head), for a total of $50,729. The direct materials are zero for beginning work in process because they are added at the end of the packaging process.

EASY FLOW
Packaging Department
Month Ended October 31, 2010

	Equivalent Units			
	Transferred In	Direct Materials	Conversion Costs	Total
Beginning work in process inventory, Sept. 30	$28,360	$ 0	$22,369	$50,729

During October, we saw $575,000 in costs transferred in from the molding department, $155,100 in direct materials costs, and $425,000 in conversion costs, for a total of $1,155,100 in costs added during October. As a check, make sure that the sum of the totals of the transferred-in, direct materials, and conversion costs equals the sum of the total beginning work in process and the total of costs added during October.

EASY FLOW
Packaging Department
Month Ended October 31, 2010

	Equivalent Units			
	Transferred In	Direct Materials	Conversion Costs	Total
Beginning work in process inventory, Sept. 30	$ 28,360	$ 0	$ 22,369	$ 50,729
Costs added during October	575,000	155,100	425,000	1,155,100
Total costs	$603,360	$155,100	$447,369	$1,205,829

Now that we have our total costs, we must divide total costs for each of the categories by the equivalent units for each respective category (as determined in requirement 1) to determine the cost per equivalent unit.

From this, we determine that the transferred-in costs are:

$$\frac{\$603,360}{125,700 \text{ units}} = \$4.80 \text{ per unit}$$

Direct materials costs are:

$$\frac{\$155,100}{110,000 \text{ units}} = \$1.41 \text{ per unit}$$

Conversion costs are:

$$\frac{\$447,369}{114,710 \text{ units}} = \$3.90 \text{ per unit}$$

	EASY FLOW Packaging Department Month Ended October 31, 2010			
	Equivalent Units			
	Transferred In	Direct Materials	Conversion Costs	Total
Beginning work in process inventory, Sept. 30	$ 28,360	$ 0	$ 22,369	$ 50,729
Costs added during October	575,000	155,100	425,000	1,155,100
Total costs	$603,360	$155,100	$447,369	
Divide by equivalent units	÷ 125,700	÷ 110,000	÷ 114,710	
Cost per equivalent unit	$ 4.80	$ 1.41	$ 3.90	
Total costs to account for				$1,205,829

We will use this to assign total costs for October in the packaging department to units completed and to units in ending work in process inventory.

Requirement 3

3 Use process costing to assign costs to units completed and to units in ending work in process inventory

Assign the costs to units completed and transferred out and to ending inventory.

Part 1	Part 2	**Part 3**	Part 4	Demo Doc Complete

4 Use the weighted-average method to assign costs to units completed and to units in ending work in process inventory in a second department

Completed and Transferred Out

Finished goods inventory consists of all three cost categories, so Easy Flow multiplies the total units transferred out by the sum of the three costs.

In this case, 110,000 units have been completed and transferred out during October. We know from requirement 2 that cost per transferred-in unit is $4.80, cost per unit for direct materials is $1.41, and the per-unit conversion cost is $3.90. The 110,000 completed units receive 100% of their transferred-in, direct material, and conversion costs. Shown another way:

$$110,000 \times \$ 4.80 = \$ 528,000 \text{ (transferred in)}$$
$$110,000 \times \$ 1.41 = \$ 155,100 \text{ (direct materials)}$$
$$110,000 \times \underline{\$ 3.90} = \underline{\$ 429,000} \text{ (conversion costs)}$$
$$110,000 \times \underline{\$10.11} = \underline{\$1,112,100} \text{ Total transferred}$$

The $1,112,100 will be transferred out to finished goods because the packaging department is the last process in Easy Flow production (debit Finished Goods, credit Work in Process).

| | Assign Costs | | | |
	Transferred In	Direct Materials	Conversion Costs	Total
Units completed and transferred out to Finished				
Goods Inventory 110,000 ×	($4.80 +	$1.41 +	$3.90)	= $1,112,100

EASY FLOW
Packaging Department
Month Ended October 31, 2010

Ending Inventory

Part 1	Part 2	Part 3	**Part 4**	Demo Doc Complete

Because direct materials are added at the end of the packaging process, they have not yet been added to the units in ending work in process.

We know from requirement 1 that the ending work in process inventory is 15,700 transferred-in units, 0 direct materials, and 4,710 conversion cost equivalent units. Shown another way:

$$15,700 \times \$4.80 = \$75,360 \text{ (transferred in)}$$
$$0 \times \$1.41 = \$0 \text{ (direct materials)}$$
$$4,710 \times \$3.90 = \underline{\$18,369} \text{ (conversion costs)}$$
$$\$93,729$$

The $93,729 ending work in process inventory will be listed as an asset on Easy Flow's balance sheet (both Work in Process and Finished Goods are inventory and, therefore, assets).

EASY FLOW
Packaging Department
Month Ended October 31, 2010

		Assign Costs			
		Transferred In	Direct Materials	Conversion Costs	Total
Units completed and transferred out to Finished					
Goods Inventory	110,000 ×	($4.80 +	$1.41 +	$3.90)	= $1,112,100
Ending work in process inventory, Oct. 31:					
Transferred-in costs	15,700 ×	4.80			= 75,360
Direct materials			0		0
Conversion costs	4,710 ×			3.90	= 18,369
Total ending work in process inventory, Oct. 31					$ 93,729
Total costs accounted for					$1,205,829

Make sure the total costs to account for, $1,112,100 + $93,729 = $1,205,829, matches with the total costs from requirement 2.

Part 1	Part 2	Part 3	Part 4	**Demo Doc Complete**

Quick Practice Questions

True/False

_____ 1. In a process costing system, a separate Work in Process Inventory account is maintained for each process.

_____ 2. In a process costing system, costs flow into Finished Goods Inventory only from the Work in Process Inventory of the last manufacturing process.

_____ 3. Wong Corporation had 25,000 units completed and transferred out and 8,000 units that were 35% complete. The equivalent units total 33,000.

_____ 4. The entry to transfer goods in process from Department A to Department B includes a debit to Work in Process—Department A.

_____ 5. The cost per equivalent unit must be computed for direct materials, conversion, and transferred-in costs in a subsequent department.

_____ 6. The number of equivalent units may be greater than the number of accountable physical units.

_____ 7. The cost per equivalent unit is calculated separately for each of the three components of cost—direct materials, direct labor, and manufacturing overhead.

_____ 8. Unique or custom-made goods would be accounted for by using a process costing system.

_____ 9. Conversion costs are generally added evenly throughout the process.

_____ 10. If a department has beginning inventory of 2,000 units, 23,000 units are started into production, and ending inventory is 1,500 units, then 22,500 units are completed.

Multiple Choice

1. In a process costing system, the number of Work in Process Inventory accounts is equal to what amount?
   a. The number of products produced
   b. The number of production departments
   c. The number used in a job order costing system
   d. Cannot be determined without additional information

2. In a process costing system, the entry to record the use of direct materials in production would include which of the following?
   a. Debit to Work in Process Inventory
   b. Debit to Materials Inventory
   c. Debit to Finished Goods Inventory
   d. Credit to Finished Goods Inventory

3. The entry to record a $24,000 transfer from the assembly department to the finishing department would include which of the following?
   a. Debit to Work in Process Inventory—Assembly

b. Debit to Finished Goods Inventory
c. Credit to Work in Process Inventory—Assembly
d. Credit to Materials Inventory

4. During the period, 50,000 units were completed, and 3,600 units were on hand at the end of the period. If the ending work in process inventory was 75% complete as to direct materials and 25% complete as to conversion costs, the equivalent units for direct materials under the weighted-average method would be what amount?
   a. 45,900
   b. 47,700
   c. 48,000
   d. 52,700

5. Beginning work in process is 900 units, units completed and transferred out in October are 3,200 units, and ending work in process is 500 units. Under weighted-average costing, what are units started into production in October?
   a. 2,300
   b. 2,800
   c. 3,200
   d. 3,600

6. Conversions costs consist of which of the following?
   a. Direct materials and direct labor
   b. Direct labor and manufacturing overhead
   c. Direct materials and manufacturing overhead
   d. Product costs and period costs

7. The Lloyd Company uses a process costing system. There were no units in beginning work in process, 1,400 were started, and 1,000 units were completed and transferred out. The units at the end of the period were 60% complete regarding materials and 40% complete regarding conversion. The cost of materials added during the current period amounted to $31,944; the cost of conversion added during the current period amounted to $30,016. What are the equivalent units for materials?
   a. 1,200
   b. 1,240
   c. 1,320
   d. 1,400

8. Refer to Question 7. What are equivalent units for conversion costs?
   a. 1,160
   b. 1,280
   c. 1,300
   d. 1,320

9. Refer to Question 7. What is the cost per equivalent unit for materials?
   a. $22.50
   b. $22.82
   c. $24.20
   d. $25.76

10. Refer to Question 7. What is the cost per equivalent unit for conversion?
    a. $22.74
    b. $23.45
    c. $25.01
    d. $25.88

Quick Exercises

20-1. Given the following products or services, identify which of the following would use a process costing system.

a. Paint
b. Surgical operation
c. Custom kitchen cabinets
d. Cellular telephones
e. Cereal

f. Airplanes
g. Soft drinks
h. Office buildings
i. Custom swimming pools
j. Personal computers

20-2. Department A has no beginning work in process inventory. During the current period, 13,500 units were placed into production. At the end of the current period, 12,000 units were transferred to Department B. The ending units in Department A were 90% complete regarding direct materials and 65% complete regarding conversion costs. Compute the equivalent units for direct materials and conversion costs.

20-3. Journalize the following transactions:

a. Issued $8,800 of direct materials to production in the Carving department.
b. Manufacturing labor in the Carving department amounted to $8,000.
c. Allocated manufacturing labor to the appropriate accounts: 90% direct labor; 10% indirect labor. The pay rate for all direct labor is $20 per hour.
d. Allocated manufacturing overhead in the Carving department at $15 per direct labor hour.
e. Transferred $8,600 of product from the Carving department to finished goods inventory.

General Journal				
Date	Accounts		Debit	Credit

General Journal				
Date	Accounts		Debit	Credit

General Journal				
Date	Accounts		Debit	Credit

General Journal				
Date	Accounts		Debit	Credit

General Journal				
Date	Accounts		Debit	Credit

20-4.   Holland Company makes a variety of chemicals. Its Grinding department reports the following information for June of the current year:

Units:	
Completed and transferred out	7,400
Unfinished units, work in process, June 30	3,500*

*100% complete for direct materials and 30% complete for conversion costs incurred.

Costs:	
Direct materials	$110,055
Direct labor	55,000
Manufacturing overhead	79,845

Requirements

1. Compute the equivalent units for direct materials and conversion costs.

2. Compute the cost per equivalent unit for direct materials and conversion costs.

3. Compute the cost of the goods completed and transferred out.

4. Compute the cost of the work in process at June 30.

20-5. Comfort Corporation manufactures air mattresses. The company uses the weighted-average method of process costing. Information for the Assembly department for the month of July is as follows:

Units:	
Work in process inventory, July 1 (75% complete for direct materials, 40% complete for conversion costs)	30,000 units
Units transferred in from Cutting dept.	150,000 units
Units completed and transferred out	140,000 units
Work in process inventory, July 31 (55% complete for direct materials, 20% complete for conversion costs)	40,000 units
Costs:	
Direct materials:	
Work in process inventory, July 1	$ 90,000
Added during July	567,000
Conversion costs:	
Work in process inventory, July 1	61,800
Added during July	721,000
Transferred-in costs:	
Work in process inventory, July 1	315,000
Units transferred in from Cutting dept. during July	1,575,000

Requirements

1. Compute the total cost of units completed and transferred out.

2. Compute the total cost of work in process inventory on July 31.

Do It Yourself! Question 1

Jiggling Jelly produces packaged jelly. Jiggling has two production departments: blending and packaging. In the blending department, materials are added at the beginning of the process. Conversion costs are added throughout the process for blending. Data for the month of June for the blending department are as follows:

Units:	
Beginning work in process	0 units
Started in production during June	32,500 units
Completed and transferred out to Packaging in June	28,000 units
Ending work in process inventory (20% completed)	4,500 units
Costs:	
Beginning work in process	$ 0
Costs added during June:	
Direct materials	15,925
Conversion costs	24,998
Total costs added during June	$40,923

Requirements

1. Use the four-step process to calculate (1) the cost of the units completed and transferred out to the packaging department, and (2) the total cost of the units in the blending department ending work in process inventory.

Steps 1 and 2

JIGGLING JELLY
Blending Department
Month Ended June 30, 2010

Step 3

JIGGLING JELLY
Blending Department
Month Ended June 30, 2010

Step 4

JIGGLING JELLY		
Blending Department		
Month Ended June 30, 2010		

Do It Yourself! Question 2

Quality Chemicals produces a chemical that it sells to hospitals. Quality has two departments: mixing and packaging. In the second department, packaging, conversion costs are incurred evenly throughout the process. Packaging materials are not added until the end of the packaging process. Costs in beginning work in process inventory include transferred-in costs of $88,000, direct labor of $44,000, and manufacturing overhead of $21,000. July data from the packaging department are as follows:

QUALITY CHEMICALS
Packaging Department
Month Ended July 31, 2010

	Units	Dollars
Beginning inventory, June 30 (80% complete)	55,000	$153,000
Production started:		
Transferred in	230,000	293,900
Direct materials		250,800
Conversion costs:		
Direct labor		189,250
Manufacturing overhead		105,000
Total conversion costs		294,250
Total to account for	285,000	$991,950
Transferred out	220,000	$?
Ending inventory (30% complete)	65,000	$?

Quality uses the weighted-average method for process costing.

Requirements

1. Compute Quality's equivalent units for the month of July.

QUALITY CHEMICALS
Packaging Department
Month Ended July 31, 2010

2. Compute the cost per equivalent unit for July.

QUALITY CHEMICALS
Packaging Department
Month Ended July 31, 2010

3. Assign the costs to units completed and transferred out and to ending work in process inventory.

QUALITY CHEMICALS
Packaging Department
Month Ended July 31, 2010

Quick Practice Solutions

True/False

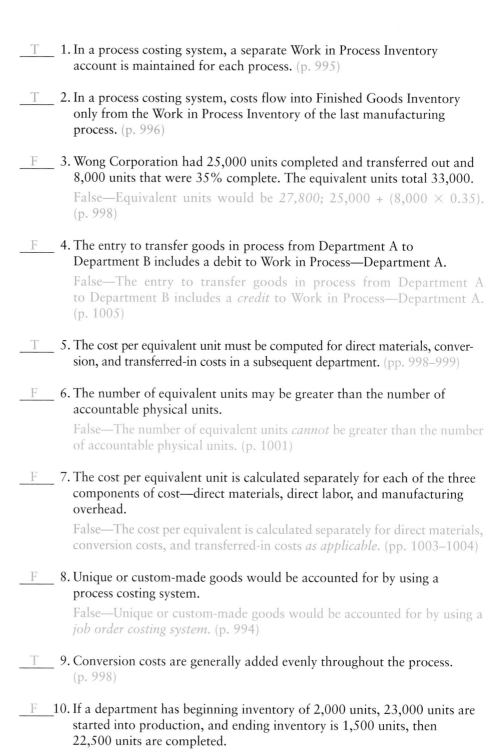

__T__ 1. In a process costing system, a separate Work in Process Inventory
account is maintained for each process. (p. 995)

__T__ 2. In a process costing system, costs flow into Finished Goods Inventory
only from the Work in Process Inventory of the last manufacturing
process. (p. 996)

__F__ 3. Wong Corporation had 25,000 units completed and transferred out and
8,000 units that were 35% complete. The equivalent units total 33,000.

        False—Equivalent units would be *27,800*; 25,000 + (8,000 × 0.35).
(p. 998)

__F__ 4. The entry to transfer goods in process from Department A to
Department B includes a debit to Work in Process—Department A.

        False—The entry to transfer goods in process from Department A
to Department B includes a *credit* to Work in Process—Department A.
(p. 1005)

__T__ 5. The cost per equivalent unit must be computed for direct materials, conversion, and transferred-in costs in a subsequent department. (pp. 998–999)

__F__ 6. The number of equivalent units may be greater than the number of
accountable physical units.

        False—The number of equivalent units *cannot* be greater than the number
of accountable physical units. (p. 1001)

__F__ 7. The cost per equivalent unit is calculated separately for each of the three
components of cost—direct materials, direct labor, and manufacturing
overhead.

        False—The cost per equivalent is calculated separately for direct materials,
conversion costs, and transferred-in costs *as applicable.* (pp. 1003–1004)

__F__ 8. Unique or custom-made goods would be accounted for by using a
process costing system.

        False—Unique or custom-made goods would be accounted for by using a
job order costing system. (p. 994)

__T__ 9. Conversion costs are generally added evenly throughout the process.
(p. 998)

__F__ 10. If a department has beginning inventory of 2,000 units, 23,000 units are
started into production, and ending inventory is 1,500 units, then
22,500 units are completed.

        False—If a department has beginning inventory of 2,000 units,
23,000 units are started into production, and ending inventory is 1,500 units,
then *23,500* (2,000 + 23,000 − 1,500) units are completed. (pp. 998–999)

Multiple Choice

1. In a process costing system, the number of Work in Process Inventory accounts is equal to what amount? (p. 996)
    a. The number of products produced
    b. The number of production departments
    c. The number used in a job order costing system
    d. Cannot be determined without additional information

2. In a process costing system, the entry to record the use of direct materials in production would include which of the following? (p. 996)
    a. Debit to Work in Process Inventory
    b. Debit to Materials Inventory
    c. Debit to Finished Goods Inventory
    d. Credit to Finished Goods Inventory

3. The entry to record a $24,000 transfer from the assembly department to the finishing department would include which of the following? (p. 996)
    a. Debit to Work in Process Inventory—Assembly
    b. Debit to Finished Goods Inventory
    c. Credit to Work in Process Inventory—Assembly
    d. Credit to Materials Inventory

4. During the period, 50,000 units were completed, and 3,600 units were on hand at the end of the period. If the ending work in process inventory was 75% complete as to direct materials and 25% complete as to conversion costs, the equivalent units for direct materials under the weighted-average method would be what amount? (p. 1011)
    a. 45,900
    b. 47,700
    c. 48,000
    d. 52,700

5. Beginning work in process is 900 units, units completed and transferred out in October are 3,200 units, and ending work in process is 500 units. Under weighted-average costing, what are units started into production in October? (pp. 1009–1015)
    a. 2,300
    b. 2,800
    c. 3,200
    d. 3,600

6. Conversions costs consist of which of the following? (p. 998)
    a. Direct materials and direct labor
    b. Direct labor and manufacturing overhead
    c. Direct materials and manufacturing overhead
    d. Product costs and period costs

7. The Lloyd Company uses a process costing system. There were no units in beginning work in process, 1,400 were started, and 1,000 units were completed and transferred out. The units at the end of the period were 60% complete regarding materials and 40% complete regarding conversion. The cost of materials added during the current period amounted to $31,944; the

cost of conversion added during the current period amounted to $30,016. What are the equivalent units for materials? (pp. 999–1005)

a. 1,200

b. 1,240

c. 1,320

d. 1,400

8. Refer to Question 7. What are equivalent units for conversion costs? (pp. 999–1005)

a. 1,160

b. 1,280

c. 1,300

d. 1,320

9. Refer to Question 7. What is the cost per equivalent unit for materials? (pp. 999–1005)

a. $22.50

b. $22.82

c. $24.20

d. $25.76

10. Refer to Question 7. What is the cost per equivalent unit for conversion? (pp. 999–1005)

a. $22.74

b. $23.45

c. $25.01

d. $25.88

Quick Exercises

20-1. Identify which of the following products or services would use a process costing system. (pp. 994–996)

a. Paint
b. Surgical operation
c. Custom kitchen cabinets
d. Cellular telephones
e. Cereal

f. Airplanes
g. Soft drinks
h. Office buildings
i. Custom swimming pools
j. Personal computers

20-2. Department A has no beginning work in process inventory. During the current period, 13,500 units were placed into production. At the end of the current period, 12,000 units were transferred to Department B. The ending units in Department A were 90% complete regarding direct materials and 65% complete regarding conversion costs. Compute the equivalent units for direct materials and conversion costs. (pp. 998–999)

Solution:

Direct materials
12,000 + (1,500 × 0.90) = 13,350

Conversion costs
12,000 + (1,500 × 0.65) = 12,975

20-3. Journalize the following transactions. (pp. 999–1005)

a. Issued $8,800 of direct materials to production in the Carving department.

b. Manufacturing labor in the Carving department amounted to $8,000.

c. Allocated manufacturing labor to the appropriate accounts: 90% direct labor; 10% indirect labor. The pay rate for all direct labor is $20 per hour.

d. Allocated manufacturing overhead in the Carving department at $15 per direct labor hour.

e. Transferred $8,600 of product from the Carving department to finished goods inventory.

General Journal				
	Date	Accounts	Debit	Credit
a.		Work in Process Inventory—Carving	8,800	
		Materials Inventory		8,800

General Journal				
	Date	Accounts	Debit	Credit
b.		Manufacturing Wages	8,000	
		Wages Payable		8,000

General Journal				
	Date	Accounts	Debit	Credit
c.		Work in Process Inventory—Carving	7,200	
		Manufacturing Overhead	800	
		Manufacturing Wages		8,000

General Journal				
	Date	Accounts	Debit	Credit
d.		Work in Process Inventory—Carving	6,000	
		Manufacturing Overhead		6,000

General Journal				
	Date	Accounts	Debit	Credit
e.		Finished Goods Inventory	8,600	
		Work in Process Inventory—Carving		8,600

20-4. Holland Company makes a variety of chemicals. Its Grinding department reports the following information for June of the current year: (pp. 999–1005)

Units:	
Completed and transferred out	7,400
Unfinished units, work in process, June 30	3,500*

*100% complete for direct materials and 30% complete for conversion costs incurred.

Costs:	
Direct materials	$110,055
Direct labor	55,000
Manufacturing overhead	79,845

Requirements

1. Compute the equivalent units for direct materials and conversion costs.

Equivalent units:

Direct materials

7,400 + 3,500 = 10,900 equivalent units

Conversion costs

7,400 + (3,500 × 0.30) = 8,450

2. Compute the cost per equivalent unit for direct materials and conversion costs.

Cost per equivalent unit:

Direct materials

$110,055/10,900 = $10.10

Conversion:

$134,845/8,450 = $15.96

3. Compute the cost of the goods completed and transferred out.

7,400 × ($10.10 + $15.96) = $192,844

4. Compute the cost of the work in process at June 30.

$$(3,500 \times 1.00) \times \$10.10 \quad = \quad 35,350$$
$$(3,500 \times 0.30) \times \$15.96 \quad = \quad \underline{16,758}$$
$$\underline{\underline{52,108}}$$

20-5.   Comfort Corporation manufactures air mattresses. The company uses the weighted-average method of process costing. Information for the Assembly department for the month of July is as follows: (pp. 999–1005)

Units:	
Work in process inventory, July 1 (75% complete for direct materials 40% complete for conversion costs)	30,000 units
Units transferred in from Cutting dept.	150,000 units
Units completed and transferred out	140,000 units
Work in process inventory, July 31 (55% complete for direct materials, 20% complete for conversion costs)	40,000 units
Costs:	
Direct materials:	
Work in process inventory, July 1	$ 90,000
Added during July	567,000
Conversion costs:	
Work in process inventory, July 1	61,800
Added during July	721,000
Transferred-in costs:	
Work in process inventory, July 1	315,000
Units transferred in from Cutting dept. during July	1,575,000

Requirements

1. Compute the total cost of units completed and transferred out.

Direct materials equivalent units
140,000 + (40,000 × 0.55) = 162,000
Conversion costs equivalent units
140,000 + (40,000 × 0.20) = 148,000
Transferred-in equivalent units
180,000 (30,000 + 150,000)

Cost per equivalent unit:
Direct materials
$657,000/162,000 = $4.06

Conversion costs
$782,800/148,000 = $5.29

Transferred-in

$1,890,000/180,000 = $10.50

Costs of units completed and transferred out

140,000 × ($4.06 + $5.29 + $10.50) = $2,779,000

2. Compute the total cost of work in process inventory on July 31.

Costs of July 31 work in process

(22,000 × $4.06) + (8,000 × $5.29) + (40,000 × $10.50) =

$89,320 + $42,320 + $420,000 = $551,640

Do It Yourself! Question 1 Solution

Requirement

1. Use the four-step process to calculate (1) the cost of the units completed and transferred out to the packaging department and (2) the total cost of the units in the blending department ending work in process inventory.

2 Compute equivalent units

Step 1: Summarize the flow of physical units;

Step 2: Compute output in terms of equivalent units.

JIGGLING JELLY
Blending Department
Month Ended June 30, 2010

Flow of Production	Step 1 Flow of Physical Units	Step 2: Equivalent Units — Direct Materials	Step 2: Equivalent Units — Conversion Costs
Units to account for:			
Beginning work in process, May 31	0		
Started in production during June	32,500		
Total physical units to account for	32,500		
Units accounted for:			
Completed and transferred out during June	28,000	28,000	28,000
Ending work in process, June 30	4,500	4,500	900
Total physical units accounted for	32,500		
Equivalent units		32,500	28,900

3 Use process costing to assign costs to units completed and to units in ending work in process inventory

Step 3: Compute the cost per equivalent unit.

JIGGLING JELLY
Blending Department
Month Ended June 30, 2010

	Step 3: Cost per Equivalent Unit — Direct Materials	Step 3: Cost per Equivalent Unit — Conversion Costs
Beginning work in process, May 31	$ 0	$ 0
Costs added during June	15,925	24,998
Total costs for June	$ 15,925	$24,998
Divide by equivalent units	÷ 32,500	÷ 28,900
Cost per equivalent unit	$ 0.49	$ 0.865

Use process costing to assign costs to units completed and to units in ending work in process inventory

Step 4: Assign costs to units completed and to units in ending work in process inventory.

JIGGLING JELLY
Blending Department
Month Ended June 30, 2010

| | | Step 4: Assign Costs | | |
		Direct Materials	Conversion Costs	Total
Units completed and transferred out to Packaging in June	28,000 ×	($0.49 +	$0.865)	= $37,940
Ending work in process, June 30:				
Direct materials	4,500 ×	0.49		= 2,205
Conversion costs	900 ×		0.865	= 778*
Total ending work in process, June 30				$ 2,983
Total costs accounted for				$40,923

*900 × $0.865 = $778.50, rounded to $778

Do It Yourself! Question 2 Solutions

 Use the weighted-average method to assign costs to units completed and to units in ending work in process inventory in a second department

Requirements

1. Compute Quality's equivalent units for the month of July.

QUALITY CHEMICALS
Packaging Department
Month Ended July 31, 2010

Flow of Production	Equivalent Units		
	Transferred In	Direct Materials	Conversion Costs
Units accounted for:			
Completed and transferred out during July	220,000	220,000	220,000
Ending work in process inventory, July 31	65,000	0	19,500
Equivalent units	285,000	220,000	239,500

 Use the weighted-average method to assign costs to units completed and to units in ending work in process inventory in a second department

2. Compute the cost per equivalent unit for July.

QUALITY CHEMICALS
Packaging Department
Month Ended July 31, 2010

	Cost per Equivalent Unit			
	Transferred In	Direct Materials	Conversion Costs	Total
Beginning work in process inventory, June 30	$ 88,000	$ 0	$ 65,000	$153,000
Costs added during July	293,900	250,800	294,250	838,950
Total costs	$381,900	$250,800	$359,250	
Divide by equivalent units	÷ 285,000	220,000	÷ 239,500	
Cost per equivalent unit	$ 1.34	$ 1.14	$ 1.50	
Total costs to account for				$991,950

Use the weighted-average method to assign costs to units completed and to units in ending work in process inventory in a second department

3. Assign the costs to units completed and transferred out and to ending inventory.

| | | | | QUALITY CHEMICALS | | | |

QUALITY CHEMICALS
Packaging Department
Month Ended July 31, 2010

	Assign Costs			
	Transferred In	Direct Materials	Conversion Costs	Total
Units completed and transferred out to Finished				
Goods Inventory 220,000 ×	($1.34 +	$1.14 +	$1.50)	= $875,600
Ending work in process inventory, July 31:				
Transferred-in costs 65,000 ×	1.34			= 87,100
Direct materials		0		0
Conversion costs 19,500 ×			1.50	= 29,250
Total ending work in process inventory, July 31				$116,350
Total costs accounted for				$991,950

The Power of Practice

For more practice using the skills learned in this chapter, visit MyAccountingLab. There you will find algorithmically generated questions that are based on these Demo Docs and your main textbook's Review and Assess Your Progress sections.

Go to MyAccountingLab and follow these steps:

1. Direct your URL to www.myaccountinglab.com.
2. Log in using your name and password.
3. Click the MyAccountingLab link.
4. Click Study Plan in the left navigation bar.
5. From the table of contents, select Chapter 20, Process Costing.
6. Click a link to work tutorial exercises.

21 Cost-Volume-Profit Analysis

What You Probably Already Know

If you decide to sign up for cell phone service, you know that there is a choice of providers and plans. Assume that you are debating whether to enroll in one of two plans. The first plan has 450 free anytime minutes, which costs $40 a month plus $0.45/minute beyond 450. The second plan has 900 free anytime minutes, which costs $60 a month plus $0.40/minute beyond 900. Your objective is to minimize your cost. To accomplish this, you are using concepts like fixed and variable costs that we will study in this chapter. The monthly amount of $40 or $60 is fixed; once the plan is selected, you will be charged that monthly amount regardless of the number of minutes you use. In addition, you will be charged a variable cost per minute if you exceed the allowed number of minutes. If you estimate that you will be using about 600 anytime minutes, which plan is cheaper? Plan one would be $40 + [(600 − 450) × $0.45] = $107.50; plan two would be $60 + 0 = $60. The second plan is cheaper.

Learning Objectives

 Identify how changes in volume of activity affect costs.

There are three types of costs—fixed, variable, and mixed. **Fixed costs** are costs that do not change over wide ranges of volume. The range of volume over which fixed costs are constant is called the **relevant range.** Building rent, furniture depreciation, and the salary of an office manager would be examples of fixed costs. If fixed costs are $100,000 and 10,000 units are produced, the fixed cost per unit is $10 ($100,000/10,000). If the volume doubles to 20,000 units, the fixed cost per unit is reduced to $5 per unit. **Variable costs** are costs that increase in total as the volume of activity increases and decrease as the volume of activity decreases. **Total variable costs** change in direct proportion to changes in volume. Direct materials and direct labor are examples of variable costs. If it costs $3 per unit for direct materials, the total variable cost when 10,000 units are produced is $30,000. If the volume doubles to 20,000, the total variable cost is now $60,000, but the variable cost per unit is unchanged at $3 per unit. **Mixed costs** have both variable and fixed components. The **high-low method** is used to separate the mixed cost into the variable and fixed elements. *Review Exhibits 21-1 and 21-2 (p. 1053) to see the impact of varying volume amounts on total variable and fixed costs.*

Use CVP analysis to compute breakeven points.

The **breakeven point** is the sales level at which operating income is zero. Sales revenue equals total fixed and variable costs. There are three approaches you can use to compute the breakeven point. The **income statement approach** uses the income statement to facilitate the calculation of breakeven units sold (see Demo Doc 1). The contribution margin is the difference between sales revenue and variable costs. The **contribution margin approach** is a shortcut to the income statement approach. The **contribution margin ratio approach** is used when you don't have detailed information on individual products. You will use these three approaches in Demo Doc 1.

Rounding Note: When calculating the breakeven sales units or sales dollars, it is possible to obtain a fractional amount. To be conservative, you should always round up to the next higher unit or dollar.

Review Summary Problem 1 for computations of breakeven sales units and dollars.

 Use CVP analysis for profit planning, and graph the cost-volume-profit relations.

As you will also see in Demo Doc 1, you can use the three approaches to compute breakeven to also determine the number of units that must be sold to create a desired net income.

The cost-volume-profit relationship can be graphed using increments of volume within the relevant range as the horizontal axis and dollars as the vertical axis. Total sales revenue is zero at zero volume and would increase linearly $10 for each unit of volume using the example in Summary Problem 1 of the main textbook (p. 1064). Total costs would start on the vertical axis at $10,000, the total fixed costs, and would increase linearly $4 for variable costs for each unit of volume. The point at which the total sales revenue line equals total costs is the breakeven point. Drawing a vertical line from that point would indicate the breakeven volume in units. *Review Summary Problem 1 for computations of sales units and dollars to achieve desired results. Review the cost-volume-profit graph in Exhibit 21-7 (p. 1068).*

 Use CVP methods to perform sensitivity analyses.

Sensitivity analysis is a "what if" technique that shows how profits will be affected if sales prices, costs, or underlying assumptions change. Using technology tools with an understanding of the interrelationship between the elements of cost, volume, and profit, it can be determined what the effect may be on net income of making business decisions.

5 **Calculate the breakeven point for multiple product lines or services.**

Most companies sell multiple product lines or services. Each product or service may have a different contribution margin. It is necessary to calculate the weighted-average contribution margin of all of the sales using a sales mix, as you will see in Demo Doc 2. A **sales mix** is the combination of products that make up total sales. *Review the Summary Problem 2 in the main textbook (p. 1074).*

Demo Doc 1

Use CVP to Plan Profits

Learning Objectives 2, 3

Crew Cut Mowing Service mows residential lawns. The average amount they charge to mow a single lawn is $30. Crew Cut has calculated the average variable cost of mowing a lawn to be about $18. Their monthly fixed cost is $1,200.

Requirements

1. Use the contribution margin approach to calculate how many lawns Crew Cut must mow in a month to break even.

2. Use the contribution margin ratio approach to determine Crew Cut's breakeven point in sales dollars.

3. Use the income statement approach to prove that your solutions to requirements 1 and 2 are correct.

4. The owner of Crew Cut currently works for another lawn service and earns $2,800 per month. He doesn't want to incur the risk of owning his own business unless he believes that he can have profit of at least the amount he currently earns. Determine the number of lawns Crew Cut must mow in a month to earn a profit of $2,800.

Demo Doc 1 Solutions

Requirement 1

2 Use CVP analysis to compute breakeven points

Use the contribution margin approach to calculate how many lawns Crew Cut must mow in a month to break even.

Part 1	Part 2	Part 3	Part 4	Demo Doc Complete

The contribution margin tells managers how much revenue is left after paying variable costs. That revenue is used for *contributing* toward first covering fixed costs and then generating a profit. The contribution margin is calculated by subtracting variable costs from the sales revenue. Therefore:

Sales price per unit

− Variable cost per unit

= Contribution margin per unit

Crew Cut's variable cost per lawn (unit) is $18. Therefore, their unit contribution margin is:

Sales price per lawn	$30
Variable cost per lawn	(18)
Contribution margin per lawn	$12

That means that after variable costs are covered, Crew Cut has $12 per lawn that they mow, which then contributes toward fixed costs until fixed costs are covered, after which point Crew Cut will begin to generate $12 profit per lawn.

Breakeven is the level of sales at which total operating revenues is equal to total expenses (fixed and variable). In other words, the level at which income is zero. To compute the breakeven using the contribution margin approach:

$$\text{Breakeven} = \frac{\text{Fixed cost}}{\text{Contribution margin per unit}}$$

$$= \frac{\$1,200}{\$12}$$

$$= 100 \, \text{lawns}$$

In this case, Crew Cut must be able to mow 100 lawns per month to break even. That's because at 100 lawns, Crew Cut has earned just enough contribution margin to cover total fixed costs. Every lawn mowed after the breakeven point contributes the unit contribution margin to profit. For example, if Crew Cut mows 101 lawns, then they would earn $12 profit.

Requirement 2

2 Use CVP analysis to compute breakeven points

Use the contribution margin ratio approach to determine Crew Cut's breakeven point in sales dollars.

Part 1	Part 2	Part 3	Part 4	Demo Doc Complete

So far, we have seen that computing the breakeven point for a simple business that sells only one product is pretty straightforward. But larger companies that don't have detailed information on individual products use their contribution margin *ratio* to predict profits, rather than using individual unit contribution margins on each of their products.

The contribution margin ratio is the ratio of contribution margin to sales revenue. In other words, they compute their breakeven point in terms of sales dollars. This enables managers to do CVP analysis with aggregated information across many products with varied selling prices. We calculate the contribution margin ratio as follows:

$$\text{Contribution margin ratio} \; = \; \frac{\text{Contribution margin per unit}}{\text{Sales revenue per unit}}$$

So, in this case, the contribution margin ratio is equal to the contribution margin per unit (determined in requirement 1 to be $12 per lawn) divided by the sales revenue per unit ($30 per lawn).

$$\text{Contribution margin ratio} \; = \frac{\$12}{\$30}$$
$$= \$0.40 \,(\text{or } 40\%)$$

This means that each dollar of sales revenue contributes 40% ($0.40) toward fixed costs and profit. To compute breakeven using the contribution margin ratio:

$$\text{Breakeven sales in dollars} \; = \; \frac{\text{Fixed cost}}{\text{Contribution margin ratio}}$$

We know that Crew Cut's fixed cost is $1,200 and their contribution margin ratio is 40%, so:

$$\text{Breakeven sales in dollars} \; = \frac{\$1,200}{40\%}$$
$$= \$3,000$$

Crew Cut must produce revenue of $3,000 per month to cover their fixed costs and variable costs (that is, break even). This is consistent with our previous calculations for breakeven (that is, 100 lawns × $30 per lawn = $3,000).

Requirement 3

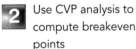

Use CVP analysis to compute breakeven points

Use the income statement approach to prove that your solutions to requirements 1 and 2 are correct.

Part 1	Part 2	**Part 3**	Part 4	Demo Doc Complete

By multiplying Crew Cut's breakeven in units, 100, by what they charge to mow each lawn, $30, we've proven that our answers to requirements 1 and 2 are the same because the result equals the same as what we calculated in requirement 2, $3,000.

Sales revenue (100 units × $30)	$3,000
Less: Variable cost (100 units × $18)	1,800
Total contribution margin	1,200
Less: Fixed cost	1,200
Operating income	$ 0

After deducting the variable cost of $1,800 for 100 lawns and the fixed cost of $1,200, the income statement illustrates that Crew Cut would produce $0 operating income at a breakeven level of 100 units.

Requirement 4

Use CVP analysis for profit planning, and graph the CVP relations

The owner of Crew Cut currently works for another lawn service and earns $2,800 per month. He doesn't want to incur the risk of owning his own business unless he believes that he can have profit of at least the amount he currently earns. Determine the number of lawns Crew Cut must mow in a month to earn a profit of $2,800.

Part 1	Part 2	Part 3	**Part 4**	Demo Doc Complete

Up until now, we've computed how many lawns (or sales revenue) Crew Cut needs to mow in order to break even. We know that it must mow 100 lawns, or the equivalent of $3,000 in sales, to break even. Anything less would be a loss. Anything more would be profit.

Now, Crew Cut wants to know how many lawns it needs to mow to generate $2,800 in profit. Because Crew Cut wants to know the number of lawns (units), we'll use the formula based on the unit contribution margin.

Using the contribution margin approach, utilize the desired profit of $2,800 as fixed cost (in CVP analysis, always think of desired profit as a fixed cost):

$$\text{Desired profit sales level} = \frac{(\text{Fixed cost} + \text{Desired profit})}{\text{Contribution margin per unit}}$$

In this way, it's very similar to calculating breakeven, except now the desired profit is treated as a fixed cost in our calculations (remember, the contribution margin per unit = selling price per unit − variable cost per unit):

$$\text{Desired profit sales level} = \frac{(\$1,200 + \$2,800)}{(\$30 - \$18)}$$

$$= \frac{\$4,000}{\$12}$$

$$= 333.33, \textbf{ rounded to 334 lawns}$$

Once you know your breakeven, another way to think of this is to divide your desired profit by your contribution margin and add the difference to your breakeven:

$$\$2,800/\$12 = 234 \text{ lawns (rounded)}$$

$$234 \text{ lawns} + 100 \text{ breakeven} = 334 \text{ lawns}$$

This analysis shows that Crew Cut must mow 334 lawns to earn a profit of $2,800 (remember, we round up in this case to avoid partial units/lawns). If Crew Cut also wanted to know how much sales revenue they would need to earn $2,800 profit, they could use this figure to do the calculation:

$$334 \text{ lawns} \times \$30 \text{ per lawn} = \$10,020 \text{ sales revenue}$$

The desired profit is treated as a fixed cost in our calculations. Using this data of 334 lawns to achieve the desired profit, the owner of Crew Cut can decide if it is worth leaving his current job to start Crew Cut. This data can also be used as a management tool to help determine marketing strategy, hiring policy, and aid in other types of decision making.

As before, you can use the income statement approach to prove these figures:

Sales revenue (334 × $30)	$10,020
Less: Total variable costs (334 × $18)	6,012
Total contribution margin (334 × $12)	4,008
Less: Total fixed costs	1,200
Operating income	$ 2,808*

The $8 operating income results from rounding a lawn [(334 − 333.33) × $12] = $8

Whenever rounding must occur in a problem, such as when we rounded up from 333.33 to 334 lawns to avoid a partial unit, there will often be a small difference when proving the numbers in this way.

Part 1	Part 2	Part 3	Part 4	**Demo Doc Complete**

Demo Doc 2

Using CVP for Sensitivity Analysis

Learning Objectives 2, 4

Hacker Golf has developed a unique swing trainer golf club. They currently have a production company produce the golf club for them at a cost of $22. Other variable costs total $6 while monthly fixed costs are $16,000. Hacker currently sells the trainer golf club for $48.

Requirements

NOTE: Solve each requirement as a separate situation.

1. Calculate Hacker's breakeven point in units.

2. Hacker is considering raising its selling price to $49.95. Calculate the new breakeven in units.

3. Hacker has found a new company to produce the golf club at a lower cost of $19 each. Calculate the new breakeven in units.

4. Because many customers have requested a golf glove to go along with the trainer club, Hacker is considering selling gloves. They only expect to sell one glove for every four trainer clubs they sell. Hacker can purchase the gloves for $5 each and sell them for $9 each. Total fixed costs should remain the same at $16,000 per month. Calculate the breakeven point in units for trainer clubs and golf gloves.

5. Use a contribution margin income statement to prove the breakeven point calculated in requirement 4.

Demo Doc 2 Solutions

Requirement 1

2 Use CVP analysis to compute breakeven points

Calculate Hacker's breakeven point in units.

Part 1	Part 2	Part 3	Part 4	Part 5	Part 6	Part 7	Demo Doc Complete

To determine how changes in sales prices, costs, or volume affect profits, let's first start by calculating the current breakeven point.

To determine the breakeven point, we first must calculate the contribution margin per unit. The contribution margin per unit is calculated by subtracting variable costs from the sales revenue. Therefore:

Contribution margin per unit = Sales price per unit − Variable cost per unit

Hacker's variable cost per club (unit) is the price they pay for each club ($22) plus their additional variable costs ($6). Therefore, their unit contribution margin is:

Selling price per club	$48
Variable cost per club ($22 + $6)	(28)
Contribution margin per club	$20

The contribution margin represents the amount from each unit sold that is available to recover fixed costs. That means that after variable costs are covered, Hacker earns $20 per club, which then contributes toward fixed costs until fixed costs are covered, after which point Hacker will begin to generate $20 profit per club sold.

Breakeven is the level of sales at which income is zero. To compute breakeven using the contribution margin approach:

$$\text{Breakeven} = \frac{\text{Fixed cost}}{\text{Contribution margin per unit}}$$

$$= \frac{\$16,000}{\$20}$$

$$= \textbf{800 trainer clubs}$$

Requirement 2

4 Use CVP methods to perform sensitivity analyses

Hacker is considering raising its selling price to $49.95. Calculate the new breakeven in units.

Part 1	**Part 2**	Part 3	Part 4	Part 5	Part 6	Part 7	Demo Doc Complete

In this case, the selling price is changing, but Hacker's variable and fixed costs are staying the same as in the original question ($28 and $16,000, respectively). The new selling price for the club is going to be $1.95 higher than the original price: from $48.00 to $49.95.

Once we update the original data to reflect the changes, the data are then processed with the same calculations. First, calculate the new contribution margin:

Selling price per club	$49.95
Variable cost per club ($221 + 6)	(28.00)
Contribution margin per club	$21.95

Using the contribution margin approach:

$$\text{Breakeven in units} = \frac{\text{Fixed cost}}{\text{Contribution margin per unit}}$$

$$= \frac{\$16,000.00}{\$21.95}$$

$$= 728.93, \textbf{rounded up to 729 trainer clubs}$$

Again, we round because Hacker cannot sell a partial unit (the .93 in the actual calculation).

With the increased selling price, breakeven has been reduced from 800 clubs to 729 clubs. The higher price means that each club contributes more to fixed costs.

You can prove this using the income statement approach:

Sales revenue (729 × $49.95)	$36,414
Less: Variable costs (729 × $28)	20,412
Total contribution margin	16,002
Less: Fixed costs	16,000
Operating income	$ 2 *

The $2 profit results from rounding 728.93 clubs to 729 (0.07 × $21.95 = $2)

Remember that as selling prices increase (provided all costs remain the same), the volume required to break even or achieve target profit goals decreases. Conversely, as selling prices decrease, the volume required to break even or achieve target profit goals increases.

Consider the following:

Selling price goes from $50 to $60, variable costs stay at $20, and total fixed costs are $60,000.

Old contribution margin was $50 − $20 = $30.

Old breakeven point in **units** was: $60,000 / $30 = 2,000 units.

New contribution margin is $60 − $20 = $40.

New breakeven point in **units** is: $60,000 / $40 = 1,500 units.

There is an *inverse* relationship between contribution margin (an increase of $10 in this case) and breakeven in units (a decrease of 500 units in this case).

Requirement 3

4 | Use CVP methods to perform sensitivity analyses

Hacker has found a new company to produce the golf club at a lower cost of $19 each. Calculate the new breakeven in units.

Part 1	Part 2	**Part 3**	Part 4	Part 5	Part 6	Part 7	Demo Doc Complete

Once costs begin to change, a new breakeven must be calculated to determine the effects of the changes. In this case, the variable cost is changing, yet fixed costs and the sales price is staying the same as in the original question ($16,000 and $48, respectively).

In this case, we calculate as we normally would, except that our contribution margin will be different:

Contribution margin per unit = Sales price per unit − Variable cost per unit

Hacker's variable cost per club (unit) is the price they pay for each club (now $19) plus their additional variable costs ($6). Therefore, their unit contribution margin is:

Selling price per club	$48
Variable cost per club ($19 + $6)	(25)
Contribution margin per club	$23

Using the contribution margin approach:

$$\text{Breakeven in units} = \frac{\text{Fixed cost}}{\text{Contribution margin per unit}}$$

$$= \frac{\$16,000}{\$23}$$

$$= 695.65, \textbf{rounded to 696 clubs}$$

With the reduced variable cost, Hacker's breakeven in units decreases from 800 clubs to 696 clubs. Using this information, Hacker's management must decide if it is worth the risk to switch to a new producer.

You can also prove this using the income statement approach:

Sales revenue (696 × $48)	$33,408
Less: Variable costs (696 × $25)	17,400
Total contribution margin	16,008
Less: Fixed costs	16,000
Operating income	$ 8 *

*The $8 profit results from rounding [(696 − 695.65) × $23] = $8

With both fixed and variable costs, remember that as these costs increase, so does the volume needed to break even or achieve target profits. Conversely, as these costs decrease, the volume needed to break even or achieve target profits also decreases.

Requirement 4

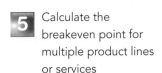

Calculate the breakeven point for multiple product lines or services

Because many customers have requested a golf glove to go along with the trainer club, Hacker is considering selling gloves. They only expect to sell one glove for every four trainer clubs they sell. Hacker can purchase the gloves for $5 each and sell them for $9 each. Total fixed costs should remain the same at $16,000 per month. Calculate the breakeven point in units for trainer clubs and golf gloves.

Part 1	Part 2	Part 3	**Part 4**	Part 5	Part 6	Part 7	Demo Doc Complete

Calculating the breakeven point is fairly straightforward when a company is only dealing with one product. But Hacker is now considering selling two products rather than just one. Now breakeven becomes a little more complicated. This is because different products will have different effects on the contribution margins because of different costs and selling prices. So the company needs to consider the sales mix (a combination of products that make up total sales) in figuring CVP relationships.

You can use the same formulas to determine the breakeven point considering the sales mix, but before calculating breakeven, you must calculate the weighted-average contribution margin of all the products first. You saw another weighted-average for process costing in Chapter 20. In this case, the sales mix provides the weights.

Step 1: Calculate the weighted-average contribution margin.

Hacker believes that they can sell one glove for every four trainer clubs that they sell. This would give them a 4:1 sales mix. So they expect that 4/5 (or 80%) of their sales will be trainer clubs, and 1/5 (or 20%) of their sales will be gloves.

Recall that Hacker pays $28 in variable costs for their clubs and sells them for $48, for a contribution margin of $20 per unit. The gloves will cost them $5 per pair and sell for $9, for a contribution margin of $4 per unit:

	Clubs	Gloves	Total
Sales price per unit	$48	$9	
Deduct: variable cost per unit	(28)	(5)	
Contribution margin per unit	$20	$4	

The weighted-average contribution margin is calculated by multiplying the contribution margin per unit by the sales mix expected for each. Once we have a total contribution margin ($80 + $4 = $84, in this case), we divide the total contribution margin by the total sales mix in units (5), as follows:

	Sales Mix Percentage		
	80% Clubs	20% Gloves	Total
Sales price per unit	$48	$9	
Deduct: Variable cost per unit	(28)	(5)	
Contribution margin per unit	$20	$4	
Sales mix in units	4	1	5.00
Contribution margin per product	$80	$4	$84.00
Weighted-average contribution margin ($84/5)			$16.80

Another way to calculate this is to multiply each product's contribution margin by its sales mix percentage:

Clubs:	$20 × 80%	=	$16.00
Gloves	$ 4 × 20%	=	$ 0.80
		=	$16.80

The $16.80 represents an average contribution margin for all the products Hacker sells. The golf clubs are weighted more heavily because Hacker expects to sell four times as many clubs compared to the gloves.

The next step is to calculate the breakeven in units for the bundle of products.

Step 2: Calculate the breakeven point in units for the total of both products combined.

Part 1	Part 2	Part 3	Part 4	**Part 5**	Part 6	Part 7	Demo Doc Complete

This is calculated using the following formula:

$$\frac{\text{Total sales}}{\text{in units}} = \frac{\text{Fixed cost}}{\text{Weighted-average contribution margin per unit}}$$

We know from the question that fixed costs will not be affected, so they should remain at $16,000. The weighted-average contribution margin, as we just calculated, is $16.80 per unit. So we compute as follows:

$$\frac{\text{Total sales}}{\text{in units}} = \frac{\$16,000}{\$16.80}$$

$$= 952.38, \textbf{rounded to 953}$$

Recall that we round up because Hacker cannot sell a partial unit.

Hacker must sell a combined 953 clubs and gloves to break even. Management needs to know how many units of each product must be sold to break even.

The next step is to determine the breakeven point in units for each product.

Step 3: Calculate the breakeven in units for each product line.

Part 1	Part 2	Part 3	Part 4	Part 5	**Part 6**	Part 7	Demo Doc Complete

Because Hacker believes that they will sell four trainer clubs for every one glove, the total breakeven, 953, is multiplied by each product's respective percent of expected total sales:

Breakeven sales of clubs $(953 \times 80\%) = 762.4$, **rounded to 763**
Breakeven sales of gloves $(953 \times 20\%) = 190.6$, **rounded to 191**
$= 954$ total units

So from this analysis, we know that Hacker needs to sell 763 trainer clubs and 191 gloves to break even. The breakeven point in sales dollars is:

$763 \text{ clubs} \times \$48 = \$36,624$
plus $191 \text{ gloves} \times \$ 9 = \$ 1,719$
for a total $= \underline{\underline{\$38,343}}$

Requirement 5

5 Calculate the breakeven point for multiple product lines or services

Use a contribution margin income statement to prove the breakeven point calculated in requirement 4.

Part 1	Part 2	Part 3	Part 4	Part 5	Part 6	**Part 7**	Demo Doc Complete

To test the calculation of the breakeven point, you would add together the revenue generated from all sales, subtract the variable costs for each of the clubs and gloves, and then subtract the total fixed costs. The result should balance to zero (or close to zero, in cases in which rounding occurs).

HACKER GOLF
Contribution Margin Income Statement

		Clubs	Gloves	Total
Sales revenue:				
Trainer clubs (763 × $48)	$36,624		
Gloves (191 × $9)		$1,719	$38,343
Variable costs:				
Trainer clubs (763 × $28)	21,364		
Gloves (191 × $5)		955	$22,319
Contribution margin	$15,260	$ 764	$16,024
Fixed costs			(16,000)
Operating income			$ 24

There is a slight $24 profit at the breakeven level because of rounding to whole units.

Part 1	Part 2	Part 3	Part 4	Part 5	Part 6	Part 7	**Demo Doc Complete**

Quick Practice Questions

True/False

_____ 1. Total fixed costs don't change as production levels decrease.

_____ 2. On a CVP graph, the vertical distance between the total expense line and the total sales revenue line equals the operating income or loss.

_____ 3. Sensitivity analysis is a "what if" technique that asks what a result will be if a predicted amount is not achieved or if an underlying assumption changes.

_____ 4. The margin of safety is the excess of breakeven sales over expected sales.

_____ 5. The contribution margin is the band of volume where total fixed costs remain constant and the variable cost *per unit* remains constant.

_____ 6. Gray Company sells two products, X and Y. For the coming year, Gray predicts the sale of 5,000 units of X and 10,000 units of Y. The contribution margins of the two products are $2 and $3, respectively. The weighted-average contribution margin would be $2.50.

_____ 7. An easy method to separate mixed costs into variable and fixed components is the high-low method.

_____ 8. Sensitivity analysis is the combination of products that make up total sales.

_____ 9. If a mixed cost has a high level of activity of 1,200 hours and a cost of $16,500 and a low level of activity of 800 hours and a cost of 12,500, the variable cost per unit is $5.

_____ 10. Using the information in Question 9, the fixed cost would be $4,000.

Multiple Choice

1. A cost whose total amount changes in direct proportion to a change in volume is what type of cost?
   a. Fixed cost
   b. Variable cost
   c. Mixed cost
   d. Irrelevant cost

2. Which of the following is a fixed cost?
   a. Salary of plant manager
   b. Sales commissions
   c. Direct materials
   d. Delivery costs

3. What is the effect on total variable costs of changes in production?
   a. Remain the same as production levels change
   b. Decrease as production increases
   c. Decrease as production decreases
   d. Increase as production decreases

4. What is the effect on fixed costs per unit of changes in production?
   a. Increase as production increases
   b. Decrease as production decreases
   c. Increase as production decreases
   d. Remain the same as production levels change

5. What is contribution margin?
   a. Fixed expenses plus variable expenses
   b. Sales revenues minus variable expenses
   c. Fixed expenses minus variable expenses
   d. Sales revenues minus fixed expenses

6. If the sale price per unit is $75, variable expenses per unit are $40, target operating income is $22,000, and total fixed expenses are $20,000, what is the total number of units that must be sold to reach the target operating income?
   a.   571
   b.   629
   c. 1,050
   d. 1,200

7. Canine Company produces and sells dog treats for discriminating pet owners. The unit selling price is $10, unit variable costs are $7, and total fixed costs are $3,300. How many dog treats must Canine Company sell to break even?
   a.   194
   b.   330
   c.   471
   d. 1,100

8. Fixed Company produces a single product selling for $30 per unit. Variable costs are $12 per unit and total fixed costs are $4,000. What is the contribution margin ratio?
   a. 0.40
   b. 0.60
   c 1.67
   d 2.50

9. Which of the following will decrease the breakeven point assuming no other changes in the cost-volume-profit relationship?
   a. A decrease in the sale price per unit
   b. An increase in the sale price per unit
   c. An increase in total fixed costs
   d. An increase in the variable costs per unit

10. Gould Enterprises sells computer disks for $1.50 per disk. Unit variable expenses total $0.90. The breakeven sales in units are 3,000 and budgeted sales in units are 4,300. What is the margin of safety?
    a. $ 780
    b. $1,950
    c. $2,580
    d. $4,500

Quick Exercises

21-1. Place an F in the space provided if the cost is typically a fixed cost, a V if it is a variable cost, or an M if it is a mixed cost.

a. _____ Packing materials

b. _____ Executive salaries

c. _____ Sales commissions

d. _____ Direct materials

e. _____ Units-of-production depreciation

f. _____ Insurance expense

g. _____ Building rent ($2,000 plus 5% of sales revenue per month)

h. _____ Property taxes

i. _____ Delivery expenses

j. _____ Photocopying machine rent (X amount per month plus Y amount per copy)

21-2. Calculate the unknowns for the following situations based on the given data.

Actual total sales revenue	$400,000
Total fixed cost	76,000
Unit variable cost	$ 15
Contribution margin ratio	40%

Requirement

1. Calculate the following items.

a. Breakeven point in dollars

b. Unit selling price

c. Unit contribution margin

d. Breakeven point in units

e. Margin of safety

21-3. Robinson Company produces swim goggles and has gathered the following information:

Total fixed costs	$156,000
Unit variable cost	$ 6
Planned sales in units	32,000

Assuming breakeven sales in units of 30,000, compute:

a. Sales price per unit

b. Contribution margin ratio

c. Breakeven sales in dollars

21-4.   Calculate the unknowns for the following situations based on the given data. All situations are independent of each other.

Total fixed costs	$180,000
Unit sale price	$ 100
Unit variable cost	$ 40

a. Calculate the breakeven point in units.

b. Calculate the breakeven point in dollar sales.

c. Assume the unit sale price increases by 10%. Other data are unchanged. Calculate the breakeven point in units.

d. Assume the unit variable cost increases by 10%. Other data are unchanged. Calculate the breakeven point in units.

e. Assume total fixed costs increase by $5,000. Other data are unchanged. Calculate the breakeven point in units.

21-5.   Ultimate Jelly Company manufactures two different types of jelly, one with sugar (Jelly) and one without sugar (Simply Jelly). The following information is available for the two products:

	Jelly	Simply Jelly
Sale price per unit	$5	$7
Variable expenses per unit	$3	$6

Total fixed expenses are estimated at $381,500. Two jars of Jelly are sold for every three jars of Simply Jelly.

Requirements

1. Determine the breakeven sales in units of both products.

2. Compute the target sales in dollars if Ultimate Jelly wants to earn $70,000 in operating income.

3. Prove the solution to requirement 2 by calculating net income using the targeted sales.

Do It Yourself! Question 1

Easy Wear T-shirts prints T-shirts for local organizations. The average amount they charge for a printed T-shirt is $10. Easy Wear has calculated the average variable cost of a printed T-shirt to be $6. Their monthly fixed cost is $18,000.

Requirements

1. Use the contribution margin approach to calculate how many T-shirts Easy Wear must sell in a month to break even.

2. Use the contribution margin ratio approach to determine Easy Wear's breakeven point in sales dollars.

3. Use the income statement approach to prove that the solutions to Requirements 1 and 2 are correct.

4. The owner of Easy Wear currently works for another T-shirt company and earns $3,200 per month. He doesn't want to incur the risk of owning his own business unless he believes that he can have profit of at least the amount he currently earns. Determine the number of T-shirts Easy Wear must print in a month to earn profit of $3,200.

Do It Yourself! Question 2

Cool Board sells a snowboard for $240 that they can purchase for $100. They have additional variable costs of $40 and a monthly fixed cost of $22,000.

Requirements

NOTE: Solve each requirement as a separate and independent situation.

1. Calculate Cool Board's breakeven point in units.

2. Cool Board is considering raising its selling price to $249. Calculate the new breakeven in units.

3. Cool Board has found a new supplier for the snowboards, who will sell the board to Cool for $95. Calculate the new breakeven in units.

4. Cool Board has had many requests from customers for bindings to go along with the board. Cool believes that for every three boards they sell, they could sell two bindings. Cool can purchase the bindings for $25 and would incur another $5 in other variable costs for a total variable cost on the bindings of $30. Cool can sell the bindings for $55. Total fixed costs should remain the same at $22,000 per month. Calculate the breakeven point in units for snowboards and bindings.

5. Use a contribution margin income statement to prove the breakeven point calculated in Requirement 4.

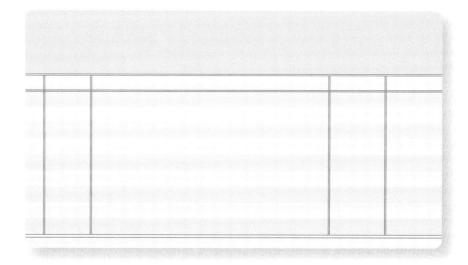

Quick Practice Solutions

True/False

_T___ 1. Total fixed costs don't change as production levels decrease. (p. 1053)

_T___ 2. On a CVP graph, the vertical distance between the total expense line and the total sales revenue line equals the operating income or loss. (p. 1062)

_T___ 3. Sensitivity analysis is a "what if" technique that asks what a result will be if a predicted amount is not achieved or if an underlying assumption changes. (p. 1066)

_F___ 4. The margin of safety is the excess of breakeven sales over expected sales.

  False—The margin of safety is the excess of *actual* sales over *breakeven* sales. (p. 1067)

_F___ 5. The contribution margin is the band of volume where total fixed costs remain constant and the variable cost *per unit* remains constant.

  False—The *relevant range* is the band of volume where total fixed costs remain constant and the variable cost per unit remains constant. (p. 1058)

_F___ 6. Gray Company sells two products, X and Y. For the coming year, Gray predicts the sale of 5,000 units of X and 10,000 units of Y. The contribution margins of the two products are $2 and $3, respectively. The weighted-average contribution margin would be $2.50.

  False—The weighted-average contribution margin would be $2.67. (p. 1059)

Sales mix: 5,000 units/15,000 units = 1/3;
10,000 units/15,000 units = 2/3;
sales mix = 1:2.
$(1 \times \$2) = \$2 + (2 \times \$3) = \$8;$
$(\$2 + \$6)/3 = \$2.67/\text{unit}.$

_T___ 7. An easy method to separate mixed costs into variable and fixed components is the high-low method. (p. 1054)

_F___ 8. Sensitivity analysis is the combination of products that make up total sales.

  False—*Sales mix* is the combination of products that make up total sales. (p. 1069)

_F___ 9. If a mixed cost has a high level of activity of 1,200 hours and a cost of $16,500 and a low level of activity of 800 hours and a cost of 12,500, the variable cost per unit is $5.

  False—If a mixed cost has a high level of activity of 1,200 hours and a cost of $16,500 and a low level of activity of 800 hours and a cost of 12,500, the variable cost per unit is *$10*. ($16,500 − $12,500)/(1,200 − 800) = $10/hour. (p. 1054)

_T___ 10. Using the information in Question 9, the fixed cost would be $4,000. (p. 1054)

Multiple Choice

1. A cost whose total amount changes in direct proportion to a change in volume is what type of cost? (p. 1052)
   a. Fixed cost
   b. Variable cost
   c. Mixed cost
   d. Irrelevant cost

2. Which of the following is a fixed cost? (p. 1053)
   a. Salary of plant manager
   b. Sales commissions
   c. Direct materials
   d. Delivery costs

3. What is the effect on total variable costs of changes in production? (p. 1052)
   a. Remain the same as production levels change
   b. Decrease as production increases
   c. Decrease as production decreases
   d. Increase as production decreases

4. What is the effect on fixed costs per unit of changes in production? (p. 1053)
   a. Increase as production increases
   b. Decrease as production decreases
   c. Increase as production decreases
   d. Remain the same as production levels change

5. What is contribution margin? (p. 1058)
   a. Fixed expenses plus variable expenses
   b. Sales revenues minus variable expenses
   c. Fixed expenses minus variable expenses
   d. Sales revenues minus fixed expenses

6. If the sale price per unit is $75, variable expenses per unit are $40, target operating income is $22,000, and total fixed expenses are $20,000, what is the total number of units that must be sold to reach the target operating income? (p. 1061)
   a.   571
   b.   629
   c. 1,050
   d. 1,200

7. Canine Company produces and sells dog treats for discriminating pet owners. The unit selling price is $10, unit variable costs are $7, and total fixed costs are $3,300. How many dog treats must Canine Company sell to break even? (p. 1057)
   a.   194
   b.   330
   c.   471
   d. 1,100

8. Fixed Company produces a single product selling for $30 per unit. Variable costs are $12 per unit and total fixed costs are $4,000. What is the contribution margin ratio? (p. 1060)
   a. 0.40
   b. 0.60
   c. 1.67
   d. 2.50

9. Which of the following will decrease the breakeven point assuming no other changes in the cost-volume-profit relationship? (pp. 1057–1066)
   a. A decrease in the sale price per unit
   b. An increase in the sale price per unit
   c. An increase in total fixed costs
   d. An increase in the variable costs per unit

10. Gould Enterprises sells computer disks for $1.50 per disk. Unit variable expenses total $0.90. The breakeven sales in units are 3,000 and budgeted sales in units are 4,300. What is the margin of safety? (p. 1068)
    a. $ 780
    b. $1,950
    c. $2,580
    d. $4,500

Quick Exercises

21-1. Place an F in the space provided if the cost is typically a fixed cost, a V if it is a variable cost, or an M if it is a mixed cost. (pp. 1052–1054)

   a. __V__ Packing materials
   b. __F__ Executive salaries
   c. __V__ Sales commissions
   d. __V__ Direct materials
   e. __V__ Units-of-production depreciation
   f. __F__ Insurance expense
   g. __M__ Building rent ($2,000 plus 5% of sales revenue per month)
   h. __F__ Property taxes
   i __V__ Delivery expenses
   j. __M__ Photocopying machine rent (X amount per month plus Y amount per copy)

21-2. Calculate the unknowns for the following situations based on the given data. (pp. 1052–1060)

Actual total sales revenue	$400,000
Total fixed cost	76,000
Unit variable cost	$ 15
Contribution margin ratio	40%

Requirement

1. Calculate the following items.

a. Breakeven point in dollars

$76,000 / 0.40 = $190,000

b. Unit selling price

$15 / (100% − 40%) = $25

c. Unit contribution margin

$25 × 0.40 = $10 or $25 − $15 = $10

d. Breakeven point in units

$76,000 / $10 = 7,600 units

e. Margin of safety

$400,000 − $190,000 = $210,000

21-3. Robinson Company produces swim goggles and has gathered the following information: (pp. 1052–1060)

Total fixed costs	$156,000
Unit variable cost	$ 6
Planned sales in units	32,000

Assuming breakeven sales in units of 30,000, compute:

a. Sales price per unit

Let X = contribution margin per unit
$156,000 / X = 30,000
$156,000 = 30,000X
X = $156,000 / 30,000 = $5.20
$5.20 + $6 = $11.20

b. Contribution margin ratio

$5.20/$11.20 = 0.4643

c. Breakeven sales in dollars

30,000 × $11.20 = $336,000 or $156,000 / 0.4643 = approximately $336,000, rounded.

21-4. Calculate the unknowns for the following situations based on the data below. All situations are independent of each other. (pp. 1057–1060)

Total fixed costs	$180,000
Unit sale price	$ 100
Unit variable cost	$ 40

a. Calculate the breakeven point in units.

$$\$180,000 / (\$100 - \$40) = 3,000$$

b. Calculate the breakeven point in dollar sales.

$$3,000 \text{ units} \times \$100 = \$300,000 \text{ or } \$180,000 / 0.60 = \$300,000$$

c. Assume the unit sale price increases by 10%. Other data are unchanged. Calculate the breakeven point in units.

$$\$100 \times 1.10 = \$110$$
$$\$110 - \$40 = \$70$$
$$\$180,000 / \$70 = 2,571 \text{ units (rounded)}$$

d. Assume the unit variable cost increases by 10%. Other data are unchanged. Calculate the breakeven point in units.

$$\$40 \times 1.10 = \$44$$
$$\$100 - \$44 = \$56$$
$$\$180,000 / \$56 = 3,214 \text{ units (rounded)}$$

e. Assume total fixed costs increase by $5,000. Other data are unchanged. Calculate the breakeven point in units.

$$\$185,000/\$60 = 3,083 \text{ units (rounded)}$$

21-5. Ultimate Jelly Company manufactures two different types of jelly, one with sugar (Jelly) and one without sugar (Simply Jelly). The following information is available for the two products: (pp. 1057–1060)

	Jelly	Simply Jelly
Sale price per unit	$5	$7
Variable expenses per unit	$3	$6

Total fixed expenses are estimated at $381,500. Two jars of Jelly are sold for every three jars of Simply Jelly.

Requirements

1. Determine the breakeven sales in units of both products.

$$\$5 - \$3 = \$2$$
$$\$2 \times 2 = \$4$$
$$\$7 - \$6 = \$1$$
$$\$1 \times 3 = \$3$$
$$\$4 + \$3 = \$7$$
$$\$7 / 5 = \$1.40 \text{ weighted-average contribution margin}$$
$$\$381,500 / \$1.40 = 272,500 \text{ sets}$$
$$272,500 \times 2 / (2 + 3) = 109,000 \text{ units of Jelly}$$
$$272,500 \times 3 / (2 + 3) = 163,500 \text{ units of Simply Jelly}$$

2. Compute the target sales in dollars if Ultimate Jelly wants to earn $70,000 in operating income.

$$\$381,500 + \$70,000 = \$451,500$$
$$\$451,000 / \$1.40 = 322,500 \text{ sets}$$
$$\$322,500 \times 2 / (2 + 3) = 129,000 \text{ units}$$
$$129,000 \times \$5 = \$645,000$$
$$322,500 \times 3 / (2 + 3) = 193,000$$
$$193,000 \times \$7 = \$1,354,500$$
$$\$645,000 + \$1,354,500 = \$1,999,500$$

3. Prove the solution to requirement 2 by calculating net income using the targeted sales.

$$\text{Revenue} - \text{Variable costs} - \text{Fixed costs} = \text{Net income}$$
$$\$1,999,500 - (129,000 \times \$3) - (193,500 \times \$6) - \$381,500 = \$70,000$$

Do It Yourself! Question 1 Solutions

Requirements

2 Use CVP analysis to compute breakeven points

1. Use the contribution margin approach to calculate how many T-shirts Easy Wear must sell in a month to break even.

Contribution margin per unit = Sales price per unit − Variable cost per unit	
Sales price per unit	$10
Variable cost per unit	(6)
Contribution margin per unit	$ 4

Breakeven in units = Fixed cost/Contribution margin per unit
= $18,000/$4 = **4,500 T-shirts**

2 Use CVP analysis to compute breakeven points

2. Use the contribution margin ratio approach to determine Easy Wear's breakeven point in sales dollars.

Contribution margin ratio = Contribution margin per unit/sales revenue per unit
= $4/$10 = 0.40 (or 40%)
Breakeven in sales dollars = Fixed cost/Contribution margin ratio
= $18,000/0.40 = **$45,000**

2 Use CVP analysis to compute breakeven points

3. Use the income statement approach to prove that the solutions to requirements 1 and 2 are correct.

Sales revenue ($10 × 4,500 units)	$45,000
Less: Variable costs (4,500 × $6)	27,000
Total contribution margin	18,000
Less: Fixed costs	18,000
Operating income	$ 0

Use CVP analysis for profit planning, and graph the CVP relations

4. The owner of Easy Wear currently works for another T-shirt company and earns $3,200 per month. He doesn't want to incur the risk of owning his own business unless he believes that he can have profit of at least the amount he currently earns. Determine the number of T-shirts Easy Wear must print in a month to earn profit of $3,200.

$$\text{Desired profit sales level in units} = (\text{Fixed cost} + \text{Desired profit})/\text{Contribution margin}$$
$$= (\$18,000 + \$3,200)/(\$10 - \$6)$$
$$= \$21,200/\$4 = \textbf{5,300 units}$$

Another way to think of this is to divide your desired profit by your contribution margin and add the difference to your breakeven:

$$\$3,200/\$4 = 800 \text{ units}$$
$$800 \text{ units} + 4,500 \text{ breakeven} = 5,300 \text{ units}$$

Do It Yourself! Question 2 Solutions

Requirements

 Use CVP analysis to compute breakeven points

1. Calculate Cool Board's breakeven point in units.

$$\text{Breakeven in units} = \text{Fixed cost}/(\text{Selling price per unit} - \text{Variable cost per unit})$$
$$= \$22,000 / (\$240 - \$140) = \textbf{220 boards}$$

 Use CVP methods to perform sensitivity analyses

2. Cool Board is considering raising its selling price to $249. Calculate the new breakeven in units.

$$\text{Breakeven in units} = \text{Fixed cost}/(\text{Selling price per unit} - \text{Variable cost per unit})$$
$$= \$22,000/(\$249 - \$140) = 201.83, \textbf{ rounded to 202 snowboards}$$

 Use CVP methods to perform sensitivity analyses

3. Cool Board has found a new supplier for the snowboards, who will sell the board to Cool for $95. Calculate the new breakeven in units.

$$\text{Breakeven in units} = \text{Fixed cost}/(\text{Selling price per unit} - \text{Variable cost per unit})$$
$$= \$22,000/(\$240 - \$135) = 209.52, \textbf{ rounded to 210 snowboards}$$

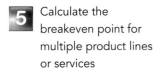

Calculate the breakeven point for multiple product lines or services

4. Cool Board has had many requests from customers for bindings to go along with the board. Cool believes that for every three boards they sell they could sell two bindings. Cool can purchase the bindings for $25 and would incur another $5 in other variable cost for a total variable cost on the bindings of $30. Cool can sell the bindings for $55. Total fixed costs should remain the same at $22,000 per month. Calculate the breakeven point in units for snowboards and bindings.

Step 1: Calculate the weighted-average contribution margin.

	Boards	Bindings	Total
Sales price per unit	$240	$55	
Deduct: Variable cost per unit	(140)	(30)	
Contribution margin per unit	$100	$25	
Sales mix in units	× 3	× 2	5
Contribution margin	$300	$50	$350
Weighted-average contribution margin per unit ($350/5)			$ 70

Step 2: Calculate the breakeven point in units for the total of both products combined.

Total sales in units = Fixed cost/Weighted-average contribution margin per unit
= $22,000/$70 = **314.28,** rounded to 315

Step 3: Calculate the breakeven in units for each product line.

Breakeven sales of boards [315×(3/5)] = **189 snowboards**
Breakeven sales of bindings [315×(2/5)] = **126 bindings**
= 315 total units

5. Use a contribution margin income statement to prove the breakeven point calculated in requirement 4.

COOL BOARDS
Contribution Margin Income Statement

	Boards	Bindings	Total
Sales revenue:			
Boards (189 × $240)	$45,360		
Bindings (126 × $55)		$6,930	$52,290
Variable costs:			
Boards (189 × $140)	26,460		
Bindings (126 × $30)		3,780	$30,240
Contribution margin	$18,900	$3,150	$22,050
Fixed costs			(22,000)
Operating income			$ 50

There is a slight $50 profit at the breakeven level because of rounding to whole units.

The Power of Practice

For more practice using the skills learned in this chapter, visit MyAccountingLab. There you will find algorithmically generated questions that are based on these Demo Docs and your main textbook's Review and Assess Your Progress sections.

Go to MyAccountingLab and follow these steps:

1. Direct your URL to www.myaccountinglab.com.
2. Log in using your name and password.
3. Click the MyAccountingLab link.
4. Click Study Plan in the left navigation bar.
5. From the table of contents, select Chapter 21, Cost-Volume-Profit Analysis.
6. Click a link to work tutorial exercises.

The Master Budget and Responsibility Accounting

WHAT YOU PROBABLY ALREADY KNOW

You may have wanted to purchase something you've had to save for over a period of time. To project how you would accomplish this, you might have made a plan. You would consider the amount of money available at the beginning of your plan plus the forecasted cash receipts less cash disbursements over the period to reach your goal. You probably already know that by addressing your financial goal and creating a cash budget, you are able to plan for the future and make decisions to facilitate achieving your goal. If the period of time is sufficiently long, you can compare your actual to your budgeted cash flows during interim periods and make changes as warranted. Some of these may include:

- Initiate steps to increase cash inflows, perhaps work more hours.
- Initiate steps to decrease cash outflows, cut back on lesser-important spending.
- Initiate steps to finance the shortfall, pursue borrowing opportunities.
- Postpone or abandon the purchase plan.

In this chapter, we will study the various budgets that companies create and appreciate the usefulness of the budgeting process for all financial entities.

Learning Objectives

 Learn why managers use budgets.

Budgeting helps managers plan and control their actions. Management creates organizational goals. Action steps are planned to achieve those goals. The budget is the anticipated financial results of taking those action steps. The actual results can be compared to the budget and corrective action taken where necessary. *Review Exhibits 22-2 and 22-3 (pp. 1103–1104) for the usefulness and benefits of budgets.*

2 Prepare an operating budget.

The sales budget is the first part of the **operating budget** that must be prepared. Expected sales units and future sales prices are used in the budget. This budget will drive the remainder of the operating budget, such as the cost of goods sold, inventory, purchase, and operating expense budgets. *Review Exhibits 22-6 through 22-8 (p. 1107) for examples of operating budgets.*

3 Prepare a financial budget.

The **financial budget** includes the cash and balance sheet budgets. The **cash budget** contains the beginning cash balance, projected cash collections, cash payments, financing required, and the ending cash balance. The period in which such items as sales and purchases on account result in cash flows must be projected and integrated into the cash budget. After completing all of the operating and cash budgets, a projection of the balance sheet account balances can be determined. This information is used to prepare the balance sheet budget. *Review Exhibits 22-10 to 22-13 (pp. 1113–1116) for components of a cash budget. Review Exhibit 22-14 (p. 1117) for the computation of balance sheet projected account balances and Exhibit 22-15 (p. 1118) for a budgeted balance sheet.*

4 Prepare performance reports for responsibility centers.

A **responsibility center** is a part or subunit of an organization whose manager is accountable for specific activities. Performance reports compare the budget to the actual results for each responsibility center. The performance of the managers of each center can then be evaluated. There are four responsibility centers:

- **Cost center**—Only costs or expenses are incurred. The human resources, accounting, and information technology departments are examples of cost centers. The goal of the manager is to minimize costs.

- **Revenue center**—Primarily revenues are incurred although there may be some related expenses. A sales department would be a revenue center. Managers are assessed based upon the revenues generated. The goal of the manager is to maximize revenues.

- **Profit center**—Responsible for revenues and expenses, and ultimately profits or net income. The goal of the manager is to exceed the profit projection. The sales and costs related to the Lipton Cup-a-Soup product line would be an example of a profit center.

- **Investment center**—Responsible for the results of the investment as well as the profits of the entity. The foods division of Lipton would be considered an investment center. Managers are responsible for making sales, maintaining expenses, and managing the investment required to generate profits.

Review Exhibit 22-17 (p. 1112) for examples of responsibility centers and responsibility accounting performance reports in Exhibit 22-18 (p. 1123).

Demo Doc 1

Master Budget

Joe University sells college sweatshirts. Actual sales for the month ended September 30, 2008, were $20,000. Joe expects sales to increase 8% in October and increase another 4% over October sales in November. Cash sales are expected to be 60% of total sales and credit sales about 40% of sales. Cost of goods sold should be 60% of total sales. Joe doesn't want inventory to fall below $4,000 plus 10% of cost of goods sold for the next month. Sales of $25,000 are expected for December. Inventory on September 30 is $6,000.

Operating expenses include sales commission, 10% of sales; rent expense of $1,000; depreciation expense of $1,200; utility expense of $800; and insurance expense of $400.

Round all figures to the nearest dollar.

Requirement

1. Prepare the following budgets for October and November:

a. **Sales budget**

b. **Inventory, purchases, and cost of goods sold budget**

c. **Operating expense budget**

d. **Budgeted income statement**

Demo Doc 1 Solutions

Requirement 1

2 Prepare an operating budget

Prepare the following budgets for October and November:

a. Sales budget

Part 1	Part 2	Part 3	Part 4	Demo Doc Complete

We prepare the sales budget first because sales impact most elements of the other budgets we will be preparing for this period.

In order to complete the sales budget, we start by calculating the total sales for each month. We will then compute the split between cash sales and credit sales for each month based on Joe's estimation that cash sales will be 60% of the total sales for each month and credit sales will be 40% of total sales for each month.

Let's begin by calculating Joe's total sales for October and November. The question tells us that actual sales for the month ended September 30 were $20,000, and that Joe expects sales to increase by 8% over that in October and another 4% over October's sales in November:

$$\text{October total sales} = \text{September sales} \times 108\%$$
$$\text{October total sales} = \$20,000 \times 108\% = \$21,600$$
$$\text{November total sales} = \text{October sales} \times 104\%$$
$$\text{November total sales} = \$21,600 \times 104\% = \$22,464$$

So we begin to build our sales budget with this data:

JOE UNIVERSITY
Sales Budget

	October	November	Total
Cash sales, 60%			
Credit sales, 40%			
Total sales	$21,600	$22,464	$44,064

Now we work backwards to calculate the split between cash and credit sales for each month. In this case, cash sales are 60% of total sales and credit sales are 40% of total sales for the current months:

$$\text{Cash sales} = \text{total sales} \times 60\%$$
$$\text{October cash sales} = \$21,600 \times 60\% = \$12,960$$
$$\text{November cash sales} = \$22,464 \times 60\% = \$13,478.40 \text{ (rounded to } \$13,478)$$

$$\text{Credit sales} = \text{total sales} \times 40\%$$
$$\text{October credit sales} = \$21,600 \times 40\% = \$8,640$$
$$\text{November credit sales} = \$22,464 \times 40\% = \$8,985.60 \text{ (rounded to } \$8,986)$$

Following is the completed sales budget:

JOE UNIVERSITY
Sales Budget

	October	November	Total
Cash sales, 60%	$12,960	$13,478	$26,438
Credit sales, 40%	8,640	8,986	17,626
Total sales	$21,600	$22,464	$44,064

This gives us a total sales budget for October and November of $44,064, with 60% of that ($26,438.40, rounded to $26,438) from cash and 40% ($17,625.60, rounded to $17,626) from credit.

Because the sales budget calculates values that you will use when preparing other budgets, it's always a good idea to check your work. These calculations can be performed in a number of ways. Here's one alternative:

$$\text{October total sales} = \text{Previous month} \times 108\%$$
$$= \$20,000 \times 108\%$$
$$= \$21,600$$

$$\text{October cash sales} = \text{October expected sales} \times 60\%$$
$$= \$21,600 \times 60\%$$
$$= \$12,960$$

$$\text{October credit sales} = \text{October expected sales} \times 40\%$$
$$= \$21,600 \times 40\%$$
$$= \$8,640$$

$$\text{November total sales} = \text{Previous month sales} \times 104\%$$
$$= \$21,600 \times 104\%$$
$$= \$22,464$$

$$\text{November cash sales} = \text{November expected sales} \times 60\%$$
$$= \$22,464 \times 60\%$$
$$= \$13,478$$

$$\text{November credit sales} = \text{November expected sales} \times 40\%$$
$$= \$22,464 \times 40\%$$
$$= \$8,986$$

2 Prepare an operating budget

b. Inventory, purchases, and cost of goods sold budget

| Part 1 | **Part 2** | Part 3 | Part 4 | Demo Doc Complete |

The inventory, purchases, and cost of goods sold budget statement takes the following format:

Cost of goods sold
+ Desired ending inventory
Total inventory required
− Beginning inventory
Purchases

So we first calculate the cost of goods sold. We know from the question that cost of goods sold is expected to be 60% of total sales for the period. From the sales budget, we know that total sales for October are expected to be $21,600, and total sales for November are expected to be $22,464. So we can calculate cost of goods sold as follows:

Cost of goods sold = 60% of budgeted sales from the sales budget
October = $21,600 × 60% = $12,960
November = $22,464 × 60% = $13,478

So here's our budget so far:

JOE UNIVERSITY
Inventory, Purchases, and Cost of Goods Sold Budget

	October	November
Cost of goods sold	$12,960	$13,478
+ Desired ending inventory		
= Total inventory required		
− Beginning inventory		
= Purchases		

Next, we need to add the desired ending inventory for each month. The question states that Joe doesn't want inventory to fall below $4,000 plus 10% of cost of goods sold for the next month. So in order to calculate the desired ending inventory for November, we need to know the cost of goods sold for December. The question tells us that December's sales are expected to be $25,000. Returning to our calculation for cost of goods sold:

Cost of goods sold = 60% of budgeted sales from the sales budget
December = $25,000 × 60% = $15,000

Desired ending inventory is now calculated as follows:

Desired ending inventory = $4,000 + (10% of cost of goods sold for the next month)
October   = $4,000 + (10% × $13,478) = $5,348
November = $4,000 + (10% × $15,000) = $5,500

We can now calculate the total ending inventory required:

JOE UNIVERSITY
Inventory, Purchases, and Cost of Goods Sold Budget

	October	November
Cost of goods sold	$12,960	$13,478
+ Desired ending inventory	5,348	5,500
= Total inventory required	$18,308	$18,978
– Beginning inventory		
= Purchases		

Beginning inventory is equal to the previous month's desired ending inventory. We are told in the question that the inventory on September 30 is $6,000, so this becomes October's beginning inventory. Once we determine beginning inventory, we subtract it from the total inventory required to determine total purchases for the period. Beginning inventory for November is the desired ending invenory for October.

JOE UNIVERSITY
Inventory, Purchases, and Cost of Goods Sold Budget

	October	November
Cost of goods sold	$12,960	$13,478
+ Desired ending inventory	5,348	5,500
= Total inventory required	$18,308	$18,978
– Beginning inventory	6,000	5,348
= Purchases	$12,308	$13,630

2 Prepare an operating budget

c. Operating expense budget

Part 1	Part 2	**Part 3**	Part 4	Demo Doc Complete

With the exception of the sales commission, which we know from the question to be 10% of sales, all expenses remain constant between October and November, as follows:

JOE UNIVERSITY
Operating Expense Budget

	October	November	Total
Sales commission			
Depreciation expense	1,200	1,200	2,400
Rent expense	1,000	1,000	2,000
Utility expense	800	800	1,600
Insurance expense	400	400	800
Total operating expenses			

So the only calculation to perform here is sales commission. We can compute sales commissions for October and November using the respective sales computations ($21,600 and $22,464) from the sales budget:

Sales commission = Expected sales × 10%
October sales commission = $21,600 × 10% = $2,160
November sales commission = $22,464 × 10% = $2,246.40 (rounded to $2,246)

So here's our completed operating expense budget for October and November:

JOE UNIVERSITY
Operating Expense Budget

	October	November	Total
Sales commission	$2,160	$2,246	$4,406
Depreciation expense	1,200	1,200	2,400
Rent expense	1,000	1,000	2,000
Utility expense	800	800	1,600
Insurance expense	400	400	800
Total operating expenses	$5,560	$5,646	$11,206

2 Prepare an operating budget

d. Budgeted income statement

Part 1	Part 2	Part 3	**Part 4**	Demo Doc Complete

The results of the budgets you've created so far are carried over into the fourth element: the budgeted income statement.

Sales revenue is traced from the sales budget in part **a.**

Cost of goods sold is traced from the inventory, purchases, and cost of goods sold budget in part **b.**

We compute gross profit by subtracting the cost of goods sold from sales revenue:

JOE UNIVERSITY
Budgeted Income Statement

	October	November	Total
Sales revenue	$21,600	$22,464	$44,064
Cost of goods sold	12,960	13,478	26,438
Gross profit	8,640	8,986	17,626
Operating expenses			
Net income			

Operating expenses are traced from the operating expenses budget from part **c.** We compute net income (loss) by subtracting operating expenses from gross profit. So our completed budgeted income statement looks like this:

JOE UNIVERSITY
Budgeted Income Statement

	October	November	Total
Sales revenue	$21,600	$22,464	$44,064
Cost of goods sold	12,960	13,478	26,438
Gross profit	8,640	8,986	17,626
Operating expenses	5,560	5,646	11,206
Net income	$ 3,080	$ 3,340	$ 6,420

So, for the period, our totals are as follows:

JOE UNIVERSITY
Budgeted Income Statement
Two Months Ending November 30, 2008

	October	November	Total
Sales revenue			$44,064
Cost of goods sold			26,438
Gross profit			17,626
Operating expenses:			
Salary and commissions		$4,406	
Depreciation expense		2,400	
Rent expense		2,000	
Insurance expense		800	
Utility expense		1,600	11,206
Operating income			$ 6,420

Part 1	Part 2	Part 3	Part 4	**Demo Doc Complete**

Demo Doc 2

Financial Budget

Joe University has prepared its sales budget; inventory, purchases, and cost of goods sold budget; operating expense budget; and budgeted income statement. Joe would now like to prepare the cash budget for the months of October and November.

Actual sales for the month ended September 30, 2008, were $20,000. Actual sales for the month ended August 31 were $16,000. Joe believes that sales will increase 8% in October and increase another 4% over October sales in November. Cash sales are expected to be 60% of sales and credit sales about 40% of sales.

Cost of goods sold is expected to be 60% of total sales. Joe doesn't want inventory to fall below $4,000 plus 10% of cost of goods sold for the next month. Sales of $25,000 are expected for December. Joe purchased $11,000 inventory during September and ended the month with $6,000 in ending inventory.

Operating expenses include sales commission, 10% of sales; rent expense of $1,000; depreciation expense of $1,200; utility expense of $800; and insurance expense of $400.

September 30 cash balance was $4,000.

Of the credit sales, Joe expects to collect 70% in the month following the sale and the remaining 30% in the next month. Purchases made by Joe University are paid for in the month after the purchase. Sales commissions are paid 50% in the month incurred and 50% in the next month. Rent, utility, and insurance are paid in the month incurred.

Requirements

1. For the months of October and November, prepare:

a. Budgeted cash collections from customers

b. Budgeted cash payments for purchases

c. Budgeted cash payments for operating expenses

d. The cash budget

Demo Doc 2 Solutions

Requirement 1

For the months of October and November, prepare:

a. Budgeted cash collections from customers

Part 1	Part 2	Part 3	Part 4	Demo Doc Complete

Armed with the budget data we calculated in Demo Doc 1 of this chapter, we can start to prepare the cash budget. We start with the budgeted cash collections from customers, which we'll use in part **d** of this demo doc to calculate total cash available for the period.

We computed the cash sales for October and November on the sales budget as $12,960 and $13,478, respectively. To this we will add any credit collections that Joe makes in this period.

Joe expects to collect on credit sales at a rate of 70% in the month following the sale and 30% in the next month. This means that in October, Joe expects to collect 70% of any credit sales made in September and 30% of credit sales made in August. Likewise, in November, Joe will collect 70% of October's credit sales and 30% of September's credit sales.

Before we can calculate how much in credit sales Joe will collect in October and November, we need to see the sales budget data for August and September because collections are being made from those two months. We know from the question that total August sales were $16,000 and total September sales were $20,000. We also know that Joe expects 40% of total sales each month to be credit sales. So if we were to figure Joe's sales budget data for August and September, credit sales would look like this:

$$\text{August credit sales} = \text{August total sales} \times 40\%$$
$$= \$16,000 \times 40\% = \$6,400$$
$$\text{September credit sales} = \text{September total sales} \times 40\%$$
$$= \$20,000 \times 40\% = \$8,000$$

Given this data, Joe's sales budget for the period August to November would look like this (although note that the only data you're interested in at this point is the highlighted data):

JOE UNIVERSITY
Sales Budget

	August	September	October	November
Cash sales, 60%	$ 9,600	$12,000	$12,960	$13,478
Credit sales, 40%	6,400	8,000	8,640	8,986
Total sales	$16,000	$20,000	$21,600	$22,464

Remember that credit sales for October and November came from the sales budget in Demo Doc 1.

So for October, Joe expects to collect 30% of credit sales made in August and 70% of credit sales made in September:

October collections from August credit sales = $6,400 × 30% = $1,920

October collections from September credit sales = $8,000 × 70% = $5,600

For November, Joe expects to collect 30% of credit sales made in September and 70% of credit sales made in October ($8,640, taken from the sales budget created in Demo Doc 1, part **a**):

November collections from September credit sales = $8,000 × 30% = $2,400

November collections from October credit sales = $8,640 × 70% = $6,048

Cash sales on the statement come directly from the sales budget. So the completed budget looks like this:

JOE UNIVERSITY
Budgeted Cash Collections from Customers

	October	November	Total
Cash sales	$12,960	$13,478	$26,438
Collections of previous month's credit sales	5,600	6,048	11,648
Collections of 2nd previous month's credit sales	1,920	2,400	4,320
Total collections	$20,480	$21,926	$42,406

Shown another way:

			October	November	Total
Month of Sale:					
August	$16,000				
Cash	60%				
Credit	40%	16,000 × 40% × 30%	1,920		1,920
September	$20,000				
Cash					
Credit		20,000 × 40% × 70%	5,600		
		20,000 × 40% × 30%		2,400	8,000
October	$21,600				
Cash	60% × 21,600		12,960		
Credit		21,600 × 40% × 70%		6,048	19,008
November	$22,464				
Cash	60% × 22,464				13,478
Credit				13,478	
	TOTALS		20,480	21,926	42,406

3 Prepare a financial budget

b. Budgeted cash payments for purchases

Part 1	**Part 2**	Part 3	Part 4	Demo Doc Complete

Purchases made by Joe are paid in the month following the purchase. So in October, Joe paid for the purchases made in September and in November, Joe paid for the purchases made in October.

The question states that Joe purchased $11,000 of inventory in September (which he will pay for in October). We know from the inventory, purchases, and cost of goods sold budget that we prepared in Demo Doc 1 (part **b**) of this chapter that Joe's purchases in October were $12,308 (which he will pay for in November):

JOE UNIVERSITY
Budgeted Cash Payments for Purchases

	October	November	Total
Purchases paid from previous month	$11,000	$12,308	$23,308
Total cash payments for purchases	$11,000	$12,308	$23,308

3 Prepare a financial budget

c. Budgeted cash payments for operating expenses

Part 1	Part 2	**Part 3**	Part 4	Demo Doc Complete

Following is Joe's operating expense budget, which we prepared in Demo Doc 1, part **c**:

JOE UNIVERSITY
Operating Expense Budget

	October	November	Total
Sales commission	$2,160	$2,246	$ 4,406
Depreciation expense	1,200	1,200	2,400
Rent expense	1,000	1,000	2,000
Utility expense	800	800	1,600
Insurance expense	400	400	800
Total operating expenses	$5,560	$5,646	$11,206

The question tells us that sales commissions are paid 50% in the month incurred and 50% in the next month. Other expenses are paid in the month incurred. So we must calculate the sales commission payments for the current month and for the previous month each for October and November.

We can calculate commissions from the current month for October and November as:

$$October = \$2,160 \times 50\% = \$1,080$$
$$November = \$2,246 \times 50\% = \$1,123$$

So far, we have sales commissions from the current month and all other operating expenses, as follows:

JOE UNIVERSITY
Budgeted Cash Payments for Operating Expenses

	October	November	Total
Sales commission from current month	$1,080	$1,123	$ 2,203
Sales commission from previous month			
Rent expense	1,000	1,000	2,000
Utility expense	800	800	1,600
Insurance expense	400	400	800
Total operating expenses			

The question tells us that actual sales for the month ending September 30 were $20,000 and that sales commissions amount to 10% of actual sales. So total sales commissions for September are $20,000 × 10% = $2,000.

Knowing this, we can compute the sales commission payments from the previous month for each of October and November as:

$$October = \$2,000 \times 50\% = \$1,000$$
$$November = \$2,160 \times 50\% = \$1,080$$

Our final statement now looks like this:

JOE UNIVERSITY
Budgeted Cash Payments for Operating Expenses

	October	November	Total
Sales commission from current month	$1,080	$1,123	$2,203
Sales commission from previous month	1,000	1,080	2,080
Rent expense	1,000	1,000	2,000
Utility expense	800	800	1,600
Insurance expense	400	400	800
Total operating expenses	$4,280	$4,403	$8,683

Shown another way, we can also compute sales commission payments from the current and previous months using each month's actual sales:

Sales commission from current month=
Current month sales $\times$ 10% sales commission $\times$ 50% payment this month:
October $= \$21,600 \times 10\% \times 50\% = \$1,080$
November $= \$22,464 \times 10\% \times 50\% = \$1,123.20$ (rounded to \$1,123)

Sales commission from previous month=
Previous month sales $\times$ 10% sales commission $\times$ 50% payment this month
October $= \$20,000 \times 10\% \times 50\% = \$1,000$
November $= \$21,600 \times 10\% \times 50\% = \$1,080$

Rent, utilities, and insurance expense are fixed amounts from the operating expense budget.

Remember that depreciation expense is a noncash expense and therefore is not included in the cash budget.

<table>
<tr><td>3</td><td>Prepare a financial budget</td></tr>
</table>

d. The cash budget

<table>
<tr><td>Part 1</td><td>Part 2</td><td>Part 3</td><td>Part 4</td><td>Demo Doc Complete</td></tr>
</table>

To prepare the cash budget, you start with the beginning cash balance and add the budgeted cash collections that you computed in part a of this demo doc. Cash payments for purchases and operating expenses are then subtracted to achieve the ending cash balance.

Beginning cash balance is from the ending cash balance of the previous month. September's ending balance as given in the question becomes October's beginning cash balance, \$4,000.

Cash collections are from budgeted cash collections from customers. Adding the beginning cash balance to the collections gives you the available cash for the month:

JOE UNIVERSITY
Cash Budget

	October	November
Beginning cash balance	$ 4,000	
Cash collections	20,480	$21,926
Cash available	24,480	
Cash payments		
Purchases of inventory		
Operating expenses		
Total cash payments		
Ending cash balance		

Cash payments for purchases of inventory are from the budgeted cash payments for purchases. Cash payments for operating expenses are from the budgeted cash payments for operating expenses, giving us the total cash payments:

JOE UNIVERSITY
Cash Budget

	October	November
Beginning cash balance	$ 4,000	
Cash collections	20,480	$21,926
Cash available	24,480	
Cash payments		
Purchases of inventory	11,000	12,308
Operating expenses	4,280	4,403
Total cash payments	15,280	16,711
Ending cash balance		

Ending cash balance is equal to cash available less total cash payments. October's ending cash balance then becomes November's beginning cash balance, and the calculations continue in this manner until the budget is complete:

JOE UNIVERSITY
Cash Budget

	October	November
Beginning cash balance	$ 4,000	$ 9,200
Cash collections	20,480	21,926
Cash available	24,480	31,126
Cash payments		
Purchases of inventory	11,000	12,308
Operating expenses	4,280	4,403
Total cash payments	15,280	16,711
Ending cash balance	$ 9,200	$14,415

Part 1	Part 2	Part 3	Part 4	**Demo Doc Complete**

Quick Practice Questions

True/False

_____ 1. Budgets provide a benchmark that helps managers evaluate performance.

_____ 2. Managers should build "slack" into the budget.

_____ 3. A company's plan for purchases of property, plant, equipment, and other long-term assets is part of the financial budget.

_____ 4. The cash budget is a projection of the cash inflows and cash outflows for a future period.

_____ 5. The cash budget is prepared before the budgeted balance sheet is prepared.

_____ 6. Sensitivity analysis is a what-if technique that asks what a result will be if a predicted amount is not achieved or if an underlying assumption changes.

_____ 7. Responsibility accounting is a system for evaluating the performance of each responsibility center and its manager.

_____ 8. Management by exception directs executives' attention to all differences between actual and budgeted variable cost amounts.

_____ 9. Most companies consider company divisions as cost centers.

_____ 10. The research and development department would be considered a profit center.

Multiple Choice

1. **Which of the following statements regarding the budgeting process is (are) true?**
   a. The budget should be designed from the bottom up, with input from employees at all levels.
   b. The budget should be approved by the company's external auditors.
   c. The budget should be designed by top management and communicated to lower-level personnel.
   d. All the above statements are true regarding the budgeting process.

2. **Which of the following budgets is an operating budget?**
   a. Capital expenditures budget
   b. Budgeted balance sheet
   c. Budgeted income statement
   d. Cash budget

3. Which of the following alternatives reflects the proper order of preparing components of the master budget?
   1. Financial budget
   2. Operating budget
   3. Capital expenditures budget

   a. 2, 3, 1
   b. 1, 3, 2
   c. 1, 2, 3
   d. 3, 1, 2

4. Desired ending inventory is 80% of beginning inventory. If cost of goods sold is $300,000, purchases will always have what relationship with cost of goods sold?
   a. Be more than cost of goods sold
   b. Be 80% of cost of goods sold
   c. Equal cost of goods sold
   d. Be less than cost of goods sold

5. During April, Cherry Company had actual sales of $180,000 compared to budgeted sales of $195,000. Actual cost of goods sold was $135,000, compared to a budget of $136,500. Monthly operating expenses, budgeted at $28,000, totaled $25,000. Interest revenue of $2,500 was earned during April but had not been included in the budget. What is the net income variance on the performance report for April?
   a. $ (8,000)
   b. $(13,000)
   c. $ 8,000
   d. $ 13,000

6. Heath Company has beginning inventory of 21,000 units and expected sales of 48,000 units. If the desired ending inventory is 15,500 units, how many units should be produced?
   a. 27,000
   b. 42,500
   c. 45,000
   d. 53,500

7. York Enterprises recorded sales of $160,000 during March. Management expects sales to increase 5% in April, 3% in May (over April), and 5% in June (over May). Cost of goods sold is expected to be 70% of sales. What is the budgeted gross profit for June?
   a. $ 54,508
   b. $112,000
   c. $127,184
   d. $181,692

8. Which of the following is an example of a financial budget?
   a. Sales budget
   b. Budgeted balance sheet
   c. Budgeted income statement
   d. Operating expense budget

9. Jay Corporation desires a December 31 ending inventory of 1,500 units. Budgeted sales for December are 2,300 units. The November 30 inventory was 850 units. What are budgeted purchases?
   a. 2,350
   b. 2,950
   c. 3,150
   d. 3,800

10. Bolin's, an elite clothier, expects its November sales to be 30% higher than its October sales of $200,000. Purchases were $100,000 in October and are expected to be $150,000 in November. All sales are on credit and are collected as follows: 30% in the month of the sale and 70% in the following month. Purchases are paid 25% in the month of purchase and 75% in the following month. The beginning cash balance on November 1 is $9,000. What is the ending cash balance on November 30?
    a. $ 87,000
    b. $114,500
    c. $140,000
    d. $149,000

Quick Exercises

22-1. Solve for the following independent situations:

   a. A sporting goods store budgeted September purchases of ski jackets at $17,900. The store had ski jackets costing $1,200 on hand at the beginning of September, and to cover part of anticipated October sales, they expect to have $4,200 of ski jackets on hand at the end of September. What was the budgeted cost of goods sold for September?

   b. A department store has budgeted cost of goods sold for October of $29,300 for its women's coats. Management also wants to have $8,000 of coats in inventory at the end of the month to prepare for the winter season. Beginning inventory in October was $6,000. What dollar amount of coats should be purchased to meet the above objectives?

22-2. Redfield Company has prepared the following forecasts of monthly sales:

	January	February	March	April
Sales (in units)	4,500	5,200	4,700	2,800

Redfield Company has decided that the number of units in its inventory at the end of each month should equal 75% of next month's sales. The budgeted cost per unit is $20.

Requirements

1. How many units should be in January's beginning inventory?

2. What amount should be budgeted for the cost of merchandise purchases in January?

3. How many units should be purchased in February?

22-3.   The sales budget of Mulls Company for the fourth quarter of 2008 is as follows:

	October	November	December
Sales	$91,000	$76,000	$108,000

Sales are 20% cash, 80% credit.
Cost of goods sold is 70% of total sales.
Desired ending inventory for each month is equal to 25% of cost of goods sold for the following month.

Collections on credit sales are as follows:
50% in the month of sale
30% in the month following sale
15% in the second month following sale
5% uncollectible

October 1 inventory is $16,000.
Expected sales for January 2009 are $84,000.
Payments for inventory are 70% in the month following purchase and 30% two months following purchase.

Requirements

1. Compute the cash collections for December.

2. Compute the cash disbursements for purchases during December.

22-4.   Soccer Forever gathered the following information as of May 31, 2008:

May 31 inventory balance	$11,100
May payments for inventory	8,300
May payments of accounts payable and accrued liabilities	9,800
May 31 accounts payable balance	5,400
April 30 equipment balance	37,500
April 30 accumulated depreciation—equipment balance	20,900
Cash purchase of equipment in May	2,700
May operating expenses, excluding depreciation (75% paid in May, 25% accrued on May 31)	4,200
May depreciation expense	600
April 30 stockholders' equity	42,485
April 30 cash balance	27,040
May budgeted sales	17,300
May cash receipts from sales on account	12,110

Cost of goods sold is 65% of sales.

May 31 accounts receivable balance is 30% of May sales.

Prepare the budgeted balance sheet on May 31, 2008.

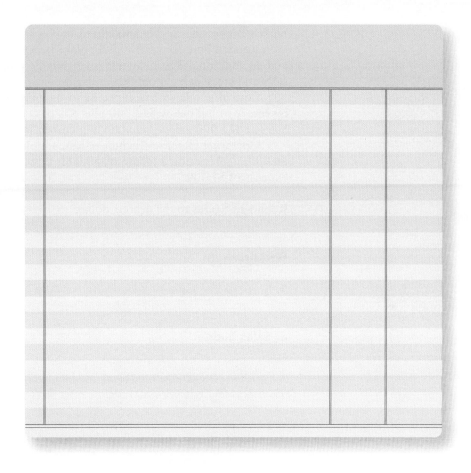

22-5. Answer the following completely.

    a. Define the term budget.

    b. Identify four benefits of budgeting.

    c. Should employees participate in the budgeting process or should management prepare the budgets alone? Explain.

Do It Yourself! Question 1

Blake's Brakes sells highly specialized brakes for travel trailers. Actual sales for the month ended June 30 was $80,000. Blake believes that sales will increase 2% in July and an additional 3% in August (over July). Cash sales are expected to be 10% of sales and credit sales about 90% of sales.

Cost of goods sold is expected to be 75% of total sales. Blake doesn't want inventory to fall below $12,000 plus 5% of cost of goods sold for the next month. Sales of $85,000 are expected for September. Inventory on June 30 is $13,000.

Operating expenses include sales commission, 5% of sales; rent expense of $6,000; depreciation expense of $4,000; utility expense of $1,500; and insurance expense of $1,400.

Round all figures to the nearest dollar.

Requirement

1. Prepare the following budgets for July and August:

a. Sales budget

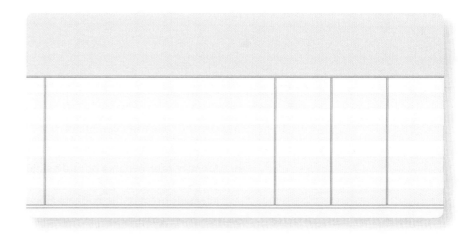

b. Inventory, purchases, and cost of goods sold budget

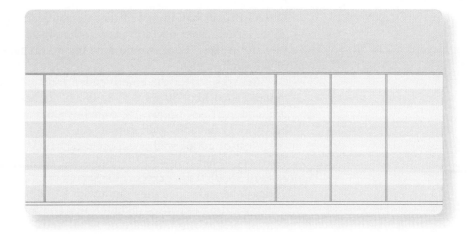

c. Operating expense budget

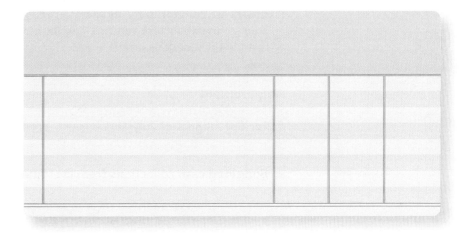

d. Budgeted income statement

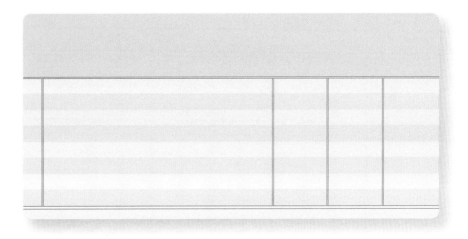

Do It Yourself! Question 2

Blake's Brakes has prepared its sales budget; inventory, purchases, and cost of goods sold budget; operating expense budget; and budgeted income statement for July and August. Blake would now like to prepare the cash budget for the months of July and August.

Actual sales for the month ended June 30 were $80,000. Actual sales for the month ended May 30 were $78,000. Blake believes that sales will increase 2% in July and increase another 3% over July sales in August. Cash sales are expected to be 10% of sales and credit sales about 90% of sales.

Cost of goods sold is expected to be 75% of total sales. Blake doesn't want inventory to fall below $12,000 plus 5% of cost of goods sold for the next month. Sales of $85,000 are expected for September. Blake purchased $56,000 of inventory during June and ended the month with $13,000 in ending inventory.

Operating expenses include sales commission 5% of sales, rent expense of $6,000, depreciation expense of $4,000, utility expense of $1,500, and insurance expense of $1,400.

June 30 cash balance is $14,000.

Of the credit sales, Blake expects to collect 20% in the month of the sale, 50% in the month following the sale, and the remaining 30% in the next month. Purchases are paid for in the month after the purchase. Sales commissions are paid 50% in the month incurred and 50% in the next month. Rent, utility, and insurance are paid in the month incurred.

Requirement

1. For the months of July and August, prepare:

a. Budgeted cash collections from customers

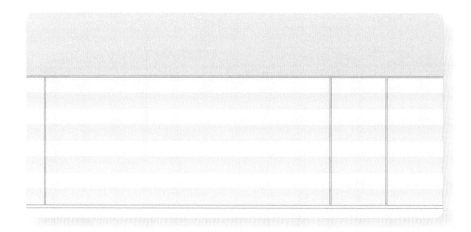

b. Budgeted cash payments for purchases

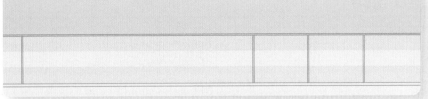

c. Budgeted cash payments for operating expenses

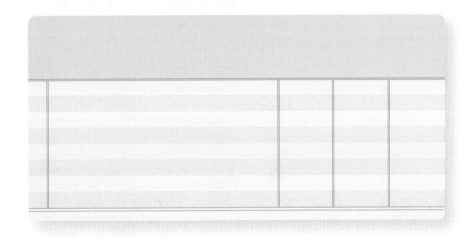

d. The cash budget

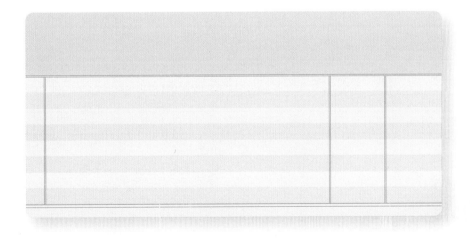

Quick Practice Solutions

True/False

___T___ 1. Budgets provide a benchmark that helps managers evaluate performance. (p. 1103)

___F___ 2. Managers should build "slack" into the budget.

> False—Managers should *not* build "slack" into the budget; it makes the budget less accurate. (p. 1119)

___F___ 3. A company's plan for purchases of property, plant, equipment, and other long-term assets is part of the financial budget.

> False—A company's plan for purchases of property, plant, equipment, and other long-term assets is part of the *capital expenditures* budget. (p. 1105)

___T___ 4. The cash budget is a projection of the cash inflows and cash outflows for a future period. (p. 1105)

___T___ 5. The cash budget is prepared before the budgeted balance sheet is prepared. (p. 1105)

___T___ 6. Sensitivity analysis is a what-if technique that asks what a result will be if a predicted amount is not achieved or if an underlying assumption changes. (p. 1119)

___T___ 7. Responsibility accounting is a system for evaluating the performance of each responsibility center and its manager. (p. 1121)

___F___ 8. Management by exception directs executives' attention to all differences between actual and budgeted variable cost amounts.

> False—Management by exception directs executives' attention to all *significant* differences between actual and budgeted amounts. (p. 1123)

___F___ 9. Most companies consider company divisions as cost centers.

> False—Most companies consider company divisions as *investment* centers. (p. 1122)

___F___ 10. The research and development department would be considered a profit center.

> False—The research and development department would be considered a *cost* center because the managers only control costs. (p. 1122)

Multiple Choice

1. Which of the following statements regarding the budgeting process is (are) true? (pp. 1102–1103)
    a. The budget should be designed from the bottom up, with input from employees at all levels.
    b. The budget should be approved by the company's external auditors.

c. The budget should be designed by top management and communicated to lower-level personnel.

d. All the above statements are true regarding the budgeting process.

2. **Which of the following budgets is an operating budget?** (p. 1105)

a. Capital expenditures budget

b. Budgeted balance sheet

c. Budgeted income statement

d. Cash budget

3. **Which of the following alternatives reflects the proper order of preparing components of the master budget?** (p. 1105)

1. Financial budget

2. Operating budget

3. Capital expenditures budget

a. 2, 3, 1

b. 1, 3, 2

c. 1, 2, 3

d. 3, 1, 2

4. **Desired ending inventory is 80% of beginning inventory. If cost of goods sold is $300,000, purchases will always have what relationship with cost of goods sold?** (p. 1108)

a. Be more than cost of goods sold

b. Be 80% of cost of goods sold

c. Equal cost of goods sold

d. Be less than cost of goods sold

5. **During April, Cherry Company had actual sales of $180,000 compared to budgeted sales of $195,000. Actual cost of goods sold was $135,000, compared to a budget of $136,500. Monthly operating expenses, budgeted at $28,000, totaled $25,000. Interest revenue of $2,500 was earned during April but had not been included in the budget. What is the net income variance on the performance report for April?** (p. 1123)

a. $ (8,000)

b. $(13,000)

c. $ 8,000

d. $ 13,000

6. **Heath Company has beginning inventory of 21,000 units and expected sales of 48,000 units. If the desired ending inventory is 15,500 units, how many units should be produced?** (p. 1108)

a. 27,000

b. 42,500

c. 45,000

d. 53,500

7. **York Enterprises recorded sales of $160,000 during March. Management expects sales to increase 5% in April, 3% in May, and 5% in June. Cost of goods sold is expected to be 70% of sales. What is the budgeted gross profit for June?** (p. 1109)

a. $ 54,508

b. $112,000

c. $127,184

d. $181,692

8. Which of the following is an example of a financial budget? (p. 1105)
   a. Sales budget
   b. Budgeted balance sheet
   c. Budgeted income statement
   d. Operating expense budget

9. Jay Corporation desires a December 31 ending inventory of 1,500 units. Budgeted sales for December are 2,300 units. The November 30 inventory was 850 units. What are budgeted purchases? (p. 1109)
   a. 2,350
   b. 2,950
   c. 3,150
   d. 3,800

10. Bolin's, an elite clothier, expects its November sales to be 30% higher than its October sales of $200,000. Purchases were $100,000 in October and are expected to be $150,000 in November. All sales are on credit and are collected as follows: 30% in the month of the sale and 70% in the following month. Purchases are paid 25% in the month of purchase and 75% in the following month. The beginning cash balance on November 1 is $9,000. What is the ending cash balance on November 30? (pp. 1113–1114)
    a. $ 87,000
    b. $114,500
    c. $140,000
    d. $149,000

Quick Exercises

22-1. Solve for the following independent situations:

a. A sporting goods store budgeted September purchases of ski jackets at $17,900. The store had ski jackets costing $1,200 on hand at the beginning of September, and to cover part of anticipated October sales they expect to have $4,200 of ski jackets on hand at the end of September. What was the budgeted cost of goods sold for September? (p. 1108)

$$\text{Let X} = \text{cost of goods sold}$$
$$\$1,200 + \$17,900 - X = \$4,200$$
$$\$19,100 - X = \$4,200$$
$$X = \$14,900$$

b. A department store has budgeted cost of goods sold for October of $29,300 for its women's coats. Management also wants to have $8,000 of coats in inventory at the end of the month to prepare for the winter season. Beginning inventory in October was $6,000. What dollar amount of coats should be purchased to meet the above objectives? (p. 1108)

$$\text{Let X} = \text{purchases}$$
$$\$6,000 + X - \$29,300 = \$8,000$$
$$X - \$23,300 = \$8,000$$
$$X = \$31,300$$

22-2. Redfield Company has prepared the following forecasts of monthly sales:

	January	February	March	April
Sales (in units)	4,500	5,200	4,700	2,800

Redfield Company has decided that the number of units in its inventory at the end of each month should equal 75% of next month's sales. The budgeted cost per unit is $20. (p. 1108)

	January	February
Next month's budgeted sales (units)	5,200	4,700
Ratio of inventory to future sales	× 75 %	× 75%
Desired ending inventory	3,900	3,525
Budgeted sales for the month (units)	4,500	5,200
Required units of available merchandise	8,400	8,725
Deduct beginning inventory	3,375	3,900
Number of units to be purchased	5,025	4,825

Requirements

1. How many units should be in January's beginning inventory?

75% × 4,500 units = 3,375 units

2. What amount should be budgeted for the cost of merchandise purchases in January?

5,025 units × $20 = $100,500

3. How many units should be purchased in February?

4,825

22-3. The sales budget of Mulls Company for the fourth quarter of 2008 is as follows:

	October	November	December
Sales	$91,000	$76,000	$108,000
Purchases	61,000	58,800	65,000

Sales are 20% cash, 80% credit.
Collections on credit sales are as follows:
50% in the month of sale
30% in the month following sale
15% in the second month following sale
5% uncollectible

Expected sales for January 2009 are $84,000.
Payments for inventory are 70% in the month following purchase and 30% two months following purchase. (pp. 1113–1114)

Requirements

1. Compute the cash collections for December.

October credit sales	=	$10,920 ($91,000 × 0.80 × 0.15)
November credit sales	=	18,240 ($76,000 × 0.80 × 0.30)
December cash sales	=	21,600 ($108,000 × 0.20)
December credit sales	=	43,200 ($108,000 × 080 × 0.50)
December cash collections	=	$93,960

2. Compute the cash disbursements for purchases during December.

October purchases	($61,000 × 0.30)	$18,300
November purchases	($58,800 × 0.70)	41,160
December cash disbursements for purchases =		$59,460

22-4. Soccer Forever gathered the following information as of May 31, 2008:

May 31 inventory balance	$11,100
May payments for inventory	8,300
May payments of accounts payable and accrued liabilities	9,800
May 31 accounts payable balance	5,400
April 30 equipment balance	37,500
April 30 accumulated depreciation—equipment balance	20,900
Cash purchase of equipment in May	2,700
May operating expenses, excluding depreciation (75% paid in May, 25% accrued on May 31)	4,200
May depreciation expense	600
April 30 stockholders' equity	42,485
April 30 cash balance	27,040
May budgeted sales	17,300
May cash receipts from sales on account	12,110

Cost of goods sold is 65% of sales.

May 31 accounts receivable balance is 30% of May sales.

Prepare the budgeted balance sheet on May 31, 2008. (p. 1118)

SOCCER FOREVER
Budgeted Balance Sheet
May 31, 2008

Assets		
Current assets:		
Cash	$15,200*	
Accounts receivable ($17,300 × 0.30)	5,190	
Inventory	11,100	
Total current assets		31,490
Plant assets:		
Equipment	40,200	
Less: Accumulated depreciation	(21,500)	18,700
Total assets		$50,190
Liabilities		
Current liabilities:		
Accounts payable	$ 5,400	
Accrued liabilities ($4,200 × 0.25)	1,050	
Total current liabilities		$ 6,450
Stockholders' equity		43,740**
Total liabilities and stockholders' equity		$50,190

*[$27,040 − $8,300 − $9,800 − $2,700 − (0.75 × $4,200) + $12,110] = $15,200
**Net income for May = $17,300 − (0.65 × $17,300) − $4,200 − $600 = $1,255
$42,485 + $1,255 = $43,740

22-5.   Answer the following completely. (pp. 1102–1105)

a. Define the term budget.

A budget is a quantitative expression of a plan of action that helps managers coordinate and implement the plan.

b. Identify four benefits of budgeting.

The four benefits of budgeting include:
1. Budgeting compels planning. Budgeting helps managers set realistic goals by requiring them to plan specific actions to meet their goals. Budgeting also helps managers prepare for a range of conditions and plan for contingencies.
2. Budgeting promotes coordination and communication. The master budget coordinates the activities of the organization. It forces managers to consider relationships among operations across the entire value chain.
3. Budgeting aids performance evaluation. To evaluate a department or activity, its actual results may be compared either to its budget or its past performance. In general, the budget is a better benchmark because it considers current changes stemming from past conditions.
4. Budgeting can affect behavior and motivate employees. The budgeting process prompts managers to look further into the future than they would look otherwise. This helps them to foresee and avoid problems.

c. Should employees participate in the budgeting process or should management prepare the budgets alone? Explain.

Employees should participate in the budgeting process so that they can bear ownership of the plan. If employees are excluded from this process and unrealistic goals are set, employee morale can be deflated, especially if the employees' performance is judged against these unfair standards. If employees help to create the budget, it can be a motivating factor to achieve the desired outcome.

Do It Yourself! Question 1 Solutions

Requirement

1. Prepare the following budgets for July and August:

a. Sales budget

BLAKES BRAKES
Sales Budget

	July	August	Total
Cash sales, 10%	$ 8,160	$ 8,405	$ 16,565
Credit sales, 90%	73,440	75,643	149,083
Total	$81,600	$84,048	$165,648

b. Inventory, purchases, and cost of goods sold budget

BLAKE'S BRAKES
Inventory, Purchases, and Cost of Goods Sold Budget

	July	August
Cost of goods sold	$61,200	$63,036
+ Desired ending inventory	15,152	15,187
= Total inventory required	76,352	78,223
– Beginning inventory	13,000	15,152
= Purchases	$63,352	$63,071

c. Operating expense budget

BLAKE'S BRAKES
Operating Expense Budget

	July	August	Total
Sales commission	$ 4,080	$ 4,202	$ 8,282
Rent expense	6,000	6,000	12,000
Depreciation expense	4,000	4,000	8,000
Utility expense	1,500	1,500	3,000
Insurance expense	1,400	1,400	2,800
Total operating expenses	$16,980	$17,102	$34,082

d. Budgeted income statement

BLAKE'S BRAKES
Budgeted Income Statement

	July	August	Total
Sales revenue	$81,600	$84,048	$165,648
Cost of goods sold	61,200	63,036	124,236
Gross profit	20,400	21,012	41,412
Operating expenses	16,980	17,102	34,082
Operating income	$ 3,420	$ 3,910	$ 7,330

Do It Yourself! Question 2 Solutions

Requirement

3 Prepare a financial budget

1. For the months of July and August, prepare:

a. Budgeted cash collections from customers

BLAKE'S BRAKES
Budgeted Cash Collections from Customers

	July	August
Cash sales	$ 8,160	$ 8,405
Collections from current month credit sales	14,688	15,129
Collections from previous month credit sales	36,000	36,720
Collections from 2nd previous month credit sales	21,060	21,600
Total collections	$79,908	$81,854

3 Prepare a financial budget

b. Budgeted cash payments for purchases

BLAKE'S BRAKES
Budgeted Cash Payments for Purchases

	July	August	Total
Payment of last month purchases	$56,000	$63,352	$119,352

3 Prepare a financial budget

c. Budgeted cash payments for operating expenses

BLAKE'S BRAKES
Budgeted Cash Payments for Operating Expenses

	July	August	Total
Sales commissions from this month	$ 2,040	$ 2,101	$ 4,141
Sales commissions from last month	2,000	2,040	4,040
Rent expense	6,000	6,000	12,000
Utility expense	1,500	1,500	3,000
Insurance expense	1,400	1,400	2,800
Total	$12,940	$13,041	$25,981

d. The cash budget

BLAKE'S BRAKES
Cash Budget

	July	August
Beginning cash budget	$14,000	$ 24,968
Cash collections	79,908	81,854
Cash available	93,908	106,822
Cash payments		
Purchase of inventory	56,000	63,352
Operating expenses	12,940	13,041
Total cash payments	68,940	76,393
Ending cash balance	$24,968	$ 30,429

The Power of Practice

For more practice using the skills learned in this chapter, visit MyAccountingLab. There you will find algorithmically generated questions that are based on these Demo Docs and your main textbook's Review and Assess Your Progress sections.

Go to MyAccountingLab and follow these steps:

1. Direct your URL to www.myaccountinglab.com.
2. Log in using your name and password.
3. Click the MyAccountingLab link.
4. Click Study Plan in the left navigation bar.
5. From the table of contents, select Chapter 22, The Master Budget and Responsibility Accounting.
6. Click a link to work tutorial exercises.

23 Flexible Budgets and Standard Costs

WHAT YOU PROBABLY ALREADY KNOW

Various budgets including a cash budget were covered in Chapter 22. Assume you had budgeted $400 as your monthly automobile expenditures and found that you actually spent $425. At first glance, it appears that there is an unfavorable difference. The budget of $400 was created assuming that your travel would be 1,000 miles and your costs consist of auto insurance of $100, gasoline $125 (1,000 miles / 20 miles per gallon × $2.50 per gallon), and $175 repayment of the car loan. If you find that you used the car 1,200 miles this month, you probably already know that you should not be held to the original, static budget. The budget should be "flexible" to allow for differences in the level of activity that impacts costs. The flexible budget for 1,200 miles should be $425 [($100 + $175) + 1,200 miles / 20 miles per gallon × $2.50 per gallon]. When the actual results are compared to the flexible budget, it appears that there is no variance. In this chapter, we will study the creation and evaluation of flexible budgets.

Learning Objectives

 Prepare a flexible budget for the income statement.

Flexible budgets are budgets that summarize cost and revenue information for several different volume levels within a relevant range. To prepare a flexible budget, the variable cost per unit and total fixed costs must be determined. You will prepare a flexible budget in Demo Doc 1. *Review the flexible budget in Exhibit 23-2 (p. 1156).*

 Prepare an income statement performance report.

The income statement performance report shows the difference between the actual results and expected results. The difference between the actual results at actual volume and the budgeted results at expected sales volume is the **static budget variance**. A component of the variance may be due to the actual sales volume differing from the budgeted sales volume; this is called the **sales volume variance**. The other component of the variance may be due to the actual amounts at actual volume differing from the budgeted amounts at actual volume; this is called the **flexible budget variance**. The **static budget variance** is the total of the sales volume variance and the flexible budget variance. *Review Exhibit 23-3 (p. 1160) for an illustration of the relationship between the static budget variance, the flexible budget variance, and the sales volume variance. Review the income statement performance report in Exhibit 23-4 (p. 1161).*

3 **Identify the benefits of standard costs and learn how to set standards.**

Many companies use standard costing because it helps them better plan and control levels of performance and provide a goal for employees to work toward. In addition, record-keeping costs are reduced because it's easier to value all inventory at standard and it provides cost information helpful to determine the sales prices. *See Exhibit 23-5 (p. 1165) for standard setting issues relating to standard costing.*

4 **Compute standard cost variances for direct materials and direct labor.**

The actual production costs are compared to the standard costs periodically. There may be a variance due to the price or the quantity used. A **price variance** measures the difference between the actual price and the standard price multiplied by the actual quantity.

A **quantity or efficiency variance** measures how well the business uses its materials or human resources. The quantity variance measures the difference in the actual and standard quantities multiplied by the standard price per unit. *Review Exhibit 23-7 (p. 1168) for an illustration of the relationship between the variances and Exhibit 23-9 (p. 1169) for a computation of price and quantity variances.*

5 **Analyze manufacturing overhead in a standard cost system.**

The total manufacturing overhead variance is the difference between the actual overhead incurred and the standard overhead. The standard overhead amount is the product of the standard overhead rate and the standard allocation base at the actual volume. Recall that the standard overhead rate is computed before the period begins as:

$$\text{Standard Overhead Rate} = \frac{\text{Expected Manufacturing Overhead Costs}}{\text{Expected Quantity of Allocation Base}}$$

The total overhead variance can be separated between the overhead flexible budget variance and the production volume variance. The **overhead flexible budget variance** shows how well management has controlled overhead costs. It is computed in exactly the same way as the flexible budget variances for direct materials and direct labor. The overhead flexible budget variance can be measured as the difference between the actual overhead cost and the flexible budget overhead for the actual number of outputs. The **production volume variance** arises when actual production differs from expected production. It is the difference between the flexible budget for the actual outputs and the standard overhead allocated to actual production. *Review Exhibit 23-11 (p. 1174) to see the total overhead, overhead flexible budget, and production volume variances and the surrounding text for the calculations of the standard prices.*

6 **Record transactions at standard cost and prepare a standard cost income statement.**

The standard cost system requires that the cost of inventory be recorded at the standard amount. This procedure permits variances to be recorded as soon as possible. If the variance is unfavorable, actual costs exceed the standard costs. The unfavorable variance is recorded as a debit to the Variance account and is treated as an expense on the income statement. If the variance is favorable, actual costs are less than the standard costs. The favorable variance is recorded as a credit to the Variance account and is treated as a contra-expense on the income statement. The recorded variances are shown on the standard cost income statement as an adjustment to the cost of goods sold. *Review the "Standard Cost Accounting System" section in the main text for sample journal entries and Exhibit 23-12 (p. 1177) for the flow of costs in a standard costing system. Review Exhibit 23-13 (p. 1178) for a sample standard cost income statement.*

Demo Doc 1

Flexible Budgets and Income Statement Performance Report

Learning Objectives 1, 2

Management at Virus Detection Sensors predicted 2010 sales of 5,400 sensors at a price of $1,000 per sensor. Actual sales for the year were 5,200 sensors at $1,050 per sensor. Following is a breakdown of their costs for 2010:

Units Sold	Budgeted 5400	Actual 5200
Variable costs	$ 620	$ 630
Fixed costs	$ 2,100,000	$ 2,050,000

Requirements

1. Why would Virus Detection prepare a flexible budget? Using Virus Protection's estimated budget values for costs and sales price, develop flexible budgets for 5,200, 5,400, 5,600, and 6,000 sensors. Would Virus Detection Sensor's managers use this flexible budget for planning or controlling? What specific insights can Virus Detection Sensors managers gain from this flexible budget?

2. Using the format shown in Exhibit 23-4 (p. 1161) of the textbook, prepare Virus Detection's income statement performance report for 2010.

3. What was the effect on Virus Detection's operating income of selling 200 units less than the static budget level of sales?

Demo Doc 1 Solutions

Requirement 1

1 Prepare a flexible budget for the income statement

Why would Virus Detection prepare a flexible budget? Using their estimated budget values for costs and sales price, develop flexible budgets for 5,200, 5,400, 5,600, and 6,000 sensors. Would Virus Detection Sensor's managers use this flexible budget for planning or controlling? What specific insights can Virus Detection Sensors managers gain from this flexible budget?

Part 1	Part 2	Part 3	Demo Doc Complete

It is difficult for management to analyze results when the actual volume differs from the static budget. Therefore, companies will produce flexible budgets, which are budgets that summarize cost and revenue information for several different volume levels within a relevant range. Virus Protection would prepare a flexible budget if they aren't sure about their projected sales volume of 5,400 sensors. Virus Protection's flexible budget would show how its revenues and expenses should vary at different volume levels.

Depending upon the volume within the relevant range, a budget can be determined for each amount of activity using the following formula:

$$\text{Flexible budget total cost} = \left(\begin{array}{c} \text{Number of} \\ \text{output units} \end{array} \times \begin{array}{c} \text{Variable cost} \\ \text{per output unit} \end{array} \right) + \text{Total fixed cost}$$

For Virus Detection Sensors, the following would be its flexible budget for 5,200, 5,400, 5,600, and 6,000 sensors:

VIRUS DETECTION SENSORS
Flexible Budget
Year Ended December 31, 2010

	Flexible Budget per Output Unit	Output Units (sensors)			
		5,200	5,400	5,600	6,000
Sales revenue	$1,000	$5,200,000	$5,400,000	$5,600,000	$6,000,000
Variable expenses	620	3,224,000	3,348,000	3,472,000	3,720,000
Fixed expenses		2,100,000	2,100,000	2,100,000	2,100,000
Total expenses		5,324,000	5,448,000	5,572,000	5,820,000
Operating income (loss)		$ (124,000)	$ (48,000)	$ 28,000	$ 180,000

Notice how the total fixed expenses stay constant at $2,100,000 across all four scenarios, yet revenue and variable expenses change. Remember that variable expenses are constant *per unit*—they are called variable because total variable costs change with level of activity.

As you can see, with an output of 5,200 units, Virus Detection would generate 5,200 × $1,000 per unit = $5,200,000 in sales revenue. Meanwhile, its expenses would be 5,200 × $620 = $3,224,000 variable expenses, plus $2,100,000 fixed expenses = $5,324,000 in total expenses.

So with an output of 5,200 units, Virus Detection would incur a loss of $5,200,000 − $5,324,000 = $124,000.

Because the output levels in the flexible budget are estimated levels of sales, these flexible budgets are being developed *before* the period to help managers *plan*. In this case, the budgets indicate that there is a danger of Virus Detection Sensors operating at a loss for 2010 at sales levels below 5,600 units. Managers should devote considerable effort to ensure that Virus Detection Sensors sells more than 5,600 sensors, or find ways to either decrease the expenses associated with manufacturing each sensor or increase the sales price per unit.

Requirement 2

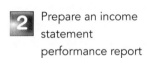 Prepare an income statement performance report

Using the format shown in Exhibit 23-4 of the textbook, prepare Virus Detection's income statement performance report for 2010.

Part 1	**Part 2**	Part 3	Demo Doc Complete

Columns 1 and 5 of the income statement performance report represent Virus Detection's actual 2010 results and its expected (budgeted) results, respectively. These figures come directly from the comparison of actual results with static budget statement for 5,400 units.

Actual results at actual prices are what actually happened. This column (1) represents Virus Detection's true income statement for 2010. This is calculated by multiplying actual quantity by actual price.

Static budget (column 5) represents Virus Detection's original budget with budgeted volume and costs. This budget uses output of 5,400 sensors, when in reality Virus Detection only had a volume of 5,200 sensors in 2010.

We can begin to build our performance report using the actual results and the static budget.

VIRUS DETECTION SENSORS
Income Statement Performance Report
Year Ended December 31, 2010

	1 Actual Results at Actual Prices	2 Flexible Budget Variance	3 Flexible Budget for Actual Number of Output Units	4 Sales Volume Variance	5 Static (Master) Budget
Output Units	5,200				5,400
Sales revenue	$5,460,000				$5,400,000
Variable costs	3,276,000				3,348,000
Fixed costs	2,050,000				2,100,000
Total costs	5,326,000				5,448,000
Operating income (loss)	$ 134,000				$ (48,000)

The next column that we can complete is the flexible budget for actual number of output units (column 3), which represents budgeted amounts based on what Virus Detection actually sold (the other two *variance* columns depend on the values calculated in this column). So for this column, we forget about the number of units that Virus Detection *expected* to sell in 2010, but we instead calculate what its operating income *would have been* had it sold the 5,200 sensors using its actual budget figures for revenues and expenses. This gives management the basis with which to compare the flexible budget variance with the sales volume variance.

Remember that a flexible budget based upon actual outputs provides the greatest ability to evaluate and control because you are comparing what you expected it to be against what it actually is.

From the question, we know that Virus Detection had budgeted to sell each sensor at $1,000. Regardless of how many sensors it *expected* to sell, if it had priced the 5,200 sensors it *did* sell at its original estimate of $1,000 per sensor, Virus Detection's sales revenue *would have been* 5,200 × $1,000 = **$5,200,000**. This is called the flexible budget for sales revenue based on actual units produced.

Virus Detection had budgeted its variable costs at $620 per sensor. If its budgeted variable costs had stayed at $620, then its **flexible budget for variable costs** would be 5,200 sensors × $620 = **$3,224,000**.

Similarly, had Virus Detection's budgeted fixed costs remained at $2,100,000, then its **flexible budget for total costs** would be $3,224,000 variable costs + $2,100,000 fixed costs = **$5,324,000**.

Given this data, then, Virus Detection's flexible budgeted operating income would be calculated as:

$5,200,000 sales revenue − $5,324,000 total costs = $(124,000) operating loss

VIRUS DETECTION SENSORS
Income Statement Performance Report
Year Ended December 31, 2010

	1 Actual Results at Actual Prices	2 Flexible Budget Variance	3 Flexible Budget for Actual Number of Output Units	4 Sales Volume Variance	5 Static (Master) Budget
Output Units	5,200		5,200		5,400
Sales revenue	$5,460,000		$5,200,000		$5,400,000
Variable costs	3,276,000		3,224,000		3,348,000
Fixed costs	2,050,000		2,100,000		2,100,000
Total costs	5,326,000		5,324,000		5,448,000
Operating income (loss)	$ 134,000		$ (124,000)		$ (48,000)

So, how do we use this data? We use it to complete the two variance columns of the income statement performance report. The differences between columns 1 and 3 are presented in column 2, which shows us the flexible budget variance.

Flexible budget variance is the difference between the actual results (at actual prices) and the flexible budget (for actual number of output units). This variance represents more or less revenue earned than expected, and more or less expenses incurred than expected, for the actual level of output. For sales revenue, the variance is favorable if the actual is greater than the flexible budget. In this case, actual sales revenue of $5,460,000 exceeds the flexible budget of $5,200,000 by $260,000, so this is a favorable outcome.

For costs, the variance is unfavorable if the actual is greater than the flexible budget. In this case, actual total costs of $5,326,000 exceed the flexible budget of $5,324,000 by $2,000, which is unfavorable. However, total operating income demonstrates a favorable result of $258,000.

VIRUS DETECTION SENSORS
Income Statement Performance Report
Year Ended December 31, 2010

	1 Actual Results at Actual Prices	2 Flexible Budget Variance	3 Flexible Budget for Actual Number of Output Units	4 Sales Volume Variance	5 Static (Master) Budget
Output Units	5,200	0	5,200		5,400
Sales revenue	$5,460,000	$260,000 F	$5,200,000		$5,400,000
Variable costs	3,276,000	52,000 U	3,224,000		3,348,000
Fixed costs	2,050,000	50,000 F	2,100,000		2,100,000
Total costs	5,326,000	2,000 U	5,324,000		5,448,000
Operating income (loss)	$ 134,000	$258,000 F	$ (124,000)		$ (48,000)

So what does this mean? The flexible budget variance of $260,000 for sales revenue indicates that Virus Detection actually received $260,000 more for the 5,200 sensors than they would have had they sold the 5,200 units at their budgeted sales price of $1,000. On average, they received $50 more per sensor than they thought they would. At the same time, they spent $52,000 more in variable costs than they expected to, and while fixed costs were trimmed by $50,000, they still spent $2,000 more than they budgeted for on total costs. Even though the overall results are favorable, management will still want to know why costs exceeded expectations.

The last column to compute is the sales volume variance column (4). The differences between columns 3 and 5 are presented in column 4.

Sales volume variance is the difference between flexible budget (for actual number of output units) and the static budget. The only reason for this variance is because the number of units actually sold differs from the static budget, but knowing whether these variances are favorable or unfavorable gives managers insight into how sales and marketing are performing in relation to the overall report.

For sales revenue, this variance is favorable if the flexible budget is greater than the static budget. That is not the case with Virus Detection, however. The flexible budget sales revenue of $5,200,000 is lower than the budgeted sales of $5,400,000. This is because the sales force sold fewer units than expected.

For costs, this variance is favorable if the flexible budget is less than the static budget. In this case, the results are favorable, with the flexible budget showing $5,324,000 in total costs and the static budget showing $5,448,000, for a favorable variance of $124,000 in total costs. However, this variance results from the fact that the sales force sold fewer units than expected. In actuality, variable costs *increased* by $10 per unit over what Virus Detection had budgeted. This is favorable only because Virus Detection budgeted costs for more units than it actually made.

VIRUS DETECTION SENSORS
Income Statement Performance Report
Year Ended December 31, 2010

	1	2	3	4	5
	Actual Results at Actual Prices	Flexible Budget Variance	Flexible Budget for Actual Number of Output Units	Sales Volume Variance	Static (Master) Budget
Output Units	**5,200**	**0**	**5,200**	**200U**	**5,400**
Sales revenue	$5,460,000	$260,000 F	$5,200,000	$200,000U	$5,400,000
Variable costs	3,276,000	52,000U	3,224,000	124,000 F	3,348,000
Fixed costs	2,050,000	50,000 F	2,100,000	0	2,100,000
Total costs	5,326,000	2,000U	5,324,000	124,000 F	5,448,000
Operating income (loss)	$ 134,000	$258,000 F	$ (124,000)	$ 76,000U	$ (48,000)

Requirement 3

2 Prepare an income
statement
performance report

What was the effect on Virus Detection's operating income of selling 200 units less than the static budget level of sales?

Part 1	Part 2	**Part 3**	Demo Doc Complete

Virus Detection's sales volume variance is $200,000 unfavorable. So, Virus selling 200 units less than budgeted reduced their sales volume by $200,000. Virus was able to more than overcome this reduction in sales volume by selling at a higher price than anticipated, as indicated by the favorable flexible budget sales revenue variance of $260,000 favorable. Had Virus Detection sold what it had budgeted for, it would have incurred a loss of $48,000. But, by increasing the sales price and reducing the fixed expense costs, even by selling 200 fewer units, Virus incurred an operating income of $134,000 instead of incurring the loss.

Part 1	Part 2	Part 3	**Demo Doc Complete**

Demo Doc 2

Standard Costs

Learning Objectives 3–6

Bumpy Road Maps manufactures road maps. Bumpy uses a standard cost system to control manufacturing costs.

The following standard unit cost information is based on the static budget volume of 120,000 road maps per month:

Direct materials (40 sq. yards @ $0.015 per sq. yard)		$0.60
Direct labor (0.10 hours @ $12.00 per hour)		1.20
Manufacturing overhead:		
Variable (0.10 hours @ $3.00 per hour)	0.30	
Fixed (0.10 hours @ $8.00 per hour)	0.80	1.10
Total cost per map		$2.90

In this example, total budgeted fixed manufacturing overhead = $0.80 × 120,000 road maps = $96,000.

Actual cost and production volume information:

- Actual production was 118,000 maps.
- Actual direct materials usage was 41 square yards per map, at an actual cost of $0.016 per square yard.
- Actual direct labor usage of 11,600 hours at $12.10 per hour, total cost of $140,360.
- Total actual overhead was $126,000.

Requirements

1. Bumpy has developed their standards. What are the five benefits of standard costing?

2. Compute the price and efficiency variances for direct materials and direct labor. Are these variances favorable or unfavorable? Why?

3. Journalize the usage of direct materials, including the related variance.

4. For manufacturing overhead, compute the total variance, the flexible variance, and the production volume variance. Are these variances favorable or unfavorable? Why?

Demo Doc 2 Solutions

Requirement 1

 Identify the benefits of standard costs and learn how to set standards

Bumpy has developed their standards. What are the five benefits of standard costing?

Part 1	Part 2	Part 3	Part 4	Part 5	Part 6	Part 7	Demo Doc Complete

A **standard cost** is a budget for a single unit. A standard is developed for the quantity and price of direct materials, direct labor, and manufacturing overhead.

Material price standards consider the cost of purchases plus freight in and receiving costs less discounts. Direct labor cost standards include the labor rates, payroll taxes, and fringe benefits. Overhead cost standards are developed by dividing estimated variable and fixed overhead costs by an appropriate allocation base. The quantity standards are usually developed using the input from knowledgeable employees taking into account an expected amount of spoilage, waste, and downtime.

Standards help managers in five areas:

1. Plan by providing unit amounts for budgeting.

2. Control by setting target levels of performance.

3. Motivate employees by serving as performance benchmarks.

4. Set sales prices of products or services by providing unit costs.

5. Simplify record keeping and reduce clerical costs.

Requirement 2

Compute standard cost variances for direct materials and direct labor

Compute the price and efficiency variances for direct materials and direct labor. Are these variances favorable or unfavorable? Why?

Part 1	Part 2	Part 3	Part 4	Part 5	Part 6	Part 7	Demo Doc Complete

Direct Materials Price Variance

The actual quantity of direct materials used was the total number of maps produced (118,000) multiplied by the amount of direct materials used per map. Actual direct materials usage was 41 square yards per map, for an actual quantity of 4,838,000 square yards of materials.

To compute the variance, multiply the difference between the actual and standard costs per unit by the actual quantity. Bumpy estimated a cost of $0.015 per square yard, but the actual cost was $0.016 per square yard, for a difference of $0.001, which multiplied by 4,838,000 yields a variance of $4,838:

$$
\begin{aligned}
\text{Direct materials price variance} &= (\text{Actual price} - \text{Standard price}) \times \text{Actual quantity of } \textbf{material} \text{ for maps produced} \\
&= (\$0.016 - \$0.015) \times (41 \text{ sq. yards usage per unit} \times 118,000 \text{ units}) \\
&= \$0.001 \times 4,838,000 \\
&= \$4,838\text{U}
\end{aligned}
$$

This variance is unfavorable because the actual price is greater than the standard price.

Direct Materials Quantity Variance

This variance measures whether the quantity of materials actually used to produce the *actual* number of output units is within the *standard* allowed for that number of outputs. This is calculated by multiplying the difference between quantities of material (actual vs. standard) by the *standard* price per unit of material.

We know from computing the direct materials price variance that the actual quantity of direct materials used was 41 square yards per map × 118,000 maps = 4,838,000 square yards. From this, we subtract the standard quantity (40 square yards per map × 118,000 maps = 4,720,000 square yards) for a difference of 118,000 square yards.

We then multiply that difference in quantity by the standard price per unit. Remember, efficiency variance is measured against the standard (flexible budget, not actual costs), for a total variance of 118,000 × $0.015 = $1,770:

$$
\begin{aligned}
\text{Direct materials quantity variance} &= (\text{Actual quantity} - \text{Standard quantity}) \times \text{Standard price} \\
&= [(41 \times 118,000) - (40 \times 118,000)] \times \$0.015 \\
&= (4,838,000 - 4,720,000) \times \$0.015 \\
&= 118,000 \times \$0.015 \\
&= \$1,770\text{U}
\end{aligned}
$$

This variance is unfavorable because the actual material used per map, 41 square yards, was greater than the standard per map, 40 square yards.

Part 1	Part 2	**Part 3**	Part 4	Part 5	Part 6	Part 7	Demo Doc Complete

Direct Labor Rate Variance

This variance measures the difference between the actual price per unit (in this case, rate per hour for labor) and the standard price per unit, multiplied by the actual quantity of input (that is, hours worked).

In this case, Bumpy estimated a rate of $12.00 per hour for labor, and actual costs were $12.10, so the difference is $0.10 per hour, which multiplied by the actual hours of 11,600 yields a variance of $1,160:

$$
\begin{aligned}
\text{Direct labor rate variance} &= (\text{Actual rate} - \text{Standard rate}) \times \text{Actual hour} \\
&= (\$12.10 - \$12.00) \times 11,600 \\
&= \$0.10 \times 11,600 \\
&= \$1,160\text{U}
\end{aligned}
$$

This variance is unfavorable because the actual hourly rate for labor, $12.10, was greater than the standard rate for labor, $12.00.

Direct Labor Efficiency Variance

This variance measures the difference between the actual quantity of input (in this case, the number of hours Bumpy actually purchased) and the standard quantity of input, multiplied by the standard price per input unit (hourly cost of the labor).

In this case, we know that the actual hours purchased was 11,600. To compute standard hours, multiply the standard rate per map, 0.10, by the actual number of maps produced, 118,000 = 11,800. So the difference between actual and standard hours is 200, multiplied by the standard price per hour of $12.00 = $2,400:

$$
\begin{aligned}
\text{Direct labor efficiency variance} &= (\text{Actual hours} - \text{Standard hours}) \times \text{Standard price} \\
&= [11,600 - (0.10 \times 118,000)] \times \$12.00 \\
&= (11,600 - 11,800) \times \$12.00 \\
&= -200 \times \$12.00 \\
&= \$2,400\text{F}
\end{aligned}
$$

This variance is favorable because actual hours used was less than standard hours.

Requirement 3

Journalize the usage of direct materials, including the related variance.

6   Record transactions at standard cost and prepare a standard cost income statement

Part 1	Part 2	Part 3	**Part 4**	Part 5	Part 6	Part 7	Demo Doc Complete

Usage of Direct Materials

Bumpy debits (increases) Work in Process Inventory for the standard price multiplied by the standard quantity of direct materials that should have been used for the actual output of 118,000 maps. This maintains inventory at standard cost. Materials Inventory is credited (decreased) for the actual quantity of materials put into production multiplied by the standard price:

Work in Process Inventory (118,000 × 40 × $0.015)	70,800	
???	1,770	
Materials Inventory (118,000 × 41 × $0.015)		72,570

So where does the rest of the debit side of this entry come from?

We learned in Requirement 2 that because Bumpy used more materials than the standard, its direct materials quantity variance was $1,770 unfavorable. This unfavorable variance increases the cost of production. Unfavorable variances will always be debited (increased).

Work in Process Inventory (118,000 × 40 × $0.015)	70,800	
Direct Materials Quantity Variance (118,000 × $0.015)	1,770	
Materials Inventory (118,000 × 41 × $0.015)		72,570

Requirement 4

5

Analyze manufacturing overhead in a standard cost system

For manufacturing overhead, compute the total variance, the flexible variance, and the production volume variance. Are these variances favorable or unfavorable? Why?

Part 1	Part 2	Part 3	Part 4	**Part 5**	Part 6	Part 7	Demo Doc Complete

Total Overhead Variance

Total overhead variance is the difference between actual overhead cost and standard overhead allocated to production.

The standard overhead allocated to production is the standard cost of the overhead per map times the number of maps actually produced. We know from the question that the standard overhead cost per map is $0.30 (variable cost) + $0.80 (fixed cost) = $1.10. So the standard overhead allocated to production = 118,000 × $1.10 = $129,800. Actual overhead cost as given in the question is $126,000, the difference being $3,800:

$$\text{Total overhead variance} = \text{Actual overhead cost} - \text{Standard overhead allocated to production}$$
$$= \$126,000 - (118,000 \times \$1.10)$$
$$= \$126,000 - \$129,800$$
$$= \$3,800F$$

The variance is favorable because the actual overhead is less than the standard overhead. Overapplied overhead is favorable because enough cost was put into production.

Part 1	Part 2	Part 3	Part 4	Part 5	**Part 6**	Part 7	Demo Doc Complete

Overhead Flexible Budget Variance

The flexible budget variance is equal to the difference between the actual overhead cost and the flexible budget overhead for the actual number of maps produced.

To compute the flexible budget overhead variance, the fixed portion of the overhead must be separated from the variable part. The variable part of the overhead is flexible, therefore the variable cost of overhead per map ($0.30) is multiplied by the actual number of maps produced (118,000); the variable part of overhead is thus $35,400.

The fixed portion of the overhead is not flexible within the relevant range, so to compute the full fixed part of the overhead, the fixed cost of overhead per map ($0.80) must be multiplied by the static expected budget output of 120,000 maps. The fixed part of overhead is thus $96,000, the same as the original budgeted amount. Total flexible budget overhead is $35,400 + $96,000 = $131,400.

We know that the actual overhead cost was \$126,000, the difference between actual and flexible thus being \$5,400:

$$\text{Overhead flexible budget variance} = \text{Actual overhead cost} - \text{Flexible budget overhead for the actual number of outputs}$$
$$= \$126,000 - [(118,000 \times \$0.30) + (120,000 \times \$0.80)]$$
$$= \$126,000 - (\$35,400 + \$96,000)$$
$$= \$126,000 - \$131,400$$
$$= \$5,400F$$

The flexible budget variance is favorable because the actual overhead cost is less than the flexible budget.

Part 1	Part 2	Part 3	Part 4	Part 5	Part 6	**Part 7**	Demo Doc Complete

Production Volume Variance

The production volume variance arises when actual production differs from expected production. It is calculated as the difference between the flexible budget overhead for the actual number of outputs and the standard overhead allocated to actual production.

Standard overhead allocated to actual production is calculated by multiplying the number of maps actually produced, 118,000, by the standard overhead per unit, \$1.10, which equals \$129,800.

We know from calculating the overhead flexible budet variance that the flexible budget overhead for the

$$\text{Actual number of outputs} = [(118,000 \times \$0.30) + (120,000 \times \$0.80)]$$
$$= \$35,400 + \$96,000$$
$$= \$131,400$$

So the difference is calculated as \$131,400 − \$129,800 = \$1,600:

$$\text{Production volume variance} = \text{Flexible budget overhead for the actual number of outputs} - \text{Standard overhead allocated to actual production}$$
$$= \$131,400 - (\$1.10 \times 118,000)$$
$$= \$131,400 - \$129,800$$
$$= \$1,600U$$

This variance accounts for Bumpy producing fewer maps, 118,000, than expected output, 120,000. Bumpy didn't use their production capacity as efficiently as possible. Whenever a business produces less than expected, the production volume variance will be unfavorable.

Part 1	Part 2	Part 3	Part 4	Part 5	Part 6	Part 7	**Demo Doc Complete**

Quick Practice Questions

True/False

_____ 1. Total variable costs change as production volume changes in a flexible budget.

_____ 2. At the end of the period, all variance accounts are closed to zero out their balances.

_____ 3. The sales volume variance arises because the number of units actually sold differs from the number of units expected to be sold according to the master budget.

_____ 4. A price variance is the difference between the actual unit price of an input and the standard unit price of the input, multiplied by the standard input quantity.

_____ 5. If the standard quantity allowed is less than the actual quantity used, the efficiency variance is favorable.

_____ 6. An efficiency variance is the difference between the actual quantity of input and the standard quantity of input, multiplied by the actual unit price of input.

_____ 7. Manufacturing overhead allocated to production equals the standard predetermined manufacturing overhead rate times the actual quantity of allocation base allowed for the standard number of outputs.

_____ 8. The overhead flexible budget variance is the difference between the actual overhead cost and the flexible budget overhead for budgeted production.

_____ 9. The production volume variance is favorable whenever actual output is less than expected output.

_____ 10. In standard costing, the journal entry to record the direct labor costs incurred includes a debit to Manufacturing Wages for the actual hours worked at the standard price for direct labor.

Multiple Choice

1. **Which of the following is true for a static budget?**
   a. Adjusted for changes in the level of activity
   b. Prepared for only one level of activity
   c. A budget that stays the same from one period to the next
   d. Also known as a fixed budget

2. Sweet Baby Diaper Company sells disposable diapers for $0.20 each. Variable costs are $0.05 per diaper while fixed costs are $75,000 per month for volumes up to 850,000 diapers and $112,500 for volumes above 850,000 diapers. What is the monthly operating income for 800,000 diapers and 900,000 diapers of volume?
   a. $22,500 and $7,500, respectively
   b. $60,000 and $45,000, respectively
   c. $45,000 and $22,500, respectively
   d. $7,500 and $60,000, respectively

3. A graph of a flexible budget formula reflects fixed costs of $30,000 and total costs of $90,000 at a volume of 6,000 units. Assuming the relevant range is 1,000 to 12,000 units, what is the total cost of 10,000 units on the graph?
   a. $100,000
   b. $130,000
   c. $160,000
   d. $180,000

4. The sales volume variance is the difference between which amounts?
   a. Number of units actually sold and number of units expected to be sold according to the static budget
   b. Amounts in the flexible budget and the static budget
   c. Actual results and amounts in the flexible budget
   d. Actual sales volume and normal sales volume

5. The flexible budget variance is the difference between which amounts?
   a. Actual results and amounts in the static budget
   b. Amounts in the flexible budget and the actual results
   c. Amounts in the flexible budget and the static budget
   d. The budgeted amounts for each level of activity in the flexible budget

6. What does a flexible budget help to measure?
   a. The efficiency of operations at the actual activity levels
   b. The amount by which standard and expected prices differ
   c. Both a and b
   d. None of the above

7. Global Engineering's actual operating income for the current year is $50,000. The flexible budget operating income for actual volume achieved is $40,000, while the static budget operating income is $53,000. What is the sales volume variance for operating income?
   a. $10,000U
   b. $10,000F
   c. $13,000U
   d. $13,000F

8. Tiger's Golf Center reported actual operating income for the current year of $60,000. The flexible budget operating income for actual volume achieved is $55,000, while the static budget operating income is $58,000. What is the flexible budget variance for operating income?
   a. $2,000F
   b. $3,000U
   c. $5,000F
   d. $5,000U

9. What does a favorable direct materials efficiency variance indicate?
    a. Actual cost of direct materials was less than the standard cost of direct materials.
    b. Actual quantity of direct materials used was less than the standard quantity for actual output.
    c. Standard quantity of direct materials for actual output was less than the actual quantity of direct materials used.
    d. Actual quantity of direct materials used was greater than the standard quantity for budgeted output.

10. Western Outfitters Mountain Sports projected 2008 sales of 75,000 units at a unit sale price of $12.00. Actual 2008 sales were 72,000 units at $14.00 per unit. Actual variable costs, budgeted at $4.00 per unit, totaled $4.75 per unit. Budgeted fixed costs totaled $375,000, while actual fixed costs amounted to $400,000.

    What is the flexible budget variance for variable expenses?
    a. $12,000F
    b. $25,000F
    c. $54,000U
    d. $54,000F

Quick Exercises

23-1. Smart Toys Manufacturing projected 2008 sales of 10,000 units at $12.00 per unit. Actual sales for the year were 15,000 units at $12.50 per unit. Actual variable expenses, budgeted at $5.00 per unit, amounted to $4.80 per unit. Actual fixed expenses, budgeted at $60,000, totaled $62,500.

Requirement

1. Prepare Smart Toy's income statement performance report for 2008, including both flexible budget variances and sales volume variances.

SMART TOYS MANUFACTURING
Income Statement Performance Report
Year Ended December 31, 2008

	1	2	3	4	5
	Actual Results at Actual Prices	Flexible Budget Variance	Flexible Budget for Actual Number of Output Units	Sales Volume Variance	Static (Master) Budget
Output Units					
Sales revenue					
Variable costs					
Fixed costs					
Total costs					
Operating income					

23-2. Dawkins Company established a master budget volume of 19,500 units for September. Actual overhead costs incurred amounted to $17,800. Actual production for the month was 22,000 units. The standard variable overhead rate was $0.50 per direct labor hour. The standard fixed overhead rate was $0.25 per direct labor hour. One direct labor hour is the standard quantity per finished unit.

Requirements

1. Compute the total manufacturing overhead cost variance.

2. Compute the overhead flexible budget variance.

3. Compute the production volume variance.

23-3. Standard Products Company recognizes variances from standards at the earliest opportunity, and the quantity of direct materials purchased is equal to the quantity used. The following information is available for the most recent month:

	Direct Materials	Direct Labor
Standard quantity/unit	6.00 lbs.	2.5 hrs.
Standard price/lb. or hr.	$8.10/lb.	$8.00/hr.
Actual quantity/unit	6.25 lbs.	2.8 hrs.
Actual price/lb. or hr.	$8.00/lb.	$7.50/hr.
Price variance	$562.50 F	$1,260.00F
Efficiency variance	$1,822.50 U	$2,160.00U
Static budget volume	800 units	
Actual volume	900 units	
Actual overhead	$11,000.00	
Standard variable overhead	$5/unit	
Standard fixed overhead	$5,600	
Overhead flexible budget variance	$900U	
Production volume variance	$700F	

Requirements

1. Journalize the purchase and usage of direct materials including the related variances.

Date	Accounts	Debit	Credit

Date	Accounts	Debit	Credit

2. Journalize the direct labor costs incurred and the application of direct labor, including the related variances.

Date	Accounts	Debit	Credit

Date	Accounts	Debit	Credit

3. Journalize the application of overhead costs including the recognition of the overhead variances.

Date	Accounts	Debit	Credit

Date	Accounts	Debit	Credit

23-4. Jeremy Industries has the following information regarding direct materials:

Actual pounds purchased and used	42,000
Standard quantity	3 pounds per finished good
Actual production	15,000 finished goods
Direct materials efficiency variance	$10,500 F
Direct materials price variance	$8,820 U

Requirement

1. Compute Jeremy's standard price per pound and actual price per pound.

23-5. Parkland, Inc., sells board games for $15.00, resulting in a contribution margin of $9.00 per game. Fixed costs are budgeted at $212,000 per quarter for volumes up to 30,000 games and $242,000 for volumes exceeding 30,000 games.

Requirement

1. Prepare the flexible budget for the next quarter for volume levels of 25,000, 30,000, and 37,000 games.

PARKLAND, INC.
Flexible Budget
Year Ended December 31, 2010

	Flexible Budget per Output Unit	Output Units (games)		
		25,000	30,000	37,000
Sales revenue				
Variable expenses				
Fixed expenses				
Total expenses				
Operating income (loss)				

Do It Yourself! Question 1

Flexible Budgets and Income Statement Performance Report

Management at Fluffy Foam Beds predicted 2010 sales of 32,000 beds at a price of $180 per bed. Actual sales for the year were 34,200 beds at $185 per bed. Following is a breakdown of Fluffy's costs for 2010:

Units Sold	Budgeted 32,000	Actual 34,200
Variable costs	$ 70	$ 75
Fixed costs	$3,000,000	$3,100,000

Requirements

1. Using Fluffy's estimated budget values for costs and sales price, develop flexible budgets for 32,000, 34,000, and 36,000 beds.

FLUFFY FOAM BEDS
Flexible Budget
Year Ended December 31, 2010

	Flexible Budget per Output Unit	Output Units (beds)		
		32,000	34,000	36,000
Sales revenue				
Variable expenses				
Fixed expenses				
Total expenses				
Operating income (loss)				

2. Prepare Fluffy's income statement performance report for 2010.

FLUFFY FOAM BEDS
Income Statement Performance Report
Year Ended December 31, 2010

	1 Actual Results at Actual Prices	2 Flexible Budget Variance	3 Flexible Budget for Actual Number of Output Units	4 Sales Volume Variance	5 Static (Master) Budget
Output Units					
Sales revenue					
Variable costs					
Fixed costs					
Total costs					
Operating income					

Do It Yourself! Question 2

Standard Costs

Circle CD manufactures CD cases. Circle uses a standard cost system to control manufacturing costs.

The following standard unit cost information is based on the static budget volume of 80,000 CD cases per month:

Direct materials (100 sq. ft. @ $0.25 sq. ft.)		$ 25.00
Direct labor (0.50 hours @ $18.00 per hour)		9.00
Manufacturing overhead:		
Variable (1 hour @ 2.00 per hour)	2.00	
Fixed (2 hours @ $5.00 per hour)	10.00	12.00
Total cost per CD case		$46.00

In this example, total budgeted fixed manufacturing overhead = $10 × 80,000 CD cases = $800,000.

Actual cost and production volume information:
- Actual production was 88,000 cases.
- Actual direct materials usage was 102 square feet per case, at an actual cost of $0.24 per square foot.
- Actual direct labor usage of 42,000 hours at $18.15, total cost of $762,300.
- Total actual overhead was $980,000.

Requirements

1. Compute the price and efficiency variances for direct materials and direct labor.

Direct Materials Price Variance

Direct Materials Efficiency Variance

Direct Labor Rate Variance

Direct Labor Efficiency Variance

2. For manufacturing overhead, compute the total variance, the flexible variance, and the production volume variance.

Total Overhead Variance

Overhead Flexible Budget Variance

Production Volume Variance

Quick Practice Solutions

True/False

T   1. Total variable costs change as production volume changes in a flexible budget. (p. 1159)

T   2. At the end of the period, all variance accounts are closed to zero out their balances. (p. 1178)

T   3. The sales volume variance arises because the number of units actually sold differs from the number of units expected to be sold according to the master budget. (p. 1160)

F   4. A price variance is the difference between the actual unit price of an input and the standard unit price of the input, multiplied by the standard input quantity.

False—A price variance is the difference between the actual unit price of an input and the standard unit price of the input, multiplied by the actual input quantity. (p. 1167)

F   5. If the standard quantity allowed is less than the actual quantity used, the efficiency variance is favorable.

False—If the standard quantity allowed is less than the actual quantity used, the efficiency variance is unfavorable. (p. 1167)

F   6. An efficiency variance is the difference between the actual quantity of input and the standard quantity of input, multiplied by the actual unit price of input.

False—An efficiency variance is the difference between the actual quantity of input and the standard quantity of input, multiplied by the standard unit price of input. (p. 1167)

F   7. Manufacturing overhead allocated to production equals the standard predetermined manufacturing overhead rate times the actual quantity of allocation base allowed for the standard number of outputs.

False—Manufacturing overhead allocated to production equals the standard predetermined manufacturing overhead rate times the standard quantity of allocation base allowed for the actual number of outputs. (p. 1172)

F   8. The overhead flexible budget variance is the difference between the actual overhead cost and the flexible budget overhead for budgeted production.

False—The overhead flexible budget variance is the difference between the actual overhead cost and the flexible budget overhead for the actual number of outputs. (p. 1174)

F   9. The production volume variance is favorable whenever actual output is less than expected output.

False—The production volume variance is unfavorable whenever actual output is less than expected output. (p. 1175)

<u>T</u>   10. In standard costing, the journal entry to record the direct labor costs incurred includes a debit to Manufacturing Wages for the actual hours worked at the standard price for direct labor. (p. 1175)

Multiple Choice

1. Which of the following is true for a static budget? (p. 1158)
   a. Adjusted for changes in the level of activity
   b. Prepared for only one level of activity
   c. A budget that stays the same from one period to the next
   d. Also known as a fixed budget

2. Sweet Baby Diaper Company sells disposable diapers for $0.20 each. Variable costs are $0.05 per diaper while fixed costs are $75,000 per month for volumes up to 850,000 diapers and $112,500 for volumes above 850,000 diapers. What is the monthly operating income for 800,000 diapers and 900,000 diapers of volume? (p. 1158)
   a. $22,500 and $7,500, respectively
   b. $60,000 and $45,000, respectively
   c. $45,000 and $22,500, respectively
   d. $7,500 and $60,000, respectively

3. A graph of a flexible budget formula reflects fixed costs of $30,000 and total costs of $90,000 at a volume of 6,000 units. Assuming the relevant range is 1,000 to 12,000 units, what is the total cost of 10,000 units on the graph? (p. 1159)
   a. $100,000
   b. $130,000
   c. $160,000
   d. $180,000

4. The sales volume variance is the difference between which amounts? (p. 1160)
   a. Number of units actually sold and number of units expected to be sold according to the static budget
   b. Amounts in the flexible budget and the static budget
   c. Actual results and amounts in the flexible budget
   d. Actual sales volume and normal sales volume

5. The flexible budget variance is the difference between which amounts? (p. 1160)
   a. Actual results and amounts in the static budget
   b. Amounts in the flexible budget and the actual results
   c. Amounts in the flexible budget and the static budget
   d. The budgeted amounts for each level of activity in the flexible budget

6. What does a flexible budget help to measure? (p. 1160)
   a. The efficiency of operations at the actual activity levels
   b. The amount by which standard and expected prices differ
   c. Both a and b
   d. None of the above

7. Global Engineering's actual operating income for the current year is $50,000. The flexible budget operating income for actual volume achieved is $40,000 while the static budget operating income is $53,000. What is the sales volume variance for operating income? (p. 1160)
   a. $10,000U
   b. $10,000F
   c. $13,000U
   d. $13,000F

8. Tiger's Golf Center reported actual operating income for the current year of $60,000. The flexible budget operating income for actual volume achieved is $55,000 while the static budget operating income is $58,000. What is the flexible budget variance for operating income? (p. 1160)
   a. $2,000F
   b. $3,000U
   c. $5,000F
   d. $5,000U

9. What does a favorable direct materials efficiency variance indicate? (p. 1170)
   a. Actual cost of direct materials was less than the standard cost of direct materials.
   b. Actual quantity of direct materials used was less than the standard quantity for actual output.
   c. Standard quantity of direct materials for actual output was less than the actual quantity of direct materials used.
   d. Actual quantity of direct materials used was greater than the standard quantity for budgeted output.

10. Western Outfitters Mountain Sports projected 2008 sales of 75,000 units at a unit sale price of $12.00. Actual 2008 sales were 72,000 units at $14.00 per unit. Actual variable costs, budgeted at $4.00 per unit, totaled $4.75 per unit. Budgeted fixed costs totaled $375,000 while actual fixed costs amounted to $400,000.

    What is the flexible budget variance for variable expenses? (p. 1160)
    a. $12,000F
    b. $25,000F
    c. $54,000U
    d. $54,000F

Quick Exercises

23-1. Smart Toys Manufacturing projected 2008 sales of 10,000 units at $12.00 per unit. Actual sales for the year were 15,000 units at $12.50 per unit. Actual variable expenses, budgeted at $5.00 per unit, amounted to $4.80 per unit. Actual fixed expenses, budgeted at $60,000, totaled $62,500. (pp. 1160–1161)

Requirement

1. Prepare Smart Toy's income statement performance report for 2008, including both flexible budget variances and sales volume variances.

SMART TOYS MANUFACTURING
Income Statement Performance Report
Year Ended December 31, 2008

	1	2	3	4	5
	Actual Results at Actual Prices	Flexible Budget Variance	Flexible Budget for Actual Number of Output Units	Sales Volume Variance	Static (Master) Budget
Output Units	15,000	0	15,000	5,000 F	10,000
Sales revenue	$187,500	$7,500 F	$180,000	$60,000 F	$120,000
Variable costs	72,000	3,000 F	75,000	25,000 U	50,000
Fixed costs	62,500	2,500 U	60,000	0	60,000
Total costs	134,500	500 U	135,000	25,000 U	110,000
Operating income	$ 53,000	$8,000 F	$ 45,000	$35,000 F	$ 10,000

23-2. Dawkins Company established a master budget volume of 19,500 units for September. Actual overhead costs incurred amounted to $17,800. Actual production for the month was 22,000 units. The standard variable overhead rate was $0.50 per direct labor hour. The standard fixed overhead rate was $0.25 per direct labor hour. One direct labor hour is the standard quantity per finished unit. (pp. 1172–1175)

Actual overhead = $17,800
Flexible budget overhead for actual production = ($0.50 × 22,000) + ($0.25 × 19,500) = $15,875
Standard overhead allocated to production = ($0.50 × 22,000) + ($0.25 × 22,000) = $16,500

Requirements

1. Compute the total manufacturing overhead cost variance.

Total manufacturing overhead cost variance = $17,800 − $16,500 = $1,300 U

2. Compute the overhead flexible budget variance.

Overhead flexible budget variance = $17,800 − $15,875 = $1,925 U

3. Compute the production volume variance.

Production volume variance = $15,875 − $16,500 = $625 F

23-3.   Standard Products Company recognizes variances from standards at the earliest opportunity, and the quantity of direct materials purchased is equal to the quantity used. The following information is available for the most recent month: (pp. 1175–1177)

	Direct Materials	Direct Labor
Standard quantity/unit	6.00 lbs.	2.5 hrs.
Standard price/lb. or hr.	$8.10/lb.	$8.00/hr.
Actual quantity/unit	6.25 lbs.	2.8 hrs.
Actual price/lb. or hr.	$8.00/lb.	$7.50/hr.
Price variance	$562.50 F	$1,260 F
Efficiency variance	$1,822.50 U	$2,160 U
Static budget volume	800 units	
Actual volume	900 units	
Actual overhead	$11,000	
Standard variable overhead	$5/unit	
Standard fixed overhead	$5,600	
Overhead flexible budget variance	$900 U	
Production volume variance	$700 F	

Requirements

1. Journalize the purchase and usage of direct materials including the related variances.

General Journal			
Date	Accounts	Debit	Credit
Req. 1	Materials Inventory	45,562.50	
	Accounts Payable		45,000.00
	Direct Materials Price Variance		562.50

General Journal			
Date	Accounts	Debit	Credit
	Work in Process Inventory	43,740.00	
	Direct Materials Efficiency Variance	1,822.50	
	Materials Inventory		45,562.50

2. Journalize the direct labor costs incurred and the application of direct labor, including the related variances.

	General Journal			
Date	Accounts		Debit	Credit
Req. 2	Manufacturing Wages		20,160.00	
	Wages Payable			18,900.00
	Direct Labor Price Variance			1,260.00

	General Journal			
Date	Accounts		Debit	Credit
	Work in Process Inventory		18,000.00	
	Direct Labor Efficiency Variance		2,160.00	
	Manufacturing Wages			20,160.00

3. Journalize the application of overhead costs including the recognition of the overhead variances.

	General Journal			
Date	Accounts		Debit	Credit
Req. 3	Work in Process Inventory		10,800.00	
	Manufacturing Overhead			10,800.00
	[($5,600/800 = $7 × 900) + $5 × 900]			

	General Journal			
Date	Accounts		Debit	Credit
	Overhead Flexible Budget Variance		900.00	
	Production Volume Variance			700.00
	Manufacturing Overhead			200.00

23-4.   Jeremy Industries has the following information regarding direct materials: (pp. 1168–1172)

Actual pounds purchased and used	42,000
Standard quantity	3 pounds per finished good
Actual production	15,000 finished goods
Direct materials efficiency variance	$10,500 F
Direct materials price variance	$8,820 U

Requirement

1. Compute Jeremy's standard price per pound and actual price per pound.

$$\text{Let } Y = \text{standard price per pound}$$
$$\text{Direct materials efficiency variance} =$$
$$[(3 \times 15,000) - 42,000]Y = \$10,500$$
$$3,000Y = \$10,500$$
$$Y = \$3.50$$

$$\text{Let } Y = \text{actual price per pound}$$
$$\text{Direct materials price variance} = (Y - \$3.50) \times 42,000 = \$8,820$$
$$Y - \$3.50 = \$8,820 / 42,000$$
$$Y - \$3.50 = \$0.21$$
$$Y = \$3.71$$

23-5. Parkland, Inc., sells board games for $15.00, resulting in a contribution margin of $9.00 per game. Fixed costs are budgeted at $212,000 per quarter for volumes up to 30,000 games and $242,000 for volumes exceeding 30,000 games. (pp. 1158–1159)

Requirement

1. Prepare the flexible budget for the next quarter for volume levels of 25,000, 30,000, and 37,000 games.

PARKLAND, INC.
Flexible Budget
Year Ended December 31, 2010

	Flexible Budget per Output Unit	Output Units (games)		
		25,000	30,000	37,000
Sales revenue	$15.00	$375,000	$450,000	$555,000
Variable expenses	6.00	150,000	180,000	222,000
Fixed expenses		212,000	212,000	242,000
Total expenses		362,000	392,000	464,000
Operating income (loss)		$ 13,000	$ 58,000	$ 91,000

Do It Yourself! Question 1 Solutions

Requirements

1 Prepare a flexible budget for the income statement	**1. Using Fluffy's estimated budget values for costs and sales price, develop flexible budgets for 32,000, 34,000, and 36,000 beds.**

FLUFFY FOAM BEDS
Flexible Budget
Year Ended December 31, 2010

	Flexible Budget per Output Unit	Output Units (beds)		
		32,000	34,000	36,000
Sales revenue	$180	$5,760,000	$6,120,000	$6,480,000
Variable expenses	70	2,240,000	2,380,000	2,520,000
Fixed expenses		3,000,000	3,000,000	3,000,000
Total expenses		5,240,000	5,380,000	5,520,000
Operating income (loss)		$ 520,000	$ 740,000	$ 960,000

2 Prepare an income statement performance report	**2. Prepare Fluffy's income statement performance report for 2010.**

FLUFFY FOAM BEDS
Income Statement Performance Report
Year Ended December 31, 2010

	1	2	3	4	5
	Actual Results at Actual Prices	Flexible Budget Variance	Flexible Budget for Actual Number of Output Units	Sales Volume Variance	Static (Master) Budget
Output Units	34,200	0	34,200	2,200 F	32,000
Sales revenue	$6,327,000	$171,000 F	$6,156,000	$396,000 F	$5,760,000
Variable costs	2,565,000	171,000 U	2,394,000	154,000 U	2,240,000
Fixed costs	3,100,000	100,000 U	3,000,000	0	3,000,000
Total costs	5,665,000	271,000 U	5,394,000	154,000 U	5,240,000
Operating income	$ 662,000	$100,000 U	$ 762,000	242,000 U	520,000

Do It Yourself! Question 2 Solutions

Requirements

1. Compute the price and efficiency variances for direct materials and direct labor.

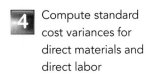
Compute standard cost variances for direct materials and direct labor

Direct Materials Price Variance

$$\begin{aligned} \text{Direct material price variance} &= (\text{Actual price} - \text{Standard price}) \times \text{Actual quantity} \\ &= (\$0.24 - \$0.25) \times (102 \times 88{,}000 \text{ units}) \\ &= \$89{,}760F \end{aligned}$$

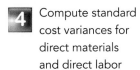
Compute standard cost variances for direct materials and direct labor

Direct Materials Efficiency Variance

$$\begin{aligned} \text{Direct materials quantity variance} &= (\text{Actual quantity} - \text{Standard quantity}) \times \text{Standard price} \\ &= [(102 \times 88{,}000) - (100 \times 88{,}000)] \times \$0.25 \\ &= \$44{,}000U \end{aligned}$$

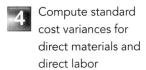
Compute standard cost variances for direct materials and direct labor

Direct Labor Rate Variance

$$\begin{aligned} \text{Direct labor rate variance} &= (\text{Actual rate} - \text{Standard rate}) \times \text{Actual hours} \\ &= (\$18.15 - \$18.00) \times 42{,}000 \text{ hours} \\ &= \$6{,}300U \end{aligned}$$

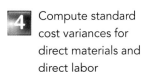
Compute standard cost variances for direct materials and direct labor

Direct Labor Efficiency Variance

$$\begin{aligned} \text{Direct labor efficiency variance} &= (\text{Actual hours} - \text{Standard hours}) \times \text{Standard price} \\ &= [42{,}000 - (0.50 \times 88{,}000)] \times \$18.00 \\ &= \$36{,}000F \end{aligned}$$

2. For manufacturing overhead, compute the total variance, the flexible variance, and the production volume variance.

Total Overhead Variance

$$\text{Total overhead variance} = \text{Actual overhead cost} - \text{Standard overhead allocated to production}$$
$$= \$980,000 - (88,000 \times \$12)$$
$$= \$76,000\text{F}$$

Overhead Flexible Budget Variance

$$\text{Overhead flexible budget variance} = \text{Actual overhead cost} - \text{Flexible budget overhead for the actual number of outputs}$$

$$= \$980,000 - [(88,000 \times \$2.00) + (80,000 \times \$10.00)]$$
$$= \$4,000\text{U}$$

Production Volume Variance

$$\text{Production volume variance} = \text{Flexible budget output for the actual number of outputs} - \text{Standard overhead allocated to actual production}$$
$$= \$976,000 - (\$12 \times 88,000)$$
$$= \$80,000\text{F}$$

The Power of Practice

For more practice using the skills learned in this chapter, visit MyAccountingLab. There you will find algorithmically generated questions that are based on these Demo Docs and your main textbook's Review and Assess Your Progress sections.

Go to MyAccountingLab and follow these steps:

1. Direct your URL to www.myaccountinglab.com.
2. Log in using your name and password.
3. Click the MyAccountingLab link.
4. Click Study Plan in the left navigation bar.
5. From the table of contents, select Chapter 23, Flexible Budgets and Standard Costs.
6. Click a link to work tutorial exercises.

24 Activity-Based Costing and Other Cost Management Tools

WHAT YOU PROBABLY ALREADY KNOW

Many colleges and universities charge a set amount of tuition for full-time students. It doesn't matter if students take 12 or 18 credits or if they are a Philosophy or Computer Science major. Is it fair that a Philosophy major taking 12 credits pays the same tuition as a Computer Science major taking 18 credits? You probably already know that Computer Science classes are held in a computer lab, which requires hardware and software and holds fewer students than a Philosophy classroom. Certainly more classes that are taken require more costs incurred by the institution for faculty and operating costs. It is clear that the number of credits and classroom support required by the nature of the course generates costs. It would be helpful for the college to know the real costs of each program. It could help the college make decisions to discontinue, reduce, or expand programs; curtail costs by understanding what drives the costs; and possibly even devise a tuition structure intended to pass program costs onto students more equitably. In this chapter, we will learn about activity-based costing (ABC). ABC is a system, as described, that assigns costs to products and services according to the action that causes the resources to be used. There are benefits to all entities to identify accurate costs of the goods and services they provide.

Learning Objectives

 Develop activity-based costs (ABC).

To develop an activity-based cost (ABC) system, the steps outlined in Exhibit 24-7 (p. 1209) must be performed. *Review Exhibit 24-3 (p. 1206) for examples of activities and cost drivers. An example of implementing the seven steps to develop an activity-based cost system is shown in Exhibit 24-7 (p. 1208). Be sure to study Exhibit 24-7 carefully to understand each step of the process.*

Use activity-based management (ABM) to make business decisions, including achieving target costs. **Activity-based management (ABM)** is the process of using activity-based costing information to make decisions that increase net income while satisfying the customers. ABC helps management make several different decisions:

- **Pricing and Product Mix**—ABC more accurately identifies product costs and consequently gross profit. Better decisions can then be made about pricing and the product mix.

- **Cutting Costs**—Identifying the cost drivers and all of the activities that are being used to manufacture the product also provides a clear understanding of what causes costs to be incurred. When companies need to cut costs, they are armed with more information as to how to cut costs or redesign the process to be more efficient.

- **Routine Planning and Control**—Management can use ABC information to create budgets and analyze variances in more detail by activities.

 Decide when ABC is most likely to pass the cost-benefit test.

The benefits of using ABC should exceed the cost of the system. ABC is usually more beneficial for companies in competitive markets because accurate costing and cost saving opportunities are critical. It is also usually beneficial to use ABC when there are products with different volumes, products requiring a varied amount of production activities, the overhead costs are materials, and the company has the electronic technology and human expertise to design and support the system.

 Describe a just-in-time (JIT) production system, and record its manufacturing costs.

A **JIT production system** obtains the required materials as needed to satisfy customer orders. The goal is to have what you need *when* you need it, a near-zero inventory level. The production takes place in work centers where employees work in a team to complete the manufacturing process.

Under JIT, the manufacturing accounting is somewhat different from job order and process costing systems. There is one account for Raw Materials Inventory and Work In Process Inventory called Raw and In Process Inventory. This account is debited for purchases of direct materials. Labor and overhead incurred are also recorded in one account, Conversion Costs. The Raw and In Process Inventory and Conversion Costs accounts are reduced (credited) for the products completed, which is debited to Finished Goods. *Review Exhibits 24-12 and 24-13 (pp. 1218–1220) for differences between the traditional and just-in-time costing.*

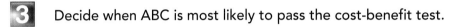 Contrast the four types of quality costs and use them to make decisions.

The four types of quality costs are as follows:

- **Prevention costs**—Costs incurred to avoid inferior quality goods or services

- **Appraisal costs**—Costs incurred to detect inferior quality goods or services

- **Internal failure costs**—Costs incurred to uncover and correct inferior quality goods or services before delivery to customers

- **External failure costs**—Costs incurred due to the lack of uncovering inferior quality goods or services until after they are delivered to customers

Review Exhibit 24-15 (p. 1222) for examples of the four types of quality costs.

Demo Doc 1

Activity-Based Costing

Learning Objectives 1, 2

Home Beauty uses activity-based costing to account for its concrete countertop manufacturing process. Company managers have identified three manufacturing activities: mold assembly, mixing, and finishing. The budgeted activity costs for the year and their allocation bases are as follows:

Activity	Total Budgeted Cost	Allocation Base
Mold assembly	$14,000	Number of parts
Mixing	$32,000	Number of batches
Finishing	$27,000	Number of direct labor hours

Home Beauty expects to produce 2,500 countertops during the year. The countertops are expected to use 10,000 parts, require 8,000 batches, and use 3,750 finishing hours.

Direct material cost is expected to be $40 per countertop and direct labor cost is expected to be $37.50 per countertop.

Requirements

1. Compute the cost allocation rate for each activity.

2. Compute the indirect manufacturing cost of each countertop.

3. Home Beauty would like to bid on selling 50 countertops to Ben Jones Builder. Assuming that Home Beauty requires a 30% markup on total costs, what bid price should Home Beauty use on the Ben Jones proposal?

Demo Doc 1 Solutions

Requirement 1

Compute the cost allocation rate for each activity.

Part 1	Part 2	Part 3	Demo Doc Complete

For Home Beauty, we have the first few steps in developing an ABC system based on the information given in the question:

Home Beauty identifies three manufacturing activities:	Home Beauty estimates the total budgeted cost for each activity:	The allocation base for each activity is the primary cost driver for each. Home Beauty identifies these:	Home Beauty estimates the quantities of each cost driver allocation base:
Mold assembly	$14,000	# of parts	10,000 parts
Mixing	$32,000	# of batches	8,000 batches
Finishing	$27,000	# of direct labor hours	3,750 direct labor hours

To compute the cost allocation rate for each activity, divide the total budgeted cost of each activity by the estimated total quantity of the cost driver's allocation base:

$$\frac{\text{Mold assembly cost}}{\text{allocation rate}} = \frac{\$14,000}{10,000 \text{ parts}} = \$1.40 \text{ per part}$$

$$\frac{\text{Mixing cost}}{\text{allocation rate}} = \frac{\$32,000}{8,000 \text{ batches}} = \$4.00 \text{ per batch}$$

$$\frac{\text{Finishing cost}}{\text{allocation rate}} = \frac{\$27,000}{3,750 \text{ direct labor hours}} = \$7.20 \text{ DL hour}$$

We will use the cost allocation *rate* for each activity to compute the indirect manufacturing cost of each countertop in the next requirement.

Requirement 2

Compute the indirect manufacturing cost of each countertop.

Part 1	Part 2	Part 3	Demo Doc Complete

To calculate the indirect cost of manufacturing each countertop, we must calculate the average *quantity* of each cost allocation base used per countertop. The average quantity of each cost allocation base used per countertop is calculated by dividing the expected total used of each base by the number of countertops Home Beauty expects to produce.

We know from the question that Home Beauty expects to produce 2,500 countertops during the year, requiring 10,000 parts, 8,000 mixing batches, and 3,750 direct labor hours per countertop. Calculations are as follows:

$$\text{Parts per countertop} = \frac{10,000}{2,500} = 4 \text{ parts per countertop}$$

$$\text{Batches per countertop} = \frac{8,000}{2,500} = 3.2 \text{ batches per countertop}$$

$$\text{Finishing hours per countertop} = \frac{3,750}{2,500} = 1.5 \text{ DL hours per countertop}$$

To compute the indirect manufacturing cost of each countertop, multiply the average quantity of each activity cost allocation base used per countertop by the cost allocation rate (as determined in requirement 1).

Activity	Actual Quantity of Cost Allocation Base Used per Countertop		Activity Cost Allocation Rate		Standard Activity Cost per Countertop
Mold assembly	4	×	$1.40	=	$ 5.60
Mixing	3.2	×	$4.00	=	$12.80
Finishing	1.5	×	$7.20	=	$10.80
Total Indirect Cost per Countertop					**$29.20**

Shown another way, you can also solve this using total costs. We know that:

Total assembly cost	= $14,000
Total mixing cost	= $32,000
Total finishing cost	= $27,000
Total indirect manufacturing cost	= $73,000

You can calculate the indirect manufacturing cost per countertop by summing the total costs and dividing by the number of countertops produced during the year:

Indirect manufacturing cost of each countertop = $73,000/2,500 = $29.20 per countertop

This is also a good way to check your work.

So Home Beauty estimates that each countertop will incur $29.20 in indirect manufacturing costs. This cost will help us compute the total cost of producing each countertop in the next requirement, which, among other decisions, helps management determine a sales price for each countertop.

Requirement 3

Home Beauty would like to bid on selling 50 countertops to Ben Jones Builder. Assuming that Home Beauty requires a 30% markup on total costs, what bid price should Home Beauty use on the Ben Jones proposal?

Part 1	Part 2	**Part 3**	Demo Doc Complete

To determine the bid price, Home Beauty must first determine the cost of producing one countertop. The cost would be direct materials + direct labor + indirect cost.

We know from the question that direct materials are expected to be $40 per countertop and direct labor is expected to be $37.50 per countertop. In requirement 2, we determined that indirect manufacturing costs amount to $29.20 per countertop. So, Home Beauty's cost of producing one countertop is:

$$\$40 + \$37.50 + \$29.20 = \$106.70 \text{ cost per countertop}$$

Because they require a 30% markup, the price that Home Beauty would charge per countertop is 130% of the cost:

$$\text{Price per countertop} = \$106.70 \times 130\% = \$138.71$$

Home Beauty is bidding on a job of 50 countertops, so the total bid price would be as follows:

$$\$138.71 \times 50 = \mathbf{\$6,935.50}$$

Again, shown another way, we can reach the same computation using total costs. We know from the question that direct material cost is expected to be $40 per countertop and direct labor cost is expected to be $37.50 per countertop. For 2,500 countertops, direct material costs = 2,500 × $40 = $100,000, and direct labor cost = 2,500 × $37.50 = $93,750. So our total costs are:

Total assembly cost	= $ 14,000
Total mixing cost	= $ 32,000
Total finishing cost	= $ 27,000
Direct material cost	= $100,000
Direct labor cost	= $ 93,750
Total cost	= $266,750

We then determine the cost per unit as total cost divided by the number of units:

$$\text{Cost per unit} = \$266,750/2,500 = \$106.70 \text{ cost per countertop}$$

This matches the cost per countertop computed earlier in this requirement. Calculations would continue as before:

Price per countertop	= $106.70 × 130% markup	= $ 138.71
Total bid price	= $138.71 × 50 bids	= $6,935.50

This is also a good way to check your work.

Part 1	Part 2	Part 3	**Demo Doc Complete**

Demo Doc 2

Other Cost Management Tools

Learning Objective 4

Healthy Heart manufactures smoothie mix for franchised retail outlets. Healthy Heart uses JIT costing. The standard unit cost of producing a case of smoothie mix is $8: $5 for direct materials and $3 for conversion costs. Direct materials purchased on account during April totaled $120,000. Actual conversion costs totaled $75,900. Healthy Heart completed 25,000 cases of smoothie mix during April and sold 24,000 cases.

Requirements

1. Prepare the April journal entries for the transactions.

2. Make the entry to close the under- or overallocated conversion costs to Cost of Goods Sold.

Demo Doc 2 Solutions

Requirement 1

4 Use the four types of quality costs to make decisions

Prepare the April journal entries for the transactions.

Part 1	Part 2	Demo Doc Complete

Companies that use a JIT system do not use a separate Work in Process Inventory account. Instead, they use two inventory accounts: Raw and In Process Inventory and Finished Goods Inventory.

The Raw and In Process Inventory account combines direct materials with work in process.

Purchases of direct material will require a debit (increase) to the Raw and In Process Inventory account.

In this case, Healthy Heart purchased $120,000 of direct materials on account in April. So the two accounts affected are Raw and In Process Inventory and Accounts Payable.

For the purchase of direct material, Healthy Heart will make the following journal entry:

Raw and In Process Inventory	120,000	
Accounts Payable		120,000

Under the JIT philosophy, workers perform many tasks. Because little labor is directly traceable to individual finished products, most companies using JIT combine labor and manufacturing overhead costs into an account called Conversion Costs.

The Conversion Costs account is a temporary account that works like the Manufacturing Overhead account.

To record the actual conversion costs, Healthy Heart will make the following journal entry:

Conversion Costs	75,900	
Various Accounts (wages payable, accumulated depreciation, and so forth)		75,900

The Various Accounts used as credits will depend on the conversion cost incurred (for example, labor → wages payable, depreciation → accumulated depreciation, utilities → accounts payable).

Goods completed are recorded at the standard cost of completing those goods.

The total cost of the finished goods is calculated by multiplying the total units completed, 25,000, by the standard cost of $8 per unit ($5 for direct materials and $3 for conversion costs) = $200,000.

Raw and In Process Inventory is credited for the standard direct material cost of the units completed:

25,000 units completed × $5 direct materials cost = $125,000

Conversion Costs is credited (increased) for the standard conversion cost of the units completed:

25,000 units completed × $3,000 conversion costs = $75,000

Healthy Heart will make the following journal entry for the 25,000 units completed:

Finished Goods Inventory (25,000 units × $8)	200,000	
Raw and In Process Inventory (25,000 × $5)		125,000
Conversion Costs (25,000 × $3)		75,000

Goods sold are recorded at the standard cost of completing the goods.

Healthy Heart sold 24,000 units with a standard cost of $8 per unit. The units sold will be recorded at a cost of $192,000:

Cost of Goods Sold	192,000	
Finished Goods Inventory		192,000

Remember, this is not recording the sales revenue, but rather Healthy Heart's costs associated with the number of cases of smoothie mix that it sold.

Requirement 2

4 Use the four types of quality costs to make decisions

Make the entry to close the under- or overallocated conversion costs to Cost of Goods Sold.

Part 1	**Part 2**	Demo Doc Complete

Just like under- and overallocated manufacturing overhead, under- or overallocated conversion costs are closed to Cost of Goods Sold at the end of the period.

Healthy Heart had actual conversion costs of $75,900 (debit) and standard conversion costs (from requirement 1) of $75,000 (credit), therefore conversion costs were underallocated.

A debit of $75,900 and a credit of $75,000 yields a credit (decrease) of $900. Healthy Heart will make the following journal entry to close the Conversion Costs account:

Cost of Goods Sold	900	
Conversion Costs		900

Part 1	Part 2	**Demo Doc Complete**

Quick Practice Questions

True/False

_____ 1. ABC costing is generally less accurate than traditional cost systems.

_____ 2. ABC systems take more effort to allocate indirect costs to products that caused the costs than do traditional cost systems.

_____ 3. The target price is what manufacturers are willing to pay to produce a product.

_____ 4. Activity-based management refers to using activity-based cost information to make decisions that increase profits while satisfying customers' needs.

_____ 5. Appraisal costs occur when poor-quality goods or services are not detected until after delivery to customers.

_____ 6. Internal failure costs occur to avoid poor-quality goods or services.

_____ 7. The cost allocation rate for each activity is equal to the estimated total indirect costs of the activity divided by the estimated total quantity of cost allocation base.

_____ 8. Overhead costs incurred are recorded in the Conversion Cost account.

_____ 9. Just-in-time costing means systematically evaluating activities in an effort to reduce costs while satisfying customers' needs.

_____10. The goal of total quality management is to provide customers with superior products and services.

Multiple Choice

1. The cost of training personnel is an example of which of the following types of cost?
   a. Internal failure cost
   b. External failure cost
   c. Prevention cost
   d. Appraisal cost

2. Which of the following is most likely to be the cost driver for the packaging and shipping activity?
   a. Number of orders
   b. Number of components
   c. Number of setups
   d. Hours of testing

3. What is the last step in developing an ABC system?
   a. Identify the activities
   b. Allocate costs to the cost object
   c. Estimate the total quantity of the cost driver
   d. Estimate the total indirect costs of each activity

4. Which of the following statements regarding activity-based costing systems is false?
   a. ABC systems can create more accurate product costs.
   b. ABC systems may only be used by service companies.
   c. ABC systems are more complex and costly than traditional systems.
   d. ABC systems are used in both manufacturing and nonmanufacturing companies.

5. Alpha Company manufactures breadboxes and uses an activity-based costing system. The following information is provided for the month of May:

Activity	Estimated Indirect Activity Costs	Allocation Base	Estimated Quantity of Allocation Base
Materials handling	$ 3,500	Number of parts	5,000 parts
Assembling	$12,000	Number of parts	5,000 parts
Packaging	$ 5,750	Number of breadboxes	1,250 breadboxes

   Each breadbox consists of 4 parts and the direct materials cost per breadbox is $7.00.

   What is the cost of materials handling and assembling per breadbox?
   a. $ 4.60
   b. $12.40
   c. $14.40
   d. $17.00

6. Refer to question 5. What is the total manufacturing cost per breadbox?
   a. $12.40
   b. $17.40
   c. $24.00
   d. $26.00

7. The cost of inspection at various stages of production is an example of which of the following?
   a. Appraisal cost
   b. Prevention cost
   c. Internal failure cost
   d. External failure cost

8. The process of designing products that achieve cost targets and meet specified standards of quality and performance is referred to as which of the following?
   a. Value engineering
   b. Developmental engineering
   c. Design engineering
   d. Total engineering

9. Which of the following is true for a JIT production system?
    a. JIT requires longer setup times than a traditional production system
    b. JIT produces goods in smaller batches than a traditional production system
    c. JIT has like machines grouped together in the production facility
    d. JIT requires higher inventory levels

10. What are the lost profits from the loss of customers called?
    a. Prevention cost
    b. Internal failure cost
    c. Appraisal cost
    d. External failure cost

Quick Exercises

24-1. Compare and contrast activity-based costing with traditional systems using a single application base for conversion costs.

24-2. Dream Sewing Machine Company uses activity-based costing to account for its manufacturing process. Following are the four activities identified with the process and their budgeted costs for the month of December:

Activity	Total Budgeted Cost	Allocation Base
Materials handling	$58,000	Number of parts
Machine setup	14,500	Number of setups
Assembling	24,000	Number of parts
Packaging	8,400	Number of finished units

Dream expects to produce 1,000 sewing machines in the month of December. The sewing machines are expected to use 25,000 parts and require 15 setups.

Requirements

1. Compute the cost allocation rate for each activity.

2. Compute the average manufacturing cost of each sewing machine assuming direct materials are $175 per machine.

24-3. Fine Hair Corporation manufactures two models of a curling iron: a standard model and a deluxe model. Using activity-based costing, three activities have been identified as cost drivers. These activities, as well as the estimated total cost associated with them for the month of December, are shown as follows:

	(1) Number of Materials Requisitions	(2) Number of Product Inspections	(3) Number of Orders Shipped
Standard	460	150	167
Deluxe	620	210	129
Estimated total activity cost	$26,500	$11,100	$19,000

Requirement

1. Determine the amount of each cost pool applied for the (a) standard model and (b) deluxe model.

24-4. Compare and contrast the major features of a just-in-time production system with a traditional production system.

24-5. Identify each of the following as a prevention cost, an appraisal cost, an internal failure cost, or an external failure cost.

a. Service costs at customer sites _____
b. Costs of designing the product _____
c. Salaries of the service department personnel who handle repairs under warranty _____
d. The cost of reworking defective product _____
e. Salaries of receiving department employees responsible for inspecting all purchased parts and materials _____
f. Lost profits from customers who did not place an order due to lack of availability of product _____
g. Salaries of the employees who inspect the final product _____
h. Maintenance costs incurred to keep the production machinery operating at full capacity _____
i. Cost of two-week training course for new employees _____
j. Customer returns due to defective merchandise _____

Do It Yourself! Question 1

Activity-Based Costing

Grand Slam uses activity-based costing to account for its baseball pitching machine manufacturing process. Company managers have identified three manufacturing activities: purchasing, assembly, and finishing. The budgeted activity costs for the year and their allocation bases are as follows:

Activity	Total Budgeted Cost	Allocation Base
Purchasing	$16,000	Number of purchase orders
Assembly	$40,000	Number of parts
Finishing	$22,000	Number of direct labor hours

Grand Slam expects to produce 1,000 pitching machines during the year. The machines are expected to require a total of 400 purchase orders, 50,000 parts, and 4,000 finishing hours.

Direct material cost is expected to be $160 per machine and direct labor cost is expected to be $80 per machine.

Requirements

1. Compute the cost allocation rate for each activity.

Purchasing cost allocation rate	=
Assembly cost allocation rate	=
Finishing cost allocation rate	=

2. Compute the indirect manufacturing cost of each machine.

Activity	Actual Quantity of Cost Allocation Base Used per Machine	Activity Cost Allocation Rate	Standard Activity Cost per Machine
Purchasing			
Assembly			
Finishing			
Total Indirect Cost per Machine			

3. Grand Slam would like to bid on selling 40 pitching machines to Pirate Family Fun Park. Assuming that Grand Slam requires a 25% markup, what bid price should Grand Slam use on the Pirate proposal?

Do It Yourself! Question 2

Other Cost Management Tools

Back to Life reconditions automobile batteries. Back to Life uses JIT costing. The standard unit cost of reconditioning a battery is $9: $4 for direct materials and $5 for conversion costs. Direct materials purchased on account during November totaled $62,000. Actual conversion costs totaled $78,000. Back to Life reconditioned 15,000 batteries during November and sold 14,000 batteries.

Requirements

1. Prepare the November journal entries for the transactions.

Date	Accounts	Debit	Credit

Date	Accounts	Debit	Credit

Date	Accounts	Debit	Credit

Date	Accounts	Debit	Credit

2. Make the entry to close the under- or overallocated Conversion Costs to Cost of Goods Sold.

Date	Accounts	Debit	Credit

Quick Practice Solutions

True/False

F   1. ABC costing is generally less accurate than traditional cost systems.

> False—ABC costing is generally *more* accurate than traditional cost systems. (p. 1209)

T   2. ABC systems take more effort to allocate indirect costs to products that caused the costs than do traditional costing systems. (p. 1208)

F   3. The target price is what manufacturers are willing to pay to produce a procuct.

> False—The target price is what *customers are willing to pay* for the products or service. (p. 1211)

T   4. Activity-based management refers to using activity-based cost information to make decisions that increase profits while satisfying customers' needs. (p. 1210)

F   5. Appraisal costs occur when poor-quality goods or services are not detected until after delivery to customers.

> False—*External failure costs* occur when poor-quality goods or services are not detected until after delivery to customers. (p. 1221)

F   6. Internal failure costs occur to avoid poor-quality goods or services.

> False—*Preventive costs* occur to avoid poor-quality goods or services. (p. 1210)

T   7. The cost allocation rate for each activity is equal to the estimated total indirect costs of the activity divided by the estimated total quantity of cost allocation base. (p. 1206)

T   8. Overhead costs incurred are recorded in the Conversion Cost account. (p. 1217)

F   9. Just-in-time costing means systematically evaluating activities in an effort to reduce costs while satisfying customers' needs.

> False—*Value engineering costing* means systematically evaluating activities in an effort to reduce costs while satisfying customers' needs. (p. 1211)

T 10. The goal of total quality management is to provide customers with superior products and services. (p. 1221)

Multiple Choice

1. **The cost of training personnel is an example of which of the following types of cost?** (p. 1222)
   a. Internal failure cost
   b. External failure cost
   c. Prevention cost
   d. Appraisel cost

2. Which of the following is most likely to be the cost driver for the packaging and shipping activity? (pp. 1205–1206)
   a. Number of orders
   b. Number of components
   c. Number of setups
   d. Hours of testing

3. What is the last step in developing an ABC system? (p. 1209)
   a. Identify the activities
   b. Allocate costs to the cost object
   c. Estimate the total quantity of the cost driver
   d. Estimate the total indirect costs of each activity

4. Which of the following statements regarding activity-based costing systems is false? (p. 1205)
   a. ABC systems can create more accurate product costs.
   b. ABC systems may only be used by service companies.
   c. ABC systems are more complex and costly than traditional systems.
   d. ABC systems are used in both manufacturing and non-manufacturing companies.

5. Alpha Company manufactures breadboxes and uses an activity-based costing system. The following information is provided for the month of May:

Activity	Estimated Indirect Activity Costs	Allocation Base	Estimated Quantity of Allocation Base
Materials handling	$ 3,500	Number of parts	5,000 parts
Assembling	$12,000	Number of parts	5,000 parts
Packaging	$ 5,750	Number of breadboxes	1,250 breadboxes

Each breadbox consists of 4 parts and the direct materials cost per breadbox is $7.00.

What is the cost of materials handling and assembling per breadbox? (pp. 1205–1206)
   a. $ 4.60
   b. $12.40
   c. $14.40
   d. $17.00

6. Refer to question 5. What is the total manufacturing cost per breadbox? (pp. 1205–1206)
   a. $12.40
   b. $17.40
   c. $24.00
   d. $26.00

7. The cost of inspection at various stages of production is an example of which of the following? (p. 1222)
   a. Appraisal cost
   b. Prevention cost
   c. Internal failure cost
   d. External failure cost

8. The process of designing products that achieve cost targets and meet specified standards of quality and performance is referred to as which of the following? (p. 1211)
   a. Value engineering
   b. Developmental engineering
   c. Design engineering
   d. Total engineering

9. Which of the following is true for a JIT production system? (p. 1217)
   a. JIT requires longer setup times than a traditional production system
   b. JIT produces goods in smaller batches than a traditional production system
   c. JIT has like machines grouped together in the production facility
   d. JIT requires higher inventory levels

10. What are the lost profits from the loss of customers called? (p. 1222)
    a. Prevention cost
    b. Internal failure cost
    c. Appraisal cost
    d. External failure cost

Quick Exercises

24-1. Compare and contrast activity-based costing with traditional systems using a single application base for conversion costs. (pp. 1205–1208)

Activity-based costing (ABC) is a system that focuses on activities as the fundamental cost objects. The activity costs are the foundation for accumulating the indirect costs of products, services, and customers. ABC systems allocate the indirect costs of manufacturing overhead to the products, services, or customers based on what caused them, the cost drivers. Each cost driver is selected for its causal relationship to an activity. The more precise the relationship, the more accurate the product cost. This method gives managers better information for decision making. In addition, developments in information technology make ABC less costly than before and much more feasible.

Single-rate costing applies indirect costs to products on the basis of a single allocation base, historically direct labor. This method is simpler than ABC and less costly. However, no single factor drives all indirect manufacturing costs. Thus, this method may distort the cost of products.

24-2. Dream Sewing Machine Company uses activity-based costing to account for its manufacturing process. Following are the four activities identified with the process and their budgeted costs for the month of December: (pp. 1206–1209)

Activity	Total Budgeted Cost	Allocation Base
Materials handling	$58,000	Number of parts
Machine setup	14,500	Number of setups
Assembling	24,000	Number of parts
Packaging	8,400	Number of finished units

Dream expects to produce 1,000 sewing machines in the month of December. The sewing machines are expected to use 25,000 parts and require 15 setups.

Requirements

1. Compute the cost allocation rate for each activity.

$58,000 / 25,000 parts = $2.32

$14,500 / 15 setups = $966.67

$24,000 / 25,000 parts = $0.96

$ 8,400 / 1,000 finished units = $8.40

2. Compute the average manufacturing cost of each sewing machine assuming direct materials are $175 per machine.

25,000 / 1,000 = 25 parts × $2.32 = $58.00

15 / 1,000 = 0.015 setups × $966.67 = $14.50

25,000 / 1,000 = 25 parts × $0.96 = $24.00

1,000 / 1,000 = 1 unit × $8.40 = $8.40

$58.00 + $14.50 + $24.00 + $8.40 + $175.00 = $279.90

24-3. Fine Hair Corporation manufactures two models of a curling iron: a standard model and a deluxe model. Using activity-based costing, three activities have been identified as cost drivers. These activities, as well as the estimated total cost associated with them for the month of December, are shown below: (pp. 1205–1206)

	(1) Number of Materials Requisitions	(2) Number of Product Inspections	(3) Number of Orders Shipped
Standard	460	150	167
Deluxe	620	210	129
Estimated total activity cost	$26,500	$11,100	$19,000

Requirement

1. Determine the amount of each cost pool applied for the (a) standard model and (b) deluxe model.

Materials requisitions:

(a) $460 + 620 = 1,080$
    $460 / 1,080 \times \$26,500 = \$11,287$ standard
(b) $620 / 1,080 \times \$26,500 = \$15,213$ deluxe

Product inspections:

(a) $150 + 210 = 360$
    $150 / 360 \times \$11,100 = \$4,625$ standard
(b) $210/360 \times \$11,100 = \$6,475$ deluxe

Orders shipped:

(a) $167 + 129 = 296$
    $167 / 296 \times \$19,000 = \$10,720$ standard
(b) $129 / 296 \times \$19,000 = \$8,280$ deluxe

24-4. **Compare and contrast the major features of a just-in-time production system with a traditional production system.** (pp. 1217–1219)

Traditional production systems often produce enormous waste in two specific areas: inventories and manufacturing processes. Inventories are maintained at high levels to guard against poor quality in raw materials, poor quality in production, machine breakdowns, long setup times on production equipment, and stock outs. However, large inventories tie up cash and hide production problems. Manufacturing processes set up machines according to function, causing raw materials and parts to travel long distances back and forth through a factory. Machines are kept busy, resulting in product being pushed through the system, regardless of downstream demand.

Just-in-time production systems have the following characteristics:

1. Production activities are arranged by the sequence of operations, reducing moving time.
2. Machine setup times are reduced through employee training and new technology.
3. Production is scheduled in small batches just in time to satisfy needs.
4. Employees are trained to do more than operate a single machine.

24-5. **Identify each of the following as a prevention cost, an appraisal cost, an internal failure cost, or an external failure cost.** (p. 1221–1222)

   a. Service costs at customer sites
     external failure cost

   b. Costs of designing the product
     prevention cost

   c. Salaries of the service department personnel who handle repairs under warranty
     external failure cost

   d. The cost of reworking defective product
     internal failure cost

   e. Salaries of receiving department employees responsible for inspecting all purchased parts and materials
     appraisal cost

   f. Lost profits from customers who did not place an order due to lack of availability of product
     external failure cost

   g. Salaries of the employees who inspect the final product
     appraisal cost

   h. Maintenance costs incurred to keep the production machinery operating at full capacity
     prevention cost

   i Cost of two-week training course for new employees
     prevention cost

   j. Customer returns due to defective merchandise
     external failure cost

Do It Yourself! Question 1 Solutions

Develop activity-
based costs (ABC)

Requirements

1. Compute the cost allocation rate for each activity.

$$\frac{\text{Purchasing cost}}{\text{allocation rate}} = \frac{\$16,000}{400 \text{ purchase orders}} = \textbf{\$40.00} \text{ per purchase order}$$

$$\frac{\text{Assembly cost}}{\text{allocation rate}} = \frac{\$40,000}{50,000 \text{ parts}} = \textbf{\$ 0.80} \text{ per part}$$

$$\frac{\text{Finishing cost}}{\text{allocation rate}} = \frac{\$22,000}{4,000 \text{ direct labor hours}} = \textbf{\$ 5.50} \text{ per direct labor hour}$$

2. Compute the indirect manufacturing cost of each machine.

Develop activity-
based costs (ABC)

$$\frac{\text{Purchase orders per}}{\text{machine}} = \frac{400 \text{ purchase orders}}{1,000 \text{ machines}} = \textbf{0.4} \text{ purchase orders per machine}$$

$$\text{Parts per machine} = \frac{50,000 \text{ parts}}{1,000 \text{ machines}} = 50 \text{ parts per machine}$$

$$\frac{\text{Finishing hours per}}{\text{machine}} = \frac{4,000 \text{ direct labor hours}}{1,000 \text{ machines}} = 4 \text{ direct labor hours per machine}$$

Activity	Actual Quantity of Cost Allocation Base Used per Machine		Activity Cost Allocation Rate		Standard Activity Cost per Machine
Purchasing	0.4	×	$40.00	=	$16
Assembly	50	×	$ 0.80	=	40
Finishing	4	×	$ 5.50	=	22
Total Indirect Cost per Machine					$78

3. Grand Slam would like to bid on selling 40 pitching machines to Pirate Family Fun Park. Assuming that Grand Slam requires a 25% markup, what bid price should Grand Slam use on the Pirate proposal?

Direct materials + Direct labor + Indirect manufacturing cost = Cost per machine

Cost = $160 + $80 + $78 = $318 per machine

Cost per machine × Markup = Sales price per machine:

$318 × 125% = $397.50 per machine

Total bid for 40 machines:

$397.50 × 40 machines = $15,900 total bid

Do It Yourself! Question 2 Solutions

Requirements

 Use the four types of quality costs to make decisions

1. Prepare the November journal entries for the transactions.

Date	Accounts and Explanation	Debit	Credit
	Raw and In Process Inventory	62,000	
	Accounts Payable		62,000

Date	Accounts and Explanation	Debit	Credit
	Conversion Conversion Costs	78,000	
	Various Accounts (wages payable, accumulated depreciation, and so forth)		78,000

Date	Accounts and Explanation	Debit	Credit
	Finished Goods Inventory	135,000	
	Raw and In Process Inventory		60,000
	Conversion Costs		75,000

Date	Accounts and Explanation	Debit	Credit
	Cost of Goods Sold	126,000	
	Finished Goods Inventory		126,000

Use the four types of quality costs to make decisions

2. Make the entry to close the under- or overallocated Conversion Costs to Cost of Goods Sold.

Date	Accounts and Explanation	Debit	Credit
	Cost of Goods Sold	3,000	
	Conversion Costs		3,000

The Power of Practice

For more practice using the skills learned in this chapter, visit MyAccountingLab. There you will find algorithmically generated questions that are based on these Demo Docs and your main textbook's Review and Assess Your Progress sections.

Go to MyAccountingLab and follow these steps:

1. Direct your URL to www.myaccountinglab.com.
2. Log in using your name and password.
3. Click the MyAccountingLab link.
4. Click Study Plan in the left navigation bar.
5. From the table of contents, select Chapter 24, Activity-Based Costing and Other Cost Management Tools.
6. Click a link to work tutorial exercises.

25 Special Business Decisions and Capital Budgeting

WHAT YOU PROBABLY ALREADY KNOW

People purchase lottery tickets in the hopes of winning the grand jackpot. On November 15, 2005, seven employees of a medical center won the Mega Millions grand prize of $315,000,000. Winners can choose to receive the money in 26 equal payments over the upcoming 25 years or in a lump sum. The seven winners decided to take a lump-sum payment. You probably already know that opting for the lump-sum payment means that something less than $315,000,000 is received. The reason for that is the time value of money. Receiving a dollar now is worth more than receiving it in a year, 5 years, or 25 years in the future. The winnings are "discounted," reduced to the present value. The seven winners received $187,100,000. In this chapter, we will study how to calculate the present value of future cash flows and how that information is used to help management make decisions.

Learning Objectives

  Identify the relevant information for a special business decision.

To make business decisions, management will compare relevant information between alternative courses of action. Relevant information includes items that will differ between alternatives and be incurred in the future. Relevant information therefore affects the decisions that are made.

  Make five types of short-term special business decisions.

Some short-term special business decisions that management makes include accepting a special sales order (*see Exhibit 25-4, p. 1255*), dropping a business segment (*see* Exhibits 25-5 *through 25-7, pp. 1256–1257*), which product to emphasize in a product mix (*see Exhibit 25-8, p. 1258, and Summary Problem 1*), when to outsource production (*see Exhibits 25-9 and 25-10, p. 1260, and Summary Problem 2*), and selling as is or processing further (*see Exhibit 25-12, p. 1262*). You will explore these types of decisions in Demo Doc 1.

In terms of product mix, **a constraint** is something that restricts the production or sale of a product, such as labor hours, machine hours, or available materials. Given sufficient demand, the products that generate the highest contribution margin *per constrained resource* will maximize operating income.

When deciding to sell a product as is or process it further, management should consider the **split-off point**, which is the point at which the product is complete and can be sold or continues to be processed further and then sold after incurring more costs. The analysis compares the revenue from selling the product as it is to the higher revenue less additional costs from selling the product after processing further. Whichever option results in a higher net revenue is the more profitable alternative.

3 Use payback and accounting rate of return models to make longer-term capital budgeting decisions.

The decision to purchase a long-term asset is referred to as capital budgeting. The focus of capital budgeting is on the net cash inflows that are projected in the future. One tool that is used to assess capital investments is the payback period. The **payback period** is the amount of time it takes to recover the initial investment. You will calculate the payback period for two different products in Demo Doc 2. *Review Exhibit 25-13 (p. 1267) for an illustration of the payback period concept.*

You can use the **accounting rate of return** to determine the rate of return from an asset over its useful life. You will calculate the accounting rate of return for two different products in Demo Doc 2.

The average annual operating income can be computed as the net cash inflow from the asset less depreciation expense. The average amount invested in the asset is the average of the cost amount and the residual value. *Review Exhibit 25-14 (p. 1269) for an accounting rate of return calculation.*

4 Use discounted cash flow models to make longer-term capital budgeting decisions.

Discounted cash flow models use the concept of **present value** or the **time value of money**. This simply means that it is more valuable to receive money now than in the future. To make the best capital budgeting decision, the value of future cash flows must be considered in terms of the current or present value. The discounted cash flow models widely used to evaluate potential expenditures are the **net present value** and the **internal rate of return (IRR)**. You will explore these methods in Demo Doc 2. *Review Exhibit 25-16 (p. 1271) for a computation of the net present value method assuming equal net cash inflows and Exhibit 25-18 (p. 1273) assuming unequal net cash inflows.*

5 Compare and contrast the four capital budgeting methods.

- **Payback period**—This is a simple method to employ, but it does not consider the project profitability or the time value of money.

- **Accounting rate of return**—This is a measure of profitability, but it does not consider the time value of money.

- **Net present value (NPV)**—NPV considers the time value of money, but it does not indicate what the projected rate of return is for the investment.

- **Internal rate of return (IRR)**—IRR considers the time value of money. The IRR determines the project's rate, but does not indicate the dollar difference between the project's present value and its investment cost.

Review Exhibit 25-20 (p. 1275) for a summary of the strengths and weaknesses of the payback period, accounting rate of return, NPV, and IRR methods.

Demo Doc 1

Special Business Decisions _____

Doctor Key produces key blanks. A Kenya company has offered to purchase 2,000 cases of keys at a per-unit price of $30. Assume selling to the Kenya company will not affect regular customers, will not change fixed costs, will not require any additional variable nonmanufacturing expenses, and will use manufacturing capacity that would otherwise be idle.

DOCTOR KEY	
Income Statement (without considering the special sale)	
Sales revenue (35,000 cases @ $38.00 per case)	$1,330,000
Less manufacturing cost of goods sold	800,000
Gross profit	$ 530,000
Less marketing and administrative expenses	410,000
Operating income	$ 120,000

Requirement 1

Assuming $500,000 of the manufacturing costs is fixed and $200,000 of the marketing and administrative costs is fixed, should Doctor accept the order from the Kenya company?

Pack-It has offered to package the key blanks for Doctor Key. Currently, Doctor packages the product themselves at the following per-case costs:

Direct materials	$30,000
Direct labor	55,000
Variable overhead	5,000
Fixed overhead	15,000
Total manufacturing cost	105,000
Cost per case ($105,000/35,000)	$ 3.00

Requirement 2

Pack-It's price per case is $2.80. Doctor would avoid all variable costs associated with the packaging and would reduce the fixed cost by $5,000 if Pack-It packages Doctor's key blanks. Should Doctor outsource the packaging work to Pack-It?

Of Doctor's 35,000 case sales, 3,000 cases are for a special blue-colored key made for one customer. The blue key sells for the same price, $38, as all the other keys, but seems to require more expenses to produce. Doctor is considering dropping the blue key. An analysis has determined that the variable cost of producing the blue key is $20 per case. If the blue key was not produced, fixed costs would not change.

Requirement 3

Should Doctor stop producing the blue key?

Demo Doc 1 Solutions

Requirement 1

1 Identify the relevant information for a special business decision

2 Make five types of short-term special decisions

Assuming $500,000 of the manufacturing costs is fixed and $200,000 of the marketing and administrative costs is fixed, should Doctor accept the order from the Kenya company?

| **Part 1** | Part 2 | Part 3 | Demo Doc Complete |

The key to this problem is to determine what effect the special sale would have on Doctor's operating income. Fixed costs will not change as a result of the sale; therefore, we will compare only the change in revenue with the change in variable costs as a result of the special sale. The decision to accept a special order will be made if the incremental revenues exceed the incremental expenses for the special order.

The increase in revenue is determined by multiplying the additional cases sold, 2,000, by the offered selling price per case of $30. Thus, the increase in revenue will be $60,000.

To determine the variable cost of producing the additional 2,000 units, we must first determine the variable cost per unit. The manufacturing cost of producing 35,000 cases was $800,000. Of the $800,000, fixed cost makes up $500,000. Therefore, manufacturing variable cost is $300,000. The variable marketing and administrative cost is determined by subtracting the fixed portion, $200,000, from the total marketing and administrative cost of $410,000, to get variable marketing and administrative cost of $210,000. Thus, the total variable cost of producing the 35,000 cases is:

$$\$300,000 + \$210,000 = \$510,000$$

The variable cost per unit is computed by dividing the total variable cost, $510,000, by the 35,000 cases, which equals $14.57 per case.

The increase in variable cost with the special sales order is:

$$2,000 \text{ cases} \times \text{ the variable cost per unit of } \$14.57 = \$29,140$$

Incremental Analysis of Special Sales Order

Increase in revenues:	
Sale of 2,000 cases × $30 per case	$60,000
Increase in variable expenses:	
2,000 cases × $14.57	29,140
Increase in operating income	$30,860

Creating a profit of $15.43 per case ($30,860 / 2,000 cases)

Doctor should **accept** the special order because it would increase operating income!

Requirement 2

1 Identify the relevant information for a special business decision

2 Make five types of short-term special decisions

Pack-It's price per case is $2.80. Doctor would avoid all variable costs associated with the packaging and would reduce the fixed cost by $5,000 if Pack-It packages Doctor's key blanks. Should Doctor outsource the packaging work to Pack-It?

| Part 1 | **Part 2** | Part 3 | Demo Doc Complete |

Outsourcing decisions consider whether management will make or buy (outsource) their products or services. Incremental analysis can be performed comparing (1) the cost to make the product, which includes direct materials, direct labor, and overhead to (2) the cost to buy, which includes the purchase price plus possibly some portion of the fixed overhead that will continue with outsourcing.

In addition, there may be a relevant opportunity cost. An **opportunity cost** represents the benefit forgone by not choosing an alternative course of action. If the production process is outsourced and the goods are purchased, there may be opportunities to use the idle resources to generate profits. The opportunity cost reduces the cost of outsourcing.

In this case, the key to this decision is to compare the Doctor's cost savings of not packaging their keys with the additional cost charged by Pack-It. On the surface, it might seem that Pack-It is making an attractive offer to package the key blanks for $0.20 cheaper per case than Doctor spends to package the key blanks themselves.

But an incremental analysis is necessary to consider the overall effects of total costs and savings on the make or buy decision.

The following shows the differences in costs between making and outsourcing (buying) the packaging:

Packaging Costs	Make	Buy	Difference
Direct materials	$ 30,000		$ 30,000
Direct labor	55,000		55,000
Variable factory overhead	5,000		5,000
Avoidable fixed costs	15,000	10,000	5,000
Purchase cost from Pack-It (35,000 units × $2.80 per unit)		98,000	(98,000)
Total cost of packaging	$105,000	$108,000	$ (3,000)
Cost per unit (divide by 35,000 cases)	$ 3.00	$ 3.09*	$ (0.09)

Rounded

This analysis makes it clear that the fixed costs have an impact on this decision. In this case, Doctor will incur that $10,000 in fixed costs whether it outsources the packaging to Pack-It or packages their own key blanks. This puts the total cost for the 35,000 cases at $3,000 higher if Doctor decided to outsource the packaging to Pack-It.

So it would make sense for Doctor to continue packaging its own product.

Requirement 3

1 | Identify the relevant information for a special business decision

2 | Make five types of short-term special decisions

Should Doctor stop producing the blue key?

As in this case, management may want to consider if discontinuing a product line, department, or component of the business would increase the operating income. The decision to eliminate a business segment may be made if dropping the segment will result in a decrease in total expenses *greater* than the decrease in revenues.

In this case, fixed costs remain the same whether or not the blue key product line is dropped; therefore, fixed costs are not relevant to the decision. Only the revenues and variable expenses are relevant.

Segment margin is calculated as:

	Sales
	Sales
Less	Variable costs
Yields	Contribution margin
Less	Discretionary fixed costs
Yields	Segment margin

In the absence of any discretionary fixed costs, contribution margin is the criteria if a product or product line should be dropped.

If the blue key product line is dropped, revenues will decrease by:

$$\text{Revenue} \quad 3,000 \times \$38 = (\$114,000)$$

Variable costs will decrease as well:

$$3,000 \times \$20 = (\$60,000)$$

Contribution margin will decrease as well:

$$3,000 \times \$18 = (\$54,000)$$

As cost savings of $60,000 are realized, and this is really a "negative" cost, then the "income" generated from dropping this line is $60,000.

The actual revenue generated from having this line is $114,000.

$114,000 is greater than $60,000 (a $54,000 difference); therefore, the company is better off by NOT dropping this product.

A decision rule might be: If the actual revenue of the product *exceeds* the cost savings (in reduced costs, either variable or fixed or both), then the product should *not* be dropped.

Demo Doc 2

Capital Budgeting

Yummy Eats produces packaged food products. They desire to produce one of two possible new products: either yogurt or cottage cheese. Each product would require an additional investment of $400,000. Yogurt would have a useful life of six years, with no residual value and cottage cheese would have a useful life of four years, with no residual value. The expected annual net cash inflows is as follows:

	Net Cash Inflows			
Useful life	*Yogurt*		*Cottage Cheese*	
Years	*Annual*	*Accumulated*	*Annual*	*Accumulated*
1	$110,000	$110,000	$140,000	$140,000
2	110,000	220,000	140,000	280,000
3	110,000	330,000	140,000	420,000
4	110,000	440,000	140,000	560,000
5	110,000	550,000		
6	110,000	660,000		

Requirements

1. Determine the payback period for each product. What is the major weakness of payback analysis?

2. Calculate the accounting rate of return. What is the major weakness of the accounting rate of return?

3. Assuming that Yummy requires a 14% return on each possible new product, what is the net present value of each product?

4. Compute the internal rate of return for each product.

Demo Doc 2 Solutions

Requirement 1

3 Use payback and accounting rate of return to make longer-term capital budgeting decisions

Determine the payback period for each product. What is the major weakness of payback analysis?

Part 1	Part 2	Part 3	Part 4	Demo Doc Complete

Payback period is a simple approach that is used sometimes to screen potential product. A company would want to recoup the investment amount as quickly as possible, assuming all other factors are constant.

In this case, payback is the length of time it takes Yummy to recover, in net cash inflows, the $400,000 initial outlay. Yogurt and cottage cheese each have equal cash inflows each year, so the payback period is calculated as:

$$\text{Payback period} = \frac{\text{Amount invested}}{\text{Expected annual net cash inflow}}$$

$$\text{Payback period for yogurt} = \frac{\$400,000}{\$110,000}$$
$$= \textbf{3.636} \text{ years}$$

$$\text{Payback period for cottage cheese} = \frac{\$400,000}{\$140,000}$$
$$= \textbf{2.857} \text{ years}$$

The payback method favors the cottage cheese because it recovers the initial investment more quickly. The major weakness of payback analysis is that it only focuses on time, not on profit. The payback period must be shorter than the useful life to provide any profit.

Requirement 2

3 Use payback and accounting rate of return to make longer-term capital budgeting decisions

Calculate the accounting rate of return. What is the major weakness of the accounting rate of return?

Part 1	Part 2	Part 3	Part 4	Demo Doc Complete

The rate of return calculated is compared to the required return set by management. The company will invest in the asset if the return is more than that required and will not invest if the return is less than the required return. If there are several alternatives, the higher the return the better it is.

The accounting rate of return is determined by dividing the average operating income from the asset by the average amount invested in the asset.

The average amount invested in the asset is calculated by dividing the cost of the asset less the residual value by two.

Average amount invested in yogurt and cottage cheese is:

$$\frac{\$400,000 - 0}{2} = \$200,000$$

To determine the average operating income, depreciation must first be calculated. The depreciation associated with the yogurt is:

$$\frac{\$400,000}{6\text{-year life}} = \$66,667$$

Depreciation associated with the cottage cheese is:

$$\frac{\$400,000}{4\text{-year life}} = \$100,000$$

The depreciation expense is now subtracted from the expected annual net cash inflows to calculate the average operating income:

Yogurt average operating income = $110,000 − $66,667 = $43,333
Cottage cheese average operating income = $140,000 − $100,000 = $40,000

The accounting rate of return can now be calculated:

$$\text{Yogurt} \quad \frac{\$43,333}{\$200,000} = 21.667\%$$

$$\text{Cottage cheese} \quad \frac{\$40,000}{\$200,000} = 20\%$$

The major weakness of the accounting rate of return is that it doesn't consider the timing of the income. The accounting rate of return doesn't consider whether the income is greater early in the life of the asset or near the end of the useful life of the asset. Management would prefer greater income early in the life of the asset so the funds could be used to generate additional income.

Requirement 3

4 Use discounted cash-flow models to make longer-term capital budgeting decisions

Assuming that Yummy requires a 14% return on each possible new product, what is the net present value of each product?

Part 1	Part 2	**Part 3**	Part 4	Demo Doc Complete

Net present value brings future cash inflows and future cash outflows to a common time period. This makes the feasibility of each product easier to compare.

The net present value (NPV) method compares the present value of the net cash inflows to the initial investment of the capital project. To obtain the present value of the net cash inflows, the minimum desired rate of return is used to find the appropriate discounting factor in the present value tables. If the cash flows are equal each year, it is considered to be an annuity and Exhibit 25-15 (p. xx) is used; if the cash flows are unequal, Exhibit 25-17 (p. xx) is used for each year's present value calculation. *If the present value of the inflows to be received is equal to or greater than that invested, the project is considered to be desirable.*

Consider the following: net present value =

	Present Value of ALL of the Cash Flows IN	(PVCFI)
less	Present Value of ALL of the Cash Flows OUT	(PVCFO)

Both of these projects expect a stream of equal periodic cash flows, which is called an annuity. The present value of an annuity is the periodic cash flow multiplied by the present value of an annuity of $1. Exhibit 25-15 (reproduced here) shows the present value of annuity factors for various interest rates and numbers of periods.

Looking at Exhibit 25-15, the present value factor for the yogurt investment, 14% and 6 periods, is 3.889.

Looking at Exhibit 25-15, the present value factor for the cottage cheese investment, 14% and 4 periods, is 2.914.

Exhibit 25-15 (partial reprduction)

			Present Value of Annuity of $1				
Period	4%	6%	8%	10%	12%	14%	16%
1	0.962	0.943	0.926	0.909	0.893	0.877	0.862
2	1.886	1.833	1.783	1.736	1.690	1.647	1.605
3	2.775	2.673	2.577	2.487	2.402	2.322	2.246
4	3.630	3.465	3.312	3.170	3.037	2.914	2.798
5	4.452	4.212	3.993	3.791	3.605	3.433	3.274
6	5.242	4.917	4.623	4.355	4.111	3.889	3.685
7	6.002	5.582	5.206	4.868	4.564	4.288	4.039
8	6.733	6.210	5.747	5.335	4.968	4.639	4.344
9	7.435	6.802	6.247	5.759	5.328	4.946	4.607
10	8.111	7.360	6.710	6.145	5.650	5.216	4.833

Appendix C-2 provides a more comprehensive table for the present value of an annuity of $1.

The present value of a project is equal to the present value factor multiplied by one period's cash flow.

The net present value is the present value less the cost of the investment, where the investment is made at time zero, or today—giving an interest factor of 1.0000, for a "present value" approach.

So to calculate net present value for each product:

Yogurt:				
	PVCFI	$110,000 × 3.889	=	$427,790
	PVCFO	$400,000 × 1.000	=	400,000
	Net present value		=	$ 27,790
Cottage cheese:				
	PVCFI	$140,000 × 2.914	=	$407,960
	PVCFO	$400,000 × 1.000	=	400,000
	Net present value		=	$ 7,960

As the net present values of both products are *positive,* accept both products, unless there is a problem with coming up with the needed funds of $800,000.

In that case, the company should choose the product with the highest net present value.

In our case, the product with the highest net present value is yogurt: $27,790.

Requirement 4

Use discounted cash-flow models to make longer-term capital budgeting decisions

Compute the internal rate of return for each product.

The internal rate of return (IRR) method calculates the estimated rate of return Yummy can expect to earn by investing in the product. The IRR uses the same concepts as the net present value. The net present value uses management's minimum desired rate of return to determine if the present value of the future net cash inflows equals or exceeds the cost of the initial investment. If they are equal, it means that the product is earning exactly the minimum desired rate of return. If the amount is positive, the product is earning a rate of return in excess of the minimum, but it is unknown. The IRR method *calculates* the projected rate of return by:

a. Identifying the projected future cash flows (as is done with the net present value method).

b. Estimating the present value of an annuity factor as:

$$\text{Annuity PV factor} = \frac{\text{Investment}}{\text{Expected annual net cash flow}}$$

c. Referring to the present value of an annuity table in Exhibit 25-15, find the number of cash-flow periods in the left column and follow that row to the right until you locate the factor that is closest to the present value of an annuity factor computed in part b. Follow that number up to the interest rate at the top of the column to determine the rate of return. *If the rate of return calculated is equal to or higher than management's minimum desired rate of return, the product is acceptable.*

To determine the internal rate of return, we must find the discount rate that makes the total present value of the cash inflows equal to the present value of the cash outflows. Work backward to find the discount rate that makes the present value of the annuity of cash inflows equal to the amount of the investment by solving the following equation for the annuity present value factor (which is, in reality, the figure obtained when calculating the payback period, as we did in requirement 1):

$$\begin{array}{l} \text{Annuity PV factor} \\ \text{for yogurt} \end{array} = \frac{\$400,000}{\$110,000}$$

$$= 3.636$$

$$\begin{array}{l} \text{Annuity PV factor} \\ \text{for cottage cheese} \end{array} = \frac{\$400,000}{\$140,000}$$

$$= 2.857$$

Looking at Exhibit 25-15, scan the row corresponding to the product's expected life—period 6 for yogurt, period 4 for cottage cheese. Choose the column with the number closest to the annuity PV factor previously calculated. The 3.636 annuity factor for yogurt is closest to the 16% column and the 2.857 annuity factor for cottage cheese is closest to 14% column. Therefore, the internal rate of return for yogurt is approximately 16% and the internal rate of return for cottage cheese is approximately 14%.

Part 1	Part 2	Part 3	Part 4	Demo Doc Complete

Quick Practice Questions

True/False

_____ 1. Relevant information is future data that differs among alternatives.

_____ 2. If the lost revenues from dropping a product exceed the cost savings from dropping the product, it should be retained.

_____ 3. Investments with longer payback periods are more desirable, all else being equal.

_____ 4. A sunk cost is a past cost that cannot be changed regardless of which future action is taken.

_____ 5. The payback method can only be used when net cash inflows are the same for each period.

_____ 6. To maximize profits, produce the product with the highest contribution margin per unit of the constraint.

_____ 7. The accounting rate of return is a measure of profitability computed by dividing the average annual cash flows from an asset by the average amount invested in the asset.

_____ 8. Fixed costs are irrelevant to a special decision when those fixed costs differ between alternatives.

_____ 9. Net present value and the payback period are examples of discounted cash flow models used in capital budgeting decisions.

_____ 10. In calculating the net present value of an investment in equipment, the required investment and its terminal residual value should be subtracted from the present value of all future cash inflows.

Multiple Choice

1. For incremental analysis, which of the following would be irrelevant?
   a. The cost of an asset that the company is considering replacing
   b. Fixed overhead costs that differ among alternatives
   c. The cost of further processing a product that could be sold as is
   d. The expected increase in sales of one product line as a result of a decision to drop a separate unprofitable product line

2. Which of the following is an irrelevant cash inflow or outflow?
   a. Future disposal value of an asset
   b. Future operating cash flows
   c. Current cash outlay to acquire a new asset
   d. Cash outlay to acquire equipment 10 years ago

3. **Lowwater Sailmakers manufactures sails for sailboats. The company has the capacity to produce 25,000 sails per year, but is currently producing and**

selling 20,000 sails per year. The following information relates to current production:

Sale price per unit	$	150
Variable costs per unit:		
Manufacturing	$	55
Marketing and administrative	$	25
Total fixed costs:		
Manufacturing		$640,000
Marketing and administrative		$280,000

If a special sales order is accepted for 5,000 sails at a price of $125 per unit, and fixed costs remain unchanged, what would the effect on operating income be?
a. Decrease by $5,000
b. Increase by $190,000
c. Decrease by $125,000
d. Increase by $225,000

4. Using the data in question 3, compute the effect on operating income if a special sales order is accepted for 2,500 sails at a price of $70 per unit, when fixed costs increase by $10,000, and variable marketing and administrative costs for the order decreases by $5 per unit.
a. Decrease by $82,500
b. Increase by $10,000
c. Increase by $22,500
d. Decrease by $22,500

5. DC Electronics uses a standard part in the manufacture of several of its radios. The cost of producing 30,000 parts is $90,000, which includes fixed costs of $33,000 and variable costs of $57,000. The company can buy the part from an outside supplier for $2.50 per unit, and avoid 30% of the fixed costs. If DC Electronics makes the part, what is the effect on its operating income?
a. $6,500 greater than if the company bought the part
b. $8,100 greater than if the company bought the part
c. $15,000 less than if the company bought the part
d. $5,100 less than if the company bought the part

6. The following data are available for the Forte Co.:

	Toaster Ovens	Bread Machines
Sale price	$60	$135
Variable costs	38	62

The company can manufacture five toaster ovens per machine hour and three bread machines per machine hour. The company's production capacity is 1,500 machine hours per month. To maximize profits, what should the company produce?
a. 4,500 bread machines
b. 2,250 toaster ovens and 3,750 bread machines
c. 3,750 toaster ovens and 2,250 bread machines
d. 7,500 toaster ovens

7. Shine Bright Company has three product lines: D, E, and F. The following information is available:

	D	E	F
Sales	$60,000	$38,000	$26,000
Variable costs	36,000	18,000	12,000
Contribution margin	24,000	20,000	14,000
Fixed expenses	12,000	15,000	16,000
Operating income (loss)	$12,000	$ 5,000	$(2,000)

Shine Bright Company is thinking of dropping product line F because it is reporting an operating loss. Assuming Shine Bright Company drops line F and does not replace it, what is the effect on the operating income?
a. Increase $2,000
b. Increase $14,000
c. Decrease $14,000
d. Increase $16,000

8. Using the data in question 7, assume that Shine Bright Company drops line F and rents the space formerly used to produce product F for $17,000 per year. What is the effect on the operating income?
a. Decrease $3,000
b. Increase $3,000
c. Decrease $14,000
d. Increase $15,000

9. Logan, Inc., is evaluating two possible investments in depreciable plant assets. The company uses the straight-line method of depreciation. The following information is available:

	Investment A	Investment B
Initial capital investment	$60,000	$90,000
Estimated useful life	3 years	3 years
Estimated residual value	- 0 -	- 0 -
Estimated annual net cash inflow	$25,000	$40,000
Required rate of return	10%	12%

The present value of $1 due 3 years from now:

8%	0.7938
10%	0.7513
12%	0.7118
14%	0.6750
16%	0.6407

The present value of $1 per year due at the end of each of 3 years:

8%	2.5771
10%	2.4869
12%	2.4018
14%	2.3216
16%	2.2459

What is the internal rate of return for Investment A?

a. 8%

b. 10%

c. 12%

d. 14%

10. Using the information in question 9, what is the net present value of Investment B?

a. $(164)

b. $6,072

c. $40,000

d. $61,528

Quick Exercises

25-1. Label each of the following items as relevant or irrelevant in making a decision.

a. Cost of insurance on a new vehicle _____

b. Cost of roof repair made on rental property last year _____

c. Original cost of old equipment that is being evaluated for replacement _____

d. Cost of new equipment under evaluation to replace used equipment _____

e. Accumulated depreciation on old equipment being evaluated for replacement _____

f. Cost of previous year's insurance policy on old equipment being evaluated for replacement _____

25-2. Dynamic Enterprises produces and sells a part used in the production of automobiles. The unit costs associated with this part are as follows:

Direct materials	$0.15
Direct labor	$0.30
Variable manufacturing overhead	$0.25
Fixed manufacturing overhead	$0.10
Total cost	$0.80

Jupiter Company has approached Dynamic Enterprises with an offer to purchase 20,000 units of this part at a price of $0.75 per unit. Accepting this special sales order will put idle manufacturing capacity to use and will not affect regular sales. Total fixed costs will not change.

Determine whether or not the special order should be accepted. Justify your conclusion.

25-3. Lightning Shoes manufactures kids' sneakers and kids' shoes. The company's product line income statement follows:

	Total	Kids' Sneakers	Kids' Shoes
Sales revenue	$841,000	$580,000	$261,000
Cost of goods sold			
Variable	220,000	116,000	104,000
Fixed	290,000	184,000	106,000
Total cost of goods sold	510,000	300,000	210,000
Gross profit	331,000	280,000	51,000
Marketing and administrative expenses			
Variable	140,000	58,000	82,000
Fixed	105,000	79,000	26,000
Total marketing and administrative expenses	245,000	137,000	108,000
Operating income (loss)	$ 86,000	$143,000	$(57,000)

Management is considering dropping the kids' shoes product line. Accountants for the company estimate that dropping the kids' shoes line will decrease fixed costs of goods sold by $50,000 and fixed marketing and administrative expenses by $6,000.

Prepare an analysis supporting your opinion about whether or not the kids' shoes product line should be dropped.

25-4.   Sharp Image Company makes a part used in the manufacture of video cameras. Management is considering whether to continue manufacturing the part, or to buy the part from an outside source at a cost of $21.30 per part. Sharp Image needs 100,000 parts per year. The cost of manufacturing 100,000 parts is computed as follows:

Direct materials	$ 765,000
Direct labor	612,000
Variable manufacturing overhead	510,000
Fixed manufacturing overhead	663,000
Total manufacturing costs	$2,550,000

Sharp Image would pay $0.30 per unit to transport the parts to its manufacturing plant. Purchasing the part from an outside source would enable the company to avoid 35% of fixed manufacturing overhead. Sharp Image's factory space freed up by purchasing the part from an outside supplier could be used to manufacture another product with a contribution margin of $59,000.

Prepare an analysis to show which alternative makes the best use of Sharp Image's factory space assuming Sharp Image:

1.   makes the part
2.   buys the part and leaves facilities idle
3.   buys the part and uses facilities to make another product

25-5.   Identify four capital budgeting models discussed in the chapter and discuss the strengths and weaknesses of each model.

Do It Yourself! Question 1

Special Business Decisions

Easy Access produces keyless entry remotes for automobiles. A Yemen company has offered to purchase 500 cases of keyless entry remotes at a per-unit price of $80. Assume selling to the Yemen company will not affect regular customers, will not change fixed costs, will not require any additional variable nonmanufacturing expenses, and will use manufacturing capacity that would otherwise be idle.

EASY ACCESS Income Statement (without considering the special sale)	
Sales revenue (5,000 cases @ $140.00 per case)	$700,000
Less manufacturing cost of goods sold	400,000
Gross profit	$300,000
Less marketing and administrative expenses	220,000
Operating income	$ 80,000

Requirements

1. Assuming $250,000 of the manufacturing costs is fixed and $100,000 of the marketing and administrative cost is fixed, should Easy Access accept the order from the Yemen company?

Great Graphics has offered to print the graphics on the keyless remotes. Currently, Easy Access does the printing themselves at the following per-case costs:

Direct materials	$20,000
Direct labor	40,000
Variable overhead	5,000
Fixed overhead	15,000
Total manufacturing cost	$80,000
Cost per case ($80,000/5,000)	$ 16

2. Great Graphics' price per case is $15. Easy Access would avoid all variable costs associated with the printing and would reduce the fixed cost by $3,000 if Great Graphics prints Easy Access's graphics. Should Easy Access outsource the printing work to Great Graphics?

Graphics Costs	Make	Buy	Difference

3. Should Easy Access stop producing the special shaped keyless remote?

Of Easy Access's 5,000 case sales, 200 cases are for a special shaped keyless remote made for one customer. The special keyless remote sells for the same price, $140, as all the other keyless remotes, but seems to require more expenses. Easy Access is considering dropping the special shaped keyless remote. An analysis has determined that the variable cost of producing the special keyless remote is $135 per case. If the special keyless remote was not produced, fixed costs would not change.

Do It Yourself! Question 2

Capital Budgeting

Office Home produces various office products. They desire to produce one of two possible new products: either pens or pencils. Each product would require an additional investment of $340,000. Useful life for the pencils would be seven years, while useful life for the pens would be four years. The expected annual net cash inflows is as follows:

Useful Life	Pencils		Pens	
Years	*Annual*	*Accumulated*	*Annual*	*Accumulated*
1	$60,000	$ 60,000	$90,000	$ 90,000
2	60,000	120,000	90,000	180,000
3	60,000	180,000	90,000	270,000
4	60,000	240,000	90,000	360,000
5	60,000	300,000		
6	60,000	360,000		
7	60,000	420,000		

Requirements

1. Determine the payback period for each product.

2. Calculate the accounting rate of return.

3. Assuming that Office Home requires a 12% return on each possible new product, what is the net present value of each product?

4. Compute the internal rate of return for each product.

Quick Practice Solutions

True/False

T   1. Relevant information is future data that differs among alternatives. (p. 1252)

T   2. If the lost revenues from dropping a product exceed the cost savings from dropping the product, it should be retained. (p. 1258)

F   3. Investments with longer payback periods are more desirable, all else being equal.

     False—Investments with *shorter* payback periods are more desirable, all else being equal. (p. 1266)

T   4. A sunk cost is a past cost that cannot be changed regardless of which future action is taken. (p. 1261)

F   5. The payback method can only be used when net cash inflows are the same for each period.

     False—The payback method can be used when net cash inflows are *equal or unequal* for each period. (pp. 1266–1268)

T   6. To maximize profits, produce the product with the highest contribution margin per unit of the constraint. (p. 1258)

F   7. The accounting rate of return is a measure of profitability computed by dividing the average annual cash flows from an asset by the average amount invested in the asset.

     False—The accounting rate of return is a method of profitability computed by dividing the *average annual operating income of the asset* by the average amount invested in the asset. (p. 1268)

F   8. Fixed costs are irrelevant to a special decision when those fixed costs differ between alternatives.

     False—Fixed costs are *relevant* to a special decision when those fixed costs differ between alternatives. (p. 1254)

F   9. Net present value and the payback period are examples of discounted cash flow models used in capital budgeting decisions.

     False—Net present value and the *internal rate of return* are examples of discounted cash flow models used in capital budgeting decisions. (p. 1270)

F 10. In calculating the net present value of an investment in equipment, the required investment and its terminal residual value should be subtracted from the present value of all future cash inflows.

     False—In calculating the net present value of an investment in equipment, *only* the required investment should be subtracted from the present value of all future cash flows. (p. 1270)

Multiple Choice

1. For incremental analysis, which of the following would be irrelevant?
   (pp. 1252–1253)
   a. The cost of an asset that the company is considering replacing
   b. Fixed overhead costs that differ among alternatives
   c. The cost of further processing a product that could be sold as is
   d. The expected increase in sales of one product line as a result of a decision to drop a separate unprofitable product line

2. Which of the following is an irrelevant cash inflow or outflow?
   (pp. 1252–1253)
   a. Future disposal value of an asset
   b. Future operating cash flows
   c. Current cash outlay to acquire a new asset
   d. Cash outlay to acquire equipment 10 years ago

3. Lowwater Sailmakers manufactures sails for sailboats. The company has the capacity to produce 25,000 sails per year but is currently producing and selling 20,000 sails per year. The following information relates to current production:

Sale price per unit	$ 150
Variable costs per unit:	
Manufacturing	$ 55
Marketing and administrative	$ 25
Total fixed costs:	
Manufacturing	$640,000
Marketing and administrative	$280,000

   If a special sales order is accepted for 5,000 sails at a price of $125 per unit, and fixed costs remain unchanged, what would the effect on operating income be? (pp. 1253–1255)
   a. Decrease by $5,000
   b. Increase by $190,000
   c. Decrease by $125,000
   d. Increase by $225,000

4. Using the data in question 3, compute the effect on operating income if a special sales order is accepted for 2,500 sails at a price of $70 per unit, when fixed costs increase by $10,000, and variable marketing and administrative costs for the order decreases by $5 per unit. (pp. 1253–1255)
   a. Decrease by $82,500
   b. Increase by $10,000
   c. Increase by $22,500
   d. Decrease by $22,500

5. DC Electronics uses a standard part in the manufacture of several of its radios. The cost of producing 30,000 parts is $90,000, which includes fixed costs of $33,000 and variable costs of $57,000. The company can buy the part from an outside supplier for $2.50 per unit, and avoid 30% of the fixed costs. If DC Electronics makes the part, what is the effect on its operating income? (pp. 1259–1261)
   a. $6,500 greater than if the company bought the part
   b. $8,100 greater than if the company bought the part
   c. $15,000 less than if the company bought the part
   d. $5,100 less than if the company bought the part

6. The following data are available for the Forte Co.:

	Toaster Ovens	Bread Machines
Sale price	$60	$135
Variable costs	38	62

   The company can manufacture five toaster ovens per machine hour and three bread machines per machine hour. The company's production capacity is 1,500 machine hours per month. To maximize profits, what should the company produce? (p. 1258)
   a. 4,500 bread machines
   b. 2,250 toaster ovens and 3,750 bread machines
   c. 3,750 toaster ovens and 2,250 bread machines
   d. 7,500 toaster ovens

7. Shine Bright Company has three product lines: D, E, and F. The following information is available:

	D	E	F
Sales	$60,000	$38,000	$26,000
Variable costs	36,000	18,000	12,000
Contribution margin	24,000	20,000	14,000
Fixed expenses	12,000	15,000	16,000
Operating income (loss)	$12,000	$ 5,000	$(2,000)

   Shine Bright Company is thinking of dropping product line F because it is reporting an operating loss. Assuming Shine Bright Company drops line F and does not replace it, what is the effect on the operating income? (pp. 1255–1257)
   a. Increase $2,000
   b. Increase $14,000
   c. Decrease $14,000
   d. Increase $16,000

8. Using the data in question 7, assume that Shine Bright Company drops line F and rents the space formerly used to produce product F for $17,000 per year. What is the effect on the operating income? (pp. 1255–1257)
   a. Decrease $3,000
   b. Increase $3,000
   c. Decrease $14,000
   d. Increase $15,000

9. Logan, Inc., is evaluating two possible investments in depreciable plant assets. The company uses the straight-line method of depreciation. The following information is available:

	Investment A	Investment B
Initial capital investment	$60,000	$90,000
Estimated useful life	3 years	3 years
Estimated residual value	- 0 -	- 0 -
Estimated annual net cash inflow	$25,000	$40,000
Required rate of return	10%	12%

The present value of $1 due 3 years from now:

8%   0.7938

10%   0.7513

12%   0.7118

14%   0.6750

16%   0.6407

The present value of $1 per year due at the end of each of 3 years:

8%   2.5771

10%   2.4869

12%   2.4018

14%   2.3216

16%   2.2459

What is the internal rate of return for Investment A? (pp. 1273–1274)

a. 8%

b. 10%

c. 12%

d. 14%

10. Using the information in question 9, what is the net present value of Investment B? (pp. 1270–1273)

a. $(164)

b. $6,072

c. $40,000

d. $61,528

Quick Exercises

25-1.   Label each of the following items as relevant or irrelevant in making a decision. (pp. 1252–1253)

a.   Cost of insurance on a new vehicle—relevant
b.   Cost of roof repair made on rental property last year—irrelevant
c.   Original cost of old equipment that is being evaluated for replacement—irrelevant
d.   Cost of new equipment under evaluation to replace used equipment—relevant
e.   Accumulated depreciation on old equipment being evaluated for replacement—irrelevant
f.   Cost of previous year's insurance policy on old equipment being evaluated for replacement—irrelevant

25-2.   Dynamic Enterprises produces and sells a part used in the production of automobiles. The unit costs associated with this part are as follows:

Direct materials	$0.15
Direct labor	$0.30
Variable manufacturing overhead	$0.25
Fixed manufacturing overhead	$0.10
Total cost	$0.80

Jupiter Company has approached Dynamic Enterprises with an offer to purchase 20,000 units of this part at a price of $0.75 per unit. Accepting this special sales order will put idle manufacturing capacity to use and will not affect regular sales. Total fixed costs will not change.

Determine whether or not the special order should be accepted. Justify your conclusion. (pp. 1253–1255)

Variable manufacturing expenses per unit:

$$\$0.15 + \$0.30 + \$0.25 = \$0.70$$
$$\$0.75 - \$0.70 = \$0.05 \text{ / unit} \times 20{,}000 \text{ units} = \$1{,}000$$
increase in operating income

Dynamic Enterprises should accept the offer as this would increase operating income by $1,000.

Points to consider:

Total fixed costs will not change

Idle capacity exists

No effect on regular sales

25-3. Lightning Shoes manufactures kids' sneakers and kids' shoes. The company's product line income statement follows:

	Total	Kids' Sneakers	Kids' Shoes
Sales revenue	$841,000	$580,000	$261,000
Cost of goods sold			
Variable	220,000	116,000	104,000
Fixed	290,000	184,000	106,000
Total cost of goods sold	510,000	300,000	210,000
Gross profit	331,000	280,000	51,000
Marketing and administrative expenses			
Variable	140,000	58,000	82,000
Fixed	105,000	79,000	26,000
Total marketing and administrative expenses	245,000	137,000	108,000
Operating income (loss)	$ 86,000	$143,000	$(57,000)

Management is considering dropping the kids' shoes product line. Accountants for the company estimate that dropping the kids' shoes line will decrease fixed costs of goods sold by $50,000 and fixed marketing and administrative expenses by $6,000.

Prepare an analysis supporting your opinion about whether or not the kids' shoes product line should be dropped. (p. 1258)

Contribution margin income statement for kids' shoes:

	Currently	If Dropped
Sales revenue	$261,000	$ 0
Variable expenses:		
Manufacturing	104,000	0
Marketing and administrative	82,000	0
Contribution margin	75,000	0
Fixed expenses:		
Manufacturing	106,000	56,000
Marketing and administrative	26,000	20,000
Operating income (loss)	$ (57,000)	$(76,000)

The company should keep producing and selling kids' shoes because operating income will decrease by $19,000 if the product line is dropped.

25-4. Sharp Image Company makes a part used in the manufacture of video cameras. Management is considering whether to continue manufacturing the part, or to buy the part from an outside source at a cost of $21.30 per part. Sharp Image needs 100,000 parts per year. The cost of manufacturing 100,000 parts is computed as follows:

Direct materials	$ 765,000
Direct labor	612,000
Variable manufacturing overhead	510,000
Fixed manufacturing overhead	663,000
Total manufacturing costs	$2,550,000

Sharp Image would pay $0.30 per unit to transport the parts to its manufacturing plant. Purchasing the part from an outside source would enable the company to avoid 35% of fixed manufacturing overhead. Sharp Image's factory space freed up by purchasing the part from an outside supplier could be used to manufacture another product with a contribution margin of $59,000.

Prepare an analysis to show which alternative makes the best use of Sharp Image's factory space assuming Sharp Image: (pp. 1259–1261)

1. makes the part
2. buys the part and leaves facilities idle
3. buys the part and uses facilities to make another product

	Make	Buy part and leave facilities idle	Buy and use facilities to make another product
Direct materials	$ 765,000		
Direct labor	612,000		
Variable manufacturing overhead	510,000		
Variable transportation		$ 30,000	$ 30,000
Fixed manufacturing overhead	663,000	430,950	430,950
Purchase price		2,130,000	2,130,000
Profit contribution from another product	0	0	(59,000)
Total cost	$2,550,000	$2,590,950	$2,531,950

Sharp Image should buy the part and use the facilities to make another product.

25-5. **Identify four capital budgeting models discussed in the chapter and discuss the strengths and weaknesses of each model.** (p. 1275)

The four capital budgeting models discussed in the chapter were the payback model, the accounting rate of return model, the net present value model, and the internal rate of return model.

The strengths and weaknesses of the different models are as follows:

The payback model is easy to understand, highlights risks, and is based on cash flows, which are of primary concern to many businesses. However, it ignores profitability and the time value of money.

The accounting rate of return model measures profitability, but it ignores the time value of money.

The net present value model and the internal rate of return model are both based on cash flows, profitability, and the time value of money. These models don't have any of the weaknesses identified with the payback method and the accounting rate of return.

Do It Yourself! Question 1 Solutions

Requirements

2 Make five types of short-term special decisions

1. Assuming $250,000 of the manufacturing costs is fixed and $100,000 of the marketing and administrative cost is fixed, should Easy Access accept the order from the Yemen company?

$$\text{Variable cost per unit} = \frac{(\$400,000 - \$250,000) + (\$220,000 - \$100,000)}{5,000 \text{ cases}} =$$

$$= \frac{\$150,000 + \$120,000}{5,000 \text{ cases}} =$$

$$= \frac{\$270,000}{5,000 \text{ cases}} = \$54 \text{ per case}$$

Increase in revenues:	
Sale of 500 cases @ $80	$40,000
Increase in expenses variable costs:	
500 cases @ $54/case	27,000
Increase in operating income	$13,000

Therefore, Easy Access should accept the special order because there is an increase in operating income.

2 Make five types of short-term special decisions

2. Great Graphics' price per case is $15. Easy Access would avoid all variable costs associated with the printing and would reduce the fixed cost by $3,000 if Great Graphics prints Easy Access's graphics. Should Easy Access outsource the printing work to Great Graphics?

Graphics Costs	Make	Buy	Difference
Direct materials	$ 20,000		$ 20,000
Direct labor	40,000		40,000
Variable factory overhead	5,000		5,000
Fixed costs	15,000	12,000	3,000
Purchase cost from Great Graphics (5,000 cases × $15 per case)		75,000	(75,000)
Total cost of labels	$ 80,000	$ 87,000	$ (7,000)
Cost per unit (divide by 5,000 cases)	$ 16.00	$ 17.40	$ 1.40

Therefore, Easy Access should not accept the printing offer from Great Graphics.

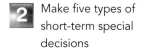

Make five types of short-term special decisions

3. Should Easy Access stop producing the special shaped keyless remote?

Reduction in revenue by dropping special keyless remote:

$$200 \times \$140 = \textbf{\$28,000}$$

Reduction in expenses by dropping special keyless remote:

$$200 \times \$135 = \textbf{\$27,000}$$

Decrease in operating income   = **$ 1,000**

As the difference between the absolute value of the loss of revenue less the cost savings from dropping the product is positive, Easy Access would not drop the special keyless remote.

Do It Yourself! Question 2 Solutions

Requirements

3 Use payback and accounting rate of return to make longer-term capital budgeting decisions

1. Determine the payback period for each product.

$$\text{Pencils Payback} = \frac{\$340,000}{\$60,000} = \textbf{5.67 years}$$

$$\text{Pens Payback} = \frac{\$340,000}{\$90,000} = \textbf{3.78 years}$$

2. Calculate the accounting rate of return.

3 Use payback and accounting rate of return to make longer-term capital budgeting decisions

$$\text{Average amount invested} = \frac{\$340,000}{2} = \$170,000$$

$$\text{Depreciation per year, pencils} = \frac{\$340,000}{7} = \$48,571$$

$$\text{Depreciation per year, pens} = \frac{\$340,000}{4} = \$85,000$$

$$\text{Average annual operating income from pencils} = \$60,000 - \$48,571 = \$11,429$$

$$\text{Average annual operating income from pens} = \$90,000 - \$85,000 = \$5,000$$

$$\text{Accounting rate of return (pencils)} = \frac{\$11,429}{\$170,000} = 6.722\%$$

$$\text{Accounting rate of return (pens)} = \frac{\$5,000}{\$170,000} = 2.941\%$$

3. Assuming that Office Home requires a 12% return on each possible new product, what is the net present value of each product?

4 Use discounted cash-flow models to make longer-term capital budgeting decisions

Pencils

PVCFI	$ 60,000 × 4.564	=	$273,840
PVCFO	$340,000 × 1.000	=	$340,000
	Net Present Value		($66,160)

Pens

PVCFI	$ 90,000 × 3.037	=	$273,330
PVCFO	$340,000 × 1.000	=	$340,000
	Net Present Value		($66,670)

Both products' net present value is negative, therefore neither product should be accepted.

Use discounted cash-flow models to make longer-term capital budgeting decisions

4. Compute the internal rate of return for each product.

$$\text{Annuity PV Factor} = \frac{\text{Investment}}{\text{Expected Annual Net Cash Flow}}$$

$$\begin{aligned}\text{Annuity PV Factor} \atop \text{for Pencils} &= \frac{\$340,000}{\$60,000}\\ &= 5.667\end{aligned}$$

Pencil internal rate of return = 6%

$$\begin{aligned}\text{Annuity PV Factor} \atop \text{for Pens} &= \frac{\$340,000}{\$90,000}\\ &= 3.778\end{aligned}$$

Pen internal rate of return = 4%

The Power of Practice

For more practice using the skills learned in this chapter, visit MyAccountingLab. There you will find algorithmically generated questions that are based on these Demo Docs and your main textbook's Review and Assess Your Progress sections.

Go to MyAccountingLab and follow these steps:

1. Direct your URL to www.myaccountinglab.com.
2. Log in using your name and password.
3. Click the MyAccountingLab link.
4. Click Study Plan in the left navigation bar.
5. From the table of contents, select Chapter 25, Special Business Decisions and Capital Budgeting.
6. Click a link to work tutorial exercises.

B Investments and International Operations

Demo Doc 1

Long-Term Investments

On January 1, 2008, Unity Corp. purchased the following investments for cash:

20,000 shares Lake Corp. stock	$60,000
4,000 shares Drop Corp. stock	$10,000

Both Lake and Drop have 50,000 common shares outstanding. During 2008, Lake and Drop had the following information:

	Net Income	Cash Dividends per Share	Market Price per Share at 12/31/08
Lake Corp.	$120,000	$0.70	$2.50
Drop Corp.	$ 60,000	$0.60	$3.00

Requirements

1. What kind of investments are these?

2. For each investment, journalize the following transactions for Unity Corp.:

a. **Purchase of investment on January 1, 2008**

b. **Dividends received from the investments during 2008**

c. **Any adjustment for net income earned by the investment**

d. **Any adjustment for the investment's year-end market price**

Demo Doc 1 Solutions

Requirement 1

What kind of investments are these?

In order to determine the investment type, we need to know what percentage of the company Unity holds.

$$\% \text{ Ownership} = \frac{\text{\# of shares held by investor company}}{\text{Total \# of outstanding common shares of investee company}}$$

$$\% \text{ Ownership of Lake Corp.} = \frac{20{,}000 \text{ shares}}{50{,}000 \text{ shares}}$$
$$= 40\%$$

An investment between 25% and 50% ownership is an **equity method** investment. The Lake Corp. shares are an equity method investment.

$$\% \text{ Ownership of Drop Corp.} = \frac{4{,}000 \text{ shares}}{50{,}000 \text{ shares}}$$
$$= 8\%$$

An investment less than 25% ownership is an **available-for-sale** investment. The Drop Corp. shares are an available-for-sale investment.

Requirement 2

For each investment, journalize the following transactions for Unity Corp.:

a. Purchase of investment on January 1, 2008

	Part 1	Part 2	Demo Doc Complete

Lake Corp.

Cash is decreased (a credit) by $60,000.
Equity Method Investment—Lake Corp. is increased (a debit) by $60,000.

	Equity Method Investment—Lake Corp.	60,000	
	Cash		60,000

Drop Corp.

Cash is decreased (a credit) by $10,000.

Long-Term Available-for-Sale Investment—Drop Corp. is increased (a debit) by $10,000.

| | Long-Term Available-for-Sale Investment—Drop Corp. | 10,000 | |
| | Cash | | 10,000 |

b. Dividends received from the investments during 2008

Lake Corp.

Cash is received, so it is increased (a debit) by:

$$\$0.70 \text{ per share} \times 20,000 \text{ shares} = \$14,000$$

Under the equity method, we are trying to capture changes in Lake Corp.'s *equity*, or more accurately, its *retained earnings*. It is as if Unity has purchased a piece of Lake's retained earnings. As Lake's retained earnings change in value, so does Unity's investment in Lake Corp.

When Lake Corp. pays a dividend, its retained earnings decrease. This means that the value of Unity's Lake Corp. Investment has also decreased (a debit) by $14,000.

| | Cash ($0.70 × 20,000) | 14,000 | |
| | Equity Method Investment—Lake Corp. | | 14,000 |

<table>
<tr><td colspan="3" align="center">Lake Corp. Investment</td></tr>
<tr><td>Jan. 1</td><td>60,000</td><td></td></tr>
<tr><td></td><td></td><td>14,000 dividends received</td></tr>
<tr><td>Bal.</td><td>46,000</td><td></td></tr>
</table>

Drop Corp.

Cash is received, so it is increased (a debit) by:

$$\$0.60 \text{ per share} \times 4,000 \text{ shares} = \$2,400$$

For available-for-sale investments, *Dividend Revenue* is also increased (a credit) by $2,400.

| | Cash ($0.60 × 4,000) | 2,400 | |
| | Dividend Revenue | | 2,400 |

Notice that the Drop Corp. Investment (available-for-sale) recorded the dividends received as *Dividend Revenue*, while the value of the Lake Corp. Investment was decreased.

c. Any adjustment for net income earned by the investment

Lake Corp.

When Lake Corp. earns net income, its retained earnings increases. This means that under the equity method, the value of Unity's investment in Lake Corp. *also* increases.

Equity Method Investment—Lake Corp. is increased (a debit) by Unity's share of Lake's net income:

$$40\% \times \$120,000 = \$48,000$$

Unity's share of Lake's net income also impacts Unity's net income. The $48,000 is also recorded as Equity Method Investment Revenue (a credit) on Unity's income statement.

	Equity Method Investment—Lake Corp. (40% × $120,000)	48,000	
	Equity Method Investment Revenue		48,000

Lake Corp. Investment

Jan. 1	60,000		
	48,000 net income	14,000 dividends received	
Bal.	94,000		

Drop Corp.

Available-for-sale investments do *not* adjust for net income. *Instead,* they adjust for year-end market price (see transaction **d**). There is no entry for Drop Corp.

d. Any adjustment for the investment's year-end market price

Lake Corp.

Equity method investments do *not* adjust for year-end market price. *Instead,* they adjust for net income (see transaction **c**). There is no entry for Lake Corp.

Drop Corp.

We are required to adjust the value of available-for-sale investments to market price at year-end (for presentation on the balance sheet).

This means that we must adjust the Drop Corp. Investment from its original balance of $10,000 to its new market value:

$$\$3 \text{ market price per share} \times 4,000 \text{ shares} = \$12,000$$

The Drop Corp. Investment has increased in value by:

$$\$12,000 - \$10,000 = \$2,000$$

However, instead of adjusting the Investment account directly, we adjust an *Allowance* account. In this way, we are able to keep a record of the original cost of the investment in the Drop Corp. Investment account, yet report the investment at market price on the balance sheet (by combining it with the Allowance account).

So the allowance to adjust investments to market is increased (a debit) by $2,000.

This increase is an *unrealized* gain (a credit) of $2,000. We know that the gain is unrealized because there is no cash involved in the transaction to ensure that the gain is "real." In the case of available-for-sale investments, we are uncertain because the stock was not actually sold. Market prices change constantly and today's gain could be tomorrow's loss. We emphasize this uncertainty on the income statement by highlighting this gain as an *unrealized* (paper) gain.

Allowance to Adjust Investment to Market	2,000	
Unrealized Gain [($3 × 4,000) – $10,000]		2,000

Part 1	Part 2	**Demo Doc Complete**

Demo Doc 2

Foreign Currency Transactions

Global Industries had the following transactions during 2008:

a. **Performed services on account for a Jordanian company for 40,000 dinar. $1 U.S. = 2.00 dinar.**

b. **Purchased equipment from an Egyptian company on account for 300,000 Egyptian pounds. 1 pound = $0.17 U.S.**

c. **Adjusted for a change in the value of the dinar. $1 U.S. now = 1.60 dinar.**

d. **Paid for the equipment when 1 pound = $0.16 U.S.**

e. **Received cash from the Jordanian company when $1 U.S. = 2.50 dinar.**

Requirements

1. Journalize these transactions for Global Industries.

2. Based on these 2008 transactions, identify whether the dinar, the pound, and the U.S. dollar are strong or weak.

Demo Doc 2 Solutions

Requirement 1

Journalize these transactions for Global Industries.

Part 1	Part 2	Demo Doc Complete

a. Performed services on account for a Jordanian company for 40,000 dinar. $1 U.S. = 2.00 dinar.

For this *initial* transaction (that is, *before* there has been any fluctuation in exchange rates), we can simply journalize the entry as usual with the calculated U.S. dollar amount.

$$\$1 \text{ U.S.} = 2.00 \text{ dinar}$$
$$\text{therefore } 1 \text{ dinar} = \$1/2.00 = \$0.50 \text{ U.S.}$$

When Global performs services, they are earning service revenue. This increases (a credit) Service Revenue by:

$$40{,}000 \times \$0.50 = \$20{,}000$$

Accounts Receivable is also increased (a debit) by $20,000.

Accounts Receivable (40,000 dinar × $0.50 U.S.)	20,000	
Service Revenue		20,000

b. Purchased equipment from an Egyptian company on account for 300,000 Egyptian pounds. 1 pound = $0.17 U.S.

Again, with this *initial* transaction, we can analyze the entry as usual.
Equipment is increased (a debit) by:

$$300{,}000 \times \$0.17 = \$51{,}000$$

Accounts Payable is also increased (a credit) by $51,000.

Equipment (300,000 pounds × $0.17 U.S.)	51,000	
Accounts Payable		51,000

c. Adjusted for a change in the value of the dinar. $1 US now = 1.60 dinar.

An adjustment will obviously change the value of the account receivable; however, it will *not* change the value of the service revenue. No new revenue has been earned (or unearned); instead, this adjustment is due to foreign currency fluctuations beyond Global's control. Therefore, the balance to the Accounts Receivable adjustment will be foreign currency gain or loss.

$$\$1 \text{ U.S. now} = 1.60 \text{ dinar}$$
$$\text{therefore } 1 \text{ dinar} = \$1/1.60 = \$0.625 \text{ U.S.}$$

The account receivable from the Jordanian company is now worth:

$$40,000 \times \$0.625 = \$25,000$$

Because the receivable is recorded at $20,000, we must increase Accounts Receivable (a debit) by:

$$\$25,000 - \$20,000 = \$5,000$$

The corresponding credit (a balancing amount) goes to Foreign-Currency Gain (gain because it is a *credit*).

Accounts Receivable (40,000 dinar × $0.625 U.S. – $20,000)	5,000	
Foreign-Currency Gain (to balance)		5,000

d. Paid for the equipment when 1 pound = $0.16 U.S.

The equipment was sold for 300,000 pounds and they expect to receive 300,000 pounds.

If 1 pound now = $0.16 U.S. the account payable is now:

$$300,000 \times \$0.16 = \$48,000$$

Therefore, Cash is decreased (a credit) by $48,000.

The liability is completely satisfied, so Accounts Payable *must* be decreased (a debit) by the full $51,000 (because there is no longer any liability to pay).

The difference is a balancing amount to Foreign-Currency Gain of:

$$\$51,000 - \$48,000 = \$3,000$$

In this case, the balancing amount is a credit, which is a gain.

Accounts Payable	51,000	
Cash (300,000 pounds × $0.16 U.S.)		48,000
Foreign-Currency Gain (to balance)		3,000

Notice it is *not* that the contract has changed, it is the value of the *U.S. dollar* that has changed.

e. Received cash from the Jordanian company when $1 U.S. = 2.50 dinar.

$$\$1 \text{ U.S. now} = 2.50 \text{ dinar}$$
$$\text{therefore } 1 \text{ dinar} = \$1/2.50 = \$0.40 \text{ U.S.}$$

If 1 dinar now = $0.40 U.S., the account receivable is now:

$$40,000 \times \$0.40 = \$16,000$$

Therefore, Cash is increased (a debit) by $16,000.

The receivable is completely collected, so Accounts Receivable *must* be decreased (a credit) by the full $25,000 (because there is no longer any further amount to collect).

The difference is a balancing amount to Foreign-Currency Loss of:

$$\$16,000 - \$25,000 = -\$9,000$$

In this case, the balancing amount is a debit, which is a loss.

Cash (40,000 dinar × $0.40 U.S.)	16,000	
Foreign-Currency Loss (to balance)	9,000	
Accounts Receivable		25,000

Requirement 2

Based on these 2008 transactions, identify whether the dinar, the pound, and the U.S. dollar are strong or weak.

Part 1	Part 2	Demo Doc Complete

The dinar went from $0.50 U.S. to $0.625 U.S. to $0.40 U.S. This means that over time, the dinar became less valuable as compared to the U.S. dollar. Therefore, the dinar is **weakening** when compared to the U.S. dollar.

The pound went from $0.17 U.S. to $0.16 U.S. This means that over time, the pound became less valuable as compared to the U.S. dollar. Therefore, the pound is **weakening** when compared to the U.S. dollar.

The U.S. dollar became more valuable relative to the pound, and more valuable as compared to the dinar. So the U.S. dollar is strong.

Part 1	Part 2	Demo Doc Complete

Quick Practice Questions

True/False

_____ 1. If a trading investment has decreased in value, the year-end adjustment requires a debit to Loss on Trading Investment.

_____ 2. Available-for-sale investments may be classified as current assets or as long-term assets.

_____ 3. The Allowance to Adjust Investment to Market account is a companion account that is used with the Short-Term Investment account to bring the investment's carrying amount to current market value.

_____ 4. An investor with a stock holding between 20% and 50% of the investee's voting stock may significantly influence decisions on dividends, product lines, and other important matters.

_____ 5. Companies owning less than 50% of the outstanding stock in a subsidiary prepare consolidated financial statements.

_____ 6. Minority interest is that portion of a subsidiary's stock that is owned by stockholders other than the parent company.

_____ 7. Goodwill is the excess of the cost to acquire another company over the sum of the market value of its net assets.

_____ 8. Held-to-maturity investments are reported on the balance sheet at amortized cost.

_____ 9. A foreign-currency transaction gain or loss occurs when the exchange rate changes between the date an order is placed and the date the merchandise is received.

_____ 10. If the U.S. dollar value of a Russian ruble is $0.035 on January 1 and increases to $0.037 on February 1, the U.S. dollar has weakened.

Multiple Choice

1. How are trading securities reported on the balance sheet?
   a. At market value as either current assets or long-term investments on the balance sheet
   b. At market value as current assets on the balance sheet
   c. At cost as current assets on the balance sheet
   d. At lower of cost or market as current assets on the balance sheet

2. Where would a loss on the sale of a trading investment appear on the financial statements?
   a. On the income statement as part of other gains and losses
   b. On the balance sheet as a current liability
   c. On the income statement as an operating expense
   d. On the balance sheet as a contra equity account

3. The entry to record dividends received from a trading investment includes which of the following?
   a. A debit to Short-Term Investment
   b. A credit to Dividend Revenue
   c. A credit to Short-Term Investment
   d. A credit to Gain from Short-Term Investment

4. A short-term investment has been properly classified by the investor as a trading investment. If the stock was bought on June 17, 2007, for $10,000, and it is now worth $13,500 on December 31, 2007, which of the following will occur?
   a. A direct increase of $3,500 to Retained Earnings that is not reported on the income statement.
   b. Dividend Revenue of $3,500 is reported on the income statement.
   c. A $3,500 gain would appear on the income statement, even though the gain is unrealized.
   d. The short-term investment will appear on the balance sheet at $10,000 on December 31.

5. Which of the following accounting treatments for available-for-sale investments is in accordance with GAAP?
   a. Available-for-sale investments are reported on the balance sheet at historical cost.
   b. Available-for-sale investments are reported at historical cost and an Allowance to Adjust the Investment to Market account is established.
   c. Available-for-sale investments are reported on the balance sheet at market value.
   d. The Available-for-Sale Investment account should be adjusted to its market value on the balance sheet date and the unrealized gain or loss of adjusting from cost to market should be shown on the income statement.

6. McGovern Corp. owns 45% of the stock of Mather Corp. Mather Corp. declares and pays cash dividends of $45,000 to McGovern Corp. Which of the following will occur on the books of McGovern Corp.?
   a. The investment in Mather Corp. on the balance sheet will increase by $45,000.
   b. Dividend revenue of $45,000 will be reported on the income statement.
   c. The investment in Mather Corp. on the balance sheet will decrease by $45,000.
   d. A gain of $45,000 will be reported on the income statement.

7. Which of the following is true for available-for-sale investments?
   a. Available-for-sale investments include all stock investments other than trading securities.
   b. Available-for-sale investments are always classified as short-term.
   c. Available-for-sale investments are intended to be sold in the very near future.
   d. Available-for-sale investments include all bond investments other than trading securities.

8. On January 1, 2009, Investor Company acquires 25% of the 20,000 shares of common stock of Investee Company and has significant influence over the Investee Company. On December 31, 2009, Investee Company reports net income of $100,000. What account should Investor Company debit?
   a. Long-Term Equity-Method Investment for $25,000
   b. Cash for $25,000
   c. Long-Term Equity-Method Investment for $100,000
   d. Cash for $100,000

9. White Corp. purchased $20,000 of 8% bonds on March 1, 2008, for a purchase price of 90. White expects to hold the bonds until their maturity date, March 1, 2013. Interest on the bonds will be paid every March 1 and September 1 until maturity. Assuming the premium or discount is amortized every interest payment using straight-line amortization, how much interest revenue will be recorded by White on September 1, 2008?
   a. $1,200
   b. $1,000
   c. $800
   d. $600

10. A U.S. company sells merchandise to a British firm for 100,000 British pounds. Assume the exchange rates for the British pound were as follows:

   Date of sale: $1.54

   Date of collection: $1.53

   Date merchandise resold by British Firm: $1.52

   What is the foreign-currency gain or loss for the U.S. company on this transaction?
   a. $2,000 gain
   b. $1,000 loss
   c. $3,000 gain
   d. $3,000 loss

Quick Exercises

B-1. In early 2008, Rocket Corporation invested some idle cash in the stock of another business. Journalize the following events that took place in 2008 and 2009:

2008:

Feb. 1 Rocket Corporation purchased 1,500 shares of stock in Missile Company for $15.50 per share. This investment was classified as a trading investment.

Nov. 15 A dividend of $1.00 per share was received on the Missile Company stock.

Dec. 31 Rocket Corporation prepares financial statements for the year ended December 31, 2008. On this date, the Missile Company stock is worth $16.25 per share.

2009:

Jan. 27 Rocket Corporation sold 750 shares of Missile Company stock for $16.50 per share.

General Journal				
Date	Accounts		Debit	Credit

General Journal

Date	Accounts	Debit	Credit

General Journal

Date	Accounts	Debit	Credit

General Journal

Date	Accounts	Debit	Credit

B-2. Zipper Corporation engaged in the following transactions involving long-term available-for-sale investments in 2007:

June 14 Purchased 3,500 shares of Button Corporation common stock for $13 per share.

Sep. 15 Button Corporation pays a $0.65 per share dividend to all common stockholders.

Dec. 31 The market price of Button Corporation stock is $13.75 per share.

Journalize these transactions.

General Journal

Date	Accounts	Debit	Credit

General Journal

Date	Accounts	Debit	Credit

General Journal

Date	Accounts	Debit	Credit

B-3.   John Corporation purchased 250,000 shares of Deere Corporation common stock on January 2, 2008, for $550,000. Deere Corporation has 625,000 shares outstanding. Deere Corporation earned net income of $330,000 and paid dividends of $100,000 during 2008.

   a.   What method should be used to account for the Deere Corporation investment?

   b.   How much revenue will be recorded by John Corporation in 2008 from its investment in Deere Corporation?

   c.   What is the balance in John Corporation's investment account at the end of 2008?

   d.   Assume all of the above facts except that on January 2, 2008, John Corporation purchased 75,000 shares of Deere Corporation. How much revenue will be recorded by John Corporation in 2008 from its investment in Deere Corporation?

B-4.   On October 1, 2007, Ace company paid $52,400 to purchase $50,000 of bonds that carry an 8% interest rate and will mature 5 years from the date of purchase. Interest on the bonds is paid September 30 and March 31 of each year. The company plans to hold the bonds until maturity and amortizes the premium or discount on bonds using the straight-line method each interest payment date. As of December 31, 2007, the bonds had a market value of $53,500.

Requirements

1. Prepare all necessary journal entries for 2007 dealing with the investment in bonds.

General Journal				
	Date	Accounts	Debit	Credit

General Journal				
	Date	Accounts	Debit	Credit

General Journal				
	Date	Accounts	Debit	Credit

2. Show how the bonds would be presented on the balance sheet at December 31, 2007.

B-5.   The Helms Company engaged in the following transactions during 2008:

Apr. 1 Purchased merchandise from a Mexican supplier at a cost of 100,000 pesos. The exchange rate on this date was $0.32 per peso.

May 5 Paid for the merchandise purchased on April 1. The exchange rate on this date was $0.31 per peso.

June 10 Sold goods to a Canadian buyer at a selling price of $83,000 Canadian dollars. The exchange rate on this date was $0.67 U.S. dollars for each Canadian dollar.

July 30 Received payment from the Canadian buyer for the goods sold on June 10. The exchange rate on this date was $0.65 U.S. dollars for each Canadian dollar.

Requirements

1. Prepare the journal entries necessary to record each of the above transactions.

General Journal				
Date	Accounts		Debit	Credit

General Journal				
Date	Accounts		Debit	Credit

General Journal				
Date	Accounts		Debit	Credit

General Journal				
Date	Accounts		Debit	Credit

2. During the periods of time covered by the transactions, was the U.S. dollar getting stronger or weaker relative to the Mexican peso and the Canadian dollar?

Do It Yourself! Question 1

Long-Term Investments

On January 1, 2008, Giant Co. purchased the following investments for cash:

10,000 shares Rock Co. stock	$ 15,000
40,000 shares Boulder Co. stock	$240,000

Both Rock and Boulder have 100,000 common shares outstanding.

During 2008, Rock and Boulder had the following information:

	Net Income	Cash Dividends per Share	Market Price per Share at 12/31/08
Rock Co.	$100,000	$0.20	$1.40
Boulder Co.	$350,000	$0.50	$6.50

Requirements

1. What kind of investments are these?

2. For *each* investment, journalize the following transactions for Giant Co.:

a. Purchase of investments on January 1, 2008

General Journal			
Date	Accounts	Debit	Credit

General Journal			
Date	Accounts	Debit	Credit

b. Dividends received from the investments during 2008

	General Journal			
Date	Accounts		Debit	Credit

	General Journal			
Date	Accounts		Debit	Credit

c. Any adjustment for net income earned by the investment

	General Journal			
Date	Accounts		Debit	Credit

	General Journal			
Date	Accounts		Debit	Credit

d. Any adjustment for the investment's year-end market price

General Journal				
Date	Accounts		Debit	Credit

General Journal				
Date	Accounts		Debit	Credit

Do It Yourself! Question 2

Foreign-Currency Transactions

Requirement

1. Journalize the following transactions for Omni Inc.:

a. Performed services on account for a French company for 2,000 euro. 1 euro = $1.11 U.S.

General Journal				
Date	Accounts		Debit	Credit

b. Purchased machinery from a Japanese company on account for 800,000 yen. 1 yen = $0.009 U.S.

General Journal				
Date	Accounts		Debit	Credit

c. Adjusted for a change in the value of the euro. 1 euro now = $1.18 U.S.

General Journal				
Date	Accounts		Debit	Credit

d. Paid for the machinery when 1 yen = $0.0089 U.S.

	Date	Accounts		Debit	Credit
		General Journal			

e. Received cash from the French company when 1 euro = $1.22 U.S.

	Date	Accounts		Debit	Credit
		General Journal			

Quick Practice Solutions

True/False

  T   1. If a trading investment has decreased in value, the year-end adjustment requires a debit to Loss on Trading Investment. (p. 1311)

  T   2. Available-for-sale investments may be classified as current assets or as long-term assets. (p. 1309)

  F   3. The Allowance to Adjust Investment to Market account is a companion account that is used with the Short-Term Investment account to bring the investment's carrying amount to current market value.

          False—The Allowance to Adjust Investment to Market account is a companion account that is used with the *Available-for-Sale account* to bring the investment's carrying amount to market value. (p. 1312)

  T   4. An investor with a stock holding between 20% and 50% of the investee's voting stock may significantly influence decisions on dividends, product lines, and other important matters. (p. 1313)

  F   5. Companies owning less than 50% of the outstanding stock in a subsidiary prepare consolidated financial statements.

          False—Companies owning *more* than 50% of the outstanding stock in a subsidiary prepare consolidated financial statements. (p. 1316)

  T   6. Minority interest is that portion of a subsidiary's stock that is owned by stockholders other than the parent company. (p. 1317)

  T   7. Goodwill is the excess of the cost to acquire another company over the sum of the market value of its net assets. (p. 1316)

  T   8. Held-to-maturity investments are reported on the balance sheet at amortized cost. (p. 1317)

  F   9. A foreign-currency transaction gain or loss occurs when the exchange rate changes between the date an order is placed and the date the merchandise is received.

          False—A foreign-currency transaction gain or loss occurs when the exchange rate changes between the date of purchase and date of *payment*. (p. 1323)

  F   10. If the U.S. dollar value of a Russian ruble is $0.035 on January 1 and increases to $0.037 on February 1, the U.S. dollar has weakened.

          False—If the U.S. dollar value of a Russian ruble is $0.035 on January 1 and increases to $0.037 on February 1, the U.S. dollar has *strengthened*. (p. 1323)

Multiple Choice

1. How are trading securities reported on the balance sheet? (p. 1311)
   a. At market value as either current assets or long-term investments on the balance sheet
   b. At market value as current assets on the balance sheet
   c. At cost as current assets on the balance sheet
   d. At lower of cost or market as current assets on the balance sheet

2. Where would a loss on the sale of a trading investment appear on the financial statements? (p. 1311)
   a. On the income statement as part of other gains and losses
   b. On the balance sheet as a current liability
   c. On the income statement as an operating expense
   d. On the balance sheet as a contra equity account

3. The entry to record dividends received from a trading investment includes which of the following? (p. 1312)
   a. A debit to Short-Term Investment
   b. A credit to Dividend Revenue
   c. A credit to Short-Term Investment
   d. A credit to Gain from Short-Term Investment

4. A short-term investment has been properly classified by the investor as a trading investment. If the stock was bought on June 17, 2007, for $10,000, and it is now worth $13,500 on December 31, 2007, which of the following will occur? (p. 1311)
   a. A direct increase of $3,500 to Retained Earnings that is not reported on the income statement.
   b. Dividend Revenue of $3,500 is reported on the income statement.
   c. A $3,500 gain would appear on the income statement, even though the gain is unrealized.
   d. The short-term investment will appear on the balance sheet at $10,000 on December 31.

5. Which of the following accounting treatments for available-for-sale investments is in accordance with GAAP? (p. 1312)
   a. Available-for-sale investments are reported on the balance sheet at historical cost.
   b. Available-for-sale investments are reported at historical cost and an Allowance to Adjust the Investment to Market account is established.
   c. Available-for-sale investments are reported on the balance sheet at market value.
   d. The Available-for-Sale Investment account should be adjusted to its market value on the balance sheet date and the unrealized gain or loss of adjusting from cost to market should be shown on the income statement.

6. McGovern Corp. owns 45% of the stock of Mather Corp. Mather Corp. declares and pays cash dividends of $45,000 to McGovern Corp. Which of the following will occur on the books of McGovern Corp.? (p. 1314)
   a. The investment in Mather Corp. on the balance sheet will increase by $45,000.
   b. Dividend revenue of $45,000 will be reported on the income statement.
   c. The investment in Mather Corp. on the balance sheet will decrease by $45,000.
   d. A gain of $45,000 will be reported on the income statement.

7. Which of the following is true for available-for-sale investments? (p. 1309)
   a. Available-for-sale investments include all stock investments other than trading securities.
   b. Available-for-sale investments are always classified as short-term.
   c. Available-for-sale investments are intended to be sold in the very near future.
   d. Available-for-sale investments include all bond investments other than trading securities.

8. On January 1, 2009, Investor Company acquires 25% of the 20,000 shares of common stock of Investee Company and has significant influence over the Investee Company. On December 31, 2009, Investee Company reports net income of $100,000. What account should Investor Company debit? (p. 1314)
   a. Long-Term Equity-Method Investment for $25,000
   b. Cash for $25,000
   c. Long-Term Equity-Method Investment for $100,000
   d. Cash for $100,000

9. White Corp. purchased $20,000 of 8% bonds on March 1, 2008, for a purchase price of 90. White expects to hold the bonds until their maturity date, March 1, 2013. Interest on the bonds will be paid every March 1 and September 1 until maturity. Assuming the premium or discount is amortized every interest payment using straight-line amortization, how much interest revenue will be recorded by White on September 1, 2008? (p. 1317)
   a. $1,200
   b. $1,000
   c. $800
   d. $600

10. A U.S. company sells merchandise to a British firm for 100,000 British pounds. Assume the exchange rates for the British pound were as follows:

   Date of sale: $1.54

   Date of collection: $1.53

   Date merchandise resold by British Firm: $1.52

   What is the foreign-currency gain or loss for the U.S. company on this transaction? (p. 1323)
   a. $2,000 gain
   b. $1,000 loss
   c. $3,000 gain
   d. $3,000 loss

Quick Exercises

B-1. In early 2008, Rocket Corporation invested some idle cash in the stock of another business. Journalize the following events that took place in 2008 and 2009: (p. 1310)

2008:

Feb. 1   Rocket Corporation purchased 1,500 shares of stock in Missile Company for $15.50 per share. This investment was classified as a trading investment.

Nov. 15 A dividend of $1.00 per share was received on the Missile Company stock.

Dec. 31 Rocket Corporation prepares financial statements for the year ended December 31, 2008. On this date the Missile Company stock is worth $16.25 per share.

2009:

Jan. 27 Rocket Corporation sold 750 shares of Missile Company stock for $16.50 per share.

General Journal			
Date	Accounts	Debit	Credit
Feb. 1	Short-Term Investment	23,250	
	Cash		23,250

General Journal			
Date	Accounts	Debit	Credit
Nov. 15	Cash	1,500	
	Dividend Revenue		1,500

General Journal			
Date	Accounts	Debit	Credit
Dec. 31	Short-Term Investment	1,125	
	Gain on Trading Investment		1,125

General Journal			
Date	Accounts	Debit	Credit
Jan. 27	Cash	12,375	
	Short-Term Investment		12,188
	Gain on Sale of Investment		187

B-2. Zipper Corporation engaged in the following transactions involving long-term available-for-sale investments in 2007: (p. 1312)

June 14 Purchased 3,500 shares of Button Corporation common stock for $13 per share.

Sept. 15 Button Corporation pays a $0.65 per share dividend to all common stockholders.

Dec. 31 The market price of Button Corporation stock is $13.75 per share.

Journalize these transactions.

General Journal			
Date	Accounts	Debit	Credit
June 14	Long-Term Available-for-Sale Investment	45,500	
	Cash		45,500

General Journal			
Date	Accounts	Debit	Credit
Sept. 15	Cash	2,275	
	Dividend Revenue		2,275

General Journal			
Date	Accounts	Debit	Credit
Dec. 31	Allowance to Adjust Investment to Market	. 2,625	
	Unrealized Gain on Available-for-Sale Investment		2,625

B-3.   John Corporation purchased 250,000 shares of Deere Corporation common stock on January 2, 2008, for $550,000. Deere Corporation has 625,000 shares outstanding. Deere Corporation earned net income of $330,000 and paid dividends of $100,000 during 2008. (pp. 1313–1315)

   a.   What method should be used to account for the Deere Corporation investment?
   Equity method

   b.   How much revenue will be recorded by John Corporation in 2008 from its investment in Deere Corporation?
   $330,000 × (250,000/625,000) = $132,000

   c.   What is the balance in John Corporation's investment account at the end of 2008?
   $550,000 + $132,000 − ($100,000 × 250,000/625,000) = $682,000 − $40,000 = $642,000

   d.   Assume all of the above facts except that on January 2, 2008, John Corporation purchased 75,000 shares of Deere Corporation. How much revenue will be recorded by John Corporation in 2008 from its investment in Deere Corporation?
   $100,000 × (75,000/625,000) = $12,000

B-4.   On October 1, 2007, Ace company paid $52,400 to purchase $50,000 of bonds that carry an 8% interest rate and will mature 5 years from the date of purchase. Interest on the bonds is paid September 30 and March 31 of each year. The company plans to hold the bonds until maturity and amortizes the premium or discount on bonds using the straight-line method each interest payment date. As of December 31, 2007, the bonds had a market value of $53,500. (p. 1317)

Requirements

1. Prepare all necessary journal entries for 2007 dealing with the investment in bonds.

General Journal			
Date	Accounts	Debit	Credit
Oct. 1	Long-Term Investment in Bonds	52,400	
	Cash		52,400

General Journal			
Date	Accounts	Debit	Credit
Dec. 31	Interest Receivable	1,000	
	Interest Revenue ($50,000 × .08 × 3/12)		1,000

General Journal			
Date	Accounts	Debit	Credit
Dec. 31	Interest Revenue	120	
	Long-Term Investment in Bonds ($2,400 × 3/60)		120

2. Show how the bonds would be presented on the balance sheet at December 31, 2007.

The investment in bonds would be classified as a long-term investment on the balance sheet.

Long-term investments:	
Long-term investment in bonds	$52,280

B-5.   The Helms Company engaged in the following transactions during 2008:
(pp. 1323–1324)

Apr. 1   Purchased merchandise from a Mexican supplier at a cost of 100,000 pesos. The exchange rate on this date was $0.32 per peso.

May 5   Paid for the merchandise purchased on April 1. The exchange rate on this date was $0.31 per peso.

June 10 Sold goods to a Canadian buyer at a selling price of $83,000 Canadian dollars. The exchange rate on this date was $0.67 U.S. dollars for each Canadian dollar.

July 30 Received payment from the Canadian buyer for the goods sold on June 10. The exchange rate on this date was $0.65 U.S. dollars for each Canadian dollar.

Requirements

1. Prepare the journal entries necessary to record each of the above transactions.

General Journal

Date	Accounts	Debit	Credit
April 1	Inventory	32,000	
	Accounts Payable		32,000

General Journal

Date	Accounts	Debit	Credit
May 5	Accounts Payable	32,000	
	Foreign-Currency Gain		1,000
	Cash		31,000

General Journal

Date	Accounts	Debit	Credit
June 10	Accounts Receivable	55,610	
	Sales Revenue		55,610

General Journal

Date	Accounts	Debit	Credit
July 30	Cash	53,950	
	Foreign-Currency Loss	1,660	
	Accounts Receivable		55,610

2. During the periods of time covered by the transactions, was the U.S. dollar getting stronger or weaker relative to the Mexican peso and the Canadian dollar?

During the periods of time covered by the transactions, the U.S. dollar strengthened relative to the Mexican peso and the Canadian dollar.

Do It Yourself! Question 1 Solutions

Requirements

1. What kind of investments are these?

$$\text{\% Ownership of Rock Co.} = \frac{10{,}000 \text{ shares}}{100{,}0000 \text{ shares}}$$
$$= 10\%$$

The Rock Co. shares are an **available-for-sale investment**.

$$\text{\% Ownership of Boulder Co.} = \frac{40{,}000 \text{ shares}}{100{,}0000 \text{ shares}}$$
$$= 40\%$$

The Boulder Co. shares are an **equity method investment**.

2. For *each* investment, journalize the following transactions for Giant Co.:

a. Purchase of investments on January 1, 2008
Rock Co.

Long-Term Available-for-Sale Investment—Rock Co.		15,000	
Cash			15,000

Boulder Co.

Equity Method Investment—Boulder Co.		240,000	
Cash			240,000

b. Dividends received by the investments during 2008
Rock Co.

Cash ($0.20 × 10,000)		2,000	
Dividend Revenue			2,000

Boulder Co.

Cash ($0.50 × 40,000)		20,000	
Equity Method Investment—Boulder Co.			20,000

c. Any adjustment for net income earned by the investment
Rock Co.

No entry.

Boulder Co.

Equity Method Investment—Boulder Co. (40% × $350,000)		140,000	
Equity Method Investment Revenue			140,000

d. Any adjustment for the investment's year-end market price
Rock Co.

Unrealized Loss [$15,000 – ($1.40 × 10,000)]		1,000	
Allowance to Adjust Investment to Market			1,000

Boulder Co.

No entry.

Do It Yourself! Question 2 Solutions

Requirements

1. Journalize the following transactions for Omni Inc.:

a. Performed services on account for a French company for 2,000 euro. 1 euro = $1.11 U.S.

Accounts Receivable (2,000 euro × $1.11 U.S.)	2,220	
Service Revenue		2,220

b. Purchased machinery from a Japanese company on account for 800,000 yen. 1 yen = $0.009 U.S.

Machinery (800,000 yen × $0.009 U.S.)	7,200	
Accounts Payable		7,200

c. Adjusted for a change in the value of the euro. 1 euro now = $1.18 U.S.

Accounts Receivable (2,000 euro × $1.18 U.S. − $2,220)	140	
Foreign-Currency Gain (to balance)		140

d. Paid for the machinery when 1 yen = $0.0089 U.S.

If 1 yen now = $0.0089 U.S. the account payable:

$$= 800,000 \times \$0.0089 = \$7,120$$

Accounts Payable	7,200	
Cash (800,000 yen × $0.0089 U.S.)		7,120
Foreign-Currency Gain (to balance)		80

e. Received cash from the French company when 1 euro = $1.22 U.S. euro.

If 1 euro now = $1.22 U.S., the account receivable:

$$= 2,000 \times \$1.22 = \$2,440$$

Cash (2,000 euro × $1.22 U.S.)	2,440	
Foreign-Currency Gain (to balance)		80
Accounts Receivable (2,220 + 140)		2,360

The Power of Practice

For more practice using the skills learned in this chapter, visit MyAccountingLab. There you will find algorithmically generated questions that are based on these Demo Docs and your main textbook's Review and Assess Your Progress sections.

Go to MyAccountingLab and follow these steps:

1. Direct your URL to www.myaccountinglab.com.
2. Log in using your name and password.
3. Click the MyAccountingLab link.
4. Click Study Plan in the left navigation bar.
5. From the table of contents, select Appendix B, Investments and International Operations.
6. Click a link to work tutorial exercises.

Glindex

A Combined Glossary/Subject Index

Payback. *The length of time it takes to recover, in net cash inflows, the dollars of a capital outlay,* 802, 809

Percent-of-sales method. *A method of estimating uncollectible receivables that calculates uncollectible-account expense. Also called the income-statement approach,* 253, 259

Period costs. *Operating costs that are expensed in the period in which they are incurred,* 568

Period inventory system. *A system in which the business does not keep a continuous record of inventory on hand. At the end of the period, it makes a physical count of on-hand inventory and uses this information to prepare the financial statements,* 125

Perpetual inventory system. *The accounting inventory system in which the business keeps a running record of inventory and cost of goods sold,* 125

Plant assets. *Long-lived tangible assets, such as land, buildings, and equipment, used to operate a business,* 297

Preferred stock. *Stock that gives its owners certain advantages over common stockholders, such as the right to receive dividends before the common stockholders and the right to receive assets before the common stockholders if the corporation liquidates,* 408–411, 420

Premium. *Excess of a bond's issue price over its maturity value. Also called bond premium,* 470

Prepaid expense. *Advance payments of expenses. Examples include prepaid rent, prepaid insurance, and supplies,* 65, 105

Present value. *Amount a person would invest now to receive a greater amount in the future,* 802, 810–812

Prevention costs. *Costs incurred to avoid poor-quality goods or services,* 776

Price (rate) variance. *Measures how well the business keeps unit prices of material and labor inputs within standards. This is computed as the difference in prices (actual price per unit minus standard price per unit) of an input multiplied by the actual quantity of the input,* 740

Principle amount. *The amount loaned out by the payee and borrowed by the maker of the note,* 467

Process costing. *System for assigning costs to large numbers of identical units that usually proceed in a continuous fashion through a series of uniform productions steps or processes,* 631

Production volume variance. *Arises when actual production differs from expected production. It is the difference between (1) the manufacturing overhead cost in the flexible budget or actual outputs and (2) the standard overhead allocated to production,* 740, 753

Purchases journal. *Special journal used to record all purchases of inventory, supplies, and other assets on account,* 188

Q

Quantity variance. *See* Efficiency (quantity) variance

R

Receivables. *Monetary claims against a business or an individual*